The Domestication of Europe

Social Archaeology

General Editor
Ian Hodder, University of Cambridge

Advisory Editors
Margaret Conkey, University of California
at Berkeley
Mark Leone, University of Maryland
Alain Schnapp, U.E.R. d'Art et d'Archaeologie, Paris
Stephen Shennan, University of Southampton
Bruce Trigger, McGill University, Montreal

Published

MATERIAL CULTURE AND MASS CONSUMPTION
Daniel Miller

EXPLANATION IN ARCHAEOLOGY
Guy Gibbon

READING MATERIAL CULTURE
Structuralism, Hermeneutics and Post-Structuralism
Edited by Christopher Tilley

THE DOMESTICATION OF EUROPE
Structure and Contingency in Neolithic Societies
Ian Hodder

In preparation

THE ARCHAEOLOGY OF INEQUALITY
Edited by Randall H. McGuire and Robert Paynter

ENGENDERING ARCHAEOLOGY
Women and Prehistory
Edited by Joan Gero and Margaret Conkey

IRON AGE SOCIETIES
From Tribe to State in Northern Europe
Lotte Hedeager

THE ARCHAEOLOGY OF DEMOCRACY
Ian Morris

The Domestication of Europe

Structure and Contingency in Neolithic Societies

Ian Hodder

Basil Blackwell

Copyright © Ian Hodder 1990

First published 1990

Basil Blackwell Ltd
108 Cowley Road, Oxford, OX4 1JF, UK

Basil Blackwell, Inc.
3 Cambridge Center
Cambridge, Massachusetts 02142, USA

British Library Cataloguing in Publication Data

A CIP catalogue record for this book is available from the British Library.

Library of Congress Cataloging in Publication Data

Hodder, Ian
    The domestication of Europe : structure and contingency in
neolithic societies / Ian Hodder.
        p.   cm. -- (Social archaeology)
    Includes bibliographical references.
    ISBN 0-631-17413-3 -- ISBN 0-631-17769-8 (pbk.)
    1. Neolithic period--Europe.   2. Agriculture, Prehistoric--Europe.
3. Architecture, Prehistoric--Europe.   4. Europe--Antiquities.
    I. Title.   II. Series.
    GN776.2.A1H63 1990
936--dc20
                                                                        90-1695
                                                                        CIP

Typeset in 11 on 12½ Garamond
by Photo·graphics, Honiton, Devon
Printed in Great Britain by T.J. Press Ltd, Padstow, Cornwall

Contents

To Christine

Acknowledgements

The author and publishers wish to thank the following for permission to redraw and reproduce figures:
Academic Press: figures 6.4, 10.1. Niels Andersen: figure 7.5. Antiquity Publications: figures 6.5 and 8.5. Eugène Belin: figure 5.6. Cambridge University Press: figures 6.3, 7.10. Aubrey Burl: figure 8.8a. Centre National de la Recherche Scientifique: figures 8.1, 8.2, 8.3, 8.4. Ceskoslovenska Akademie: figure 6.1. Edinburgh University Press: figure 6.6. Linda Ellis: figures 3.2a, 4.3, 4.4. Mike Ilett: figure 5.7. Institute of Prehistoric Archaeology, University of Copenhagen: figures 7.3, 7.7, 7.8. Jysk Arkaeologisk Selskab: figures 7.6, 7.9b. Lili Kaelas: figure 7.9a. J. Lüning: figures 5.2, 5.3. James Mellaart: figures 1.1, 1.2, 1.3, 1.4, 2.3. Museum für Ur- und Frühge-schichte, Freiburg: figure 4.1. Odense University Press: figure 7.4. Ouest France: figures 8.6, 8.8b. Oxford University Press: figure 8.7. Prehistoric Society: figures 7.1, 9.4. Presses Universitaires de France: figure 5.10. P. Raczky: figures 3.2b, 3.4. Regents of the University of California: figure 4.5. Regents of the University of Michigan: figure 5.1. Routledge & Kegan Paul: figure 5.4. Royal Anthropological Institute: 9.2, 9.3. Society of Antiquaries of London: figure 9.6. Thames & Hudson: figures 2.1, 2.2, 7.2. I. Thorpe: figures 9.1, 9.2, 9.3, 9.5. Henrieta Todorova: figure 4.2.

Preface

There is a widely used formula, seen at the beginning or end of books or articles, whereby those who have commented on first drafts of a typescript are thanked, while their responsibility for the ideas or errors in the final text is disclaimed.

I have never really understood these formulaic disclaimers. Any other member of the discipline within which one works is at least partly responsible for what one writes, and certainly those who have commented and helped form a particular text are more closely involved than most. The people listed below did not agree with everything they read but they cared enough to criticize some unwarranted ideas and to nurture others. They domesticated my wilder claims and 'mothered' my early thoughts. They helped to form and structure this book. Although they have contributed to the effacing of the 'I', what remains of that entity is deeply grateful to them for their time, interest and care.

Richard Bradley, Ian Kinnes, Torsten Madsen, Chris Scarre, Andrew Sherratt, Joan Oates, and Alisdair Whittle read and commented on substantial portions of the text. In particular I owe a considerable debt to Barbara Bender for her extensive and critical comments on the volume. I also thank Charlotte Damm and Mark Edmonds for reading parts of the book, Ruth Tringham for help with south-east European references, Anick Coudart for sorting out some illustrative problems for me, and Jose John and Nigel Holman for help with the typing and printing.

The largest part of the book took shape while I was a Fellow at the Centre for Advanced Study in the Behavioural Sciences at Stanford, California (with partial support by National Science Foundation, grant BNS 8411738). I wish in particular to thank Gardner Lindzey for his support there.

I have tried in this book to balance symbolic and structural analyses with consideration of the pragmatic and the economic, including the everyday world of consequences and implications. My thinking more carefully about these latter issues is due in large measure to the influence of my wife, Christine Hastorf. She has been the person above all who has structured my ideas and new directions, tamed my wandering diversions, and brought my abstract structures down to earth – an unlikely but effective 'mother goddess'.

These and other people and institutions influenced me heavily. The already structured domestic and wider 'homes' within which we all work channelled and ordered my 'naturally' vagrant thoughts. It is difficult not to be wholly dependent on (and here I wish to continue to indulge in this series of apparently mixed metaphors, the reason for which will I hope become clear later in the book) the pot of knowledge on which we all subsist, difficult not to be dominated by the discipline which surrounds and nurtures us. We acknowledge others, thanking them, but disclaiming their responsibility, identifying our own work as original and distinctive. But the real question, and here one of my themes has already been broached, is whether there is anything of the 'I' in this book at all.

1

Introduction

There is no beginning to this book; no starting point. There has been a stream of becoming as bits and pieces were brought together, suggesting to me a structure that I had already created. And there is, in the way of writing I have chosen, a first page, and a first word just as, undoubtedly, there will be a last. The book is already structured even though my thoughts seem disorganized, provisional, unready, continually changing. Already, then, tensions emerge between representation and experience, between code and felt reality, between structure and contingency.

A partial solution: make the first page the last. But I do not want to avoid the issues, even if I am not yet sure, at least not coherently, verbally, consciously sure, what the issues are.

I cannot decide, on the first page, whether to write the book. But you know that I have done. Our positions and our readings are different. In writing I create a past to be read, but before me is only blank whiteness; an uncertain future. You read the text as structured in past time and in space. You see its form and you read a structure. I write the text apparently uncertain as to where it will lead me, as I try, groping, to fit experience to structure.

At least I can say how I got to where I am now in my train of thought, and how an idea began to coalesce. In providing this little personal history I want to show that my writing is provisional and contextual, how it results from apparently haphazard interactions but also from interpretations of those interactions in terms of social, economic, and conceptual structures that had already found me. Or rather, the ideas in the book came about through the interaction of structure and experience, including the experience of writing this book. We think through experience, but we organize that experience by our thoughts. As a result it seems both as if the book is already written as I sit down to write, and as if I discover or at least objectify the structures in the writing.

I cannot be sure of the exact sequence of events, but I can at least give a trace of how the idea for the book came about. I had given a talk, it little matters about what, in the Smithsonian in Washington. . .

But before I tell this story, it seems that you the reader and I the writer are already closer together because we have something of a common history – the text so far. I have less choice in what I can say if I wish to maintain some coherence to the text. The stage has already been set and the structures of thought are ready to be played out. I the writer must spend time reading what I have written and reading what I want to say in terms of what I have already said. And you the reader begin to write the text in the sense that you begin to create patterns and meanings in my text. But the longer and more structured my text, the less you have to write within it. The more my text is organized into coherent relationships, the less room you have to create your own 'writings' within my text, although you perhaps have more room to generate your own texts in relation to the structures I have 'created'.

I had given this talk – perhaps it does matter that it was about ethnoarchaeological research I had conducted amongst the Nuba in Sudan. The audience was a mix of anthropologists, archaeologists, men and women, professionals and amateurs, crowded between display cases and columns in the museum. At the end the questions led to nowhere in particular and we dispersed amongst the cabinets and chairs drinking wine out of polystyrene cups. I was talking amongst a small group of people, including a tall social anthropologist with greying hair. I cannot remember his name. And I cannot remember what we were talking about. But I do remember that it struck me when this tall anthropologist said: 'I've often thought that the Palaeolithic cave art of south-west France could not have been made anywhere else except in Europe.' And I have remembered the remark ever since.

I think he was talking seriously. He certainly looked serious. At first the comment sounded and sounds ridiculous – and extremely unanthropological in that the tall anthropologist seemed to be imposing his own concepts of art on the Palaeolithic. Again I do not remember exactly our discussion. The only other thing he said in order to clarify his point, was that the styles of Mesoamerican or Chinese or Indian art were somewhat different from Palaeolithic art.

For those who live in European-derived cultures, the Palaeolithic art, he thought, appears familiar. Yet, I felt, it might only appear familiar because we look at it with our own eyes – Palaeolithic eyes would have looked at the art very differently. The tall anthropologist would have been trained to be critical in this way. Yet here he was suggesting that the art was *made* in a distinctly European style.

It's a wild idea, unconventional and unacceptable. Spoken in a busy room, it had a fluidity and an ambiguity that suggested a myriad of vague images. Set down here on paper the thought seems more fixed, with less potential. Yet I have not written it down before, and for several years the thought has remained with me as a worrying question, restlessly disturbing. The thought was unthinkable, but once thought, paths seemed to lead everywhere.

Some more fragments. Someone I had met long ago asked me to write an article for the Jubilee Edition of the Bulletin of the Institute of Archaeology in London, as part of the Institute's commemoration of its fiftieth anniversary. The proposal was to collect together a group of writers associated with the Institute, including past students. I had always retained a strong affection for the 'Institute', as it was and is called, since my time as an undergraduate there. In fact I was in the first group of undergraduates ever admitted to the Institute in 1968. I have wide-eyed images of Sir Mortimer Wheeler, flamboyant even in the small lift, and Professor Grimes, distinguished and immaculate throughout his long slow lectures, transformed by a white carnation in his lapel. I hardly ever went back to the Institute after I left in 1971, yet I remained very attached emotionally. It seemed like an old familiar friend to me. So I wanted to write something for the Bulletin.

At first, all I could think of was something theoretical, on ethnoarchaeology and material culture studies. But in the end I used those ideas for a conference in Rome. And anyway I wanted to do something more substantial for the Institute. I decided, apparently out of the blue, to do a paper interpreting the symbolism of Çatal Hüyük, a Neolithic site in Anatolia excavated by James Mellaart who teaches at the Institute. His lectures about Çatal Hüyük had been highly evocative for me as an undergraduate – and I remember too being attracted by Mellaart's enthusiasm.

But the reason for choosing Çatal was quite different. Someone (I think it might have been Nicholas Postgate, who taught Near Eastern archaeology at Cambridge) had seen my book *Symbols in*

Action (Hodder 1982a), or had heard me talk about my brief visit to the present-day Nuba, in Sudan. The Nuba have an elaborate style of decoration on the interior walls of their compounds, involving painting, incision, and clay moulding. Much of the symbolism of this domestic art concerns women, including women's breasts, and I had interpreted the symbols in terms of positive and negative attitudes towards female sexuality. As in many cultures Nuba women are both powerful and subordinate, reproductive yet dangerous. If it was Nicholas who knew of this work of mine, he said in an offhand, abrupt way, as we crossed the road, or sat down to eat in his college: 'You know, you should do an analysis of Çatal Hüyük. It is one place which has got clear evidence of symbolism, such as vultures' beaks in women's breasts. Just like the Nuba stuff.'

I had not remembered any such things from James Mellaart's lectures, but soon afterwards I went to the Haddon Library in Cambridge and flipped through Mellaart's (1967) *Çatal Hüyük. A Neolithic town in Anatolia*. Sure enough, there were photos of protuberances from house walls, interpreted as breasts, with the beaks of vultures protruding from the nipples. Other breasts covered the jaws and tusks of wild boar. The violence of this imagery made a vivid impression on me so that, although I could not re-read much of the book at the time, I put it away in my mind for future use. And so when the chance came of writing for the Institute's Bulletin, I was glad to be able to return to this most fascinating of sites.

The paper that I finally wrote ended up coming to much the same set of conclusions as reached by Mellaart in his various publications about Çatal Hüyük. I tried to be critical about my interpretations, but it proved difficult to disagree with Mellaart, even though his interpretations often seemed overly imaginative when first encountered. Mellaart had written his text for his own purposes, but I wanted to use it in a context in which 'scientific' archaeology expected statements to be supported by quantified data. I could not use his text for my purposes with any ease. The site had not been published with detailed plans and tables of, for example, artifact numbers in each room, or each part of a room. So when giving talks about my reading of the Çatal data, I have often been criticized for the quality of the data. Unfortunately such problems are often an unavoidable part of syntheses of European prehistory at the present stage of development of archaeological research in many areas.

Despite the lack of quantified data and detailed publication, it seemed to me that the richness of the symbolism of Çatal Hüyük is such that various oppositions and associations could be identified with some confidence, and I discussed these, as critically as I could, in my article. For example, the interior walls of the houses do indeed frequently have what Mellaart interprets as female breasts. As well as the beaks of the Griffon Vulture (*Gyps fulvus*) and boar tusks, these 'breasts' contain the teeth of a fox and a weasel's skull.

The first question to ask was, 'how do we know these are breasts?' After all, the clay protuberances sometimes occur singly rather than in pairs, and the pairing is sometimes vertical, with one 'breast' above the other on the wall. Overall it seemed possible that the protuberances, or at least some of them, do evoke breasts because of the close stylistic affinity between the breasts modelled on the walls and those modelled on undoubtedly female figurines. In both cases the nipples are sometimes shown as open or inverted. The symbolism thus could be 'read' to suggest a link between women (and in particular the reproductive, child-rearing, or sexual aspects of women as perhaps indicated by the breasts) and wild animals (and in particular the death-dealing beaks, tusks, and teeth of those animals). These associations are certainly evocative. But how reliable are they? After all, we cannot be sure for example that the clay protuberances do represent breasts.

At Çatal Hüyük there are other reasons for linking women with danger and the wild. The figurine material shows a close association between women and felines, probably leopards. Women are shown holding leopard cubs and sitting beside or on leopards (figure 1.1). Another aspect of the Çatal Hüyük symbolism appears to make the same point even more forcefully. Mellaart claimed in his publications that women are depicted on the house walls giving birth to animals including horned bulls. I had not been convinced of the published drawings purporting to show these acts of birth. When I sent a first draft of my article to James Mellaart at the Institute, he replied openly and constructively. He argued strongly that there is indeed good evidence of the birth-giving scenes. The child or animal heads appear between the widespread legs of figures that can be identified as female on the basis of, for example, depictions of swollen abdomen, vulva, menstruation, breasts, facial features, long black tresses, female attire, and bonnets. With all this as yet unpublished evidence, the notion of female reproduction being linked to the wild and danger might be made more secure.

I do not think that I consciously used the Nuba as an analogy, although my work there is referred to in the Çatal Hüyük article

Figure 1.1 Statuette from Çatal Hüyük.
(Source: Mellaart 1967)

(Hodder 1987). But the similarities were very evocative. My lasting
memory of the Nuba is the wonder evoked when I first entered one
of the dark compounds of the Mesakin sub-group. Crouching low
through a key-hole entrance, one enters a covered central space
surrounded by walls and huts. It takes some time for one's eyes to
become used to the dark and to the smoke from the fire in the
centre, on which rests a blackened pot. Gradually one makes out
grinning faces, arms decked in gleaming bangles, with beads around

the ears of the young women. Painted on the walls is a density of design and representation, including female breasts, fantastic creatures, and feared objects including aeroplanes. On spikes above the hut entrances are found agricultural and other symbols of protection. Later I was to realize that the jaws of various animals were placed above the entrances and within the eaves of the houses.

In his book on Çatal Hüyük, Mellaart had included a drawing of an imaginative reconstruction of the inside of one of the Çatal houses (figure 1.2). It showed humans dressed as vultures bringing offerings of skulls, in a painted and darkened room, with the light shafting through from a small window. The scene, however incorrect in detail, reminded me of the Nuba experience. Overall the parallels are strong: elaborate decoration on the insides of the dwelling units, often showing women and various wild or fearful creatures.

Later, I came to know of other ethnographic accounts which explored the representation of women in small-scale societies (e.g. Ortner 1972; MacCormack and Strathern 1980; Barstow 1978; Meeker et al. 1986) or which examined the links between women

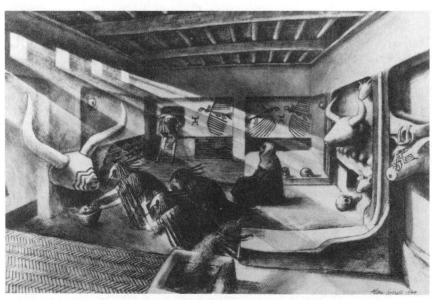

Figure 1.2 Reconstruction of a funerary rite taking place in a house in level VII at Çatal Hüyük. It is based on the actual discovery of wall paintings of vultures with human legs and human skulls on platforms below them found against the north wall, and skulls found in baskets below each bull's head on the west and east walls.
(Source: Mellaart 1965)

and dangerous things and I came to understand some of the interpretive debate such links had caused (e.g. Lakoff 1987). But at the time, as a result of having read Mary Douglas and her cross-cultural discussion of purity and pollution taboos (1966), I came in a fairly straightforward manner to interpret the Nuba symbolism in terms of male–female relationships. Thus the dangers associated with women were seen as occurring in societies in which absolute male power was in some way contradicted or frustrated by powers held by women. Certainly my experience amongst the Nuba to some degree predetermined my interpretation of Çatal Hüyük – or rather it produced a readiness to accept the outlines of Mellaart's interpretations of the site. Certainly my initial excitement at the possible human breasts containing the beaks of vultures derived in part from my Nuba and Mary Douglas background. But I also came to feel that there were sufficient contextual links within the Çatal Hüyük data to justify the reconstruction of a symbolism concerning a power and danger associated with female representation.

For example, we can follow another set of contextual links leading from the 'breasts' containing vulture beaks. Wall-paintings in three houses at Çatal Hüyük show the Griffon vulture together with headless human figures, often lying contracted on their left sides. Mellaart interpreted these scenes as depicting part of the burial process, as is supported by the following evidence. First, the position of the body (contracted on the left side) is apparently found for many of the burials which occur beneath the house floors at Çatal Hüyük. Second, human skulls are found on house floors (where they could have been placed after the occupation of the house) separated from their bodies. Third, Mellaart suggests that there is evidence among the burial remains for excarnation (the removal of flesh prior to burial). Fourth, Griffon vultures are carrion eaters. If the Griffon vulture is associated with death in the wall-paintings, the link between vultures and women in the 'breast' depictions further draws women and death into the one complex.

Within other aspects of the data it becomes possible to tease out further some of these symbolic associations and oppositions. For example, the houses are internally organized in a repetitive way (figures 1.3 and 1.4). Entering the house by a ladder from the roof one arrives at the southern end which contains hearth and oven but little symbolic elaboration. The walls in this part of the house are generally undecorated. It is also relevant that the domestic pottery at Çatal Hüyük remains undecorated throughout most of the phases

Figure 1.3 Plan of level VIB at Çatal Hüyük.
(Source: Mellaart 1967)

of occupation. It is the northern, inner part of the house which contains the elaborate wall decoration, bucrania, and burials beneath the floors. But there is also a gender distinction here in that according to Mellaart male burials occur to the north of female burials. (Male burials occur beneath the north-eastern platform and female burials occur beneath the east-central platform. The north-western platform also contains burials but no repeated pattern is mentioned here).

Male burials are associated with hunting points and weapons and what appear to be men are shown in the wall-paintings hunting large bovids. As we have seen, much of the wall symbolism concerns wild animals (including leopards, wild boar, fox, vultures, bovids) and death. It would thus be possible to suggest that the northern, inner-most part of the house is associated with men, the wild and death. In contrast, the southern, outermost part of the house is associated with women (as seen in the location of burials) and the domestic (as seen in the southern location of hearths and ovens). Of course these oppositions and associations relating to men and women are

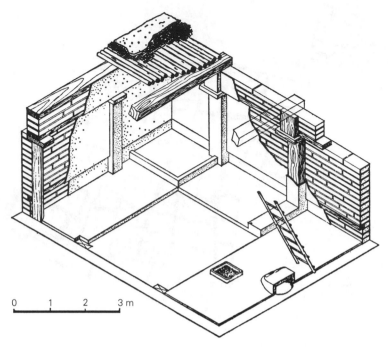

Figure 1.4 Diagrammatic view of a typical house at Çatal Hüyük showing timber
framework, panelling, platforms, bench, hearth, oven, and ladder.
(Source: Mellaart 1967)

representational. The symbolic relationships do not necessarily trans-
late into divisions of labour and task differentiation.

It would not be difficult to impose the following set of rules on
the representational system.

| male | inner (back) | death | wild |
| female | outer (front) | life | domestic |

It would also be appropriate to note that most of the elaborate
symbolism, decoration, painting, relief sculpture is located towards
the inner 'male' part of the house. The main overt expression of
elaborate symbolism envelops death, the wild and the fearful.
Dangerous symbols are caught within an elaborate decorative code,
and they are also 'domesticated' spatially within the house, separated
and controlled by the 'female' area. The argument begins to emerge
– and here I am moving from my original Çatal Hüyük text to a
theme that will come to dominate this book – that early Neolithic

material symbolism is involved in the celebration and control of
the wild, and that the control relates to social power through the
representation of male and female and through the organization of
domestic space.

The figurine material, too, shows women associated with the wild
as much as controlling it. On the one hand the woman in figure 1.1
is shown sitting on wild animals, her hands resting on their heads,
'lording' over nature. She is shown in control, almost proud and
serene. On the other hand, she is associated with the wild leopards
and with danger. The bared breasts perhaps evoke other breasts on
the house walls. Given these contextual associations, it might have
been possible at Çatal Hüyük to look at the figurine and ask 'are
there vulture beaks, is there death, in those breasts?'

Much of the symbolism at Çatal Hüyük thus seems to evoke
concerns about death and the wild in relation to the ordered, controlled, and 'cultured'. Of course, the wild and the natural are
not themselves 'natural' categories. They are themselves constructed
within the social process. To be unclothed is only 'natural' if opposed
to a clothed 'cultural' state. The wild, nature, and death are created
as categories in order to form the domesticated and the cultural, and
vice versa. In the opposition and juxtaposition of the cultural and
the wild society is dialectically created out of its own negative
image. In the association between reproduction and death, society is
renewed and given life.

The full range of the complex of meanings is lost to us. In
particular the role of cattle within the symbolism is difficult to grasp.
Perhaps this was intentional. Perhaps the symbolic role of cattle was
intentionally kept ambiguous. Certainly bucrania play a major part
in the Çatal Hüyük representational sculpture and painting. Mellaart
claims that they are associated with bearded, and therefore male,
figures but the published depictions remain unconvincing for me.
Small 'stick' figures that may be male are shown in the wall-paintings
hunting cattle with bows and arrows, and certainly arrowheads are
associated with men in burials. If cattle are to be associated with
males in certain contexts at Çatal Hüyük, then it is interesting to
note that the cattle bones found on the site are largely domesticated.
Cattle, then, may also be involved in both wild and domestic realms.

Some General Considerations

In the paragraphs above I found it necessary to refer to general themes that I only intended to 'discover' later in the book. While thinking about this book I was at the same time teaching at Cambridge, reading, talking to colleagues in different parts of the world. Somewhere in that continuum of events I came across the remarkably original work of Jacques Cauvin on symbolism in the early Neolithic of the Near East (1972 and 1978). He noted that cattle bones and placed cattle skulls occur in the eighth millennium bc at Mureybet in the Levant prior to cattle domestication and that much of the early symbolism in the Neolithic of the Near East concerns cattle. He argued that *Bos primigenius* (aurochs or wild cattle) would have been an ideal symbolic expression of internal psychological and social fears. The domestication of wild cattle and of the external wild more generally could thus be seen as an attempt to domesticate and control internal and social problems. I developed this general theme by linking the control of social problems to the control of people. Put simply it seemed possible to argue that the process of domestication – the control of the wild – is a metaphor and mechanism for the control of society.

Thus I return to the problems identified at the beginning of the chapter concerning the relationship between the reader and the writer. I cannot write this book in such a way as to involve you fully in the process of discovery since I have already, to some extent, discovered before I start to write. I cannot write without selecting certain events in the process of discovery as significant. And this selection (which comes after the event of having identified certain structures as of interest to me) is necessary in order to make my story coherent. The coherence produced has been artificially created by me as the writer.

I find it necessary therefore to state at the outset the general issues of which I was only vaguely aware at the beginning, which structured my work and writing, but which only became clear contingently, during and after the writing. These are the general concerns within which I set the discussion. I found in the writing, in my haphazard acquaintances with other people and with other interpretations of the data, that I had been absorbed by a number of parallel issues involved in the relationships between code and practice, structure and event, which are often difficult to disentangle. I will clarify these main areas of interest as I now see them having written the first draft of this book.

The first issue concerns the relationship between symbolic and social structures. By symbolic I mean the secondary connotations evoked by the primary associations and uses of an object or word. These secondary meanings tend to refer to abstract and general concepts and they tend to be organized into oppositional structures which can take various forms (for example, as we have already seen, male:female, back:front, death:life, wild:domestic). These symbolic structures are manipulated and organized cognitively, but they do not in my view reside solely in the mind. Rather they are public structures that are given contextual (localized, changing, contradictory, and conflicting) meanings in relation to the strategies and pragmatics of individuals in their daily lives. The public symbolic structures are reproduced in the social practices. But here a problem emerges in any attempt to distinguish symbolic and social structure. If the symbolic structures are produced in the social realm then there is likely to be a close tie to social structures. By the latter I mean organized relations of kin, gender, age set, class, etc. which are themselves often integrally related to divisions and relations of production, reproduction, and exchange. But of course it can be argued that these social structural relations are themselves partly produced in certain instances by and through the symbolic structures and through other structures of signification including language.

While I will endeavour in this text to distinguish symbolic and social structures it must be stated at the start that the symbolic and conceptual structures discussed here are conceived of by me as being more social than cognitive. I accept that many aspects of social relations should not be reduced to symbolic relations but I assert that it is often difficult, on the other hand, to distil symbolic relations from their social contexts.

The problem, however, is exacerbated in archaeology, leading to a further elision of the symbolic and the social. Archaeologists cannot yet with any confidence identify kinship relations and they can rarely directly 'see' social relations of production in that they can never see who works for whom, who exchanges prestige items, what is the social basis for organizing production, what are the rules of inheritance, and so on. Of course, many archaeologists will object and show how they have been successful in demonstrating the exchange of valued objects between elites, the location of larger centres in relation to land and resources, the exclusive relationship in burials between men or elites and certain artifacts of production indicating privileged access or control. But ultimately most if not all of these relationships are represented to us through a system of signification rather than being directly observed. Burials, houses, settlements, artifacts, and refuse are produced in relation to social organization but they may symbolically and strategically reorder that organization. This point will become clearer by the final chapter in this volume. I have already begun to suggest that representational systems in which male and female are involved do not tell us directly about the social relations of men and women. The relationship between social and symbolic structures is complex, meaningful, and itself socially construed. Archaeologists have to 'read' the symbolic structures in order to infer the social realm. The separation of symbolic and social in my account will be difficult to maintain.

The second issue is often phrased in archaeology in terms of the interactions between normative and expedient components in artifact production and discard. More generally the issue concerns the relationship between general structure and concrete events. As already noted, the symbolic process involves generalization beyond the particular. It involves comparison and the construction of general categories, including social categories, which are by definition abstract. A distance thus emerges between general categories and particular events. The categorical system has to be both coherent in its own terms and able to account for concrete instances. Yet there is always a risk that the practical, the situational, or unintended consequences will produce contingent events that cannot be accommodated within existing social and symbolic structures. It could be argued that archaeologists have a unique ability to monitor the way in which general structures interact with experience. By following the way in which the structures identified at Çatal Hüyük become transformed in relation to environmental change and in relation to events produced intentionally and unintentionally within existing structures, the interaction between structure and event could be studied.

Closely related to this second issue is the degree of determinism involved. What role can be given to human agents? At one extreme it would be possible to argue that actors at Çatal Hüyük and the writer of this book were entirely determined by structures in relation to events. Thus, given an array of symbolic and social structures, and given a set of concrete conditions, certain solutions can be predicted. Within this view, human agents provide the medium for the playing out of structures, but they are entirely determined by those structures. According to this view history could not have been otherwise, except perhaps for random variation or 'error'. At the other extreme, social life is generated by knowledgeable human actors, monitoring the results of their actions, conflicting in their demands, pursuing varied social goals. Even if agents act within and through symbolic and social structures, they are able to transform the structures strategically. According to this view, history could have been otherwise. It is not fully predictable. There is an open moment of interpretation in the linking of structure to event and it is this individual creativity which is the distinctive characteristic of the human condition. In exploring the relative importance of these two views the archaeologist might study the way in which long sequences of structural transformation seem to be predetermined, or might examine different reactions of the same structure to similar external conditions. Can alternative plots be conceived? Could history indeed have been otherwise?

A final, and again closely related issue, concerns the nature of power. I understand power to be the ability to act in relation to interest, including the interest in controlling others and resources. Most discussions of power and domination have concentrated on distributions of economic resources. Thus it is argued that social and ideological domination depend ultimately on privileged access to goods, labour or land. Social change concerns competition over these resources and structures of signification are underpinned by their distribution. There are a number of difficulties here. First, power may be based on the control of social or esoteric knowledge rather than on the control of economic resources. Second, goods, labour, and land have to be evaluated within a symbolic system before they can be used as the basis for social domination. The power to act assumes some knowledge of an interest, but that interest is itself partly constructed within a system of signification. It can be argued therefore that all power relations depend on the structures of signification within which they take place. Put rather differently, the central issue is the relative importance of prestige and economy in constituting power. Are human actions determined more by cultural values and systems of prestige or by the distribution of economic resources? Archaeologists might hope to contribute to this debate by examining over the long term the durability of symbolic codes in the face of changing relations of production. As radical economic change takes place, associated with changes in structures of social domination, do the symbolic codes seem to determine or be determined by the changes in the economic structures? Is it possible, as Duby (1980) has argued in another study of long term processes, in Medieval Europe, that the superstructure can at times act as infrastructure, playing a dominant role?

Catal Hüyük and Hacilar Through Time

I intend to worry about the above closely related issues throughout this book. The apparently haphazard encounter with Çatal Hüyük led me in certain directions and encouraged me to look at other data in Europe and the Near East in similar ways. New paths were opened to me by that experience although it may be that I was already travelling on the same route. Perhaps I read the Çatal Hüyük experience in predetermined ways. The general themes outlined above were partly suggested by the data that I examined and they partly structured the way I looked at the data.

The general themes will be explored in this book in relation to a range of data, but with particular reference to the domestication of plants and animals. The 'origins of agriculture' refer to a long period in the Near East and Europe (from the tenth to the fourth millennia bc) in which certain plants and animals were increasingly brought under human control. Often associated with the formation of sedentary communities, agricultural origins have long exercised the minds of prehistorians. On the whole, however, the transformation has been examined in economic, environmental, social, and population growth terms. The questions I wish to ask of this important period centre on changes in symbolic structure which correspond with other types of change. Is there a widespread transformation of symbolic structure which goes hand in hand with the economic domestication of plants and animals? How widely relevant is Çatal Hüyük? Was the change the result of contingent events after the end of the last glaciation, or was it the result of the relentless unfolding of symbolic and social structures? To what extent can it be argued that all the elaborate symbolism often associated with the early Neolithic in Europe and the Near East is linked to a process of social control?

In addition to exploring general questions of this type in relation to the early Neolithic, I wish to examine the general issues defined above in relation to middle and later Neolithic developments. These later transformations of Neolithic society can again be introduced by reference to cultural change at Çatal Hüyük.

The various levels at Çatal Hüyük cover the late seventh and early sixth millennia bc. Mellaart also argues (1970) for cultural similarities with the Turkish site of Hacilar, the levels of which cover the middle and late sixth millennium bc. The excavations at these two sites thus allow gradual changes in the material symbolism to be recognized, although there is unfortunately less good evidence for the accompanying social and economic changes. One distinctive general trend at the two sites is that the elaborate symbolism gradually becomes less 'within-house' and more 'between-house'. At Çatal Hüyük the wall decoration occurs only on the inside walls of the houses and particularly on the innermost walls furthest from the entrance. Burial occurs under the floors of the houses. The symbolism is not found to the same degree on pottery and on other portable artifacts except figurines. But in the upper (later) levels at Çatal Hüyük the wall plaster reliefs and the paintings tend to die out, at least partly as a result of worse conditions of preservation in the upper levels. By contrast, pottery begins to be painted in the uppermost levels.

These trends are continued at Hacilar where painting and relief sculpture are absent from walls. Pottery, on the other hand, becomes gradually more elaborate and painted except in the uppermost level at Hacilar. Mellaart argues for a continuity in themes from the Çatal Hüyük wall symbolism to the equally complex Hacilar pottery. He also suggests that the pots at Hacilar were used largely for eating and drinking rather than for cooking. The decoration of portable pottery perhaps relates to an increased symbolic emphasis on relations between houses rather than within houses. Nevertheless, the pots are found, together with female statuettes, clustered around hearths and ovens. Domestic activities remain visible and central at Hacilar. The hearths and ovens are often centrally placed within rooms, but ovens and 'kitchens' also occur outside the enclosed house area. Burial too is no longer within the house and is presumed largely to have taken place outside the settlement.

It is as if the dark recesses of the Çatal Hüyük houses have been banished to an outer, less domestic arena. An increased emphasis on larger social entities is also seen in other evidence. In the Çatal Hüyük levels, an elaborate and structured code is developed which is general and abstract in that it is repeated around the site and applied to a variety of contexts, from female figurines to the spatial layout of houses. The main theme in this code seems to involve the bringing in of death and the wild and surrounding them with a cultural order. The main locus of this code is the house, and there seems to be a great deal of similarity in layout from house to house. Perhaps the similarity between houses suggests a social order and discipline. Through time there is evidence for an increase in the degree of group cohesion or definition. At Hacilar, the settlement becomes defended with walls, and the central part of the site appears to be a pottery workshop in Hacilar II.

How are we to conceive of these changes? Why does the within-house symbolism decline as the definition of larger social units increases? Do the changes take place within a structured symbolic code, or do the changes alter the underlying structure? In whose interests do the transformations take place?

Attempts at answering these questions will have to await more detailed comparative studies to be provided later in this book. Certainly the Çatal Hüyük–Hacilar sequence shows how existing structures are reinterpreted in new contexts, as when a range of symbols and ideas surrounding bucrania and female bodies are transposed from house walls to more portable pottery. By this creative leap the idea of, for example, culturing the wild can be retained and given a new, wider social focus. But we will have to await the evidence from other areas to know whether other paths could have been taken. For example, is the move from burials within houses to extra-settlement locations widely found? Is pottery always extensively decorated as tighter villages are formed?

The specific instances of Çatal Hüyük and Hacilar do not allow full answers to the issues raised earlier. On the one hand, there is a need for richer data. By comparing sites with fuller information and over wide areas and times it may be easier to focus on the general issues identified in the chapter. It will be necessary, therefore, to expand outwards from Çatal Hüyük and from Anatolia and to interpret the symbolism of other areas during the period of the initial adoption and intensification of agriculture. On the other hand, there is a need for a richer interpretive framework. Already an interpretive position has been sketched out that will allow the more general questions to be addressed.

I have begun to describe the adoption of agriculture as a social-symbolic process. The natural (wild) is made cultural (domesticated, agri-cultured). Animals, plants, clay, death, and perhaps reproduction are all 'natural' phenomena which are 'cultured' and brought within the control of a social and cultural system. These ideas, these structured thoughts, will be explored and expanded as I read the data in their terms.

With additional data, and with a particular interpretive framework I will try, especially towards the end of the book, to answer the main questions so far identified. Was the whole process of domestication actively created within a changing context in order to have certain social dramatic effects? Or is the Neolithic simply a prime example of rule following – a determinable response to a changing social and physical environment?

These questions boil down to simple general issues that are issues of our time, not of the Neolithic. This book appeared to come about in a haphazard way, but the events that I have described as leading to the book merely objectified worries that any child of the 1950s to 1970s in Western Europe is likely to have confronted. From Camus's *The Outsider,* to the Vietnam war and the events of soix-ante-huit, from socialism to yuppiedom, from modernism to post-modernism, the issues of structure in relation to change, society in relation to the individual and of science and economy in relation to culture were often at the fore. So the events and the archaeological data that I have described as leading up to this book did not generate entirely new thoughts, new structures. Rather they were interpreted by me in relation to existing structures. It was only through the experience of these events, including writing this book, that the issues became thinkable and the structures became clear. We can only think through experience.

In my view the importance of archaeology in the modern world is that it provides another experience – the experience of the past – through which one can objectify and think our present thoughts. We can only change the structures that bind us once they have been thought. The artifacts from the past, excavated in material contexts and ordered partly by material constraints, provide a wealth of experience through which the present can be thought about and thus changed. This is the ultimate reason that I delve, in the following chapters, into the complex and detailed information for the European Neolithic.

2

The Domestication of Society

Çatal Hüyük and I, we bring each other into existence. It is in our joint interaction, each dependent on the other, that we take our separate forms. But to what extent is this dialectic merely a playing out of larger structures? One of the questions I wish to ask in this book is whether the world of individuals and events, however constructed or contingent it might be, is simply the medium through which a larger script is written.

Thus I began this book with Çatal Hüyük because it was in that context that my ideas appeared to me to begin to take shape. I will need to return to the Neolithic of Anatolia and the Levant later in this chapter, but the book is not about the Neolithic of the Mediterranean region. I have largely confined myself in this book to south-east, central, and north-west Europe for the following reason. Although the domestication of many of the most important European plants and animals begins in the Near East and spreads throughout Mediterranean Europe by the early sixth millennium bc, the long-term social and cultural transformations to which the economic changes correspond in the Mediterranean seem to me to follow a somewhat different path from the rather later development of 'the Neolithic' in other parts of Europe. Given that I want to follow the unfolding of long-term structures, my initial focus is on a coherent sequence that I believe I can see in the spread of the use of domesticated plants and animals from the eastern Mediterranean into south-east Europe and then into central and north-west Europe. I hope to follow the rather different sequence in the Mediterranean as a whole in later writing.

My aim is therefore to conduct a long-term contextual analysis of the European Neolithic. By 'contextual', I mean an analysis which attempts to 'read' or interpret the evidence primarily in terms of its internal relations rather than in terms of outside knowledge. In particular an emphasis is placed on internal symbolic relations rather than on externally derived concepts of rationality. This distinction between an interpretive prehistory and an anthropological archaeology is not in my view equivalent to that between inductive and deductive reasoning. In my interpretation of internal symbolic relations I intend to use both inductive and deductive procedures as I work between data and conceptualization. Indeed my overall concern is to move beyond localized contextual variation to produce historical generalizations of considerable scale and duration. Another recent volume on the European Neolithic (Whittle 1988b) has rightly drawn attention to the great variability in the evidence, spatially and temporally. I wish to use this variability to identify some general themes, some widespread and long-term structures. Having identified this larger-scale context in which similar meanings are assigned to similar objects it will be possible to compare and contrast more localized contexts and to understand the dimensions in terms of which variability occurs.

In beginning the main part of this book with the Neolithic of south-east Europe, it is natural to focus on the Iron Gates region of the Danube and on Lepenski Vir. As at Çatal Hüyük, the rich material found at Lepenski Vir encouraged its excavator, Srejović, to publish a full interpretation (1972) and to discuss symbolic structures at some length. My discussion here is heavily based on his published account.

Lepenski Vir is one of a number of sites which occur in the Iron Gates region on the Yugoslavian–Romanian border in eastern Serbia. The sites show continuous occupation in this area from 12,000 bc into the early Neolithic. By the mid sixth millennium bc there begins the Lepenski Vir culture with a Romanello-Azilian flint industry. This culture is known from at least 11 sites (including Lepenski Vir itself and Vlasac and Padina) and represents one of a number of specialized late Mesolithic adaptations to particular resources in SE Europe, perhaps allowing greater sedentism. The only domesticated plant or animal found at the Lepenski Vir sites is the dog.

At Lepenski Vir itself, there are four main levels, themselves subdivided. After a scanty proto-Lepenski Vir level, Lepenski Vir I and II are without domesticates but with trapezoidal houses and C14 dates ranging from 5400 to 4700 bc. Lepenski Vir III is separated from II by a thin sterile layer. It has Atlantic as opposed to Boreal

Table 1 Simplified chronological chart showing the main phases (including some sites) discussed in the volume. Conventional radiocarbon (C14) dates as used in the text are shown. The corresponding calendar dates produced by C14 calibration are provided for comparison.

Calendar years	Mid 7th mill. BC	Early 6th mill. BC	Mid 6th mill. BC	Early 5th mill. BC	Mid/later 5th mill. BC	Early 4th mill. BC	Late 4th mill. BC	Mid 3rd mill. BC
Radiocarbon years	5500 bc	5000 bc	4500 bc	4000 bc	3500 bc	3000 bc	2500 bc	2000 bc
STEPPES				A	B1 Tripolye	B2	C1	C2
HUNGARIAN PLAIN		Körös	Alföld — Szakálhát →	Tisza — Pre-Cucuteni	Tiszapolgár — Cucuteni	Bodrogkeresztúr →	Baden	Kostolac → Vučedol
WEST BALKANS		Starčevo (Lepenski Vir)	Early Vinča		Late Vinča	Bubanj	Kostoloc — Baden →	Vučedol
BULGARIA		Karanovo I–II Veselinovo	KIII	KIV KV Maritsa	KVI	Gumelnitsa (Varna)	Ezero	

RHINELAND   Linear   Grossgartach
                pottery   Hinkelstein Rössen   Michelsberg   Corded ware

N. FRANCE   Linear   Late
                              pottery Cerny Rössen Chassey-Michelsberg   SOM

KUJAVIA   Linear   Sarnowo
                              pottery Lengyel Pikutkowo Wiórek Luboń

                                                                        Globular
                              Linear   Stroke   Salzmünde   Amphorae   Beaker
C. GERMANY   pottery   pottery   Rössen Baalberg   W-Bernburg Corded ware

                                                                            Fuchsberg MNIII
S. SCANDINAVIA   Ertebølle   EN   MNI II IV V Corded ware

Radiocarbon years 5500 bc 5000 bc 4500 bc 4000 bc 3500 bc 3000 bc 2500 bc 2000 bc pollen, a full range of domesticates, and a lack of trapezoidal houses. There is some uncertainty as to the dating of the earliest Neolithic in the northern part of SE Europe, but it is likely to have begun in the latter part of the sixth millennium and so to overlap, at least partially, with Lepenski Vir I and II.

As Srejović has himself emphasized, the overall impression at Lepenski Vir I and II is order (figure 2.1). The village in its various levels appears 'planned', with equivalent houses oriented in the same way on a horseshoe-shaped shelf overlooking the Danube. The houses face east, and each is characterized by a hardened clay plaster floor and similar internal arrangement. In some sub-phases there is a larger central house which has no special artifacts but which does have more cult objects, altars, and sculptures than other houses. Stone tools and refuse are found within the houses rather than scattered about the village. Srejović contrasts the overall order and control in the village with the wild untamed landscape outside. Apart from domesticated dog the main resource appears to be deer, while

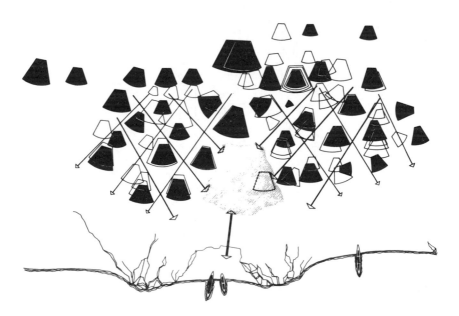

Figure 2.1 Lepenski Vir. Layout and main communication routes.
(Source: Srejović 1972)

fishing was also important. Indeed, Lepenski Vir is the name of a whirlpool on the Danube which provides good fishing. At the village level, therefore, we see social control, social order, in relation to the wild. This point is emphasized by the contrast between Lepenski Vir I and II and Level III where the village plan appears more haphazard, refuse occurs all over the settlement rather than just within the houses, and house shape varies from oval to rectangular.

How was this wider social control achieved? The larger central houses at Lepenski Vir do not seem to suggest marked social ranking and centralized monopolies on force, power, and prestige. Even if some degree of central control did exist, the problem still remains of explaining how the social order was constructed and accepted. What was the discourse of power that led it to be accepted as truth? I will suggest that the major struggles within all houses at Lepenski Vir concern the control of death and the control of the wild, and I will argue that it was this internal discipline which provided the logic for the wider social control.

Each house is trapezoidal in plan, with the hearth at the eastern end, towards the Danube. Around the hearth are often found settings of stones placed in a V shape. In one case the setting is replaced by a human jaw. Whether or not all the V stone settings should be read as representing jaws and death, there is at least some association of the hearth with death. But equally, Srejović argues that one stone associated with a hearth at the site is carved with a representation of a vulva. Although this carving could probably be given other interpretations it remains possible that fire, and perhaps its transformative capacities in the hearth, was associated with the transformations of both death and birth.

By and behind the hearth are found burials beneath the floors, 'altars', stone 'head' and other sculptures (figure 2.2). In Lepenski Vir I and II, burial of adults, both male and female, involves extended north–south laying out of the body, often with several individuals buried in a house over a period of time. Child burial is rare. The antlers of stags are placed along the body in all burials.

Also towards the narrower and darker back part of the house are found stone boulders sculpted in a variety of ways from simple or complex abstract designs to human heads bearing a certain resemblance to fish. Srejović argues (1972, 120) that the skulls of men were commemorated by the carved boulders, and in one case at least a sculpted head is found directly above and associated with the skull of a child (ibid., 119).

(a)

(b)

Figure 2.2 Lepenski Vir houses with (a) 'altar' and (b) sculptures behind hearth.
(Source: Srejović 1972)

Death, or representations of the dead, thus dominate the house at Lepenski Vir. The pervasiveness of death in the Lepenski Vir house is accentuated if we can accept a further suggestion provided by Srejović. In the Proto-Lepenski Vir level was found a male grave laid out so as to form a similar arrangement to the later trapezoidal houses. The triangular to trapezoidal grave contained a body lying on its back with the legs bent and knees apart so as to fill the whole grave with a triangular-trapezoidal shape. The broader end of the grave faced east, as in the later houses. In addition, the skull was propped up, looking forward and eastward in exactly the same way as the later sculpted heads look eastward from the back of the trapezoidal house. It is thus possible that the houses of Lepenski Vir I and II recall earlier burials in their overall shape and internal arrangement.

As at Çatal Hüyük, death at Lepenski Vir is closely associated with the wild. Stag antlers occur in the graves and as 'offerings' behind the hearths. Fish remains also occur here and in relation to the 'altar'. We have also seen that boulder art links humans, death and fish. The two main wild resources exploited at Lepenski Vir thus both seem closely associated with the main symbolic metaphor used within the house – death.

In making sense of this evidence it would be possible to identify a series of oppositions into which death and the wild can be placed. The data do not provide unambiguous indications of such oppositional structures. It would be possible to argue, however, that the eastern (sunrise) entrance end of the house with the light burning in the fire, is opposed to the darker, western (sunset) back end. Although evidence of death is associated with the hearth itself, the main concentration of burials and markers of the dead occurs in the back area of the house. It would thus be possible to oppose death to the life-giving properties of fire, food preparation around the hearth and so on. It would also be possible to argue that the main evidence for the wild (stag antlers and fish offerings) occurs in the back end of the house in opposition to any domestic activities associated with the hearth. Thus wild is opposed to domestic. In addition, the association of a possible vulva with the hearth might allow a provisional hypothesis that the back part of the house was especially linked to male and the front part to female. The following scheme can thus be suggested.

back	west	dark	death	wild	male
front	east	light	life	domestic	female

Even within the evidence we have available to us, the scheme cannot be as simple and straightforward as this. For example, death is also directly associated with the front, light end of the house. And there are cross-cutting divisions. For example, tools and ornaments of stone and bone are only found in the peripheral area of the house, away from the central area with hearth, altar and boulders (ibid., 131). This centre–periphery distinction suggests a ritual–mundane opposition which does not fit well with the 'domestic' functions given to the hearth above.

Indeed, the evidence, limited as it is, seems almost to rejoice in its own ambiguity. The carved 'head' boulders in particular seem to play on the boundary between human and fish. The V settings of stones around the hearths are clearly not constructional since uneven numbers are found on either side of the hearth. But whether they do or do not all refer to the human jaw is uncertain. And does the house shape 'really' recall earlier burials?

I am not sure that we should be dismayed at our inability to fit our fragmentary archaeological data into neat oppositional structures. It may be the notion of oppositional structures which is itself weaker than the archaeological evidence. I am not sure either, that if we could talk to the inhabitants of Lepenski Vir we would necessarily be much the wiser. The site was inhabited for a long period of time with people of different ages, sexes, and perceptions. And even if they could tell us with some conviction that the sculpted heads did or did not refer to fish or the dead, would we take their opinions at face value? I think we would have to assume that there might be underlying, non-discursive concepts which the inhabitants used in their lives even if they could not be very articulate about them.

The evidence from Lepenski Vir is not clear. But perhaps it never was clear. Perhaps the model of oppositional structures is inadequate. This is not to argue that the types of opposition between front/back, life/death did not exist but rather to argue that they were used strategically and contextually.

So how were they used? The rather dry description of symbolic oppositions that I have so far provided ignores a central component in Srejović's text and in the displays of the Lepenski Vir material that I have seen. The site is wonderfully evocative and atmospheric. The ritual, art, and symbolism seem to reach to us and react on us not through their dry 'linguistic', precise meanings, but through emotive experience. The ambiguous sculpted heads, the all-pervasive presence of death, the ordered arrays of houses, the deep gorges of the Danube all seem to appeal directly to our senses. It is as if the houses provide a setting for some drama – an ideal scene for the performance of some plot.

And without drama, what would these structures be doing anyway? Who would believe them, accept them, if they were only abstract rules? It is only through the emotional experience, through fear of death, joy in life, the comfort of home, the danger of the wild, that the structures have any force. In other words, the structures have to be performed in the events within the house if they are to have power. Movement within the house, taking objects from front to back, burying bodies, carving and placing the stones, lighting the fire, are all enmeshed within a dramatic setting. The daily events themselves are the drama, but only because they have been 'set' up as such.

That this is an active performance can be seen by focusing attention on the main theme of the Lepenski Vir drama – death. The dead body is treated in a certain way. It is made use of to create a drama. In particular the dead body is brought into the house. Death is continually brought to one's attention, not to be forgotten. The jaw by the hearth, and the sculpted heads above the hidden human skulls contribute to that. The historical associations of the house shape itself perhaps set the scene in death. The natural fear and danger of death is further played upon, elaborated, heightened by associating the dead with a wild stag, perhaps one of the largest wild animals in the vicinity, and with its dangerous antlers.

But the antlers may have been taken from an animal killed and controlled by man. The dead body has been brought into the house, controlled within the domestic arena, literally domesticated. And not only brought into the house, but framed within the innermost part of the house. The sculptures too are clearly cultural products, depicting the wild and retaining the form of natural boulders, certainly, but carved in a distinctive cultural form with a human technology. As at Çatal Hüyük the main focus of symbolic elaborations is associated with the death-linked part of the house. The Lepenski Vir 'art' adds to the dramatic effect which heightens social and emotional awareness of the feared while at the same time framing and 'culturing'.

The domestication of death and the wild occurs in all the houses. Within each separate unit control is internalized. The dramatic events create the structures of control, but the structures are 'objectified' in the emotional experiences of the events. The control of the wild and of the social relations within each house allows the control of the wild in the society at large. The well-ordered equivalent houses and the other aspects of societal-wide organization identified above could all have been created through the building block of control within each individual house.

This is not to argue that the whole drama was simply stage-set by one dominant group – such as by men, or by male and female elders, or by one family. Rather, the evidence suggests an overall concern with identifying the place of the individual in relation to the social. Each individual house, in domesticating death and the wild is also domesticating itself according to structures which are general to the larger group. In domesticating the wild according to general social rules, each individual is also domesticating his or her own potential individuality – that potential unsocial 'wildness', which threatens to 'be the death' of society. Another aspect of this same idea which will become clear later in this book is the practice of secondary burial after decomposition of the body (ibid., 117). The individuality of the flesh has been removed at Lepenski Vir before the dry, social bones are placed within the home.

Of course it is possible to argue that I am not identifying anything specific at Lepenski Vir. The culture/nature duality is the very stuff of all human society. The imposition of cultural categories is everywhere the mechanism by which the social world is ordered. Similarly, presumably the domestic world from Palaeolithic caves to contemporary suburban semi-detached houses is widely used as one way in which the cultural and the social are constituted. However, I have already begun to suggest two more specific components of domestic symbolism associated with the origins of agriculture. First, domestic architecture and activities seem to have taken on a special importance at this time. Houses generally become more complex and elaborate and the larger social units expressed archaeologically at 'villages' such as Lepenski Vir contain little evidence of other types of architecture. Thus the larger social units are themselves largely constructed in terms of collections of domestic units. Second, I have begun to suggest that within the general idea of the house as a metaphor for the domestication of society there is a more specific ordering of spatial and symbolic relationships. As the book develops I hope to be able to substantiate these two points more fully.

Before leaving Lepenski Vir and considering later developments in SE Europe, it is important to note the striking similarities with Çatal Hüyük. Perhaps I have simply imposed the Çatal Hüyük ideas on the less rich Lepenski Vir data. But even if I have, the data do allow at least certain aspects of the transference. In both cases death and the wild are located within the domestic unit within a wider 'village' grouping. In both cases hearths are at the front of the house and death, the wild and symbolic elaboration concentrated in the back portions. And yet the specific contents of the two cultural assemblages are very different. While John Nandris (1970) has demonstrated numerous cultural similarities between Anatolia and the Balkans, Çatal Hüyük and Lepenski Vir remain separated in time, space, and culture. But this is a theme to which I will need to return later in this volume.

Perhaps the clearest difference between Lepenski Vir and Çatal Hüyük is that the former does not have agriculture. The possibility exists, therefore, that domestication in the social and symbolic sense occurred prior to domestication in the economic sense. Indeed, as hinted earlier, the agricultural revolution may have been an epiphenomenon of deeper changes.

Domestication as a Discourse of Power

There is some controversy about the dating of Lepenski Vir in relation to the first agriculture in the region (see Whittle 1985, 316 n. 16), but it seems likely that Lepenski Vir I and II are contemporary with agricultural Starčevo sites (see below). Nevertheless the tradition of trapezoidal houses in the Lepenski Vir micro-region extends back through similar sites in the Iron Gates region. Thus, whatever the precise dating of Lepenski Vir I and II, this site does give an indication of the actions of individuals within a sedentary hunter-gatherer group immediately prior to or contemporary with early agriculture.

It occurs to me, however, that given the paucity of evidence from other Mesolithic sites in south-east Europe for the social and cultural transformations leading to the domestication of plants and animals, there might be some value in following through my initial ideas about the symbolism associated with domestication in the Near East. Although the latter area is not the main concern of this book, the evidence for gradual indigenous domestication is clear and more complete and the sequence is relevant to that in Europe. The Lepenski Vir material, as I came upon it, reinforced my general idea that economic domestication is associated with or is preceded by social and symbolic domestication. Is this idea valid in an area (the Near East) with a continuous and relatively well documented sequence of indigenous change? Could I clarify my views about the domestication process by considering again the Near Eastern data before embarking on the European journey in earnest? This toing and froing between Europe and the Near East may seem irksome to the reader, but then this book is not only about structure and contingency in the Neolithic past. It is also about structure and contingency in the present – in my research process. The neat structures which we try to produce in writing books hide the dialectical relation between structure and contingency, code and experience. By retaining something of the contingent character of my research in the book I hope to probe more completely the complex relationships between apparently chance events and the structures which seem to bind all we do.

The date that one gives for the 'origin of agriculture' in the Near East depends very much on the animal or plant species being considered and on the type of measurement of domestication that is used. In general, intensive use of wild resources and some degree of sedentary life begin before genetic changes in plants and animals can be identified. Thus, sheep may have been domesticated at Zawi Chemi at about 9000 bc on the basis of the high percentage of immature animals found (Oates and Oates 1976), but genetic changes to sheep or goat occur only in the eighth and seventh millennia in the Near East. Similarly, there is evidence for the intensive gathering and collecting of plants in the Near East from at least the tenth millennium bc, but the evidence from pollen of human use of cereals comes from Mureybet at 7700 bc (Cauvin and Cauvin 1982) while domesticated cereal grains occur at Jericho perhaps from 8000 bc (PPNA), and certainly from 7000 bc.

Given this long slow process of domestication in the Near East (Hole 1984; Moore 1985) it is not possible to identify a point in time and say 'this is when domestication of plants and animals began'. But it is at least clear that the growth of Neolithic symbolism does not occur *after* the domestication of the economy. Indeed, if the symbolic and social parts of the process do not occur before the economic, they are certainly integrally connected with it.

Within the Kebaran, or late Pleistocene culture in the Levant, it is not yet possible to talk of villages or of real sedentism even though some grinding of wild food within the settlements occurred (Cauvin and Cauvin 1982). At Névé-David a Kebaran male burial has been found, dated to approximately 11,000 bc, associated with three mortars. One of the mortars had been placed covering the skull and another between the legs (Kaufman and Ronen 1987). It is in the following Natufian, 10,300–8500 bc (Bar Yosef 1982), that evidence of the processing of wild plants on sites increases considerably. Grinders, mortars and pestles, and glossed sickle blades abound, the latter sometimes set in elaborate carved sickle shafts. Hunting of gazelle in particular, and fishing were also important components of the economy.

Natufian sites can be divided into base camps and seasonal camps (Bar Yosef 1982), but some degree of mobility has even been suggested for the base camps (ibid., and Cauvin and Cauvin 1982), some of which reach 2000 m² (Eynan) and 3000 m² (Rosh Horesha). The internal organization of the houses in these settlements often shows some degree of order. Eynan had about 50 round houses in each of three building phases. The houses, 3–9 m in diameter, had a lining of rubble. One house in the lowest level had a paved stone floor with red-painted plaster on the walls. Each hut had, usually near the centre, a stone-built hearth, sometimes surrounded by a stone pavement of flat slabs. In one case a large mortar was placed near the hearth (figure 2.3). Storage pits are found inside and outside the houses.

Thus, already in the Natufian we can see that the process of domesticating plants involves an emphasis on the house and settlement in a wider sense. The plants are at least partly ground and prepared near and in the hearth in the house. An increased social control is seen in the larger settlements with equivalent and ordered habitation units, perhaps with some informal degree of social ranking beyond age and sex divisions (Bender 1978; Wright 1978). This social control may be linked to the control of resources within the home. The household appears to be the main unit of production, and conceptually too attention is focused on the house. The hearth itself is emphasized and the house is sometimes painted. The wild is brought in and controlled.

It is thus of interest that burial of the dead in the Natufian occurs in the settlement and in the house. Burials are found in and near houses, including in storage pits. Scattered human bones occur in occupational debris, and there is evidence of both primary and secondary burial. The skeletons show evidence of head decoration, necklaces, bracelets, belts, etc. Death, too, was controlled culturally and domesticated.

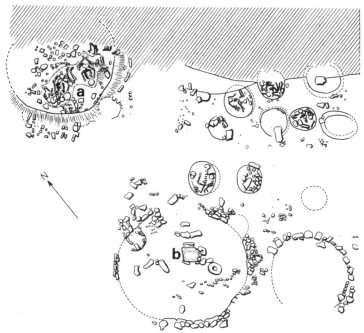

Figure 2.3 Plan of part of the Natufian settlement at Eynan (Ain Mallaha), level III, with round houses and storage pits, some reused for burials: (a) tomb inside a house; (b) hearth with mortar to the right, fixed in the floor.
(Source: Mellaart 1965, after Perrot)

An increasing emphasis on house and settlement continues into the beginning of the eighth millennium, in the Pre-Pottery Neolithic A. Indeed, the encircling stone wall and towers, and the first use of mud-brick at Jericho in PPNA, together with the still slight evidence of heavy dependence on morphologically changed plants and animals, suggest that the primary forces may have been social and symbolic and that the economic domestication played a central but not dominant role.

PPNA sites are generally larger, with most reaching 2–3 ha (Cauvin and Cauvin 1982). The greater social constraints implied by the increasing settlement size and by the organization of labour needed for the construction of the massive walls and towers at Jericho, have the house as their source in the sense that the house becomes increasingly the focus of cultural activity. This process is perhaps best seen at Mureybet (Cauvin 1979 and 1986) in levels II and III. The houses are round and not usually more than 4 m in diameter and in level III the first internal divisions occur in the houses. All the houses are plastered by level III, one with geometric painting. Within a clay bench within a level II house was found a bucranium, and cattle horns were found in the walls. As at PPNA Jericho, human burials are found inside and outside houses, the rite including the separation of the head from the body.

The cattle, which become an important part of the diet in Mureybet II and III, are still morphologically wild, and it is this fact which led Cauvin to claim (as was discussed briefly in chapter 1) that cattle were first domesticated symbolically – brought into the house, controlled within cultural categories and within a 'cattle cult'. Cereals too were still morphologically wild, but there was an increasing cultural interest in the control of food within cultural categories and domestic containers. Some stone bowls and dishes have zigzag moulding, and some precociously early pottery in level III has some rather crude decoration of incised lines (Cauvin 1974). The degree of firing of these early Mureybet pots, occurring well before the main development of ceramics in the sixth millennium, is variable but nevertheless indicates a concern to experiment with the transformation of clay into fired ceramic, thus also transforming the 'wild' contents into a 'domestic' product.

But it is in Mureybet IVB (7300 bc) and in other PPNB sites such as Jericho and Beidha that the process of cultural and economic domestication reaches its apogee. Morphologically wild plants and animals are still common on sites until at least the sixth millennium bc (Moore 1985) but there is a growing number of permanent villages (Oates and Oates 1976) and more intensive exploitation of sheep, goat, cattle, and pig (Moore 1985). Houses are generally rectangular and show greater evidence of internal differentiation. At Mureybet, a skull cult which had begun to emerge in the Natufian is identifiable. Human skulls are placed on the floor of a house, against walls, and on red clay supports. Burials also occur beneath the floors of houses. At Jericho, houses have several rooms grouped around courtyards. The floors are plastered and are often painted, and several buildings have been interpreted as shrines. Figurines (mainly female) increase in number. In PPNB Jericho, ten human skulls (both male and female) with facial features modelled in clay have been found, with the eyes inset with shells. Such skulls are also known from Beisamun (Oates and Oates 1976) and from Ramad (dated to about 6200 bc). At the latter site headless seated clay female figures, c. 25 cm high, coated with plaster and with traces of red paint, may have acted as skull supports. At Ain Ghazal, burial is most common beneath house floors with skulls removed and placed separately beneath floors. Ochre decoration of walls increased through time. Pits containing human statuettes had been dug into abandoned house floors, and plastered human skulls occurred in a courtyard pit (Rollefson 1983, 1986).

It was not until the Pottery Neolithic at Jericho that gazelle was replaced by sheep or goat as the primary meat source (Oates and Oates 1976), although we have seen an intensification and increasing selection of use of resources since at least the Natufian. At Beidha too in the PPNB phase, full use of domesticates was not achieved. Moore (1985) suggests more generally that agriculture and stock raising came to dominate hunting and gathering more completely in the Pottery Neolithic A (sixth millennium bc). Despite all the variability and difficulty of definition of 'domestication', it seems clear that the origins of agriculture take place within a complex symbolic web that centres on the house and on death. In addition, through time clear trends in this symbolism can be identified, both in the Levant and south-east Europe. The early elaboration of the house involves the use of burial. Thus in the period up to about 6000 bc in the Levant, and rather later at Çatal Hüyük and Lepenski Vir, burial occurs beneath the floors of houses and is referred to within the domestic context in a number of ways (e.g. by wall-paintings or stone head sculptures). But after 6000 bc in the Levant, in the early Pottery Neolithic burial is commonly outside the settlement (Moore 1985). At the same time the multi-roomed rectangular houses become unpainted, pottery is introduced and increasingly decorated, and there are fewer arrowheads found on sites indicating a decline in the visibility of hunting associated with the increased importance of agriculture and stock raising. In Anatolia too I have noted the switch at Hacilar towards burial outside the domestic context, less symbolic elaboration of house interiors, and increased use of decorated pottery. In SE Europe we shall find the same preference after Lepenski Vir for burial away from houses and for decorated ceramics. There is general structural change here which is larger than any individual local sequence. In all cases considered so far, it is as if the incipient stages of domestication are associated with death in the domestic context, closely associated with productive and reproductive activities and with ordered village plans. As the economic process of domestication intensifies, however, death is distanced from the house (although the dead may still have been referred to symbolically by the use of figurines, for example).

Although it is not my aim to conduct a detailed analysis of Neolithic symbolism in the Levant, this brief review does support a hypothesis that I will outline here and then explore in more detail in Europe.

In any historical account, it is difficult to know at what point to break into the chain of events. It is always necessary to start some-where by taking certain things as 'given', unexamined and unexplained. Otherwise it becomes necessary to push back endlessly in time to 'the' original cultural event. In the final chapter in this book I will suggest an overall view of preceding events in the Palaeolithic that lead up to and produce the origins of agriculture. This will be a matter of tracing certain ideas backwards and so I must leave my conjectural foray into the Palaeolithic to the end of the book when the ideas will have been developed. For my present purposes, I wish to start my story with a presumed importance of 'the house' amongst Pleistocene hunters and gatherers. I expect that the house was always a safe haven, providing warmth and security, the focus of a child's early life, and the centre of domestic production.

I also take for granted for present purposes that in the late Pleistocene and early Holocene in the Near East, social groups began to aggregate and become more sedentary. The conditions leading to this process are not important here. They will be discussed in chapter 10. But whatever the events which provided the necessary conditions for increased sedentism, human individuals could have avoided the need for sedentism in a variety of ways – for example by dispersing, decreasing population levels through infanticide, or by relocation. Why did they choose sedentism and the increased labour involved in the more intensive gathering of wild resources? To live in a larger, sedentary social unit involves sacrificing the flexible and immediate response of the small unit to the needs and demands of the larger whole. There is some degree of order in the layout of early settlements in the Near East. There is evidence of storage in Natufian sites. The protection of the household's stored resources implies the need for some increased degree of societal-wide control on behaviour. There was probably joint labour investment in the gathering and hunting of resources. Woodburn (1980) has shown that in intensive hunter-gatherer economies such as those encountered in the Natufian there is a delayed return for labour investment. In other words, the labour invested in joint economic projects is not returned in the form of food until a later date. In order to protect the individual's investment, the wider social whole provides a durable set of social relations and authorities in which the individual can have confidence. Social structures become longer term and more established. There is also the possibility for increasing social dominance, as has been suggested for the Natufian (see above). Bender (1978) has in fact argued that it is lineage competition for social dominance which may have led to the intensification of production, and hence to the adoption of agriculture.

But how was all this achieved? Why did individuals not react in a different way? Why did they give themselves to the constraints of the larger whole? How was the desire for sedentism and intensification created? The evidence suggests that the house became the central metaphor, and I have also suggested that in early societies the house would have evoked certain emotions including security and the social and cultural as opposed to the wild and natural. It seems possible, therefore, that in the Natufian if not earlier, a creative link was made which was to have lasting and expanding consequences. The household is a production unit and it is through that production that the larger social unit is to be constructed. But it is also a conceptual unit opposed to the wild, the dangerous and the unsocial. By linking the matter and ideal of the house to the matter and ideal of social reproduction, the social desire for aggregations and intensification was channelled.

It is rarely possible over the long run to discipline 'from the top down' without the awakening of desire 'from the bottom up'. Domination involves negotiation from different points of view. Structures of power are linked to structures of signification. It is certainly possible that the changes in the Neolithic of the Near East were manipulated by special interest groups, such as the elders. But it is equally likely that other groups in society played equally active roles. Whatever the details of that negotiation, I would argue that the discourse of power was conducted in terms of the house and the activities associated with it. This wider set of activities and concepts I intend to call the domus. I will define this term more carefully in chapter 3, but for the moment it can roughly be translated as 'home', referring to the specific attributes of 'home' found in different Neolithic contexts. Whatever the social, economic, and environmental variables or 'causes' involved, it was through the domus that the origins of agriculture were thought about and conceived.

The domus was put centre stage. The house was paved and painted, and later plastered and divided functionally. Death was brought in and controlled, cultured beneath the house floor. By PPNA wild animals were being brought in and 'controlled' within the domestic unit. 'Wild' plants too were brought in and converted into a cultural product. The domus became the conceptual and practical locus for the transformation of wild into cultural. There is little evidence for rituals or areas of authority or production outside the house unit. Rather it was in the internal 'self'-control that the larger societal control was generated. The wider social unit had its roots in the internalized desire for the control of individualistic, unsocial, 'wild' behaviour. The domus provided a way of thinking about the control of the wild and thus for the larger oppositions between culture and nature, social and unsocial.

In particular, individual family feelings regarding their dead were controlled within the family home. The placing of the dead below a house floor or in a storage pit created a drama in which dark fears were linked to basic loves. The home protected one from the wild and even from death. This internal drama was also a public drama, at least in so far as it repeated an accepted, societal-wide code. Each house referred to other houses. It was within the cultural control of the wild within each house that the larger social unit could be created. The evidence supports the idea that it was the domus which provided the enabling conceptual and practical mechanism for social and economic transformation. Existing attitudes to and practices within the home created the possibility of both the increased symbolic control of 'the wild' within 'the domus' and economic domestication.

The intended and unintended consequences of the creation of society through the idea of 'domus' are far-reaching. They unfold with an almost inexorable logic. Any social conflict, whether between men and women, old and young, local group and local group, could be negotiated in terms of the need better to control 'the wild' by bringing it within the control of 'the domus'. The extension of social control, the giving of feasts in order to gain social prestige and the expansion of group size in order to increase productive advantages (Bender 1978) would all have been related to the domus (for example by holding feasts in relation to burial ceremonies in houses or in relation to the periodic painting of houses). As a result, both cultural and economic domestication increase. Figurines and pottery containers involve the transformation of 'wild' clay into cultural products. The house becomes more elaborate and internally differentiated and more clearly linked to the control of the wild, and as part of that social-symbolic process wild plants and animals are continually brought into a closer relationship with humans, leading ultimately to genetic change.

But the older issues concerning the relationship between the individual or individual family (both potentially in conflict with wider societal interests and hence 'wild') and the social remain and in fact become increasingly problematic. As the size of social unit increases and the economy intensifies, the desire for social control is increasingly undermined by the awareness of social constraint. A problem emerges as central: what is the relationship between the individual human body which dies and decays, and the more permanent social role which he or she fills? Where does the authority of the individual (elder male, elder woman, etc.) reside? As the long-term social structures of the type described by Woodburn (1980) and briefly discussed above increase, the notion of the domus itself becomes problematic. On the one hand the house is the locus for the reproduction of the individual, and for his or her productive activities. It thus provides a basis for loyalties that cross-cut societal-wide interests. On the other hand, the domestication process has become the metaphor for society itself.

One attempt to deal with this problem emerges through time concerning the drama surrounding death. Increasingly, there is evidence of public symbolism concerning the separation of the individual temporary flesh of the human body from the more durable bones. There is more evidence for secondary burial, and in particular the separation of the head from the body. In addition, the clay modelling of facial features on skulls, and the replacing of the eyes as shells, evokes in an extraordinarily dramatic way, basic fears about mortality and the decay of the human flesh. To whatever specific social issues these dramas were addressed, they seem to concern the individuality of the human flesh. The frequent location of skulls inside houses situates that concern within the contradictions of the domus. But ultimately, the individuality of the body is separated from the social metaphor within the house. I have also shown that the symbolic evocations surrounding death are increasingly taken out of the house. In this way the power of the individual house as the locus for the domestication of death is reduced. Also pottery, more visible and portable and hence more public, becomes more elaborately decorated than the insides of houses at Hacilar. It is as if some aspects of the domestication process had moved to a wider societal domain.

Conclusion: the Origins of Agriculture

I have argued that a concept of 'home' – the domus – was used as a metaphor for the domestication of society and the creation of larger social units in the early Holocene in the Near East. But the domus was not only the metaphor for change. It was also the mechanism of change, and it was through this dual role that what we normally talk about today as domestication and the origins of agriculture in the Near East came about.

As metaphor, the idea of the domus used existing fears and emotions to create the channel for structural change. The origins of agriculture need never have happened. People could have reacted in other ways. However haphazard and unintentional the whole process, some intentionality was necessarily involved and some moment of desire is implicated. I suggest that the social will to sedentism and intensification which ultimately led to economic domestication was created through drama, in the sense that emotions, feelings, and fears were aroused in the interplay of concepts surrounding the domus. It was drama that created the will to control the wild and thus to transform culture into nature. And it was through the experience of that cultural domestication within the self that the social whole was constructed. The domus was more than a way of thinking about society. It was also the source of a desire.

As mechanism, the domus is the locus of the production and reproduction which constitute society and social relations. The meagre evidence which we have suggests that storage and processing of food were clearly linked to the household. The wider social structures which enabled those productive tasks were themselves created in those tasks. Whether we are considering joint field labour, the protection of storage, or the exchange of food, feasts, or prestige items such as obsidian or shells, the household appears to be the mechanism for the provision of the productive resources on which these socio-structural relations depend. The relations of production/ reproduction involving joint endeavours, exchanges, etc. were increasingly channelled through the household rather than, as may have been the case in earlier social configurations, being channelled through a criss-crossing circuit of relations. In a very practical way then, the control of the wild within the domestic unit constituted the control of the relations between people within society. Even more important, individuals became enmeshed in long-term dependencies. The delayed return for agricultural labour investment meant that individuals became trapped within broader social and economic structures. Social control and the regulation seen in planned villages were created through the mechanism of agriculture. The adoption of more intensive production techniques, leading to agriculture, served the interests of dominant groups in society in that the new economic regime ensnared people within social and economic structures on which they came to depend. The symbolic confrontation of culture and nature, the reproductive and destructive, nurture and death created society through the opposition between domestic and wild, but the practical process of domestication also created real dependencies between domestic units. Through this dual symbolic and practical process individual domestic units could be 'settled' in villages.

In this chapter I have increasingly found myself indulging in a highly imaginative reconstruction. In fact I already know as I write that I can support the argument better in relation to the European evidence which is the main focus of this book. Nevertheless, the story does seem to fit the Near Eastern data equally well and it was partly suggested by them. Even though the Near East is the start of the story that unfolds gradually across Europe, the story is not fully dependent on the partial surviving data from any one region. I found myself telling the story in some detail here, in order to show the potential relevance of the Near Eastern data. But in order to transform the story into history I will need to consider the European data in greater detail in the following chapters.

Perhaps more important, I do not claim at this stage to have provided an adequate account of the processes involved in the origins of agriculture. I have left many aspects hanging loose. In particular I have not tried to explain why sedentism comes about at a particular juncture in the post-Pleistocene period. Neither have I adequately explored the strategies of social domination involved in the domestication process. Perhaps most seriously, I have not resolved the issue I raised in chapter 1 concerning the relative roles of structures and contingencies. If anything the data seem to be suggesting to me the playing out of structures over vast areas. These are all unresolved problems which I hope the European data will help to elucidate.

When my story is transferred to Europe, Lepenski Vir clearly recalls the beginning of the process I have so far hypothesized. Here burials are placed within the house and death is seemingly ever present within its 'fixtures and fittings'. The drama in the house still emphasizes the death and history of the individual family as the basis for social participation. It is only later in SE Europe that we might expect the contradiction inherent within the strategy to be played out.

3

The Domus in the Neolithic of SE Europe

As I wrote this book I gradually came to realize what I meant by the term domus. It was somewhere towards the end of chapter 8 that I finally felt comfortable with the concept. My definition of the term came about through my haphazard experience of the data. I gradually accommodated my own preconceptions derived for example from my visit to the Nuba and from my understanding of English and Latin, to my re-examination of the regional prehistoric sequences and contextual information. It became necessary, as will be shown in later chapters, to redefine the term in the different regions. This shifting contributes to the mobile and uncertain nature of the overall concept. The domus is not a well bounded term with hard and fast scientific meanings. The meanings vary depending on what the term is associated or contrasted with.

Nevertheless, it is necessary, having finished the first draft of the book, to return to this point in my account in order to forewarn the reader what I mean by the concept, at the most general level. Perhaps most important, the term is specialist. It is not as overloaded with contemporary associations as are the nearest equivalents such as 'home'. I wanted to use general ideas to make a specific interpretation of the data, and the use of a specialist term contributes to that endeavour.

The domus involves practical activities carried out in the house, food preparation and the sustaining of life. But it is also an abstract term. Secondary, symbolic connotations are given to the practical activities, leading to the house as a focus for symbolic elaboration and to the use of the house as a metaphor for social and economic strategies and relations of power. Practical acts such as the preparation and provision of food, the placing of female figurines in the house, and the burial of women and children in and around the house associate the house with the more general idea of nurturing. The provision of shelter and the storage of food associate the house with caring. The domus as defined here is the concept and practice of nurturing and caring, but at a still more general level it obtains its dramatic force from the exclusion, control and domination of the wild, the outside (which I shall later describe as the 'agrios'). Culture, then, is opposed to nature, but in an historically specific manner.

I was also attracted to the use of the term domus (and other related terms such as 'foris' and 'agrios' which I will define later) because of the possibility that many of our contemporary concepts do have prehistoric roots. Most dictionaries link domesticate to domestic to Latin *domus*, to Greek *domos*, to Sanskrit *damas*, to Old Slavonic *domu*, to Old Irish *doim* and to the Indo-European *dom-* or *dem-*. Further links are also made to domicile, dominant, dominus (whence don, donna in the sense of a distinguished or important man or woman), dome (house, mansion, cathedral church), domain, dame, and tame. Although Benveniste (1973, 251) argues that the Indo-European root should be divided into three distinct units (the sense of a house or building, the sense of *domare* or to tame, and the sense of a family or social unit) the evidence for radical distinctions seems slight. I would prefer to accept the overall conclusion that 'in the light of *domus* and the related forms we can assess the richness and specificity of a terminology which must be counted among the most ancient of the Indo-European world' (ibid., 257). Regardless of whether the first farmers in Europe and the Near East were in any sense Indo-European (Renfrew 1987), I find it fascinating that our language should link houses with the economic process of domestication and with the social processes of the formation of larger and more clearly defined social units involving some form of societal domination and constraint – since these are exactly the links made by the archaeological data for the early Neolithic of Europe and the Near East.

But of course I cannot know if there is a direct link between those linguistic and archaeological data, between the present words and the Neolithic experience. Indeed my main reason for using terms such as the domus is that they allow a sleight of hand. On the one side, it is as if I am using a linguistic tie to the distant past in order to think the archaeological data in 'their' terms, using words with common Indo-European roots, perhaps spoken by 'them', or at least closer to words spoken by 'them'. The use of possibly common terms makes it seem as if I am getting closer to the past, closer to the general archaeological ideal of getting back into the past. Or to put it another way, it appears as if I am thinking about the past (and the present) in the past's terms.

On the other side, it is blatantly and painfully clear that the words as we use them today have more recent and modern meanings. The first farmers in Europe may have used languages unrelated to Indo-European. The term domus may have more recent roots. The distances between the past and the archaeological remains (which are themselves partly constructed in the present), between the meanings of Indo-European terms and contemporary equivalents, and between the material traces of the past and the modern meanings of words used to describe them are so great that no one can really imagine that 'their' and 'my' meanings coincide. The interpretive problems caused by encounters with 'other' worlds are faced equally by historians, archaeologists, and anthropologists. But the great expanses of time involved in the archaeological case highlight the difficulty of translation between 'their' and 'our' languages.

The use of terms such as the domus, which are familiar yet strange, points to the uncertainties and difficulties of interpretation. The use shows that our comfortable scientific terms (I could have used culture–nature instead of domus–agrios for example) are themselves historically produced and ever changing in meaning. The passage of time transforms the meanings, but always within given historical structures. By playing on, punning with, terms such as domination, domestication, focus, forest, and agriculture I hope to draw attention to the fact that we think the past through language which is both constructed in the present and constructed in the past. In the latter sense, the language also constructs us in the present (since we think through language) and constructs the way we look at the past. To push the point even further, the material remains from the past, in so far as they can be seen as texts constructed in the past, also construct our thoughts in the present. We reconstruct the past as much as we construct it. My account in this book is both of the past and of the present. The aim in my rewriting is to contribute knowledge about ourselves both as historical and as contemporary beings.

Having provided a broad definition of the domus and attempted to justify use of the term, I wish to return to my original text in which the term is used in gradually shifting ways. In this and the following chapter I intend to develop the concept of the domus in relation to the Neolithic of SE Europe. In doing so I will be providing a general overview which pays insufficient attention to regional variation. Indeed, the Neolithic of SE Europe is frequently treated as an entity (Tringham 1971; Whittle 1985). Despite the many internal variations, there is a common tradition (including house construction, pottery style, figurines and other miniatures, and occurrence of 'tells') which, together with the absence of other traditions such as long houses and long burial mounds found else-where in Europe, defines a continuity over space and time in SE Europe. Because of the inadequacy of data from most sites in most areas of Europe, some 'pooling' of information is necessary. While this approach perhaps assumes what it should set out to prove – the 'wholeness' of the SE Europe Neolithic – the strategy is necessary in practice and lends itself to later contextual revision and critique. Nevertheless the dangers of such a strategy are particularly acute in SE Europe where 'Balkanization' seems especially marked. Regional cultures such as the Hamangia are organized in markedly different ways from the general pattern described here. The sequence in the Great Hungarian Plain differs substantially from that found in central Bulgaria. There is major variation in subsistence economies, and the rate at which tell-like settlements and painted pottery are adopted differs markedly from region to region. I hope at a later stage to write about the way in which different historical trajectories 'bounce' off each other to produce 'co historical' regional traditions. For the moment, however, I wish to argue that despite the regional variation within SE Europe, certain general trends can be identified. While I will point to some of the regional and temporal variation below, it is to the more general processes that I wish to address myself.

As a further caveat, it should be recognized that many of the biases in the archaeological data for this period and area derive from the way in which information has been collected. The overall prevalence of information on houses and settlements results from the ease of identifying tell sites. The archaeology of the region has often focused on tells to the detriment of the less visible cemeteries and smaller settlement and activity sites. I will argue below, however, that the present visibility of the domus in the archaeological data may be at least partly linked to its past centrality within Neolithic society.

The final limitation of the data that I wish to consider here concerns depositional processes. I will be discussing at some length in this and the following chapter the distributions of artifacts within houses. I shall be arguing that the artifacts found within the houses give clues as to the nature of the domus. In the SE European context it is extremely difficult, if not impossible at the moment, to know whether relatively complete but broken pottery and other artifacts found on the floors of houses represent *in situ* use of the house or *in situ* abandonment or post-abandonment behaviour (such as symbolic closure, or use of the house as a store or for refuse). While some recent excavations have attempted to distinguish primary and secondary refuse (see below), the interpretation of 'primary' *in situ* deposits remains uncertain. The possibility has to be retained, therefore, that much of the symbolic patterning to be identified below is the result of abandonment rather than use. Despite this difficulty, the principles identified in that patterning remain of interest.

The Early Neolithic

Contemporary with the Lepenski Vir settlement discussed in chapter 2, the Neolithic economy spread into SE Europe in the second half of the sixth millennium bc, although some degree of indigenous development has been suggested (Dennell 1983). While domesticated plants and animals occur widely on sites in the late sixth and early fifth millennia, the dependence on wild resources remains relatively high. For example, wild animals often make up 35–50 per cent of the animal bones from a site. But there is much local variation. In the Starčevo levels at Anza in Yugoslavia, wild animals comprise less than 5 per cent of the animal bones (Gimbutas 1976), while at the Starčevo site of Obre 1, 25 per cent of the bones are from wild animals (Benac 1973). In the Körös variant of early Neolithic culture, hunted mammals and birds make up 6–62 per cent of the animal bones and fishing, shellfish, and snails are important at many sites (Kosse 1979).

On the other hand, sites are often located on easily worked and drained arable land (e.g. Dennell and Webley 1975), and the settlements of Bulgaria and southern Yugoslavia show continuous occupation and a clear reliance on domesticated cereals. The animal bones in the Starčevo levels at Obre 1 suggest year-round occupation (Markotic 1984). In the Körös and Criş sites in the northern part of the area there are no tell sites, but the analysis of bird bones from

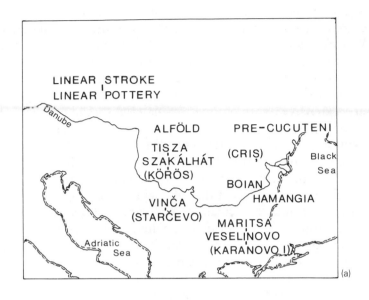

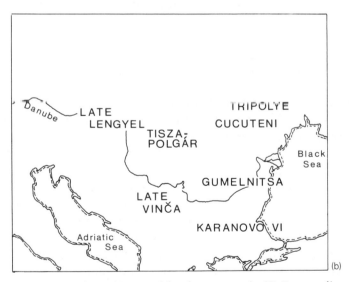

Figure 3.1 Main cultural groupings and local sequences in SE Europe discussed in the text: (a) sixth to early fourth millennia (with sixth to early fifth millennia groups in brackets); (b) late fourth millennium.

Körös sites indicates year-round occupation and some occupation layers are up to 3 m thick (Kosse 1979). On the other hand, Kaiser and Voytek (1982, 330–1) summarize the evidence for the Starčevo sites, including the thinness of occupation horizons, site location, and animal bone assemblages, and conclude that Starčevo settlements were semi-sedentary and short-term. In eastern Hungary, Körös sites are 'extensive', with occupation material spread over large river-side zones (Sherratt 1982a; 1983a). The linear scatters probably represent a pattern of settlement drift over several generations, formed by the movement of dispersed clusters of houses (ibid).

Overall, then, early Neolithic sites are generally firmly established in an agricultural lifestyle although dependence on wild resources and a degree of mobility remain considerable at least in certain areas. In conjunction with this evidence, where the sizes of contemporaneous occupation layers can be identified, the sites are often small. For example, few Starčevo settlements are larger than 1 ha (Kaiser and Voytek 1982), and they are internally undifferentiated.

Perhaps because of the relative impermanence of settlements, there are few reliable house plans and settlement plans from this period. Certainly, as at Lepenski Vir, the house is an important focus of productive and symbolic activities. But it is in the early Neolithic only a faint trace of what it is to become in the later Neolithic and Copper Ages in SE Europe. Indeed, the relative 'invisibility' of the early Neolithic house is not an accidental, mechanical product of semi-sedentary occupation. Even in the tell sites of this period the houses are small and less elaborate than they later become. Rather, we have seen in chapter 2 that a link exists in the Near East between sedentism, the formation of larger social units, and an emphasis on the domus. It is thus not surprising to find that in the early Neolithic groups of SE Europe, the small social units that often depended heavily on wild resources and were often only semi-sedentary, are not associated with great symbolic elaboration of the house.

On the other hand, the ideology of the domus is already present in the early Neolithic of SE Europe and it provides the basis for social life in these small settlements. Houses are rectangular, with walls made of daub on a wooden or wattle frame. They are generally small (e.g. 4 × 8 m to 6 × 7 m) and do not usually show any internal divisions, although a Körös site (Tiszajenő) in south-east Hungary has a slight portico and one room containing a hearth, storage pot set in the ground, and conical clay weights possibly from a loom (Tringham 1971). In the tell site of Karanovo in Bulgaria, level I has single room houses. At one of the corners on the outside wall of the house is a small 'cupboard' for storing grain (Mikov 1959), and millstones are found next to the hearth. In general, in the early Neolithic of SE Europe there is one hearth or oven per house, and evidence for both the grinding of plant material and its storage is particularly associated with the area around the hearth. Ovens and storage pots and pits are also found outside, but again in close association with the houses. The focus of activities around the hearth is perhaps best seen at the late Starčevo/early Vinča site of Obre 1 in which coarse ware sherds, stone querns, and stone paving are clustered around the hearth (Benac 1973).

The latter site also provided evidence for the deposit of animal bones beneath an outside hearth and the placing of animal bones as a 'foundation deposit' within the house (ibid., 339). Evidence for symbolic elaboration within the house includes the red and white painting of walls at Karanovo (Tringham 1971) and the occurrence of Körös house models with an animal head on the gable end (Kalicz 1970). Whether such models provide an accurate representation of houses or not, their very existence indicates an interest in the symbolic representation of the house. Gimbutas (1974, 67) refers to Starčevo house models beneath house floors, as 'foundation deposits'.

There is, however, no clear link between the houses and death. There is, for example, no regular pattern of burials being found beneath houses as at Lepenski Vir or Çatal Hüyük. In general burials are rare and many bodies may have been exposed or otherwise dealt with outside settlements. Burials do occur in settlements in grave pits or in pits initially used for storage with or without grave goods. But at Obre 1, for example, the burials are all of children, while other human bones occur in occupation debris. At Anza, the settlement burial sample was biased in favour of young individuals and females (Chapman 1983).

The high frequencies of children's burials in the settlements at Obre 1 and Anza suggests the idea that the settlement itself has become particularly associated with child-care activities, in contrast to the external world. It is not as easy in the early Neolithic to link women closely to this inner domain as it is later on. But some Körös anthropomorphic pots indicate the emerging centrality of representations of women in the domestic sphere. There are a number of small anthropomorphic pots from Körös sites with exaggerated buttocks and widely interpreted as female on comparison with figurines and later similar pots. One of these pots (the 'Venus of Gorza') contained the burnt fragments of a human skull (Kalicz 1970). Early Neolithic pottery is closely associated with the settlements and with the houses within them. That some of the pots are depicted as female is thus of interest.

But for the early Neolithic these links are weakly developed. Indeed the number of figurines from this period, mostly representing women, are small and their within-site context is uncertain given excavations which rarely record precise locations or distinguish between primary and secondary refuse. The figurines seem generally to occur broken in rubbish pits or in secondary refuse deposits (Tringham 1971). They are rare in Starčevo sites, particularly early Starčevo sites (Benac 1973, 372), and in the early Neolithic as a whole they are frequently absent from occupation horizons.

In summary, the early Neolithic of SE Europe shows the beginning of a social strategy that later becomes more elaborate. Settlement units remain relatively small and are often semi-sedentary. There is some 'planning' within settlements (i.e. houses in rows or with similar orientations) and thus some degree of social constraint within the group. Individual family units mainly bury their dead away from the settlement, and the economic strategy involves some common participation within long-term structures (see chapter 2). The domus, and particularly the hearth, are associated with drama and symbolism while at the same time they are the focus (a word deriving from the Latin, meaning fireplace, hearth – fireside, home) of productive activities including plant food. My general model that the domestication of society is achieved through the ideology of domesticating the wild seems relevant to these data. But the system is weakly developed. We obtain only glimpses of an emerging strategy.

It is important to note that the domus ideology can be glimpsed in the sixth and early fifth millennia before more sedentary and larger social units emerge widely in the following millennia. However the tell sites in central Bulgaria develop the more complex domus quicker than the areas to the north such as eastern Hungary. Sherratt (1983c) has described the northward movement of stable tell settlements containing concentrations of houses. Already in the early Neolithic in Bulgaria, the ideology and practice of the domus are used to create stable, aggregated and long-lived social units.

The Concept of the Domus in the Late Fifth and Fourth Millennia bc

The idea of the creation of larger social groups and greater social domination through the metaphor of the domestication of the wild corresponds to economic changes. Following the mechanisms outlined by Bender (1978), social groups increased and intensified production by for example increasing their size so that they could engage competitively in feasting and exchange. The underlying basis for this process was domestic production and the productive activities were couched within the ideology of the domus as the guarantor of social life against the wild. The domus was where the wild was brought in and controlled or where the cultural was separated from the natural. Any competition for social control took place in these terms. And the early Neolithic ideology surrounding the home had, as it were, provided an under-used set of concepts with a rich potential for development and manipulation, in order to generate the game. As social and economic competition and intensification increased they did so in terms of the domus concept. The latter reinforced the domestic locus of production while at the same time becoming reinforced and elaborated itself. Through time the stronger domus scheme was further manipulated in order to provide a metaphor for larger scales of production. The domus thus provided the medium for the dialectical relationships between economy, society, and symbolic meaning.

In what follows I wish to consider SE Europe in the late fifth and fourth millennia as a whole since there are many cultural similarities between the various areas. The data will mainly derive from the following cultural groupings: Tisza, Vinča, Gumelnitsa, Karanovo VI, and Cucuteni-Tripolye. There is, however, a considerable danger in grouping these various cultural units because of the spatial and temporal variation identified earlier in this chapter. In particular, the grouping incorporates two major phases. The first, covering the late fifth millennium bc and the period up to about 3500 bc might be termed the late or 'mature' Neolithic in which many aspects of the domus reach their most developed form. The cultural units include Vinča, Tisza, and Boian. In the following phase (termed Copper Age by Sherratt 1982a, 1983a), lasting until about 2700 bc, the domus remains central in the tell sites of the Gumelnitsa and Cucuteni groupings but there are also dispersed patterns of settlement in the Tiszapolgár and Bodrogkeresztúr cultures in eastern Hungary and cemeteries such as at Varna and Tiszapolgár-Basatanya become more frequent. The Copper Age thus represents a transitional phase. Because the domus remains central in this period in many areas I have decided to retain a broad view of the late fifth and fourth millennia evidence. As the account progresses I will introduce the chronological sequence as a major component.

The house

It is the house which represents the durable material expression of Neolithic and Chalcolithic life in SE Europe. Many activities, including burial, have left little trace. Those activities that can be identified are again often linked to the house.

This centrality of the house is also seen in the increasing size and internal differentiation of houses that occur in the late fifth and fourth millennia bc. Throughout the whole of SE Europe the same trend towards bigger and more internally divided houses can be identified – at Karanovo and in the Vinča, Tisza, Gumelnitsa, and Cucuteni cultures. For example, in Vinča sites, houses mainly have one room, but two or three-roomed houses are known (Markotic 1984). Where there are three rooms in Vinča houses, the middle room frequently has the hearth and has most evidence of domestic activities (ibid., 96). Other Vinča sites show a varied pattern. At Gomolava in a three-roomed house, one room had storage jars buried in the floor, and one had an oven. At Divostin a three-roomed house had a hearth in each room. At Banjica two rooms of a three-roomed house held hearths (ibid.).

Vinča houses average 4–6 × 6–13 m (Markotic 1984), while Gumelnitsa houses average 5–6 × 12 m (Tringham 1971). The latter often have a porch and thick clay floors over a layer of logs. By the Cucuteni B phase (= Tripolye CI) there is a tendency towards the construction of two to four-roomed houses, such as that from Kolomijščina (figure 3.2), while house models from this cultural grouping appear to show two storeys (Ellis 1984, 49). Two-storeyed houses have been excavated at Herpály in eastern Hungary (Raczky 1987).

Evidence of painted or incised decoration on the inner or outer surfaces of house walls comes from many sites including Azmak (Georgiev 1965), Obre II (Benac 1973), and Tîrpeşti (Marinescu-Bîlcu 1981). At Vinča sites, house walls are usually painted on the

(a)

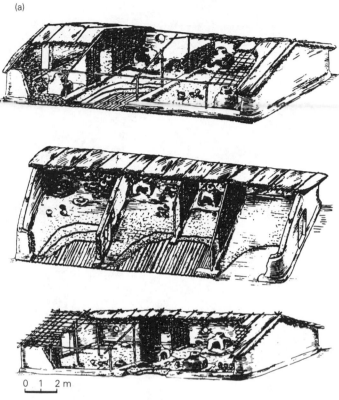

Figure 3.2 (this page and overleaf) Examples of houses in SE Europe: (a) Kolomijščina I, dwellings 24 (top), 11 (middle) and 2 (bottom); (Source: Ellis 1984)

inside and outside, commonly in blue or blue and red. Decorative slabs have been found on the walls of the houses at Kormadin, and at Banjica the exteriors of walls were decorated with three-dimensional spirals. Ornamented plaster has been found at Trnovaca, Baranda, Vinča itself, and Grivac (Markotic 1984, 94). In the Karanovo VI levels at Azmak, one large three-roomed house had 15 layers of plaster on the floor, while another two-roomed house, 19 × 9 m in size, had the insides of the walls ornamented with geometric, mainly rectilinear white and red designs (Georgiev 1965). Walls are frequently decorated in the Tisza area (Raczky 1987). But perhaps the best evidence for the amount of symbolic elaboration invested in the house comes from Ovcarovo in north-east Bulgaria (Todorova 1978). The outsides of the houses carry painted designs,

(b)

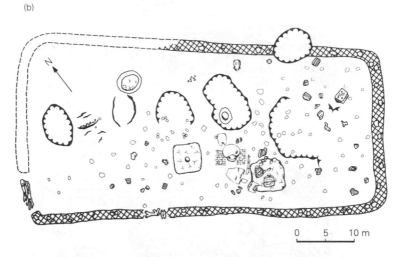

0   5   10 m

Figure 3.2 (b) Tisza house from Veszto-Magor, level 4.
(Source: Raczky 1987)

while the inside walls and floors are painted in monochrome – a different colour being used for each replastering of the floor. Indeed one house in Ovcarovo had been replastered in this way 47 times.

The insides of houses are often well-furnished. For example, in the Tisza, Herpály, and Czöszhalom Late Neolithic groups in the Tisza region, houses contain either open or domed ovens, clay-plastered grinding areas, oval or quadrangular in form, and flat clay tables, often surrounded by quernstones and stone or bone artifacts. One characteristic built-in feature are clay bins either plastered onto the floor or standing on legs, and large vessels. The grain remains inside these bins and vessels suggest that they were used for grain storage. 'Altars' and basins and big clay figurative reliefs applied onto the walls also occur (Raczky 1987, 19).

The well excavated houses at the Vinča site of Opovo (Tringham et al. 1985) also give some indication of house contents. Complete but crushed pots, clay weights, figurines, grindstones, polished and flaked stone tools, bone tools, and bone (meat) debris were found. Since many excavations did not make a distinction between *in situ* finds and redeposited refuse, it is often difficult to disentangle the spatial patterns. But in those cases in which *in situ* material does appear to have been identified, it is clear that not all areas on the house floor were equally important. In many cases much of the floor space is empty, with activities concentrating around the hearth or oven.

The oven

We have already seen at Lepenski Vir how the hearth can become the focal point of the house. In the fourth millennium, the hearths, which are frequently 'domed' and are perhaps best interpreted as ovens, often form the foci of domestic activities. For example, in phase V at Karanovo, the larger front room of two-roomed houses generally contains no cultural remains, while the smaller back room contains oven, mill, food storage, and domestic utensils (Mikov 1959). At the site of Obre II in the Butmir group, the concentration around the oven is even more specific (Benac 1973). As is shown in figure 3.3, pots, grinding stones, small axes, spindle whorls, and scrapers occur by the oven, and repeatedly mainly on the left side of the oven. In Vinča sites, food processing usually occurs around ovens or silos (Chapman 1981). Gumelnitsa houses frequently have a saddle quern dug into the floor next to the oven at the back of the house (Tringham 1971).

A model of the interior of a house from Ovcarovo provides an exact representation of the interior of the houses excavated at that site (Todorova 1978). I will discuss the nature of these models later in this chapter. For the moment, it is of interest to note that the 'oven' in the house model has a sloping gabled roof and openings

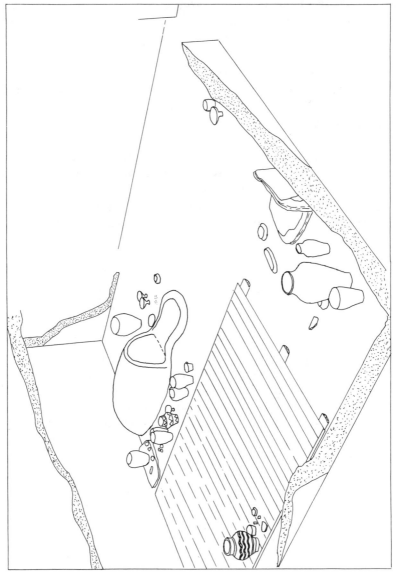

Figure 3.3 Interior layout of a room at Obre II, level 3.
(After Benac 1973)

in the front and side walls. Indeed this 'oven' looks like a 'house' model. 'The shape of the ovens is so much like that of the houses, that during excavations models of ovens have sometimes been mistaken for models of dwellings' (ibid., 52). Certainly many house models do have sloping roofs, but it is unclear whether they should be reinterpreted as ovens, or whether the ovens mimic houses, or whether the Ovcarovo house model oven should be reinterpreted as a 'shrine'. Whatever the answer to this problem, it seems likely that the centrality of the oven within the house was sometimes reaffirmed by drawing symbolic parallels between houses and ovens.

But the oven was clearly not only a symbolic focus. It also was the focus of domestic production. I have already referred to examples of houses in which the grinding and storage of plant foods are closely linked to the oven, with the grinding stones and storage vessels often fixed permanently into the ground. More generally, pottery is frequently placed around the oven. For example, in the Cucuteni A levels at Tîrpeşti, in at least one case pottery is clustered *in situ* around the oven (Marinescu-Bîlcu 1981, 74). In many sites the sherds near the oven are from coarse storage vessels. At Obre II, the pots near the oven include big storage vessels and pots containing charred grain (Benac 1973).

Throughout SE Europe, storage pits and pots also occur outside houses, even though they have a special focus around the oven. It may also be the case that storage facilities inside houses generally increase through time from the sixth to the fourth millenium. This trend has been noted most clearly at Selevac (Tringham pers. comm.). In the earlier (Vinča-Tordoš) layers at the site, with a still semi-sedentary economy, storage pits are found outside houses. But in the fully sedentary Vinča-Pločnik village, storage pits are found inside houses, as also at Opovo and Gomolava. This type of change could be interpreted in two apparently contradictory ways. On the one hand, it could be argued that as sedentism increased so the dependency on storage of food products increased leading to greater need to protect stored food within the production unit. This argument disregards the specific historical associations of the house oven by which the stored food is often located. On the other hand, it could be argued that the bringing of food storage into the house was part of an active social strategy which may have made use of but also created the greater sedentism. It has been estimated at the site of Herpály that sufficient storage jars were present in each house for a storage capacity of several hundred litres (Raczky 1987, 122). Social control over substantial resources may have been the driving force behind both sedentism and in-house storage. That increasing control seems to have been mediated by, and enmeshed within, the expanding domus idiom.

Ovens and figurines

Anthropomorphic and zoomorphic figurines in SE Europe can be linked to the house in a variety of ways. Overall, the frequencies of figurines of clay, bone, and marble increase in time from the sixth to the fourth millennium in the same way that house size and complexity increase. For example, at Anza, phase I (equivalent to the Aegean early Neolithic) has five figurines, phases II and III (Starčevo) have 16 figurines, and phase IV (early Vinča) has 48 figurines. By the early fourth millennium most sites in SE Europe have figurines, at some areas and sites in high frequencies (Chapman 1981).

The within-site distribution of figurines is complicated by the fact that most figurines are found broken and discarded as redeposited refuse. As a result, most figurine fragments are found outside houses. However, figurines do often occur in houses, and the *in situ* nature of such cases is shown by the unbroken condition or by the seating of the figurines on small stools (Tringham 1971; Todorova 1978).

At the Vinča site of Opovo (Tringham et al. 1985) one house (feature 2) had a clear oven floor with pottery, figurine and clay weight beside it. By the oven was a clay pedestal with an associated hollow clay 'head' with two 'ears' that may have been set on the pedestal. In the Pre-Cucuteni layers at Tîpeşti (Marinescu-Bîlcu 1981, 26) one oven had a figurine attached to its kerb. A similar association is seen in the late Cucuteni model from Popudnia. On the bench to the right of the oven in the model there is 'a female figurine with hands on her breasts' (Gimbutas 1974, 69–70). A remarkable house at Sabatinovka (early Cucuteni) contained a large oven, at the base of which a female figurine was found (ibid., 72). Near the oven were pots (one containing burnt cattle bones), five saddle querns and five terracotta figurines. On a nearby platform were found 16 female figurines on stools. As a further example from the Cucuteni cultural group, at Kolomijščina I 21 figurines, all in seated position, were discovered in the oven area. Eighteen were female and three male (ibid., 74). At Ovcarovo, too, in north-east Bulgaria, figurines and miniature models of houses have been found close to ovens (Todorova 1978, 52). In the Tisza culture large hollow figurines or anthropomorphic pots are found 'such as the two from Kökénydomb which were both lying together by the hearth of a house' (Tringham 1971, 186).

The link between figurines and ovens thus seems secure. More generally, figurines are linked to the range of activities surrounding the ovens. We have seen figurines linked to storage silos (at Selevac: Chapman 1981, 65) and grinding stones as well as to the oven itself. At the late Vinča house at Medvednjak clay figurines are closely associated with specific weaving, grinding, food preparation, and storage activities (ibid.).

Figurines and women

One reason why the firm association of figurines with the activities around the oven is of interest, is that figurines are themselves closely linked to women. For example, Markotic (1984, 145) notes that an overwhelming majority of the Vinča figurines depict humans which are female as identified by breasts, pubic 'triangle' and lack of penis on a nude form. From the Vinča settlement itself, Markotic provides the following counts for figurine types: standing female, 481; sitting female, 60; male, 17; animal, 18. In a similar vein, Todorova (1978, 83) suggests that over 90 per cent of the figurines found in the fourth millennium bc in Bulgaria depict women. Of the 250 figurines from Sitagroi, not one can clearly be identified as male, and only about 1 per cent of the anthropomorphic figurines from this site can be considered as possibly portraying men (Gimbutas 1986, 226). In the Pre-Cucuteni levels at Tîrpeşti, almost all the very large number of figurines represented women except for a few animal figurines (Marinescu-Bîlcu 1981). Most of the figurines mentioned above because of their associations with ovens and houses are female.

Women and pots

The vast majority of figurines in the fourth millennium bc in SE Europe depict women. But the saturation of the area around the oven with the cultural category 'woman' is further increased when it is realized that much of the pottery also occurs within that category. As we have seen, the *in situ* evidence implies a close link between pots, houses, and the areas around the ovens.

Pots in the shape of human or animal forms or with human or animal depictions placed on them are common in SE Europe in the period being considered here (e.g. figure 3.4), although as we have seen they also occur in the early Neolithic. While the sex of the anthropomorphic depictions is often uncertain, many are clearly female, as for example in Tisza sites (Raczky 1978) and in Gumelnitsa contexts. In other cases a female figure is shown holding a pot. For example, a Tisza figurine from Novi Becej shows a woman sitting on a decorated stool and holding a vessel in her hands (Sevic and Kostic 1974).

Generally, the type of decoration found on the figurines resembles that found on the pottery. Even where detailed differences between the pottery and figurine designs are claimed (e.g. Marinescu-Bîlcu 1981, 38), the general similarities remain. Certainly figurine decoration includes the same broad swirls found on the pottery. It is also important to note that the same designs occur as house wall decoration on surviving daub fragments and on the walls of house models. For example, wall remains from House 2 at Gorzsa in the Tisza culture are decorated with designs identical to those found on pots

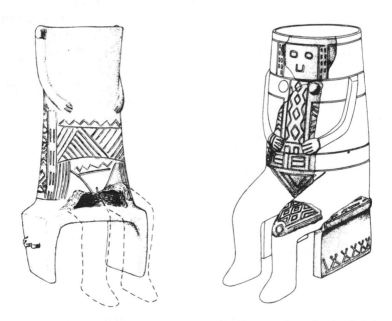

Figure 3.4 Reconstruction of Tisza vessels from Kökénydomb (heights 33 and 24 cm).
(Source: Raczky 1987)

and on an anthropomorphic figurine from the same site (Raczky 1987, 34). In SE Europe as a whole, the distribution of related decorative motifs links women, pots and houses, and reinforces the spatial associations already identified in which pots and figurines are often found in the house or clustered around the oven.

The significance of the occurrence of a similar decoration on figurines (which we have seen are largely female), pots and house walls is increased if we can accept Marinescu-Bîlcu's reference (1981, 66) to 'the absence of decoration on male representations' in the Cucuteni A levels at Tîrpeşti. Gimbutas (1974, 55) refers to decoration on male figurines from the Vinča and east Balkan cultural groupings, but even here the amount of decoration or decorated clothing shown on the male figurines is not marked. Further research needs to be carried out before the associations of unambiguously male figurines can be discussed with any security. But overall there seems to be a strong association between women and figurines and pots. A number of different lines of evidence seem to point in this same direction – the spatial associations of pots and female figurines around the ovens and in the houses, the forming of pots in the shape of women, the occurrence of similar decoration on pots, female figurines, and house walls, and the depiction of women holding pot-shaped vessels. (The rather different evidence from the Hamangia culture will be discussed further in chapter 4).

Pots, women, and miniatures

The links already identified are further strengthened by considering a broader 'set' of miniature items in which female figurines play a dominant role. Indeed, the interpretation of the female figurines should not be considered in isolation from a broader class of miniature representations which includes miniature pots, houses, ovens (for a miniature oven at Sitagroi see Renfrew et al. 1986) and stools.

I have already referred to the data from Sabatinovka and Kolomijščina I where female figurines were found associated with miniature stools. Similar associations between female figurines and stools are found on Gumelnitsa sites (Tringham 1971). Perhaps the clearest example of a 'set' of miniature representations comes from an early Karanovo VI house at Ovcarovo. Here were found three clay 'altars', 'shaped like the pedimented facade of a house', four female figurines, three tables, three stools, three 'drums', three miniature pots with lids, and two larger miniature dishes (Todorova 1978, 80). All were painted in red designs of the general spiral-meander type found widely in SE Europe.

Another 'set' of items in which miniatures including female figurines occur is defined by those objects which are marked with 'signs' sometimes referred to as 'pre-writing', in the fourth millennium bc in SE Europe (Winn 1981). For present purposes it is sufficient to note that a conventionalized and standardized corpus of signs is found on a range of objects in SE Europe. A detailed study of the occurrence of such signs in Vinča contexts has demonstrated that they are mostly incised on clay objects prior to firing and that they occur on spindle whorls, figurines (virtually always female figurines) and other miniatures, and pottery (Winn 1981).

Thus, both the set of items depicted as miniatures and the set of items with 'signs' again link women to pots and houses. Evidence of weaving from within houses will be demonstrated below. Thus the occurrence of spindle whorls in these sets is not surprising. But how much significance can be given to these linkages? After all, my main evidence for the centrality of the cultural category 'woman' in the data considered is the preponderance of female figurines. Perhaps figurines had little social significance. What was their role and the role of other miniatures?

There has been a long discussion in archaeology concerning the 'meaning' of figurines. Despite Ucko's (1969) timely warning that the figurines from Greece and SE Europe could have had a range of functions, including use as toys, most archaeologists have continued to assume that they had some special symbolic significance. In other words, it is widely felt that the figurines were not just toys or teaching devices. Why has a 'ritual' or 'symbolic' interpretation stubbornly been retained? Is this just the result of modern romantic notions about Mother Goddesses?

I think not. There are some contextual factors concerning the SE European figurines which suggest that they had more than a primary utilitarian function. In other words, I would argue that the figurines were truly symbolic in that they evoked secondary meanings beyond the obvious sign which says 'this is a woman' or 'this is a stool'. First, the figurines and miniatures are often well made, highly polished, and carefully incised or painted. Second, we have seen examples of the specific spatial localization of the *in situ* miniatures near ovens and even attached to the oven. They were not used or placed haphazardly on the sites. Third, the female figurines occur in 'sets' of miniature objects which include|miniature houses (and perhaps ovens), tables, chairs, and pots. As far as we can see these items are, in their normal sizes, also linked to the house itself. Finally, the female figurines themselves do not attempt to be 'true' depictions of women. Many are mere stumps with breasts, buttocks, and pubic triangle shown. The face, and particularly the mouth, as well as the hands and feet are often not executed in detail. In all these ways, then, there is evidence of a standardized selection and categorization of aspects of womanhood in relation to the domestic world. In considering the secondary evocations of the female figurines, I have been continually brought to the area of the oven and to the house. What exactly was the image of women that was represented in the domestic area?

The woman in production in the house

A late Cucuteni house model from Popudnia, western Ukraine shows a figure interpreted as a woman working, perhaps grinding grain, within the house (Gimbutas 1974, 70). There are no easily identifiable breasts on this figure in the drawings of the model that I have seen, and the interpretation as a woman is uncertain. But it would be possible to argue that we are not dependent on such evocative but in some aspects blurred 'snapshots' of daily life in the fourth millennium bc in SE Europe for evidence that women played a major role in domestic production.

I have so far demonstrated that a strong link occurs between women, the house, the oven area, and pottery. This is already more than a conceptual link in that the ovens were presumably used to prepare food and the pots to cook and store grain and other products. Indeed pots containing charred grain have frequently been found, and there are some instances of pots containing animal bones. However, archaeologists have less access to gender roles in the practice of everyday life in prehistory than they do to concepts about that life. Thus while I can demonstrate conceptual links between women and the house and the oven, I cannot be certain that men did not do all the actual cooking and food storage in pots. Even if the Popudnia model shows a woman at work, it remains a representation. Archaeologists do not observe behaviour directly, only representations of behaviour.

The productive activities which I have already noted as associated with the oven area in the house in SE Europe include food preparation (in the oven itself) and the grinding of plant foods. Certainly hearths do occur away from the oven and outside the houses within the settlements, but the main focus for the transformation of plants into food seems to be the female-associated area within the house. On some sites several grinding stones are found together, perhaps indicating a greater scale of production, but the overall domestic basis of plant food production is clear. Certainly it must be assumed that many of the stages of crop-processing (such as threshing and winnowing) occurred outside the house. Inside the house, Dennell (1978) found that the carbonized botanical remains from floors of earlier Neolithic houses were probably the result of crop processing such as cleaning and sieving. These residues contrast with the fully processed grain found in the ovens but they also differ from the more mixed midden and other non-floor deposits. A similar pattern might be expected for the late fifth and fourth millennia. At least the final stages of transformation of grain and other plant products into usable food may have occurred in the house. An interesting contrast with the distribution of animal bones occurs at Obre II, where no animal bones were found inside some houses, only grain (Benac 1973). In general, as we have seen, and with certain exceptions, depictions of animals do not play a major role in the figurine material associated with the houses, although the importance of animal depictions may increase through time in some areas (Raczky 1987).

There is little clear evidence of the involvement of women in agricultural production. For example Gimbutas (1986, 245) notes that 'sometimes actual grains were inserted in the belly of Cucuteni figurines, and a large number of Pre-Cucuteni (Tripolye A) figurines bear grain impressions on both the thigh and belly areas.' Until further work of this type is carried out, all that can be claimed overall, is that women are conceptually associated in the houses with the grinding and preparation of plant foods. Certainly we have seen that there is good evidence that they were symbolically associated with food storage, either in 'bins' or fixed pots near the oven.

The frequency of crushed whole pots is generally high inside houses, either near the oven or near the inside walls. Given the strong link already noted between representations of women and decorated pottery, it is important to consider the uses to which the pottery was put. Ellis (1984, 200) provides a discussion of the functions of fine painted pottery in the Cucuteni-Tripolye culture area. She notes that fire and soot marks from cooking are seldom observed but that through time there is increasing evidence for the use of painted wares for food storage. Vessel sizes get larger and more uniform. Some vessels are up to 1 m in height. Their restricted orifices, considerable weight and difficulty of manoeuvre preclude their use for everyday food preparation. Ceramic lids or covers are also increasingly common. Many vessels contain charred grain or animal bones. Also certain rooms without ovens seem to be put aside and packed with large vessels. A storage function seems likely for these and for the similar vessels found in rooms with ovens.

Pottery assemblages associated with fourth millennium bc sites in SE Europe include a wide range of types which presumably had a variety of functions, including cooking and serving food and drink. But at least a substantial proportion of the pots were used for storage. Women and houses in which most *in situ* pots are found are thus clearly associated with the storage, and hence to some extent with the domestic redistribution of vital resources.

Evidence for spinning and weaving also occurs within the houses and in relation to the cluster of associated attributes identified as the domus. Spindle whorls are clearly linked by the 'signs' on them to pottery and female figurines (Winn 1981). At the Vinča site of Banjica several houses contained evidence of looms near the wall opposite the food-processing area (Chapman 1981). In the Tisza culture, clusters of loom weights on floors indicate the former presence of wooden looms within houses (Raczky 1987, 19).

Other evidence for craft production begins to take us away from the house (although of course not necessarily from the domestic unit of production). Certainly there are indications from within houses of flint blade and stone axe production, of the working of red deer antlers and copper and pottery production. Full consideration of these spheres of activities shows that they do not contribute substantially to the symbolism of the domus. Yet the very fact that all these types of activities occur in the house, as will be demonstrated below, points again to the centrality and power of the domus in fourth millennium bc SE Europe.

Overall, therefore, it is possible to link a set of ideas associated with women to productive activities within the house such as the processing and storage of grain and weaving and spinning. But it is not possible to argue that these activities were carried out by women rather than by men, or that women did or did not carry out other activities, such as flint knapping, that we know sometimes took place within the house. All I can say is that certain activities within the domus are given symbolic emphasis through their spatial and stylistic organization. The use of decoration, miniatures and 'signs' links together a series of activities in which representations of women are central.

It should be clear therefore that I am not arguing for a 'matrifocal' society in the Neolithic of SE Europe. On the evidence available I am not able to propose that women played central roles in production and in relations of social dominance. I certainly cannot say whether these societies were matrilineal, matrilocal, or matriarchal. All I would pretend to say is that certain aspects of womanhood came to be used as a metaphor for certain aspects of social and productive activities. The domus, in which certain aspects of womanhood were incorporated, can best be seen as a discourse of power, a way of talking about social relations, and a way of mediating (making sense of) strategies of domination. To put it over-simply, women may or may not have had any real power in the Neolithic of SE Europe, but certain aspects of being a woman were conceptually central. This abstract centrality is part of the definition of the domus.

Conclusion

In this chapter I have argued that a cluster of traits, summarized in the upper part of figure 3.5, defined a broad and loose concept that I have termed the domus. The concept of the domus partly derives from practical activities within the house. It concerns the use of objects and resources. But it is also a wider emotive concept linking aesthetics (in the use of decoration and modelling of clay figurines), abstract codes (perhaps represented in the 'signs'), social roles (mother and woman), and basic needs (warmth, shelter, and nourishment). It is particularly in the final stages of the transformation of raw food into cooked product that the domus plays its role. The underlying theme linking activities and concepts within the domus, is the woman as transformer of wild into domestic – the woman as domesticator, or as domesticated.

Some caveats are necessary before leaving this chapter. First, I have found it necessary in presenting the data to depict a rather static picture. I have not found space yet to consider the wider social and economic changes within which the domus played a prominent role. This will be the task of the following chapter in which sequences of change within SE Europe will be discussed.

A second caveat concerns the possibility that the domus is not equivalent to 'the private'. I do not wish to assume that the house

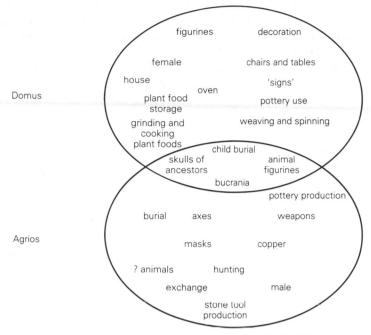

Figure 3.5 Associations of the domus and agrios in SE Europe.

is a private domain in opposition to an outside public world. Indeed, it seems possible that the 'performances' associated with the use of figurines around the oven in the houses were very 'public' in the sense that they were participated in by many members within the domestic or wider social unit. Indeed the high visibility of the pottery and figurine decoration, and the wide areas over which formally similar performances are found support the attempt to situate the public within the 'private' domestic world. It is one of the contentions of this book that the creation of larger and more differentiated social units in the Neolithic took place through the concept of the domus.

Third, we have begun to see that the activities in the house are often repeated outside the house. Evidence of cooking does occur between houses within settlements. Much plant food processing occurred outside the house. And the 'signs' on the famous Tartaria tablets show that the 'set' of items linked by the 'signs' should include objects other than spindle whorls, female figurines, and pots. Indeed I have blatantly oversimplified a complex picture in arguing for the cluster of attributes associated with the domus. For example,

I have included women, pots, chairs, stools, and houses within that cluster partly because of their common occurrence as figurines or miniatures. But we know that animals and men are also, albeit rarely, depicted as clay miniatures. Why have I not included them within the concept of domus? Still worse, we shall see that cattle heads and skulls (bucrania) occur in the houses. Why have I not included them here?

The response to these questions is partly statistical. Given the large number of female figurines, the depictions of men and animals are rare. But the response is also interpretive. In the chapter that follows I will argue for a linked set of concepts which overlap with the domus but take us beyond.

4

Domus and Agrios in SE Europe

In chapter 3 I mainly discussed what I was being shown. And I was shown what 'they' wanted me and probably other members of 'their' and neighbouring societies to see. By the early fourth millennium bc the houses in SE Europe are highly visible – substantial, well constructed, decorated, and repeated as models. Females and pottery are very visible. Everything which is placed permanently (such as storage pots and grinders) occurs around the oven. The archaeology of this period in SE Europe is settlement archaeology. It is the settlements which have survived, often as tells, and which attract attention. And within the settlements everything focuses on the house and oven, even in sites which have undergone extensive excavation (Todorova 1978).

Of course, it can be argued that if I could see the perishable, if I could see the prehistoric actions and hear the spoken prehistoric words, then other activities in the house might be equally visible. I have only defined the domus in relation to archaeologically visible remains. As a result I may have misdefined a difference between the domus and its less visible opposite. However, it can equally be argued that the 'inscription' of events in durable materials (that will survive archaeologically) is itself a meaningful categorization of the world of events. In the SE European case, the non-perishables seem to be connected by the use of decoration, 'signs', etc. They form a coherence which can be described conceptually. What survives is not haphazard, but results from a certain emphasis on durability, objectivity, or muteness (Braithwaite 1982) in the making of a material statement. However biased our data may be, they are biased in meaningful ways.

In this chapter I wish to delve into the less visible and the transient in SE Europe before turning to those aspects of the house (the bucrania and animal figurines for example) which do not fit into the concept of domus as I have defined it. A distinctive feature of the earlier fourth millennium bc in SE Europe is the relative invisibility of death. Cemeteries are rarely found and burial ritual has left little trace. The contrast with the ever-present evidence of the house in SE Europe is stark.

A note about chronology is necessary here. As already noted, in discussing the domus I have painted a static picture. The difficulties in such an approach are exacerbated when considering the various components of the non-domus. For example, cemeteries become increasingly common in the Copper Age (after 3500 bc), and the major cultural changes associated with Baden (after 2700 bc) are again associated with changes in burial rite. I hope gradually to introduce evidence for the temporal sequence (see table 1).

Death

For the early Neolithic we have seen that burials are rare but that they occur in settlements in pits (sometimes reused storage pits), outside houses, with or (more frequently) without grave goods. There is some evidence that burials in settlements are mainly of young individuals and females (see p. 51). In addition, one female anthropomorphic pot contained burnt human skull remains (see p. 52). The evidence is limited, but early Neolithic burial within settlements is associated to some degree with women and children.

For the cultural groups of the late fifth and early fourth millennia bc, a wider range of burial practices is known including individual pits in or near houses, groups of individual burials between houses, or in unoccupied parts of settlements, and increasingly, through time, cemeteries (Chapman 1983). But once again, the major factor is the overall absence of burial data. As Ellis (1984, 172) notes for the Cucuteni-Tripolye culture area, 100 years of research have failed to bring to light consistent data on burial ritual. This may be largely the result of a failure to survey and excavate outside settlements. But given the length of research and the density of present-day building and land-use in SE Europe as a whole, the lack of evidence for burial ritual is perhaps significant. At the Vinča site of Opovo, the secondary refuse outside the houses included fragments of burned human bone, some with gnaw marks (Tringham et al. 1985). Such evidence suggests that bodies may have been exposed outside the settlement, and the bones brought in by dogs. Certainly, the overall poverty of burial evidence in SE Europe indicates that the main burial rite is not visible to us. It is likely to have involved some form of exposure or burning of the body, most probably outside the settlement.

But what of those bodies that were interred within the settlement? In the fifth and fourth millennia, graves begin to appear in recognizable groups within unoccupied parts of settlements, as for example in Tisza settlements (Raczky 1987; Kalicz 1970), although isolated graves continue to be found either inside or outside houses. As in the early Neolithic, the single or small groups of burials within settlements are often of children. For example, at Obre II no cemetery was found, but the skeletons of 11 children were recovered in small graves without grave goods, usually flexed and lying on the left side, between the houses. Children's burials occur under Boian house floors at Glina in Romania and under Tripolye house floors at Luka Vrublevetskaya (Chapman 1983). At Herpály, 75 per cent of the human remains belonged to infants or children. This pattern was not found at Szegvar-Tüzköves, although here there were sufficient adult burials to show that males were buried contracted on their right side and females on their left side, and that male graves tended to contain stone blades and axes whereas pottery was largely recovered from female burials (Raczky 1987, 58 and 121). It is also of interest that human skulls are found on or under house floors in Vinča, Gumelnitsa, and Cucuteni-Tripolye sites (ibid.). This latter evidence supports the idea suggested above that exposure or pretreatment of the body involving the removal of flesh may have been part of the main, but sadly largely invisible, burial rites in SE Europe.

Adult burial does take place within houses and between houses within settlements. Witness the adult burial inside a Vinča house at Parta or the cluster of Boian graves within the Andolina settlement (Chapman 1983). But through time in the fourth millennium adult burials occur more frequently in cemeteries in which males are associated with more numerous or 'richer' finds. For example, amongst three cemeteries in north-east Bulgaria (Vinitsa, Devnya, and Golyamo Delchero) 34 per cent of the finds come from male burials, 22 per cent from female burials, and 14 per cent from child burials (30 per cent of the finds derive from cenotaphs, to be discussed below). At these cemeteries, men dominate in all categories – tools, jewellery, ochre, copper objects, vessels. On the other hand, 'perfunctory attention was paid to deceased infants' in these

Figure 4.1 Male grave at Varna.
(Source: Biegel 1986)

cemeteries (Todorova 1978, 75). In the Varna cemetery, some difficulties were encountered in identifying the sex of skeletons, but of
those that could be identified 29 were thought to be male and only
9 female (Marinow and Yordanov 1978). The only sexed skeleton
with rich burial furnishings, including gold objects, at Varna was a
male (figure 4.1; Ivanov 1978). At the Devnya cemetery there is a
uniformly high status of male graves (Chapman 1983). The emphasis

on adults and males in cemeteries is not universal. For example, the very late Tripolye cemetery at Vykhvatintsy in Soviet Moldavia contained 63 burials, 36 of which were children 14 years of age or under (Ellis 1984, 172).

Nevertheless, a listing of the finds from cemeteries begins to introduce us to objects that did not figure largely in chapter 3 because they do not seem to play a central role in the symbolism and activities of the domus. For example, the Vinča cemetery at Botoš had at least 21 graves (Markotic 1984), which Chapman (1981) has divided into two sections of the cemetery: a western sector with poor graves, and an eastern sector with rich graves. In the latter were found lamps and figurines, polished stone axes, mace-heads, chisels, armbands, stone animal heads, beads, and bracelets. At Varna, rich graves contained gold handles for 'sceptres', copper axes, stone shaft-hole axes, and a wide range of gold ornaments including diadems, cheek plaques, ear-rings and sheet-gold depictions of cattle. At the Tisza-polgár-Basatanya cemetery, partly of Bodrogkeresztúr date and thus late in the period being considered here, men are associated with stone knives, obsidian arrowheads, antler and stone axes, maces, copper awls, copper and gold jewels, and wild boar or domesticated pig mandibles. Women are associated with shell or stone beads, copper or gold jewels, and bone pins (Kalicz 1970). Sherratt (1982b) has shown that at this cemetery there is a tendency for shaft-hole axes and copper daggers to be associated with adult men.

Chapman (1983) has noted that with a few exceptions, female figurines do not occur as grave goods in cemeteries and intramural burials. The exceptions are clear. Figurines do occur in the Vinča Botoš cemetery, and they occur in the Tartaria burial pit (Winn 1981). They are also common in the cemeteries of the Hamangia group. Chapman (ibid.) suggests that the Hamangia cultural area sees a reversal of the pattern found elsewhere in SE Europe. Figurines of marble, clay, or bone are common in graves, but there is a virtual absence of all but the most fragmented or poorly made figurines from Hamangia settlements. I do not intend to pursue this structural inversion in this context except to note that it is part of the marked regional diversity in the SE European Neolithic to which I have already pointed.

The general paucity of female figurines from graves, in contrast to their frequent occurrence in settlements, points to other differences between settlement and cemetery assemblages. Apart from the greater 'visibility' of men in the later fourth and third millennia cemeteries, the overall character of the finds in the cemeteries is marked by tools, hunting and other weapons, items such as metal traded over long distances and jewellery. Of course, all these items are found in settlements and their contexts of production and use will be discussed below. But they form a set which overlaps only inexactly with the characteristic items found *in situ* around the oven in the house.

The distribution of different types of axes provides an example of the distinctive nature of the cemetery assemblages. Chapman (1983) has compared the finds from cemeteries and settlements from three Transdanubian and East Bulgarian locations and has found that several axe types are only associated with males and that the types of axes found in cemeteries are always different from those found in settlements.

Simple stone axes had existed in SE Europe from the early Neolithic. By the later fifth millennium bc shaft-hole battle axes had appeared, for example at Karanovo III (Mikov 1959), and by the mid fourth millennium copper shaft-hole axes are found throughout much of SE Europe (although they remain rare in the Vinča cultural group). Many of the stone and copper shaft-hole axes do not show signs of heavy use (Todorova 1978, 69) and the axe handles covered with gold at Varna certainly suggest a special symbolic purpose. These types of 'special' axes are rare in settlements.

Some of the differences between settlements and cemeteries are chronological, since many of the cemeteries discussed here are rather later than the settlements described in chapter 3. The dynamism in the oppositions being described here will become an important part of my account. But it is clear that even in contemporary settlements and cemeteries discussion of artifacts associated with graves takes us into a world in which males are more visible, there is more evidence of status display, and more tools, weapons, and widely exchanged valuables.

But the rarity of cemeteries needs to be re-emphasized. In a general review of fifth and fourth millennia bc burials, Chapman (1983) refers to less than ten cemeteries in contrast to the many hundreds of settlements known. Death ritual left fewer durable remains. In the same way, even within cemeteries there seems to be evidence for the hiding or masking of death. In the north-east Bulgarian cemeteries of the later fourth and early third millennia bc, many graves are in fact 'cenotaphs' without bodies but with rich grave goods. The richness of these cenotaphs correlates more closely with the richer male burials than the poorer female burials (see above, p. 74).

At Varna, approximately 60 graves were excavated, 21 of which were cenotaphs (Ivanov 1978). In the latter, the contents and their arrangements were identical to the graves with bodies. Three of the cenotaphs were extremely 'rich', with many hundreds of gold pieces per tomb, including a gold skeuomorphic 'axe' on a gold handle as well as copper and stone shaft-hole axes. The finds in these rich cenotaphs again suggest a 'male' character, supported by the fact that the one 'rich' grave with a skeleton that could be sexed was male. Three cenotaphs contained clay masks over the place where the head should have been, and the graves contained full normal equipment. The masks were of low-fired or sun-baked clay. Gold diadems, cheek plaques, mouth plaques, and ear-rings were placed on the masks.

There are also a number of partially preserved skeletons in the graves at Varna, and a parsimonious explanation of the cenotaphs would be that the bones in them had completely decayed leaving only the accoutrements of the burial ritual. Certainly the graves occur at different depths, and different soil conditions may have affected the bones so that some survived, some partially survived, and some totally decayed. The 'invisibility' of the bodies at Varna may have more to do with natural post-depositional factors than social and cultural depositional processes.

Such an argument, however, ignores the masks. We have encountered clay modelling of facial features on human skulls at a developed stage in the Neolithic sequence in the Near East (see p. 35). In the east Balkans, the masks occur in a context again associated with death, and in which the dead are not normally given permanent and durable markers. It appears in a context of social display which is overt. There is great variation at Varna between 'rich' graves with much gold and copper and 'poor' graves. Does the mask hide the individuality of those involved in competitive display?

Rich graves with metal finds are not found in the west Balkans. However, here too, it has been argued by Gimbutas (1974) that the mask already played an important role well before Varna appeared to the east. Many of the Vinča figurines of the fifth and early fourth millennia bc show angular projections extending clear of the face. On very few Vinča figurines is the face depicted in the round. Reduced and stylized facial features are found throughout the SE European Neolithic, and it is possible that the Vinča figurine faces are simply schematic representations rather than masks. However, many examples show such a clear separation of the 'face' from the head, that a mask interpretation seems reasonable. Although clear masks do occur on female figurines, they seem especially associated with men (ibid., 60). In a general discussion of the Vinča culture, Markotic (1984, 146) suggests that 'the male statuettes seem to show a greater number of masks than the female figurines.'

The association of masks with men in Vinča and Varna, and the association of masks with death at Varna is important given the overall differences between settlements and burial contexts. Throughout the fifth and fourth millennia bc, it is rare to find obvious variation in the size and complexity of the female-centred houses in the settlements, particularly in those settlements that have been fully excavated such as Polyanitsa and Ovcarovo (figure 4.2). On the other hand, the differences at Varna between those graves with few

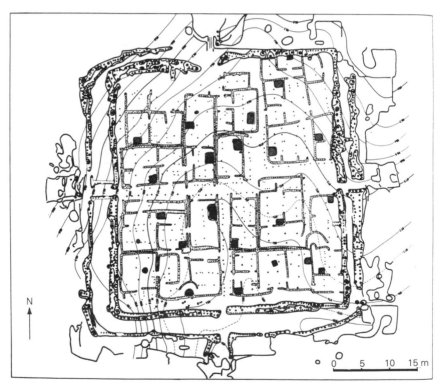

Figure 4.2 The Polyanitsa settlement mound, level 3.
(Source: Todorova 1978)

objects and those with hundreds of gold objects is marked, and Chapman (1983) has identified differences between 'rich' and 'poor' graves at a number of cemeteries in SE Europe. As I have already described, symbolism concerning females is less prominent in burial contexts and children's graves are often absent from cemeteries. On the other hand male graves are particularly richly adorned in cemeteries where they are associated with prestigious objects and overt symbols of power including copper and gold axes.

Overall, then, evidence of burial becomes more prevalent through time. Cemeteries become increasingly common, and as they do so, the archaeological evidence for male hunting and warring equipment and overt symbols of status and prestige increases. Burials which were initially poorly furnished become richly decked in ornament and display by the later fourth millennium bc. In the eastern Balkans, for example, agglomerated settlement and the prevalence of the domus continue in many areas into the same period. But in the late fourth millennium Tiszapolgár phase in eastern Hungary, the appearance of cemeteries is associated with settlement dispersal and a decline in the evidence for the domus (for example figurines are less overtly female: Sherratt 1984). The detail of regional sequences only serves to clarify the overall trends. For example, in the Tisza culture of eastern Hungary in the early fourth millennium, at the height of the representation of the domus, the number of deposited grave goods, including prestige items, gradually increases through time (Raczky 1987, 24).

Production and Exchange Outside the Domus

In order to understand the symbolism surrounding death in relation to the domus, it will be useful to consider other activities which seem to take place as much outside as inside the house. The discussion encompasses many of the types of objects which play a more important role in burial ritual.

In the Balkans as a whole, cold hammering and smelting of copper occur from the fifth millennium bc, as is seen for example in the Boian culture cemetery of Cernica, and mainly concern small objects and ornaments such as needles, awls, and beads. Casting of copper to produce a wider range of objects including shaft-hole axe hammers occurs from 3700–3200 bc in the east Balkans, and copper mines are found both in the west Balkans at Rudna Glava and in the east Balkans at Ai Bunar.

Certainly there is some link between copper production and the domus. At Cascioărele two moulds for simple flat copper axes were found in a house in a Gumelnitsa B1 horizon. Copper slag appears in late Vinča houses at Gomolava, Stapari, and elsewhere (Chapman 1981). Although the Rudna Glava malachite mines are 40 km from the nearest known Vinča site (ibid.), there is no evidence of manufacture there (Markotic 1984). Nevertheless, furnaces for smelting the ore are not frequently found on sites and most of the preparation and casting of the ore must have taken place outside settlements (Todorova 1978; Chapman 1981) or in special 'workshops'.

Evidence for in-settlement pottery manufacture has been widely claimed in SE Europe. For example, at the Sadievo tell, clay ready for pot forming has been found on site (Kancev 1978). Ovens or kilns containing large numbers of stacked vessels have been found in burnt houses in Karanovo and Ovcarovo (Todorova 1978). A pottery workshop has been claimed at the Boian-Gumelnitsa site of Rasev although on weak evidence (Evans 1978). The best evidence for pottery production comes from the Cucuteni-Tripolye area where Ellis (1984) shows that pottery kilns occur mainly on the margins of settlements and often within or associated with 'workshops', although in certain cases at least the latter appear similar to normal domestic houses, and the kilns similar to ovens. The Cucuteni-Tripolye kilns and workshops are associated with large planned villages with up to 498 domestic structures (at Petreny) or even 1700 structures at Majdanets'ke (ibid., 186 and see figure 4.3), and Ellis provides convincing evidence of a degree of craft specialization. In much of SE Europe, however, the evidence is less clear and any specialization in craft production which did take place could well be associated with domestic production units as suggested by the frequent occurrence of isolated or small groups of kilns within the interiors of settlements (Kaiser and Voytek 1982, 342). Nevertheless, Ellis's general review of the location of kilns does show that they are frequently marginal, placed away from houses on the edges of the settlements.

The production of flint and stone tools also extended outside the house. At the late Vinča site of Stapari there is evidence for the production and working of flint blades, axes, and red deer antlers in houses. At Banjica (Vinča) there are indications of the use of yards for stone-working and indoor production of flint tools and

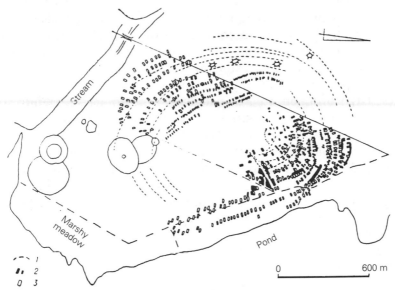

Figure 4.3 Survey results at Majdanets'kc. 1 = concentric plan of buildings; 2 = house platforms detected by aerial survey; 3 = house platforms detected by surface surveys.
(Source: Ellis 1984)

axes (Chapman 1981). However, the detailed excavations at the Opovo site (Vinča), produced no evidence of debitage (manufacturing waste) although tools and retouched pieces were plentiful. At the same site, stone axes and chisels were common but there were no waste products, indicating that stone tool production took place outside the settlement. Evans (1978) suggests that in upland areas, near the sources of flint, work-stations such as Madara in north-east Bulgaria are found with slight evidence of occupation but good evidence of the preparation and production of stone tools.

Overall, it is extremely difficult to identify where craft production was carried out in the fourth millennium in SE Europe and who was doing it. The degree of craft specialization or centralization of production appears locally varied and often extremely limited although the range of products from pottery, copper, and stone to bone, gold, and shell is wide. Given the low degree of craft specialization, it is likely that much production was organized through and by the domestic group. But there does seem to be some spatial differentiation within that production. For all the materials discussed above the house plays a part, pointing again to the strength of the domus as a practical economic unit. But production also extends well outside the house. In contrast to the evidence for grinding of grain, storing and cooking food, and weaving and spinning inside the house, the 'outside' production includes pottery, stone and flint tools, copper tools, ornaments, and symbols of power. Many of these latter products are associated with the domus. Certainly stone and flint tools occur around the oven and they must have been frequently used there. However, with the exception of pottery, it was not possible to link them closely into the domus concept in chapter 3. Apart from pottery, they do not play a major part in the decorative symbols and the symbolic practices surrounding female representations and the house and oven. Where they do seem to take on significance in defining age and sex groupings is in the cemeteries (see above).

Another possible difference between the domus and the world outside the domus concerns subsistence production. Evidence for the storage and processing of plant products, especially cereals, within the house is substantial. Animals, like men, are relatively invisible, both in the figurine material and in the activities around the oven. Certainly storage jars containing bones do occur in the house, but I have already referred to a possible case in which cereal grains were found inside a house and animal bones outside (see p. 66). Many of the bones found in houses do not seem to be primary refuse, and animal bone densities are often higher outside houses. There is no hard and fast rule. Cattle, in the form of bucrania, do play a role in the domus as will be discussed below. And yet the symbolism on pots, houses, and figurines within the domus does not give cattle the important place which we know they had within the economy. Although there is some variation in the relative proportions of the various domesticated animals at sites, cattle bones normally dominate.

The use of wild resources, by definition, takes us outside the domus. In the period being considered here the frequencies of wild animal bones on sites vary considerably, although in certain cultural groups such as the Tisza they are often high. In Vinča sites wild animal bones vary from 7.8 per cent at Anza and 9 per cent at Rast, to 27 per cent at Liubcova (Markotic 1984), while at Opovo at least 62 per cent of the fauna is wild (Tringham et al. 1985). In Pre-Cucuteni and Cucuteni sites the main wild fauna is deer, and the percentages for the minimum number of wild individuals on sites vary from 13 to 66 for Pre-Cucuteni sites and from 19 to 64 for Cucuteni sites (Ellis 1984). Hunting equipment is also apparent in this period. In Vinča sites bone harpoons (for fishing or hunting) and points are numerous and in Gumelnitsa sites there is for the first time evidence that hunting equipment included arrowheads of chipped stone (Tringham 1971).

Finally, long distance exchange of valuables is not especially associated with the domus. Rather the valuables are mainly used for tools, weapons, and jewellery. Obsidian is exchanged from, for example, the Tokaj source in the north-west Carpathians. Raw lumps and cores of obsidian are found in graves in the Tiszapolgár and Bodrogkeresztúr groups. High frequencies of obsidian are found in some larger Vinča sites. *Spondylus* shell is used for jewellery in the Vinča cultural area (Chapman 1981), perhaps deriving from the Aegean area. There are major and minor sources of copper throughout the Carpathians and to the south in the Balkans. Two copper mines in the west and east Balkans have already been mentioned. In the Tisza area, Sherratt (1982b) suggests that cattle too were traded in the middle and later Neolithic. He notes that most sources of flint, stone, and obsidian occur in the uplands surrounding the Great Hungarian Plain. What was exchanged for these upland resources? Sherratt notes that the well-watered open plains were ideal for cattle breeding and that faunal remains from sites in the plain show 50–75 per cent cattle, with very high proportions of wild forms especially in the eastern part. The mixture of sizes and morphological characteristics between domestic and wild forms of cattle at some of these sites has been taken as evidence of local domestication (Bökönyi 1962). The plain could have been used for breeding cattle and domesticating new stock for export to upland areas.

Outside the Domus: the Agrios

I have so far in this chapter identified a number of cultural attributes in the late fifth and fourth millennia in SE Europe which are not found in the concept of the domus. There is of course a danger in assuming that all the things which are not found primarily in the house have some coherence. To say that certain items are 'less frequently found in the house' is to say very little. But it was not only statistical association that led to the definition of the domus in chapter 3. The term domus represents a concept (rather like 'home') as well as a thing. The conceptual themes which link together the attributes of the domus include mothering (women and children), nurturing (providing food), and caring (storage). The concepts which link attributes outside the domus are less visible, indeed invisibility and impermanence may initially be essential attributes. The main underlying themes that we can see associate men with warring, exchange, prestige, hunting, wild and domestic animals, and death. Outside the domus I have also identified various aspects of domestic material production.

The importance of the conceptual as well as the statistical definition of the domus is clear when considering items found within houses but not included within the description of the domus above (figure 3.5). Stone tools, for example, were sometimes made in houses but they do not form a regular part of the symbolic practices which take place in relation to the house. Similarly, because of the rarity of animal representations amongst figurines and in pottery decoration, I excluded cattle from the domus. And yet we have seen that in the fourth millennium cattle were the main domesticated animal. At this time cattle may have been used for meat and milk (Bogucki 1984 and Sherratt 1981) so they provided sustenance probably through domestic production. It would be easy to accept, therefore, that cattle nurtured, cared, and provided and that they played a central role in the domus. It is thus not surprising that there are cattle figurines and that cattle symbolism does occur in the house. Unfortunately it is not always easy to identify species in animal representations. I have already mentioned (p. 51) Körös house models with an animal head on a gable end, and similar examples are found in Vinča sites (Markotic 1984). Bucrania (clay-moulded cattle skulls with horns) also occur in Vinča contexts. They are often not well baked, which led Markotic (1984) to suggest that they were not placed outside on gable ends but inside houses. At the late Vinča site of Jakovo-Kormadin, the middle room in a three-roomed house contained a bucranium above the oven. At this site bucrania either occur in conjunction with a normal domestic assemblage or with a range of special features including in one case an 'altar', pillar, decorated wall plaster, a throne figure, and another figurine (Chapman 1981). Bucrania thus occur right at the heart of the domus.

Another clear 'problem', where the outside intrudes into the heart of the domus, was discovered when considering burial ritual. Why are human skulls found on or beneath the floors of the houses? Why was death, the opposite of nurturing, caring, and providing, and the denial of these dynamic processes, brought in to confront the domus? In this as in the cattle example, it would be possible to argue that the domus is defined through, and gains its authority from, the idea of controlling, taming, and ordering the wild and dangerous and from the idea of renewal out of death and danger. While death was increasingly removed from the domestic arena for reasons to be discussed further below, symbolic traces (of the danger of death to society, of the individual versus the social, of decay, etc.) needed to be retained within the house in order to legitimate the domus as carer and provider.

Equally, in a few instances stone axes were given a central role within the symbolism of the domus (Raczky 1987, 23). For example, at Kökénydomb, polished stone axes were deposited under each corner and under the middle of a large storage bin plastered onto the floor of a house and decorated in a manner similar to the pottery (Banner and Foltiny 1945). It could be argued here that the domus is dependent on the idea of controlling the power of the axe (as used in clearing the forest or in protecting and killing human beings) within its own symbols and practices.

At one level, then, there were no oppositions, only a centering around the domus. The domus was the focus. Everything derived from it and referred to it. Even those aspects of life which might be most dangerous to it, including cattle, death, and axes were seen as deriving from the domus. The definition and status of families and of social groups derived from the idea of controlling or taming the wild and the dangerous. It was only by emphasizing this opposite and the threat that it posed to social interests that the domus could be used as a principle of social discourse.

At another level, therefore, an opposition to the domus necessarily existed (figure 3.5). It was not simply the case that everything derived from the domus. Cattle did play a subordinate role in the performances around the oven, death was largely separated from the house, and axes are rarely central to the symbolism within the house. I have shown that many of the items used in the domus can be linked to a diametrically opposed set of concepts concerning individual display, hunting, warring, death, and males. At this second level, the outer, male-associated world 'presenced' itself within the house (Ray 1987).

In the first draft of this book I simply called this non-domus principle 'the outside'. But this term contained none of the ambiguity and double meaning of the domus. In using a straightforward English phrase like 'the outside' the 'movement' between past and present was lost, the dependence on language was hidden from view, and the emphases on continuity and critique were dissipated. In searching for the Indo-European opposites to the domus I turned to Benveniste, and found that he had identified two opposites (1973, 256–7). The first, the 'foris', appears to have less relevance in SE Europe but will come to be of use in considering the central European data in chapters 5 and 6. The second concerns the Latin opposition between *domus* and *ager* (field), from which comes *peregrinus* (stranger, foreign). The English word pilgrim (one who journeys far; a wayfarer, especially one who wanders in a strange country) comes from this word. Other Indo-European languages associate the word for field with the outside. The Greek adjective derived from *agros* (field) is *agrios* which means wild, savage. This whole group of words, including acre and agent, is probably formed on Indo-European *ag-* meaning drive, do, act. But the main reason for using a term linked to *ager* and *agrios* is that a play can be made on the idea of 'agri-culture' as a 'culturing' of the 'wild'. The 'origins of agriculture' are connected, via the domus–agrios opposition, to the more general process of social and cultural domestication. At the same time, reference to agriculture and to the links between field, outside and wild emphasizes that while the house may have been the symbolic focus of the domus, domestication of the wild also took place in the wild outside.

The domus and the agrios are ideas which have some external statistical basis but which are also created by me, using the linguistic structures of my thought, in order to have some internal coherence. The practices to which they refer show much overlap and it will be necessary to examine that overlap further. But there does appear to be some 'objective' basis for distinguishing the domus from the agrios. It would certainly be good to have more evidence of the associations and oppositions that I claim to be able to see. Some readers will feel that I should await more and better excavations, more data, before attempting to build complex interpretations. Symbolic and social interpretation does depend on rich data and perhaps I write too early. And yet my ideas can be and will be refuted through a discussion of the data. It is this belief in argument in relation to the data which makes interpretation worthwhile.

There are some still more abstract concepts that have begun to emerge from considering the domus and the agrios. The domus is fixed, permanent, visible, and very 'present'. It also brooks little individual variation. There is often a repetition of the individual domestic unit which leads to a strong sense of the equivalent and the communal. The agrios, on the other hand, is initially 'absent' and less visible. It involves exchange and hierarchy, competition and individual display. It is closer to the wild. In order to understand the agrios more clearly and its relationship to the domus it is necessary to reject the static picture that I have drawn so far. In fact the relationship between the two principles changes through time. It is from the interplay between the two principles that we can begin to understand the transformations of Neolithic society in SE Europe, and it is the temporal evidence which further validates and emphasizes the existence of and opposition between the principles themselves.

Patterns of Change

First it is necessary to clarify the social and economic changes that occurred. For example, Vinča sites show a process of landscape infilling in relation to the earlier Starčevo sites, increased location in interfluves, and increased size. Although Vinča sites range from 1 ha to 100 ha, most are between 1 and 10 (Kaiser and Voytek 1982) and show evidence of a planned layout with streets (Markotic 1984, 97). Sites were occupied for several centuries, and perhaps up to 500 or 600 years in some cases. Settlement boundaries appear in later Vinča phases (Markotic 1984). There is a trend in the economy towards an emphasis on cattle husbandry, and greater attention seems to have been paid to crop purity and crop processing activities (Kaiser and Voytek 1982). Chapman (1981) suggests that Vinča sites see agricultural innovations such as the cultivation of flax and the higher yield crop bread wheat, and the use of an ard or plough. However, I will show below that a much later date has been argued for the introduction of the plough in SE Europe. Nevertheless, the indications of agricultural intensification are numerous, including greater specialization in barley (ibid.).

Other cultural areas show similar patterns of settlement agglomeration associated with economic intensification. In eastern Hungary, Szakálhát and Tisza sites become increasingly aggregated (Sherratt 1982a) and show evidence of internal planning and enclosure ditches. True tells appear and cattle become the major domesticate. There is a penetration into the uplands. In the Bulgarian tell sites, there is good evidence for a planned internal layout, and terrain and ditches are used for enclosure and fortification (Todorova 1978). The sites average 2.5 ha, with 19–20 houses, but some larger mounds reach 15 and 25 ha. On the basis of the numbers of houses in fully excavated sites, population estimates for these larger sites reach 600 people in 100–20 houses and 1000–1200 people in 190–200 houses. Cattle dominate in most regions.

In the Cucuteni-Tripolye area, sites occur in naturally fortified positions along major river systems and are further provided with defensive ditches (Ellis 1984). During Cucuteni A and B there is a development towards larger, denser settlements. The completely excavated site in north-east Romania called Truşeşti has 95 Cucuteni A houses which are not arranged in any clear plan, but Vladimirovka, dated to Tripolye B, has 200 buildings arranged in a semicircular fashion. In some late Tripolye sites possibly as many as 2000 buildings can be observed (ibid.). There has been little excavation of these very large sites (figure 4.3). For example, only 8 of the 498 structures at Petreny were excavated at the turn of the century. But aerial photography has revealed the arrangement of buildings at Petreny into 10 concentric rings with pathways. Overall settlement patterns show dense distributions of sites (figure 4.4), although many of the larger agglomerations may be later than many of the smaller settlements. A wide variety of wheats and barleys was cultivated, and cattle were the main domesticated animal with domesticated horse appearing in the latest phases.

All the evidence, then, points to an increasing definition and closer integration of larger social units within settlements, coupled with economic intensification. Craft production shows a not dissimilar pattern. In the Vinča area, the site of Selevac shows a change from semi-sedentary to fully sedentary occupation contemporary with the change from Vinča-Tordoš to Vinča-Pločnik (Tringham et al. 1980). At the same time at this site there is a change in procurement patterns which become more selective and organized, and an intensification of production. For example, the number of imperfectly reduced pots decreased over time, indicating a greater control over the process of ceramic production, and a greater variety of pots and a greater volume of pots are produced. There is also change and intensification in lithic production. For example, the early horizons at Selevac have little evidence of core preparation or complete systematic reduction of cores. But in the later horizon are found polyhedral cores, micro-cores, and standardized blades resulting from improved core treatment (Kaiser and Voytek 1982).

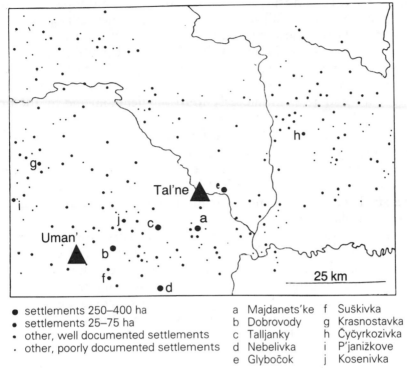

- settlements 250–400 ha
- settlements 25–75 ha
- other, well documented settlements
- other, poorly documented settlements

a Majdanets'ke f Suškivka
b Dobrovody g Krasnostavka
c Talljanky h Čyčyrkozivka
d Nebelivka i P'janižkove
e Glybočok j Kosenivka

Figure 4.4 Tripolye settlements in the Uman' region, Ukraine.
(Source: Ellis 1984)

A change towards more organized, intensive, and specialized production has also been noted in the Cucuteni-Tripolye area (Ellis 1984). During the Pre-Cucuteni/Tripolye A period, ceramic production varied considerably in terms of clay preparation, decoration, and firing. Pottery was fired in pits in uncontrolled atmospheric conditions and the duration of firing was relatively short. Later, however, there was a high degree of clay refinement, the firing of ceramics in complex updraught kilns to temperatures up to 1000° C (including ceramics without temper), the use of an early form of the pottery wheel, and the pre-fire application of slips.

The settlement agglomeration and economic intensification that took place in the late fifth and fourth millennia were substantial. Individuals submitted themselves to the rules and constraints of larger and more closely-tied social units, with little if any centralized control. They undertook to increase labour input and to release control over certain aspects of production as specialization and differentiation increased. Whatever the causes of these changes, to be discussed below, how were they conceived? Why did people not react in other ways? How did the changes become thinkable?

The settlement and economic changes correlate with the elaboration of symbolism in houses discussed in chapter 3. By the time of late Vinča and Tisza in the early fourth millennium and by the time of Gumelnitsa and Cucuteni in the later fourth millennium, houses had become larger and more differentiated, decorated, substantial, and long-lasting. The oven had become the clear focus of activities. Female figurines had become more common and sets of miniatures had appeared. Pottery types had become more varied. In short, all the attributes of the domus, already present in the early Neolithic, became elaborated.

Thus as large and more permanent settlements formed, it was the domus which became still more of a central focus. It can thus be argued that the social and economic changes were thought through the domus. By extending the idea of domesticating the wild into all areas of production the principle of control could be used as a metaphor in a larger arena. But the extension of the domus was not only conceptual. The larger social units that were formed and the intensification of production involved individuals in greater economic and social dependencies. The greater social order and control were thus linked to greater constraint on the individual. As that constraint increased, the agrios seems to have become an ever more attractive alternative metaphor in social life.

Many of the attributes associated with the agrios became more marked during the course of the fourth millennium bc and into the third. They became increasingly more visible. Chapman (1983) describes a process whereby more and larger cemeteries gradually appeared through time. We have seen that weapons and symbols of power such as shaft-hole stone and copper axes gradually appeared through time. Many of the more distinctive Vinča bucrania are late in date, and the human skulls brought into the house are late too. During the Tisza period in eastern Hungary a perceptible decline in human representations has been noted at Gorzsa, with an increased importance of animal figurines in late Tisza (Raczky 1987, 43), including bucrania. The proportions of wild animal bones also increase through time (ibid., 24).

Evidence for the decline in the importance of the domus is clear for example in eastern Hungary, where the domus is most evident in Tisza sites. In the following Tiszapolgár culture (Sherratt 1982a, 1982b, 1983a), large settlement agglomerations disappear and houses are less elaborate. The pottery is predominantly plain. Figurines are absent. Large formal cemeteries appear, such as Tiszapolgár-Basatanya (discussed on p. 75) which is not directly associated with an adjacent settlement. Specific status-linked items are found, such as daggers of stone and copper, gold ornaments, and shaft-hole axes. Daggers and shaft-hole axes are specifically associated with men. Settlements are still less visible in the Bodrogkeresztúr culture which follows although cemeteries are known. Much of the pottery remains undecorated (Sevic and Kostic 1974). Sherratt (1983a, 40) notes that only about 5 per cent of Bodrogkeresztúr pottery is decorated or otherwise diagnostic of cultural affiliation – a much lower proportion than in earlier phases in the same area.

In the ensuing Baden culture, from about 2700 bc, there are both open and fortified settlements. Regional survey on the Great Hungarian Plain has shown that Boleraz and Baden sites are on average smaller than in the Tiszapolgár phase (Sherratt 1983a, 37). Evidence is found of substantial upland expansion of settlement (Sherratt 1982a, 311). Pottery is decorated but the major focus of the evidence is burial. There is considerable variation in burial rite including inhumation (which dominates) and cremation, single and communal interment, flat graves and graves with a small earth mound. Burials occur either singly within or outside settlements, or in large cemeteries (including examples with 400 graves). Some rich burials are found, with for example copper diadems. At Alsónémedi two human burials each contained two skeletons of cattle. Wheeled vehicles are also known as seen in the clay cart models from the Budakalasz cemetery and elsewhere, which sometimes show oxen in harness. At Alsónémedi, for example, male graves are 'richer' than female graves. Much of this evidence 'reads' like the agrios discourse that I have already described. The emphasis is on burial, men, cattle, and individual display. Anthropomorphic pots, including examples with breasts, do now reappear. But now they are as urns, in burial contexts. It is now the outside which dominates and gives meaning to material culture. The domus is much less visible.

Throughout the rest of SE Europe a similar pattern is found, with the evidence for female figurines, elaborate houses, and highly decorated pottery gradually declining to be replaced by cemeteries and ultimately by the individualistic display in burial contexts associated with the beginnings of the Bronze Age. Understanding of this

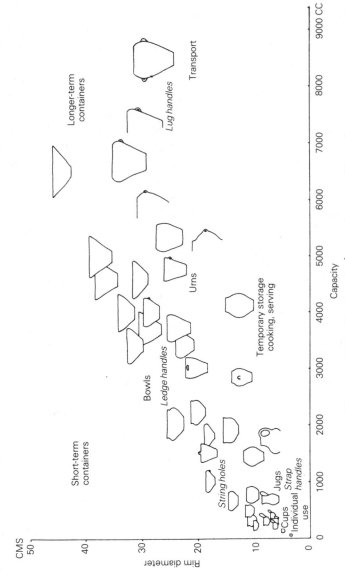

Figure 4.5 Distribution of pottery shapes at Sitagroi.
(Source: Sherratt 1986b)

change is marred by a poverty of reliable evidence (Whittle 1985). At the beginning of the third millennium bc many of the Bulgarian tells show evidence of interruption followed by levels with less decorated pottery, few anthropomorphic figurines, and few of the artifacts primarily associated with the domus. In the second half of the third millennium, individual burials under tumuli are widely found, sometimes accompanied by stone stele, probably representing males, holding or wearing in their belts hafted axes. The tumuli which extend from Baden eastwards have their centre of distribution in the Pontic steppe and it is reasonable to assume a steppe intrusion of ochre-grave groups into SE Europe (Sherratt 1987, 86).

However, overall change to a more individualistic burial rite, incorporating symbols of hunting or warring and particularly emphasizing males, can be linked to more gradual internal processes such as changes in the pottery assemblages of the third millennium bc. Apart from the general decrease in the decoration of ceramics, the assemblages show the addition of a new range of small vessels closely linked to drinking, pouring, and serving (figure 4.5). In the Baden cemeteries of Alsónémedi and Budakalasz the rich burials are associated with an elite drinking set of jug, dipper, cup, and bipartite bowl (Sherratt 1986b, 442). While the liquid used may have been water or milk, the expansion of viticulture at this time, as seen in the change in the morphology of grape pips in Sitagroi phase IV (Renfrew et al. 1986), suggests that the liquid may have been wine although a substitute such as mead is perhaps more likely (Sherratt 1986b and 1987). The pattern fits the concept of the agrios already defined. Males were linked to the control of the wild. The inebriated, the uncontrolled, is also linked to men through the burial associations. And the small individual pots again emphasize social advancement through personal mastery. Sitagroi phase V, dated to the last half of the third millennium bc and early second millennium, has a 'Burnt House' in which drinking jugs or cups with rising handles are not found in the area of the house used for cooking, storing, and preparing food. How widely such a separation of domestic and drinking activities might be found is uncertain at the moment.

It is important to emphasize that the processes of change that I have described in this chapter do not involve radical replacement of one cultural trait by another except in the case of the ochre graves. Rather, there is a gradual process of transformation and a shifting of emphasis within a pre-existing cultural code. The domus certainly does not disappear. It simply loses its centrality and importance.

For example, the Burnt House in Sitagroi phase V retains many of the characteristics of the domus found so widely a millennium earlier. At the back of the house are found oven, evidence of storage and fixed pots, querns and grinders, much as in the domus. But the figurines and general elaboration of this area of the house are not found. Indeed excavation could not at first identify the apsidal wall around the oven area because, unlike the main room in the house, the wall was less substantial and not provided with a plaster face (Renfrew et al. 1986). Similarly, the agrios only increased in importance by manipulating existing structures. For example, it can be argued that the increasing importance of cattle was prefigured in the placing of bucrania within houses. The increasing importance of individual, ostentatious burial also came about through gradual transformation of the domus. The cemeteries, which gradually increase in number, introduce many agrios dimensions to the durable cultural map. But they comprise collections of graves, rather like collections of houses in the settlements, with little surface evidence of individual variation. Cemeteries partly refer to the domus and its communal ethic. But having made this extension, it was possible to expand further in a new direction so that burial became the stage-setting for individual social action and competition through the agrios.

Conclusion

The seeds of collapse of the centrality of the domus existed in its fabric since the beginning. Of course some components of the domus never had a beginning. Or rather, the beginning of some basic notions about home are as old as culture itself. Equally, the concept of domus did not totally disappear in the third millennium bc. Aspects were retained to be reused in new ways within new social structures. But at the beginning of the Neolithic the domus was given a particular definition and a particular place defining the domestication process.

At Lepenski Vir it is possible to see the development of an idea of the domus such that the house and the hearth, and the more general domestication of the wild, became metaphors for the formation of larger social units. Culture and society are contrasted with nature and the individual; and house and home are used as the main mnemonics. The control of death and the wild within the house is used to insert general social rules into the practices within individual houses. The communal is asserted over the individual. We know little of the social strategies underlying these ideas, but it is likely that social groups such as those at Lepenski Vir were able, through their joint labour, to compete successfully regarding resources, feasts, marriage alliances, and prestige exchange (cf. Bender 1978). Whoever's interests were involved, they were well served by manipulating the domestication metaphor.

But the scheme as I have described it was one-sided, top heavy. The creation of society through the idea of domesticating the wild rested precariously on the social manipulation of symbolic relations. Already at Lepenski Vir some practical intensification of production was involved. But it was not until the domestication of plants and animals that humans could be more fully domesticated, caught within longer-term dependencies, engrained more deeply with the practices of delayed returns for labour. The concept of the domus was used to achieve the economic change, but in the early Neolithic a more balanced relationship between concept and practice within the domus could be achieved. Individuals were constrained both in theory and in practice. Perhaps this is one of the reasons that the ever-present symbolic reference to death could increasingly be removed from the house, as the house and settlement became a more practical social and economic unit.

I pointed out that the gradual removal of burial from underneath house floors, as in the change from Lepenski Vir to the Neolithic in SE Europe, occurs in the Near East although at a rather later stage in the process of the adoption of agriculture. I argued in the Near East that during the Neolithic the communal and the social were increasingly emphasized in relation to the individual. Individual households associated with death and with their individual ancestors might have frustrated the attempts of dominant social groups (perhaps elders or those lineages more successful in exchange and feasting relations) to extend the authority of the domus through the settled community as a whole.

Such an argument, which seems equally relevant in SE Europe, assumes that the overall social strategy of dominant groups was to forge closer or more extensive community ties through time, presumably in order to allow increased community production and thus greater ability to participate in competitive processes of exchange and domination. Certainly in SE Europe both the idea and the practice of domestication seem to have been used to create larger social entities during the Neolithic. I have shown in this chapter that

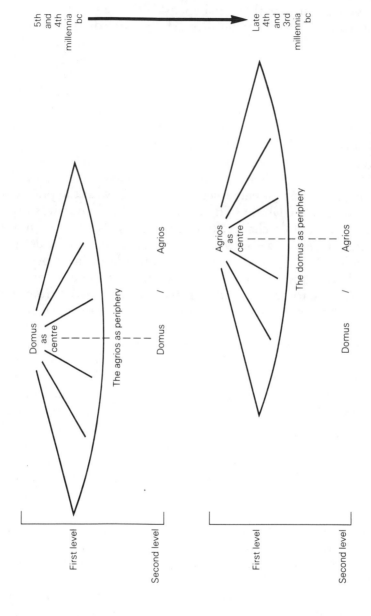

Figure 4.6 The shift in the relative importance of the domus and agrios through time. At one level domus and agrios are opposed, but at another level either the domus or the agrios is used as the central metaphor for social life.

the formation of large settled villages with their associated evidence for economic intensification and some degree of specialization can be linked to the full development of the domus ethic in different parts of SE Europe at different times in the fourth millennium bc. Figurines, miniatures, pottery types, and wall decoration proliferated. The metaphor of the domestication of the agrios was continually referred to by, for example, placing human skulls beneath floors, axes within decorated boxes, and bucrania within or on houses. Over and against the wild, savage, strange, foreign agrios, the domus provided the conceptual framework of caring and nurturing through which social constraint was constructed and larger communities were built.

The domus was metaphor and practice all rolled into one. It implied an increasing use of plants and animals separated from their natural state, dependent on human labour. It implied social interdependence over the long term as labour was invested in the creation of a domestic environment of cleared land and agricultural tools. It implied the need for social control and constraints on individual action in order to build planned villages, common defences, and communal cemeteries. But the social control could not simply be built from the top down. Its rationale was dispersed within the framework of the domus itself, within the overall metaphor of domestication and taming.

Right from the beginning the use of the domus was associated with constraint and a common social order imposed on individual units of production. As that constraint increased through time, the agrios could be developed as an alternative mechanism and metaphor of power. For example, a more flexible, dispersed settlement pattern was attained by the expansion of settlement into a wider range of environments and use of a wider range of resources. From one perspective this extension of settlement was simply a further extension of the domus and of the idea of domesticating the wild. The settlement change could be created within domus principles but it had the effect of allowing small group action outside the authority structures of the large villages.

Another effect produced by the expansion of the domus was the increased reliance on defence. As local groups in settled villages engaged in closer competition over resources, defence and warring became more important. The practices and ideas of the agrios could thus be highlighted at the expense of the domus. The whole metaphor associated with warring, hunting, and status display became a more appropriate discourse through which groups competed and organized their production.

That the change of centrality from the domus to the agrios was not only conceptual but also practical is clear from the evidence of economic change. Sherratt's (1981, 1983b, 1986a; Chapman 1982) important and persuasive model of the Secondary Products Revolution suggests that in the third millennium bc in Europe, particularly in the Baden culture in SE Europe and in the middle Neolithic TRB culture (see chapter 7) in N Europe, there is evidence for the use of animals for pulling carts and ploughs. The use of animals for wool is seen as occurring at the same time or slightly later. The plough allowed the use of a wider range of soils and secondary animal products permitted greater use of upland areas and a generally more extensive system. In the terms I am using in this book, the Secondary Products Revolution fitted into the cultural transformations which were already underway and allowed the further pursuit of social and economic strategies based on the agrios. The plough and the importance of cattle and ox traction seen in Baden contexts are thus incorporated within an existing scheme and they have effects depending on that scheme. In this sense, then, the technological innovations do not cause anything. Rather they are perceived within existing structures and can be manipulated in order to change those structures. The effects may be partly unintended. Sherratt has shown that the use of secondary products is often associated with certain types of social and economic system. The very practice of the shift to a greater dependence on cattle, the plough, and secondary products may have enhanced the authority of the agrios idiom by linking it to an appropriate economic practice in which dispersal and small group independence were more viable and to an appropriate social practice in which opportunistic and competitive exchange relationships became more important in defining social power than one's position in settled, long-term village and lineage structures.

The details of my account are unclear and the overall model of conceptual, social and economic change has been sketchily introduced. I hope to provide a more substantial basis for my interpretation in the chapters which follow. But in broad outline I have tried to provide an account in which structures follow a logical sequence, an 'unfolding', through time while I also allow for social strategies and human actions in the course of events. I have tried to find a middle path between determinism and voluntarism. The domus–agrios structure has its own logic and internal tensions which, when put into play, seem to determine the outcome of events. This is partly because the structure is as much social, economic, and practical as it is symbolic. Thus the 'playing out' or the following of the logic of the structure has certain effects (such as economic change, settlement dispersal, etc.) which necessitate a rereading and a rewriting of the structures of signification.

But it is easy to become involved in too abstract an account. For the structures to 'work' they depend on practical performance. For example, to bring the bucranium into the oven area of the house creates multiple and ambiguous meanings. These were probably just as ambiguous then as they are now, if not more so, as we might see if the evidence was more complete. Does the bucranium indicate that cattle have to be controlled so that they can nurture like the house, or does it indicate that the house is wild and dangerous like oxen? The event may delight in the ambiguity between structures which it produces. But given all the ambiguity the act would have to have been brought off well, competently, with panache. It would have to have been well performed. Bringing the power of cattle into the domus was a creative act thought through and using existing structures, but not determined by them. The performance around the oven creates tensions in order to resolve them, or rather to appear to resolve them. Badly performed, the structures would quickly disintegrate and become meaningless. Structure is the medium for, but depends on, good performance in practical social contexts.

The different ways in which social actors manipulate structures and the historical and environmental differences between regions should produce radical differences in the way in which the same or similar structures are transformed through time. In remaining parts of the book I wish to explore similarities and differences between SE Europe and the sequences known in other regions. The concern is whether 'history could have been otherwise', and the lurking suspicion is that just possibly the answer is not, as I have so far argued 'yes', but 'no'.

5

Dominating Boundaries and Entrances: the Earlier Neolithic in Central Europe

The explanation of other sequences of change in Europe has two related aims. First, I wish to examine the relationship between local historical sequences and what appear to be wider trends. Is there indeed some pan-European, or even universal, developmental process in which regional groups and localized cultures became engaged? To what extent can history be otherwise? Given a set of social and conceptual structures and a local environment does history follow predetermined paths? Or does human action involve an interpretive, creative component? Similar questions have been addressed by scholars over many centuries. Does archaeology have anything to contribute? Second, I wish to ask related questions of my own writing. Is my writing already written? Do I simply impose assumptions on the data? In a sense I found what I expected in SE Europe. The pattern fits nicely what I had wanted (see chapter 1) as a result of visiting the Nuba, reading Mary Douglas, and reading various books and articles referred to in chapter 1 concerning the representation of women in non-complex societies. Particularly the emphasis on female representation in the SE European Neolithic fits into some of these schemes and into the modern social interest in gender relations. So am I simply interpreting the archaeological data according to pre-existing schemes, or can I interpret the data in order to contribute to, comment on, and in some small way transform the structures within which we live? Can I be sensitive to different historical trajectories, using any uniqueness of experience which they contain, to contribute to our experience of ourselves?

The Fifth and Fourth Millennia bc in Central Europe

It is often assumed that the Neolithic spreads across Europe, and by this is often meant that movements of people were involved. However, it remains possible that the change from the Mesolithic to the Neolithic was largely undertaken by indigenous groups, resulting in a local colonization of fertile and easily worked loess soils which had previously been avoided for the most part. But even if few people moved across Europe, many of the domesticates and much of the knowledge and cultural influence derived from SE Europe. As a result, the Neolithic did not 'begin again' in each new locality or region as farming spread through Europe. The Linear Pottery or Linearbandkeramik (LBK) 'early' Neolithic in central Europe derives from cultures in SE Europe at a certain point in time and carries the previous experience and history of those groups with it. The LBK carries a cultural experience, a memory, with it as it spreads. It does not start afresh.

Western Linear Pottery is unpainted and dark burnished, decorated with incised bands which form spirals and meanders. It originates in Hungary in approximately 4500 bc, at the same time as the formation of the Vinča and other dark burnished pottery groups with spirals and meander decoration in SE Europe. To be more specific, in the area of the Hungarian Plain already occupied by agricultural sites, the Alföld Linear Pottery develops from the local Körös and Szatmár populations with strong Vinča influence. In a new area of Hungary west of the Danube, the widespread western branch of the Linear Pottery makes its first appearance (Sherratt 1982a, 297). From these two Hungarian groups the two facies of the Linear Pottery culture developed, one in the east centred on the Carpathian Basin, and one in the west stretching through Czechoslovakia, to central Poland, Germany, Holland, and the Paris Basin. It is mainly the latter that will be considered here.

The Linear Pottery Culture acts as the source for a number of 'Danubian' cultures and styles that develop and transform up to approximately 3300 bc. The Linear Pottery Culture itself endures until 4000–3950 bc. In the Rhineland there follows a sequence resulting in Rössen (c.3500–3300 bc), in Bohemia, S. Poland, and C. Germany Stichbandkeramik (SBK or Stroke Linear Pottery) is followed by Late Lengyel or Rössen, and in W. Hungary, Slovakia,

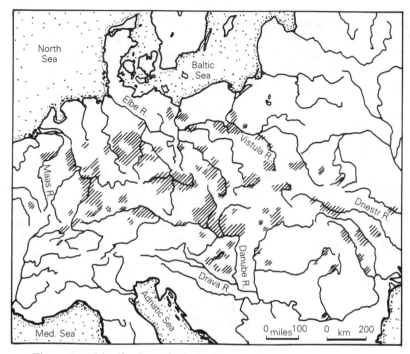

Figure 5.1 Distribution of Linear Pottery sites in central Europe.
(Source: Milisauskas 1986)

and Moravia painted Early Lengyel pottery is followed by plain Late Lengyel pottery (see table 1). In all these areas, the Danubian tradition ends around 3300 bc, to be followed by a distinctively new tradition incorporating TRB (Trichterrandbecher or funnel-necked beaker), Michelsberg (in the Rhineland), and Chassey (in the Paris Basin). Because of the essential coherence of the Danubian cultures up to 3300 bc, I intend intitially to treat them as a group before discussing change within the period 4400 to 3300 bc. Later transformations after 3300 will be considered separately in chapter 6.

Similarities and differences between central and SE Europe

Given the origin of the Linear Pottery culture in SE European cultures, it is not surprising that the data immediately appear familiar in that again it is the house which dominates our understanding. There is great variety in the size and layout of the houses, but

Danubian archaeology is again settlement archaeology. The numerous small and large scale excavations have been concerned mainly with uncovering the traces of long houses and their associated features. The houses occur initially loosely scattered along river terraces, on rich loess soils which have attracted intensive agriculture ever since. As a result, occupation horizons have largely been destroyed by heavy ploughing. Despite this massive destruction, the post-holes of the large houses remain substantial and enduring. Six to 8 m wide and up to 45 m and later 60 m long, the houses show complex post patterns and internal divisions, for example, with double posts at the south-eastern end, sometimes a 'Y' arrangement of posts in the central section, and a continuous wall bedding trench around the north-western section (figure 5.2). The size and elaboration of these houses, despite the millennia of destruction, impose their authority on the information that survives from this period.

And so the notion of the domus again seems appropriate, at least after an initial inspection. This first impression is strengthened by several aspects of the data. For example, the house is the centre of activities. Storage of grain takes place in pits by the house or in stores within the house. While there is some evidence that as in SE Europe the interiors of the long houses were cleaned out (Milisauskas 1986, 177), the house remains the focus of productive activities as evidenced by the contents of the refuse pits around it. At Olszanica, a late fifth-millennium bc site from south-east Poland with LBK (more specifically Notenkopf (Music Note) and Zeliezovce) pottery, has highest concentrations of refuse in pits nearest the long houses. With distance away from the long houses, the amounts of fine pottery and flint tool debris decline (ibid.). The entire sequence of flint tool production took place in the settlement, focused around the house, together with artifact use (ibid., 84). Extensive excavations on the Aldenhoven Plateau, near Köln in West Germany have shown that an area between houses at Langweiler 9 may have been used for pit digging, craft activities, refuse deposition, and so on, although many artifacts and pits show clusters around the houses themselves. At Langweiler 8 an activity zone of radius 25 m around the house was identified including long pits along the sides of the house, and at least one extra pit to each of the sides and the back of the house and sometimes also to the front (Lüning 1982) (figure 5.3).

In a small late Lengyel site adjacent to the main settlement at Brześć Kujawski in central Poland, Bogucki and Grygiel (1981) have identified a range of activities including storage and burial, and

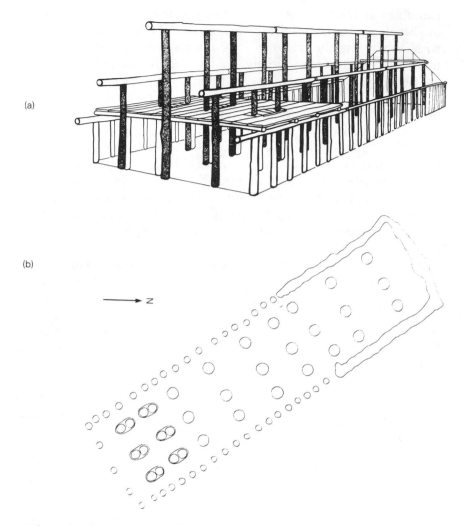

Figure 5.2 Reconstruction (a) and groundplan (b) of Linear Pottery house.
(After Lüning 1982)

rubbish pits, associated with the house (figure 5.4). Higher densities
of refuse occurred in rubbish pits nearer the entrance to the house.
At Cuiry-les-Chaudardes in the Paris Basin the side ditches of the
long houses have higher densities of sherds towards the south-eastern
entrance, although here there are also high densities in the long
ditches adjacent to the north-western corner of the house (Ilett et

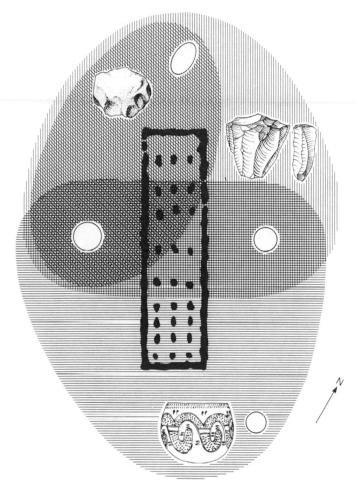

Figure 5.3 Model of some of the activity zones around a Linear Pottery house at Langweiler 8. Circles indicate pits.
(Source: Lüning 1982)

al. 1982). Returning to Brześć Kujawski, flint working was done close to the house and ground stone tools were manufactured on the site itself, rather than arriving as finished products (Bogucki and Grygiel 1981). The production of antler axes was also a major on-site activity, although the finished axes were not found on site. Where they do occur in settlements in the Brześć Kujawski area, they are found in graves and hoards (ibid.).

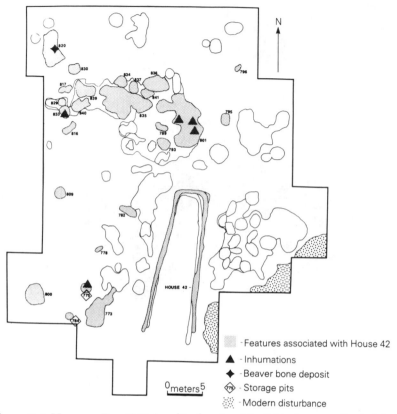

Figure 5.4 House at Brześć Kujawski, showing Neolithic features. Shaded features are those contemporary with house 42.
(Source: Bogucki and Grygiel 1981)

There is some slight evidence for differences in activities along the length of the long house or in the areas outside it. Higher densities of sherds nearer the entrances of the houses have already been noted. At Langweiler 8, specific categories of finds are divided in unequal proportions among the pits around the house. This pattern may also reflect differences in activity within the house (Lüning 1982) although this is less certain. An example of the patterns found at Langweiler 8 is shown in figure 5.3, where pottery, especially undecorated pottery, dominates to the south-east of the entrance area, whereas flint tools and artifacts in above average quantities occur to the north-west. These two zones overlap in the small side pits away from the house. The north-west corner of the house has a preponderance of stone rubble.

As well as being the focus of activities within the settlement, the house also contains certain aspects of the symbolism found in the domus in SE Europe. The walls were daubed with mud taken from long irregular pits along the longer sides of the houses. There is evidence from a few sites that the walls of Linear Pottery houses may have been painted (Hodder 1984, 58; Lichardus and Lichardus-Itten 1985, 277). Foundation deposits occur in house post-holes (ibid., 284). In a number of the later, trapezoidal long houses, for example at Postoloprty, Bylany, and Bochum-Hiltrop, there is an alcove on the right after entering, between the antechamber and the central room. In the site of Postoloprty in Bohemia, dated to a period immediately after SBK, a trapezoidal house 33 m long is subdivided into three rooms, the central room containing four hearths. By the alcove between the antechamber and central room, a deposit was found in the foundation trench for the house. In it was a stone box made of grinding stones containing pottery, a bone pin, and bones including a pig's skull (Soudský 1969). Unlike in SE Europe, where special deposits were associated most closely with the hearth, at Postoloprty the careful deposition of objects occurs in the walls in the entrance area of the house. Hearths have not generally survived in the Danubian houses on the heavily ploughed loess, so it is difficult to make comparisons in this regard with SE Europe. However, the paucity of evidence of hearths, hearth structures, oven fragments, models of ovens, etc. could be taken as implying that a limited significance given to hearths and ovens has contributed to their non-survival.

Given the enormous number of long houses that have been excavated in central Europe, the evidence for wall decoration and special deposits is slight. Other similarities with the SE European domus can nevertheless be sought. For example, at Cuiry-les-Chaudardes in the Paris Basin, three of the LBK houses are associated with child burials, and Coudart (1987) has suggested that adult inhumations may be rare in Danubian villages. This pattern, if confirmed by analysis, would recall the association between settlements, women, and children in SE Europe. On the other hand, in the late Lengyel site of Brześć Kujawski 3, adult burials are found in storage pits near the long house (figure 5.4) (Bogucki and Grygiel 1981). Bone does not survive well in many decalcified loess situations. The burial evidence will be examined more carefully below.

More general links between other components of the domus can be found however. We have seen that fine decorated pottery is associated spatially with the long houses. Temporally too there is a link since, as we shall see, elaborately decorated Danubian pottery often dies out at the same time as the long houses disappear. It does not seem to be coarse or storage pottery that is decorated, but the main fine decorated shapes are initially open bowls, with necked or 'beaker' bottle forms becoming increasingly important. Sherds from sieves also lack the characteristic Linear Pottery decoration (Bogucki 1984). Following another possible line of argument, Soudský (1962, 198) has claimed that analyses of fingerprints on Linear Pottery ceramics indicated that the fingerprints are consistently female, although whether the sex of the fingerprints can be determined in the absence of a large sample of Neolithic fingerprints of both sexes is questionable (Milisauskas 1986, 218).

In the south-eastern part of the Linear Pottery culture, the familiar modelling of pots in the form of women is found, but how far this pattern can be extended over the Danubian area as a whole is uncertain. Some human figurines and other anthropomorphic representations do occur in Linear Pottery and Stroke Linear Pottery contexts (e.g. Behrens 1973) and Wamser (1980) has plotted the distribution in central Europe of early Linear Pottery depictions of women holding pots (as in the example from Erfurt).

After an initial look it might seem reasonable to associate decorated pots and houses with women and with the providing and giving of food and drink, but away from the influence of SE Europe, the associations and the symbolism are weakly developed and the evidence is tenuous. Other aspects of the domus symbolism do occur in Danubian groups, but again they are rare outside the Carpathian zone. Figurines are rare, often not well finished and representing animals as much as people (Milisauskas 1986). Miniatures sometimes occur (ibid.), although only of pots.

Because of the cultural links between the western Linear Pottery and its domus-dominated eastern counterpart, and because of the continuities between SE European and central European cultures, it seems reasonable to argue that some components of the domus are to be found in the Danubian province. In particular the house itself is important, as is pottery, especially the finer wares involved in the preparing, presenting, and eating of food. But the differences with SE Europe are stark. Where hearths do survive, they are not surrounded by fixtures and elaborate furnishings. Representation of the human body and expressions of female sexuality are rare. Milisauskas (1986, 210) has attempted to identify male and female activity areas at the Linear Pottery site of Olszanica, suggesting that female tasks were carried out along one side of the long house and male tasks on the other, but neither the spatial segregation of tools, nor the gender associations are clear cut. There is no clear zone of female-linked activities in the house nor any clear association between houses and women. Of course, it could be argued that the greater destruction of the long houses has led to a loss of the essential information. But on the other hand, even poor survival of occupation floors would have allowed baked clay female figurines and models of houses to be recovered from refuse deposits, as well as accidentally fired wall decoration and oven and house paraphernalia. That so little of this survives is certainly significant. Some aspects of the domus are present in central Europe, but they are reduced or given less or different importance.

If the domus has less or different prevalence in central Europe, what happens to its potential opposite, the agrios? I will argue that this oppositional structure again appears to exist, but that it is expressed differently in central Europe. There is in fact a variety of burial rites in Danubian cultures. For example in the Linear Pottery phase there are scattered burials in graves or reused pits near houses in settlements (see figure 5.4). There are also small or large cemeteries, sometimes near settlements as at Elsloo (Modderman 1975). These cemeteries increase in frequency as one moves north and west in the Linear Pottery area. They may have less than 20 graves or more than 100. The graves were certainly marked in some way as there is rarely any overlap between them (e.g. Dohrn-Ihmig 1983a) and at Sondershausen a possible mortuary hut has been identified (Kahlke 1958). The orientation of the graves is variable (Whittle 1988b) but is often west/east. In most cases crouched inhumations are found, although extended inhumations and cremations also occur.

Thus, the Linear Pottery culture does not strongly oppose the life-giving properties of the house with burial and bodily decay. There is less evidence of complex flesh-removal procedures, both sexes are equally represented in the cemeteries, the graves are visible and durable, and they are sometimes oriented in a similar way to the houses. They are often grouped into cemeteries in much the same way that, as we shall see, the houses are grouped into settlements, although in some cases at least the graves appear more concentrated than the houses (Whittle 1988b). The artifact associations in the graves too, do not oppose a male burial sphere with a female domestic sphere as they had done in SE Europe. Rather, there is an overall clear difference between male and female grave contents, although the precise way in which this is expressed varies. For example, *spondylus* shells are found in adult male graves in the Nitra cemetery in Slovakia (Sherratt 1982b), but in female graves in Sondershausen, E. Germany (Kahlke 1958) and in the Paris Basin (Burkill 1983b). At Nitra, Sondershausen, Aiterhofen in Bavaria, and Rixheim in France, adult males are associated with polished stone axes and adzes, with projectile points, and sometimes with chipped stone tools, although flint blades occur with women at Aiterhofen. The overall link between men and axes and arrowheads is clear and again shows in a reduced form the structure found in SE Europe. Female graves contain ornaments and, in Aiterhofen, querns and awls. But they are not everywhere less 'rich' or less visible in the cemeteries. In the Paris Basin, for example, some of the female graves are very 'rich'. At Frignicourt, a woman was buried with 817 cardium beads, 6 *spondylus* beads, a pendant and 2 bracelets in *spondylus*, a schist bracelet, and a bone bead (Burkill 1983a).

Similar patterns continue through time. The variety of burial continues and even in the late Lengyel at Brześć Kujawski burials are found in graves and pits within the settlement. But cemeteries also occur. In the Hinkelstein cemetery of post-Linear Pottery date in the Rhineland, arrowheads, perforated tools, and shoe-last celts are associated with men, while grinding stones, pottery ornaments, and light stone tools are associated with women (Lichardus and Lichardus-Itten 1985). In the Rössen culture there are some big cemeteries involving single inhumation burials with pots, tools, hunting equipment, and ornaments. However, at the Rössen cemetery itself, there are perhaps greater similarities with the type of opposition observed in SE Europe. Of the graves 18 contained males, and only 6 females and 5 children. Despite the small sample of women in this cemetery, of the 7 shaft-hole axes found, all were in male graves. Of course it is possible that female graves have survived less well or been less easy to identify than male graves, but the male dominance in this cemetery departs from the usual pattern in central Europe.

In the burial data as a whole it is possible to link men to hunting and to axes and thus perhaps to warring, cutting down the forest, and control of the wild. The polished Linear Pottery axes and the shaft-hole axes and adzes which appear after the Linear Pottery in the Rhineland may have had both functional and prestige value, although the latter is far from clear. Stone axes are frequently found as stray finds and in non-settlement contexts. Females may thus have been linked more to the house and food preparation and males more to the outside wild and its control. But this opposition does not 'resonate' strongly throughout the cultural material. Male is not strongly contrasted with female in all spheres. Female symbolism is strong in burial and it is not clearly associated with the house, so that male–female cannot be linked to burial–settlement, invisible–visible, and so on.

Another aspect of the central European pattern that does not 'resonate' as in SE Europe concerns the opposition between the social (communal) and the individual. In central Europe we shall see that the relationship between the individual and the social is again a major focus of concern. But the importance of the communal seems to have been argued in several ways in addition to the house, settlement, and cemetery. One of the most distinctive aspects of the Neolithic outside SE Europe is the appearance of communal structures or camps often termed 'ritual' because of the lack or paucity of normal occupation residues within them (Whittle 1988a). To the south-east within the Danubian province, these enclosures seem mainly associated with Early Lengyel and SBK phases. They clearly differ from the enclosed settlements and tells in the Balkans discussed in chapter 4. In Moravia, the site of Těšetice-Kyjovice (figure 5.5) is important because, in this intermediary area, it links the camps with the domus complex of SE Europe and emphasizes the transformations that occur in the move from SE to central Europe. The site, dated to early Lengyel, with encircling ditch and interrupted palisades, did not contain settlement traces in its interior although such traces were found outside. In the ditches 6 m wide and 3.5 m deep were found enormous numbers of baked clay anthropomorphic figurines, much animal bone, stone tools, and some human bone (Lichardus and Lichardus-Itten 1985). Specific interpretations are difficult, but in general terms it appears that the monument is communal in that it serves a local group of houses. It incorporates material which is associated with the domus but in a context outside

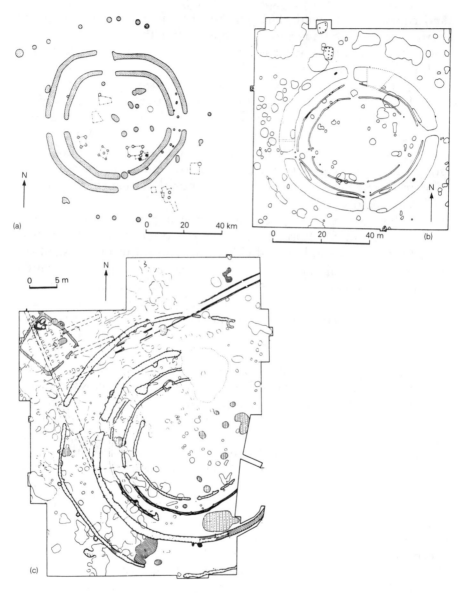

Figure 5.5 Central European enclosures: (a) Kothingeichendorf; (b) Těšetice-Kyjovice; (c) Vochov. (a and b after Behrens and Schröter 1980, c after Pavlů 1982)

the house. There is something new here, from the SE European perspective. The communal is spatially separated from the house. The enclosure is associated with the domus but no longer embraces its traditional representative – the domestic dwelling.

Whittle (1985, 190) discusses similar sites from Slovakia, again with four opposed entrances, while a remarkable early Lengyel example has been found at Svodín (Whittle 1988a, 4). In Bohemia, Vochov is a partially excavated circular ditched enclosure (figure 5.5) of Linear Stroke Pottery date, although it also has some Linear Pottery (Pavlů 1982). There are two ditches backed by three concentric palisades. This and other similar enclosures from Bohemia are generally assumed to have non-domestic functions (ibid.) because of the lack of evidence of buildings in them and because there sometimes seem to be too many rings for the small size of the interior. They appear imposing, marking out an area with multiple ditches and palisades. It is possible that they are simply stock enclosures and that the multiple rings represent different phases of construction. However, the exact placing of the concentric rings argues for contemporaneity between at least some of the rings. Thus, even if the enclosure did have some economic, storage, feasting, or settlement purpose, it nevertheless makes a powerful statement about the control of space, and it links that control to the community as a whole since the spatial distribution of the enclosures suggests they 'served' a local area of settlements (ibid.).

At Kothingeichendorf in Bavaria (figure 5.5) a small double-ditched enclosure with Linear Stroke Pottery and Linear Pottery has four opposed entrances as in the Moravian and Slovakian examples. Precisely similar enclosures do not occur at this time to the north in the Danubian region. However, distinctive characteristics of the enclosures so far discussed are the multiple entrances and discontinuous ditches. Indeed, Lichardus and Lichardus-Itten (1985) compare Bochum-Harpen with Vochov and Těšetice-Kyjovice, arguing for a similarity in function. The enclosure dates from the Grossgartach-Rössen transition, has numerous interruptions in the ditch, and has no trace of habitation in the interior. Interrupted ditch enclosures and enclosures with multiple concentric ditches occur in the Rhineland from Linear Pottery through to Rössen and later phases (Whittle 1977b). In many cases, evidence of occupation is found outside them and they sometimes appear to 'serve' more than one settlement. There is great variety in the profiles of their ditches, their plans, sizes, and location, so that Whittle suggests they may not all have had the same function. Neverthless, the common attributes of the early central European enclosures are distinctive in contrast to the enclosed settlements in SE Europe. The enclosures are communal but they do not contain individual long houses. Rather, they are placed outside the immediate sphere of the house, even though the evidence from Těšetice-Kyjovice and Svodín suggests they may be closely linked to the domestic domain.

It does not seem possible to understand the central European material in the same terms as were used for SE Europe. The house and domestic pottery remain foci of symbolic elaboration, and similar male–female oppositions are encountered. But the cultural material as a whole does not seem to be structured in equivalent ways. How can we begin to understand this new system, and what are its distinctive properties?

The Early Danubian Evidence

I wish to start with the long house because it so clearly is an important node in the durable archive. And I wish to start at the beginning, with the early Linear Pottery culture. To what extent can we recapture the lives of the early Linear Pottery inhabitants of the long houses despite the poor survival of occupation horizons? The first point is simply that the house is often large and internally complex. Numerous substantial timbers are required in its construction (Startin 1978). Longitudinally there are three rows of posts between the walls (figure 5.2). Extending up to 45 m, these lines of posts add to the sense of linearity within the house. But the house is also divided into three sections. The entrance is in the narrow south-eastern end of the house. On analogy with later houses such as Postoloprty, the central section of the Linear Pottery house, sometimes with a distinctive 'Y' arrangement of posts, was probably the main living area. Charcoal in the post-holes of the central areas of Linear Pottery houses supports this interpretation (Whittle 1985, 81). The back area of the house is sometimes surrounded by a continuous bedding trench. Each of the three areas of the house is marked by different post arrangements. The continuous bedding trench at the north-western end and the presence of pits outside the long sides of the house imply that the only entrance was through the main entrance at the narrow south-eastern end. Space was thus differentiated or graded in a linear sequence from front to back. The longitudinal lines of posts emphasize linearity. The cross-cutting tripartite divisions grade the linear space. To reach the back of the house one had to walk through the front two 'rooms'. In certain respects it is the central section of the house which appears dominant since in many houses one or both of the end sections may be absent (Modderman 1970). But the central section always remains. In a 'complete' long house, access to the central section is controlled by passage through the entrance section.

Estimates of the numbers of people inhabiting a long house vary. If only the central portion of long houses was inhabited, the size of this section (up to 6 × 15–20 m) is not so much larger than the single houses in SE Europe that we need to suppose a more complex social unit. Rather, despite the evidence of four hearths at Postol-oprty, it is easier to assume single, if larger, social units in the long houses. Startin (1978) has suggested that the construction of the house would have involved more than one household unit.

We have, then, a small social unit inhabiting a very substantial house in which space is graded from front to back in a long linear sequence. That the inhabiting social unit would have become closely associated with the house itself is supported by the long period of occupation of each house. Estimates of the use-life of the houses, based on experimental, historic, and environmental factors vary from 20 to 50 years or more. The house might then be rebuilt nearby, but rarely on top of existing house locations. The same 'settlement' could thus be used over many centuries through the gradual shifting and replication of the long house. Starling (1985a) has noted for the Elbe–Saale region in central Germany that in the Linear, Stroke, and Rössen phases, about 80 per cent of sites in each phase continue from earlier phases (see also Lüning 1982).

But what is meant by a Linear Pottery 'settlement' or 'site'? We have seen that the house is associated, at least in the Linear Pottery phase, with side pits for daub later used for rubbish, storage pits, activity areas, and sometimes graves. Such household units can either exist singly or in loose agglomerations. Excavated settlement plans may initially look densely packed with long houses, but only when contemporary houses are identified is it realized that at any one time a settlement consists of less than 20 and frequently less than 10 houses, with each house separated by up to 40 m or even 100 m. It often appears as if the scattered settlement pattern extended more or less continuously along the loess-covered terraces immediately above rivers and streams (Kruk 1980; Kuper et al. 1977).

Many of the early long houses were thus relatively loosely grouped, sometimes into small settlements. Despite the apparent independence or separation of individual houses, there is a remarkable conservatism in house plan throughout the whole Linear Pottery area. The highly complex internal ordering is repeated over vast areas in Europe. The long house itself plays an important part in defining the cultural and social in relation to the 'wild' which begins outside the settled zones. The size and ordered complexity of the long house create an elaborate and powerful cultural domain.

The idea that the house helps to create the cultural in respect to the natural is supported by considering the environmental and economic evidence for the Linear Pottery culture. Pollen evidence is often difficult to interpret especially if only sporadic sampling points distant from settlement areas have been studied. It is necessary to bear in mind factors such as the filtering effect of woodland on pollen rain. However, the overall evidence from pollen and other sources suggests that, in most areas, a wooded environment remained. Pollen, soil, and snail evidence from the Elbe–Saale region suggests that the landscape in the Neolithic was a 'forest steppe', wooded in the lower moister valleys, and largely treeless on the interfluves but with isolated clumps and small stands of trees (Starling 1983). By the Middle Neolithic in this region there was still little evidence of deforestation due to human impact. In the Rhineland too, pollen diagrams give no indication of large scale early deforestation (Bakels 1978). In north-west Bohemia, a combined pollen diagram from Komorany Lake appears to show that in the Linear Pottery and Linear Stroke Pottery phases there are a few cerealia but little change in the non-arboreal pollen and only a very localized impact on the Mixed Oak Forest (Neustupný 1985). In a pollen sequence from Pleszow in south-east Poland (Milisauskas 1986), the appearance of the first Linear Pottery occupation correlates with the presence of a few cereals. At the same time, elm and ash declined and traces of charcoal begin to appear, suggesting some woodland clearance by fire, while hazel and pine increased, the hazel at least quickly regenerating in the cleared areas. Estimates of settlement population size and land use involve difficult assumptions and many unknown parameters. For a small region in south-east Poland, Milisauskas (1986, 163) has estimated that only 1.7 per cent of the total available arable land was used by the Linear Pottery population. Even if wildly inaccurate, this estimate agrees with the general evidence of slight impact on the environment. We have to conceive of most Linear Pottery houses and house clusters as relatively isolated within a wooded river valley environment.

It seems likely that the fields of household units were also near individual houses since there is evidence that large areas were not cleared for the growing of crops. The plant remains recovered from Linear Pottery sites suggest that the sizes of fields were quite small and that the fields were overshadowed by forest edges or hedges (Knörzer 1971, Bakels 1978, Willerding 1980), since shade-loving varieties are found amongst the weeds associated with cereal crops. Because of the uniform composition and repetition of weed associations in Linear Pottery sites in the Rhineland, the fields were either used permanently or were always laid out in the same sequence, using the same methods (Bakels 1978). Experimental planting of crops on the loess has shown that the soils are sufficiently rich not to be quickly or easily exhausted (Milisauskas 1986, 162).

The evidence thus supports the notion that the inhabitants of the Linear Pottery long houses conducted hoe agriculture in small permanent or rotating fields in clearings around the house. Although cattle, sheep, goat, and pig were also grazed in the areas around the houses, the overall transformation of the natural environment was slight. The house remained, stable, used and rebuilt over long periods of time, as a bold assertion of the cultural in a largely untamed world. The wild, uncontrolled, began close to the house walls, but it was distanced by the monument of the house itself and by the complexity of its internal cultural ordering. Certainly there was a dependency and interaction with the wild. Arrowheads are only common in certain areas (for example the Netherlands). The bones of wild animals including cattle and deer occur on Linear Pottery sites. But in comparison with later periods, the proportions of wild animal bones in site faunal assemblages are low, generally less than 10 per cent (Lichardus and Lichardus-Itten 1985), although depending on the method of counting used, 20–30 per cent of wild animal bones are found on sites in Poland (Milisauskas 1986) and 18 per cent in the Paris Basin (Ilett 1983). At least in bone deposition practices, the wild was relatively distanced from the tamed. The low percentages of wild animal bones are particularly emphatic in view of the propinquity of houses to the relatively untamed forest in which game probably occurred.

Can we then use the idea of the domus to describe the Linear Pottery long houses of central Europe? Before the formation of bounded villages and ditched enclosures in the later Linear Pottery and following phases, the house played a major part in defining and creating the cultural and the social order. Without the house there was no society. Linear Pottery settlements occurred in riverine loess environments in which pre-existing hunter-gatherer populations were sparse. The loose scatters of individual household units of production maintained close contacts as seen in the widespread similarities of house, pottery and burial forms. But the domestication of the wild remained largely a matter of individual domestic production centred on the house. The long house expressed a cultural order over the natural. The economic taming of the wild was part of that same expression, closely linked to the cultural transformation. The taming of the wild formed a metaphor for the formation of society because the house was, in the same moment, the primary social unit, the model of cultural order, and the unit of economic production. The house set itself against the wild, boldly, impressively, elaborately. In the drama of that act, the social, cultural, and economic were fused.

In its relationship with the wild the long house thus embodies the social and cultural process of domestication that seems to go hand in hand with the domestication of economic resources in Europe. In this sense, therefore, the idea of the domus is appropriate. The long house is the focus of the domination of the wild. Certainly the Danubian concept of domus is different from that in SE Europe. There is less visible emphasis on nurturing and on female representation, and many of the oppositional structures are put together in different ways. But the essential idea of the house as the link between the social, cultural, and economic processes of domestication remains. But how could I capture the observed differences between SE and central Europe? Here it becomes necessary to face historical individuality, as described at the beginning of this chapter. How could I interpret the domus in its transformed state in central Europe?

Without any comparable ethnography, of my own or published by other people, to assist, the task of answering these questions initially seemed hopeless. Despite having stared at, and taught, the data on the Danubian cultures for 20 years, they had remained largely intractable to me, at least in so far as symbolic interpretation was concerned. The breakthrough, if one can call it that, came from considering the obvious. It is often what is under one's nose that one finds most difficult to see. I already knew, before beginning this chapter, that I was working towards comparing long houses with the later long burial mounds (see below). It occurred to me that much Danubian pottery was described in similar terms – 'linear' 'band' keramik, stich 'band' keramik. Facile as it seems, the major cultural items in the area in which I was dealing had all been described as long or linear: long houses, long barrows, and linear pottery. It is of course unlikely that linear decoration on the pottery has much to do with the linear organization of the houses and tombs and I do not intend to make that argument here. Nevertheless, patterns began to resonate once I keyed the idea of linearity into them. As the chapter unfolds I will marshal these patterns together, and try to convince you of their coherence. I have already discussed the organization of space within the long houses. They are of course long and the linearity is emphasized by the five rows of posts, sometimes stretching back 45 m from the entrance. Space is organized linearly in that actors would have had to move 'along' the house from room to room. The linear sequence is, however, punctuated by the entrance and by the differences in activities and rooms along the house. Space within the house, and outside it, is graded. Activities are ordered by their distance from the door, or back of the house. Activity, person, or room 'A' is nearer the door (for example), than activity, person, or room 'B'.

Rather than talk of a long house, we might therefore equally well talk of a linear house. The cultural ordering which opposes the wild is a linear ordering. As one moves from the natural to the cultural along this sequence, one might expect to find that the boundary between culture and nature would be emphasized. At first that boundary surrounds the house as a whole. But the dramatic effect of sequence and order are maintained by channelling movement along the linear space. By marking points along that space, seclusion, exclusion, and inclusion can be expressed. In particular, the separation of the cultural from the natural can best be emphasized by drawing attention to the entrance in the narrow end of the house. Indeed, as we move through time in central Europe the entrance area becomes increasingly important.

Later Danubian Developments

Danubian long houses go through several changes up until the time of their disappearance around 3300 bc (figure 5.6). In some cases they become bow-sided, swelling in the central area as if to emphasize the already noted importance of the central section of the house (Dohrn-Ihmig 1983b). But the most common development is that they

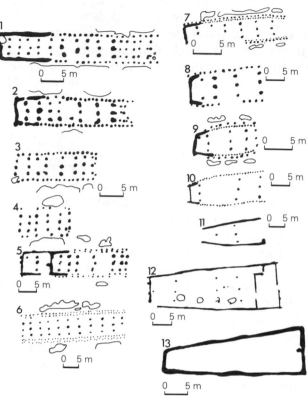

Figure 5.6 Danubian houses in (a) central Europe and (b) (facing page) the Rhine-land.

(Source: Coudart 1987)

(a) 1 Bylany – middle Linear Pottery
2 Bylany – late Linear Pottery
3 Bylany – late Linear Pottery
4 Bylany – latest Linear Pottery
5 Hinheim – late Linear Pottery
6 Zwenkau-Harth – latest Linear Pottery
7 Zwenkau-Harth – early Stroke Pottery
8 Libenice – Stroke Pottery IV
9 Zwenkau-Harth – late Stroke Pottery
10 Hinheim – Stroke or post-Stroke Pottery
11 Zwenkau-Harth – latest Stroke Pottery
12 Postoloprty – Stroke Pottery V
13 Brześć Kujawski – Lengyel

(b) 1 Elsloo – middle Linear Pottery
2 Langweiler 2 – late Linear Pottery
3 Elsloo – late Linear Pottery
4 Bochum – late Linear Pottery
5 Rosdorf – late Linear Pottery
6–7 Bochum-Hiltrop – final Linear Pottery
8 Bochum-Kirchharpen – Grossgartach
9 Hasselsweiler – Grossgartach
10 Bochum-Laer – Rössen
11 Schwäbish-Hall – Rössen
12 Bochum-Hiltrop – Rössen
13 Deiringsen-Ruploh – Rössen III

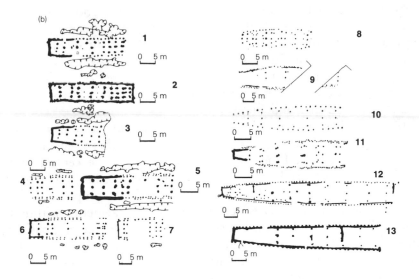

become trapezoidal (figure 5.4). The back portion becomes signifi-
cantly reduced in many cases, and the wider south-eastern end
contains the entrance (e.g. Jürgens 1979). The trapezoidal shape,
whatever its aerodynamic qualities in the face of north-westerly
winds, results in a grading of space from front to back. The front
has the largest width and it is often assumed that it had the greatest
height. It contains the entrance. When internal divisions occur, they
most frequently mark off the entrance antechamber (figure 5.6). I
have already described the alcoves and the Postoloprty ritual deposit
in the antechamber. At the late Lengyel sites of Brześć Kujawski 3,
the rubbish pits nearest the entrance of the house had the densest
concentration of refuse (Bogucki and Grygiel 1981). A possibly
similar pattern occurs at Biskupin (ibid.), and at Cuiry-les-Chaudardes (Ilett et al. 1982).

By way of contrast, as the entrance becomes more clearly marked
and more clearly a focus of activities, so the back and interior parts
become less important. The continuous bedding trench around the
back part of the house is often very reduced, while the post-holes
which had been such a prominent feature of the Linear Pottery
house interiors become smaller and fewer in number. Coudart (1987)
argues that the early walls of Linear Pottery houses were not load-

bearing. In later houses the walls did support the roof and as they became more substantial, the interior post-holes became shallower and the posts they contained probably played little of a direct supporting role. The increased importance of the walls is also seen in the appearance of 'buttresses' on the outsides of walls, as for example in the case of the trapezoidal Rössen houses from Inden-Lamersdorf (Kuper and Piepers 1966).

Overall, there is a trend in long house layout from an emphasis on the interior to an emphasis on the boundary between the inside and the outside. In Linear Pottery houses it is the central of the three sections of the house which is most significant and it is the interior posts which hold up the building. The complexity of the cultural ordering is focused on the post arrangements within the house. By the time Rössen houses are being built, the emphasis has shifted from the central to the front section, and from the inner posts to the outer walls. In addition, entrance through the walls becomes increasingly marked by internal divisions and special deposits.

The Linear Pottery houses are inward looking because, relatively isolated in the natural landscape, the focus of society is within the house. We shall see that through time, Danubian houses increasingly form into tighter social clusters and into villages. In these larger social units it is perhaps not surprising that the house is built in order to express more of its character to the outside world. The outside walls become more important. In particular, attention is drawn to movement into and out of the house by the elaboration and expansion of the entrance area. The sides of the house expand outwards, like the sides of a stage, and draw the eye to the front. The perspective of the house draws the visitor in but at the same time emphasizes the threshold. The house is put on display, but the exclusion of outsiders from insiders is emphasized.

As the display and the boundaries of the house become more important, so the evidence for expansion of and competition between households increases. Lichardus and Lichardus-Itten (1985, 298) in fact suggest that the increased importance of the walls results from a desire to place the interior posts farther apart in order to obtain more room. The hearths in the central rooms at Postoloprty may imply larger social or multiple social units. Increasing size of the domus social unit is also suggested by the appearance of yet longer houses in the Rössen phase. Examples are known up to 50 m long at Deiringsen-Ruploh and up to 60 m long at Bochum-Hiltrop. However most Rössen houses remain in the 9–30 m length range.

The greater variation in Rössen house sizes (Coudart 1987) is simply an extension of an earlier pattern. Linear Pottery house clusters include both very small and very large examples. For example, Olszanica in Poland contains houses varying in length from 7 to 41 m, and Bylany in Czechoslovakia has a range from 6 to 45 m. In addition, the largest houses in certain phases at Bylany also have an attached fenced enclosure and this pattern is also found later. In the Aldenhoven Plateau, only 19 per cent of the Linear Pottery houses are full long houses with all three compartments. At Langweiler 8, longer houses have more associated pits, they are richer in material with more decorated pottery, and there are more weeds and wheat chaff in the botanical remains (Lüning 1982). Because there is the same number of wheat grains and the same number of querns in the long and shorter houses, Lüning (ibid., 17) suggests that the cleaning and processing of grain may have been carried out more in the long houses even though grain was consumed at all houses. Varied interpretations of these data are possible. However, it is of interest that variations in production are suggested on other sites. For example, one of the largest (although by no means the largest) houses at Cuiry-les-Chaudardes in the Paris Basin contained over half the waste flint flakes and blades and half the flint cores of the whole site and it had an especially low ratio of tools to waste.

Some differences in production between Danubian houses are thus suggested. However, there is no evidence from the internal layout of the houses to suggest that longer houses formed a different category or provided an entirely different function. They appear simply the same but bigger and with more of the same productive activities. Thus I would prefer to see the variation in contemporary house size in a settlement as expressing varying degrees of performance and ability in using the house and the idea of domus as a mechanism and goal in social life. Some of the variation in house size may relate to different points in a family's life cycle (Lane 1987), but the continuum of house sizes may also be the result of varying success in the various economic and social practices of the household, including subsistence production, feast giving, and marriage exchange. The house does not simply reflect these activities. Its construction and use are also creative economic and social practices themselves. The construction and use of a yet larger, more impressive and dramatic long house, involving cutting down the forest, organizing the necessary labour, and receiving people into the house, constitute relations of dependence and authority. The house is a massive triumph of culture over nature and it might thus appropriately recreate the domus idea of control over nature and link it with social control. In the Rössen culture we have seen that certain houses reach substantial sizes. On the Aldenhoven Plateau (Lüning 1982, 21), some farmsteads go through long periods of occupation and many phases of rebuilding, while others have shorter lives. There is little identifiable social variation other than gender or age distinctions in cemeteries. It seems as if the domus with all its ideological and productive functions, becomes the medium for competition between household units. The boundary of the domus becomes increasingly important both in terms of display and in terms of internal social control. After all, social standing in the wider social arena depends on control within the domus.

There is a limit to the extent to which the individual domus can extend its size and control over resources. There is a limit to the size of feasts it can give, the number of fields it can plant, or the number of spouses it can attract. A logical result of the expansion of the domus principle is thus to expand the principle into 'the settlement' and create larger social units, organized by the same ethic. And indeed, settlement formation is increasingly found associated with increasing evidence for bounding or 'defending' the settlement.

We have seen that in the Linear Pottery phase, most 'settlements' are really scattered loose associations of houses along river systems. Up to 17 contemporary houses may occur within a broad cluster. In some cases, as at Cuiry-les-Chaudardes (figure 5.7), the linearity principle is again present at the settlement scale. The houses are arranged in rows extending away from the river. Not all the houses are contemporary but the linear pattern is maintained. More generally, in Linear Pottery settlements there is rarely any overlap between houses. Rather than being built on earlier houses, later houses are built beside earlier houses so that through time the settlement may gradually move in a linear sequence, as for example at Sittard and Geleen in the Netherlands.

Through time settlements not only become larger, as at Brześć Kujawski (Bogucki 1987, 7), they also become more clearly bounded. The Linear Pottery enclosures from the Rhineland have already been discussed and it was noted that many do not contain houses or traces of settlement as at Langweiler 3 and 8. Some of the houses inside the enclosure at Köln-Lindenthal may be contemporary with it but even here there is some doubt (Whittle 1977a and b). These enclos-

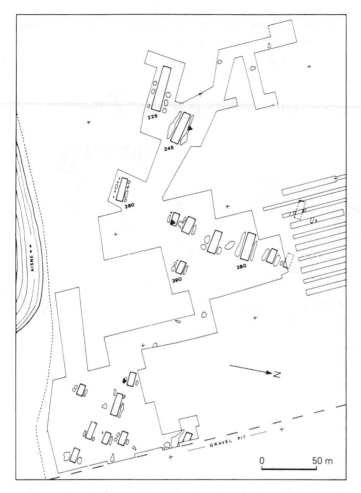

Figure 5.7 Linear Pottery features at Cuiry-les-Chaudardes. Black triangles indicate
child burials.
(Source: Ilett et al. 1982)

ures may have been involved in defining bounds around non-settlement resources such as cattle or stored food. They may also have
had other conceptual and social functions to do with wider group
definition. They are similar to later enclosures which did contain
houses (see below). Perhaps the creation of larger bounded social
units had to be conceived and legitimated initially outside the increasingly clustered settlements themselves. Perhaps the extension of the

domus principle to incorporate larger groupings was initially difficult, involving persuasion and the drama of collective practices.

By the Rössen phase, villages with groups of houses surrounded by a boundary occur for example at Inden-Lamersdorf, and at Wahlitz in the Elbe–Saale region there is a cluster of houses with a surrounding ditch (Starling 1985a). Late Rössen defences occur at Berry-au-Bac in the Paris Basin (figure 5.8, Ilett 1983). The latter

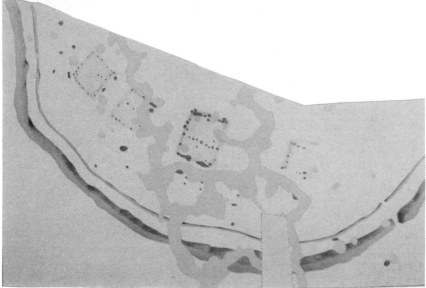

Figure 5.8 Reconstruction and plan of Berry-au-Bac.
(Source: Coudart and Pion 1986)

enclosure covers an area of between 2 ha and 3 ha and contains houses which did not extend outside. It is defined by a ditch and internal palisade, both continuous in the excavated area except for one narrow entrance. It is assumed (ibid.) that there was a gravel and earth bank behind the palisade. The majority of refuse in the ditch was concentrated on either side of the entrance.

One of the most important ways in which human groups conceive of the relationship between themselves and others is through attitudes to dirt and impurity (Hodder 1982c). The 'other' is often thought to be dirty and unclean, whereas 'we' define 'ourselves' as pure. Distributions of refuse on settlement sites thus give an insight into the location of the principal boundaries between 'self' and 'other' (Hodder 1982a). In Linear Pottery sites we have seen that refuse is deposited immediately outside the house, in the rubbish pits along the side walls and particularly in the pits toward the front of the house. We have seen some slight evidence that the insides of the houses were kept relatively clean. This evidence supports the general notion that in Linear Pottery society, the domus itself was the principal unit of social life. The relatively isolated houses formed loose agglomerations of self-defining productive units.

Through time in the Danubian sequence, refuse is separated from the houses (figure 5.6, Coudart 1987). The construction pits that are used for rubbish deposition are dug away from houses and towards the edges of the settlement at Inden-Lamersdorf. Whatever the primary reasons for the construction of these pits, rubbish was now being carried away from houses to pits that might be used by several houses and which were either distant from the house or not linked to any particular house at all. Even the discard of refuse in the enclosure ditch at Berry-au-Bac, however appropriate or practical, nevertheless had the effect of setting up a boundary between inside and outside. In all these later examples the communal is confirmed over the individual social unit. The changes in discard practices have conceptual and social effects consistent with the construction of boundaries around the larger community.

The interrupted ditched enclosures such as Těšetice-Kyjovice, Vochov, and Bochum-Harpen all of Linear Stroke Pottery and Rössen date (above p. 111), with their general lack of internal occupation may have played related roles. Their large size suggests that they involved communal practices in their construction and perhaps a communality of use as expressed by the multiple entrances. In addition they are often located such that they appear to 'serve' several social units. Their distinctive character has to do with boundaries and entrances. The multiple consecutive rings of palisades and ditches (figure 5.5) emphasize the separation of outside from inside. By the same means, the entrances become important. Indeed, to walk through the enclosing ditches and palisades at, for example, Těšetice-Kyjovice, involves walking through graded space from outside to inside and back again, in a linear sequence. The impression gained is not dissimilar from movement through the graded space of the house. The basic ideas of bounding and grading space in a sequence and drawing attention to entrances and exits is similar in both the house and in the interrupted ditched enclosure.

In the villages, the entrances of the houses draw attention to the movement from the individual social unit to the wider communal grouping. So too, the multiple entrances of the ditched enclosures link the communal centre to the multiple individuals outside. Even if the ditched enclosures had other primary functions such as cattle control, cattle exchange, food storage, or exposure of the dead, the practice of their use must have linked individuals or individual social units coming through multiple entrances to a common centre. In the village the multiple individual entrances of the houses are on the inside of the community boundary. In the unoccupied enclosures, by an elegant twist, the multiple entrances are on the outside. The communal becomes central.

It is certainly unlikely that 'the communal' would have been entered into lightly. Village formation is likely to have involved the need for some increased labour and greater social constraint and Bogucki (1987, 7) has discussed some of the ecological and economic problems associated with Danubian settlement nucleation. There is some limited evidence for economic intensification at this time. In the Rhineland, for example, carbonized plant remains from Rössen sites include much greater amounts of barley than in Linear Pottery sites. They also include spelt and compact wheat in addition to einkorn and emmer (Whittle 1977a and 1985; Knörzer 1971).

It is no longer possible to assume that the desire for settlement nucleation and increased labour input resulted from population increase, settlement expansion, and pressure on resources. Starling (1985a) has shown convincingly that in several areas of Europe Danubian settlement gradually retracted through time, abandoning productive loess regions and forming settlement clusters and villages. In other words, people were not forced to start nucleating because they had filled up the landscape. It is uncertain whether population increased at all. In certain areas it may even have declined. As Starling concludes, some social mechanism must have created the will to form villages.

The social mechanism I have described emanates from the domus as conceived in central Europe. Social negotiation and competition occur in the currency of bounded and graded space. Individual units which perform better, both economically and dramatically, build larger and more imposing houses. Social power is based on inclusion within and exclusion from strongly bounded entities. The logic of this competitive process leads to the desire to include more than one house unit. The logic is inherently incremental and dynamic (see Gregory 1980 for a different view), as individual social units try to expand their size and increase their productive and prestige potential. Individual houses increase in size but a successful domus manages to extend beyond the constraints of the independent house and create the beginnings of the village unit. The transformation is argued and the will to agglomerate is created through existing principles centred on the domus. Rubbish deposition moves from the house exterior to the village exterior. Boundaries and entrances are recreated in relation to a communal focus in circular ditched enclosures. The boundaries and entrances between the social and the individual, between the cultural and the wild, are emphasized and established physically on the ground. Gradually the dominant ethic is extended outwards from the house unit, proliferating and controlling in many spheres and at many scales.

In SE Europe I contrasted the domus with the agrios, and it seems possible to argue for a similar opposition in central Europe. On the other hand, I have described how the domus–agrios relationship is less evident in the data for the period in central Europe that has been considered so far. In contrast, there is a new emphasis on boundaries and entrances along linear graded space. Entrances to the house are emphasized in the deposition of artifacts and increasingly in the trapezoidal shape and in special foundation deposits. Entrances to the community are emphasized in the enclosures. It is as if there is a back–front, inside–outside opposition which does not correlate with domus–agrios. Rather, the front end of the house has to do with entering and leaving, and it seems to become more important as the wider community agglomerates and competitive display between house units in 'villages' becomes more marked. The front is thus linked to social relationships between household units. At least that was how I interpreted the evidence. It was therefore of interest to find that Benveniste opposes domus to two terms in the Indo-European family of languages. As well as domus–agrios, there is domus–foris. Benveniste (1973, 256) notes that Latin established a distinction between *domi* 'at home' and *foris* 'outside'. The Latin word for door (*fores*) has Indo-European roots as is seen also in Greek *thura* (door) and English 'door'. In Latin *foranus, foresticus*, and *forestis* all refer to the outside, extraneous world. In Italian *forestiere* means foreign, and the English word 'foreign' derives from the foris root, as does the word forum, from the Latin for a market-place or place of public business.

So once again, in the structure of our language, a set of concepts (the forest, the foreign, the wild, the public) is defined in terms of the house – in this case its door. I intend to use the term 'foris' to refer to the emphasis on boundaries and entrances which is of changing importance in the Neolithic of central Europe. In doing so I do not mean to argue that the inhabitants of Rössen villages spoke proto-Indo-European or used a term akin to foris to describe the front ends of their houses, although they may have done. Rather, my reason for using this terminology is to draw attention to our own structures of thought which already, as expressed in language, link forest, foreign, forum, and door. We give words like door specific meanings in the world in which we live, and those meanings are partly historically derived. We use these words in archaeology, apparently objectively, to describe parts of houses. But the terms are not neutral. They incorporate historical and contemporary assumptions and we think the world (and the past) through an already structured language, using words already heavy with meaning. I want to use a specialist language which may or may not be linked historically to Neolithic European societies in order to undermine our blindness to our own words, and in order to engage in long-term critique.

The process of increasing emphasis on the foris, seen so clearly in the development of the entrance ends of Danubian houses, has also been identified above in the multiple entrances of community enclosures. I wish to show that the same process occurs at other scales and in other spheres. First, I will consider still larger patterns of settlement distribution and second, different scales of patterning in pottery production.

The linear scatter of Linear Pottery houses along the first terraces of river valleys must have reinforced the various linear tendencies that we have seen in the organization of space within houses and settlements. Gradually the linear continuum became divided as settlement became increasingly clustered. However, already in the Linear Pottery phase in south Poland, Kruk (1980) has shown that groups of settlements existed with a variety of functions. Through time in south Poland (see also Milisauskas and Kruk 1984), these local clusters gradually expanded in size (in the Lengyel phase). Gradual expansion of zones of settlement, concurrent with the increasing size of houses and settlement agglomerations, has been noted in several areas. For example, in the Paris Basin, immediately after the Linear Pottery culture, there is an expansion of settlement both onto interfluves and outwards to Normandy and the lower Seine basin (Ilett 1983, 24). In the Rhineland, Rössen sites begin to extend higher up the sides of valleys and they move outwards, both south to the north Alpine foreland and north onto the north European plain beyond the loess.

While, at some scales and in some areas, the area of Danubian settlement gradually expands, at other scales and in other areas, there is clear evidence of settlement retraction. For example, in the Elbe–Saale region of central Germany, the numbers of sites decrease quite dramatically from Linear Pottery to Linear Stroke Pottery to Rössen, and settlement becomes increasingly clustered and restricted. Some sites continue to be inhabited from phase to phase but others on equally good soils are abandoned, leading to greater separation between settlement clusters. Starling (1985a) notes the same pattern in Bohemia. Rather in the same way that some houses get very big while others are very small, some villages and micro-regions succeed while others do not. These various scales are probably closely connected in that successful performance at the level of the household allows the same domus–foris–agrios principles to be repeated at other more inclusive levels.

On the other hand, the extension of the domus principle to larger social groupings begins to change the relationship between the domus and the house. We have seen that the domus–foris idea, while initially concentrated on the house, is gradually extended outwards to include and order larger spheres of settlement. This process results in both expansion of the social group and more clear definition of its boundaries. In certain regions, surrounding settlement is 'sucked in' so that some local groups increase in size and perhaps also prestige and productivity. As the emphasis on larger communal definition increases, the small social unit within the house, which had started the whole process off, becomes increasingly contradictory to the interests of the larger whole. The interests of the individual house-hold conflict with the emphasis on communal socialized production. The logical outcome of the extension of social and cultural bound-aries is the devaluing of the smaller bounded unit which was the medium through which the process began. In at least one area, the Aisne valley, at the late Rössen village of Berry-au-Bac around 3400 bc, the defensive boundary ditches are clear, but the houses are reduced in size and visible significance (figure 5.8). The display of the domus within the house and the markings of the house bound-aries have become inappropriate strategies within the new larger and more clearly defined social units. This process of a decrease in house size and elaboration continues after 3300 bc (see chapter 6).

A very similar process can be identified in changes in pottery styles and production. As already noted, it is tempting to argue that the linearity in the organization of space in Linear Pottery houses and settlements extends to the use of linear bands on the pottery itself. For the moment, however, there is little evidence to support such a link, even though pots are closely tied in their depositional patterns to houses (see p. 103). Whatever the specific meaning of the bands of linear pottery decoration, they do become increasingly differentiated and contrastive through time in the same way that the boundaries of the houses become increasingly marked.

A typical pattern of Linear Pottery development is shown in figure 5.9 (Hodder 1982b). The earliest pots show little separation of decoration into distinct zones or bounded areas. Through time there are three main ways in which contrasts are built up on the surface of the pot. First, the bands of decoration are increasingly differen-tiated from the background by, for example, filling the bands with densely packed impressions. Second, the bands of decoration are increasingly divided internally by, for example, breaking the line (forming a zigzag), placing dots or lines at intervals along the band, or by alternating the type of infill decoration. Third, a band of rim decoration is increasingly differentiated from the band of decoration on the body of the pot. After Linear Pottery in the Rhineland, decoration gradually changes in these directions until by the early Rössen phase (see figure 5.10) several horizontal zones of decoration occur with densely filled bands containing contrasting zigzag motifs. Similar sequences occur in all areas of central Europe (Lichardus and Lichardus-Itten 1985; Milisauskas 1976). In the Elbe–Saale region, the contrast and complexity of the pottery decoration increases through Linear Stroke Pottery and into early Rössen. Here Lichardus

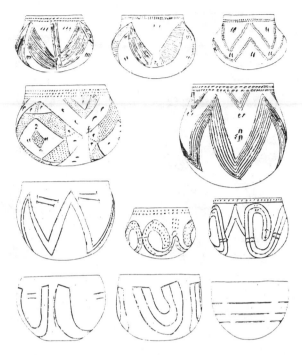

Figure 5.9 Stylistic changes in Linear Pottery from Geleen, Sittard, and Elsloo. Lower row: period 1b. Upper row: period IIcd. 2nd and 3rd rows: intermediate styles.
(Source: Hodder 1982b, after Louwe Kooijmans)

(1976) has defined three phases within Rössen based on pottery associations. After phase I the amount of decoration on pots gradually declines as does its complexity.

Up until middle Rössen, pottery decoration thus gradually becomes more complex and dense. The range of shapes also gradually increases. Most Linear Pottery forms are simple bowls (figure 5.9). 'Bottle' or 'beaker' shapes with upright or everted neck gradually increase in frequency (figure 5.10, no. 31), sometimes with pedestal bases (figure 5.10, no. 24) in Rössen contexts. Open dishes also occur in Rössen (figure 5.10, no. 26). Thus, the categorical boundaries between different pottery functions are increasingly emphasized in conjunction with the increasing zonation and boundary formation within the decoration. However, right at the end of the sequence decoration declines, and in Lichardus's Rössen phase III there is a

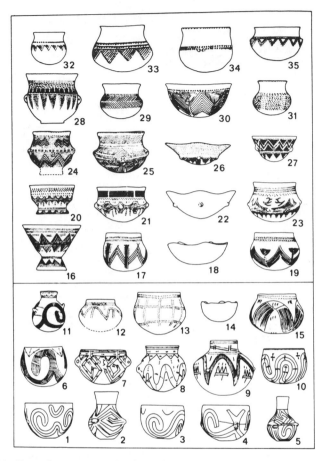

Figure 5.10 Ceramic sequence in the Rhineland. 1–15, western Linear Pottery. 16–19, Hinkelstein. 20–3, Grossgartach. 24–7, early Rössen. 28–31, mid Rössen. 32–5, late Rössen.
(Source: Lichardus and Lichardus-Itten 1985)

restriction in the range of shapes since pedestalled 'bottles' are no longer found.

How can we interpret these changes? The correlations with the changing house patterns are striking. There too boundaries in the use of space are increasingly emphasized and right at the end the size and elaboration of houses decline, at least regionally as at Berry-au-Bac. It has consistently been possible so far in this book to relate early and middle Neolithic pottery production and use to the domestic context. In central Europe we have seen that fine decorated pottery is found clustered around the house. Evidence such as figure 5.3 also showed that pottery as a category might be especially associated with the entrance area of the house. We have seen that, through time, the entrance of the house and its boundary with the outside world become increasingly important. The degree of elaboration of the decoration of pottery and the numbers of types of pottery shape have a similar trajectory. Pottery is certainly transportable and highly visible. Strongly associated with the house, it would have played a central role in expressing to the outside world the success of the domus in obtaining, preparing, and providing food and drink. The increasingly elaborate decoration drew attention to and celebrated these domestic processes. Participation in food and drink within the domus helped to define its boundaries with the outside world and, indeed, there is considerable and increasing variation in pottery style. Equally, the giving of food and drink to others, perhaps even the giving of feasts using elaborately decorated pottery, would have helped to establish relations of alliance, dependency, and domination. Thus in contrast to SE Europe where pottery appears clearly tied to the domus, in central Europe pottery played perhaps its more important role in the foris, in the relationships between the household unit and the 'foreign'.

Through time, it is as if the process of competitive display and boundary formation becomes 'saturated'. It is difficult to see what more could be done to the early Rössen pots in figure 5.10 to make them more elaborate or contrastive, given the principles in use, and Rössen houses 60 m long seem almost extravagant. It is as if the whole process of expanding the domus and elaborating its boundaries had reached its own limits. But these limits are not only internally produced. They also result from the contradiction that gradually emerges between domestic production and community production. Social actors may increasingly elaborate the boundaries of the domestic unit in order to create, compete for, and control prestigious social relations within and between communities. But as will be shown in the following chapter, houses and pottery decoration ultimately decline as emphasis on the boundaries between one house unit and another is overtaken by the extension of the domus–foris principle to a community scale.

Regional distributions of pottery decoration styles tell a similar story as they change over time. Linear Pottery styles are widely similar over much of central Europe. By the end of the Linear Pottery culture regional styles of pottery emerge, such as the Rhine–Main,

Rhine–Maas, and Gering groups (Dohrn-Ihmig 1974). Within the following Linear Stroke Pottery, Lengyel, and Rössen styles there are further subdivisions including the various groups within the Paris Basin, a separation between Rhineland and Elbe–Saale groups, and localized groups within, for example, the Elbe–Saale area, such as Gatersleben (see however Lichardus 1976). Towards the end of or just after Rössen, a large number of small groups can be identified (Lichardus 1976; Whittle 1977a). Through time, therefore, as Danubian settlement clusters become more segregated, so too do pottery styles increasingly bound off regional groups. There is once again a process of boundary display and boundary formation as groups try to incorporate and exclude. The process is a local one, but it has 'knock-on' effects at other scales. At the local level households and communities increasingly define their boundaries. At a larger scale the local distinctions produce increasing distinctions between regional pottery styles.

Conclusion

I now feel more confident that I did not simply impose the Nuba on Çatal Hüyük and the SE European Neolithic. In those areas the Nuba seemed to have some relevance. In central Europe it was possible to identify some of the same principles. The house and material associated with the house such as domestic pottery again dominate the archaeological evidence. The house is massive and the internal arrangements of posts are initially complex. The house contains the remains of relatively few wild animals. So once again the domus is based on its opposition to the wild. Arrowheads and axes occur in Linear Pottery graves so that at least some attributes of the agrios can be recognized as in SE Europe.

On the other hand, the domus in central Europe seems to have been defined in a rather different way. It is not so obviously the case in central Europe that female representations are linked to houses and male representations to graves. In the central European houses there is less emphasis on hearths or ovens, although this may largely be due to differing patterns of survival on the loess of central Europe in comparison with the tells of SE Europe. There are few models and miniatures of houses, ovens, or women. Similarly, the agrios seems to have been defined in a rather different way. Cemeteries occur from early on and there are 'rich' female graves.

I have also claimed to be able to interpret the rather different central European domus. The house itself domesticates nature in the cutting down of large trees, and in the creation of a complex ordering of space within dwellings relatively dispersed across the landscape. The domestication of plants and animals is thus linked to a monumental work – a drama of sheer scale. Startin (1978) has shown that the community beyond the household would have been involved in the construction of the linear house. The house is both concept and doing. The idea of the domus and its execution in the house involve the organization of labour, and joint investment in durable property. Society is thus created through an idea and its practice.

So one aspect of the new central European domus is that the transformation or domestication of nature is viewed in terms of the monumental. The domus in this area is less linked to caring and nurturing (although these attributes may have remained to some degree), and more tied to monumental intervention and control of the wild – the creation of a monument which dominates and separates off nature, creating social relations as it does so.

Within the new monumental form of the house, older ideas about the arrangement of space and about the distinctions between, for example, front and back take on a new significance. The linear grading of space is the second aspect of the rather different domus principle in central Europe. The whole idea of line, lineage, and lineal descent was attractive to me in view of data that will be discussed in later chapters. But initially the idea of the linear house derived from linking the form of the Linear Pottery houses themselves to general anthropological ideas about space that is socially controlled or 'deep' (e.g. Donley 1982). The linear grading of space allows one to think in terms of graded social space from inside to outside.

The linearity of the house has added significance when discussed in terms of the foris. In the Near East and in SE Europe the particular character of the domus derived from making a simple opposition with the wild – the agrios. But by emphasizing a distinction between domus and foris in central Europe, the door and the entrance area take on an enhanced significance. Indeed many of the changes in house plan through time can be interpreted as leading to a greater emphasis on boundaries and entrances at the front ends of houses. Social competition and social display seem closely linked to the going in and coming out at house entrances. The domus, therefore, is defined in terms of the control of movement from foreign to domestic. A linear ordering of space is created in which the movement along graded space to the heart of the domus defines society and its boundaries. The domus is that which has been controlled and dominated in the domestication process but which has also been brought in.

Thus through time, instead of seeing greater emphases on hearths, female representations, and cemeteries as the domus–agrios opposition becomes the main preoccupation in SE Europe, there is an increasing emphasis in central Europe on boundaries and entrances as social strategies are initially pursued principally in terms of the domus–foris opposition. Households emphasize their entrances and the movement through entrances as they create closer links and dependencies with other households. Perhaps 'foreigners' were 'domesticated' by involving them not only in house building but also by bringing them in to feasting and food exchanges in which increasingly elaborate decorated pottery was used.

The definition of the domus in terms of the foris is seen most clearly in the enclosures. The unoccupied sites often have multiple boundaries and entrances which emphasize the linear grading of space between outside and inside. It is through this idea of bringing people in to some kind of 'forum' that larger scale community relations are created and maintained. On this basis, increasingly agglomerated settlements can be formed, which collect housing daub from and deposit rubbish towards the edges of the community, thus dividing the clean from the unclean. I have already suggested, and the argument will be followed in chapter 6, that the expression of the domus–foris principle at the community scale of social organization seen in the enclosures came into conflict with the retention of the same principles at the level of individual houses.

In reference to a point made at the beginning of this chapter, I would claim that I have been able to interpret unique historical expressions – to interpret the differences between SE and central Europe. But it is a much more difficult matter to explain why these differences came about and to decide whether they are determined by economic and environmental factors. For example, it would be possible to argue that the different social and cultural processes surrounding domestication in SE and central Europe followed paths determined by different experiences of economic change. Even if few people moved into central Europe, it is possible that more aspects of the Neolithic economy were introduced from outside than in SE Europe. By the time the farming technology spread into central

Europe it was already well developed. The transformation in central Europe was thus more abrupt. Small communities (whatever their local or distant origin) faced large expanses of hunter-gatherers and relatively unoccupied forest. In relation to the wild, the agrios, the problem was how to create social links between dispersed small-scale communities – how to maintain relations of dependence and domination in the face of fragmentation and potential fission. It could be argued, therefore, that the conceptual and practical emphasis on the door, the entrance, the foris provided a mechanism for social relations in such a natural and social environment. Mutual house construction was used to create relations of dependence and domination. The monumental 'home' fixed people and domesticated them into regularized and graded social relations.

However, these attempts at explanation of the differences between SE and central Europe are far from convincing. It is difficult to argue that the social or natural environment in central Europe in the early Neolithic created conditions which determined a particular transformation of symbolic structures, such that monumentality, linearity, and the domus–foris opposition became dominant themes. While the central European domus was well suited to and clearly engaged with the environment in which it was utilized, that environment is not sufficient cause of the particular character of the domus. Similar practical problems as outlined above for central Europe would have occurred to some degree in SE Europe.

It might be possible to argue that the differences between SE and central Europe in the Neolithic resulted from different Mesolithic backgrounds and from different historical perceptions of the domestication process. Sadly, in the present state of the data, we know little of the social, economic, and conceptual structures current in central Europe immediately prior to the adoption of agriculture.

Even if it was possible to argue that the central European domus was structured by indigenous pre-Neolithic ideas and practices, and by central European interpretations of the SE European domus in relation to the natural and social environment of central Europe, there is little evidence that these various influences would determine what I have found in central Europe. Further work on this matter is clearly needed. The conditioning factors need to be examined in detail and with care. For the moment it seems most likely to me that the central European domus will not readily be explained by reference solely to conditions and precedents. Rather, it is created actively by individual actors who have themselves interpreted the

world in a particular and unique way. What they produced is coherent and logical in its own terms and it is this coherence which I have
tried to recapture in my account. While we can explain how the
domus as reformulated in central Europe worked and why it was
appropriate in the circumstances of the time, I do not believe, at
least not yet, that we can explain the creative act itself as being
entirely predetermined.

However, the argument is especially weak while the data for the
Mesolithic in central Europe are poor. The Neolithic differences in
Europe may be predetermined by Mesolithic differences. The impact
of Mesolithic structures on the development of Neolithic society will
be examined more fully in Scandinavia (chapter 7). Consideration of
the transformation of the domus into the later Neolithic in central
Europe in chapter 6 will in the meantime allow similar questions
about long-term historical determinism to be examined in a context
with more complete data. Perhaps then the provisional conclusions
reached here (or have they already been decided?) will need revision.

6

Towards a Higher Domain: the Later Neolithic in Central Europe

In the preceding chapter I argued that the domus–foris opposition in central Europe was used and extended as part of the process of social competition and display. Boundaries and entrances were increasingly emphasized in houses and larger-scale enclosures. Much of the argument may have seemed rather general and abstract. After all, the hypothesis that the wider village communities that emerged during the fourth millennium bc were constructed in terms of the same ethic that was used in the house unit could probably be applied in many societies. The notions of inclusion, exclusion, boundaries, and entrances are widely found. Worse, there is little direct evidence to support a link between the two concepts of the village and the household. Certainly changes through time in the village and household seem to be closely correlated and each level is constructed in terms of the other. For example, the village community is partly defined by the placing of domestic refuse, and the boundaries of the village and household become more marked in tandem. It seems likely that the concept of community was created through the concept of domus. But the evidence is unclear.

In the later Neolithic there is, in my view, more secure evidence which suggests that the domus principle was extended to other domains. Before about 3300 bc, we have seen that symbolic elaboration, the control of boundaries and space, centred on the settlement sphere. Burials were ordered in cemeteries in a somewhat similar manner to the ordering of houses within settlements and villages. In contrast to the earlier phases in SE Europe, Danubian burial is 'present', durable, and direct. There were few stages of body preparation and flesh removal, and artifacts were placed in individual graves. The relationship between the individual and the social was clearly stated.

After 3300 bc, in central Europe, the domus ethic was extended to death ritual in a well-documented fashion. To understand the reasons for this change it will be necessary to discuss the overall flow of events in which the changing burial ritual plays a part. For after 3300 bc there are important developments in the frequently undecorated pottery assemblages. Houses are small and enclosed settlements often become more substantial. Overall settlement and economic practices alter and the importance of warring and hunting gradually increases. All this will have to be discussed. For the moment, however, I wish simply to document the link between long houses and the long burial mounds which appear in central Europe after 3300 bc.

It is difficult however, to organize the relevant information. I am in this chapter broaching the subject of megaliths. Yet megalithic burial is normally discussed as a phenomenon of north and west Europe. Long tombs appear throughout the area discussed in chapter 5. Yet the central European examples can only be fully understood in relation to their northern and western counterparts. So the problem in presenting the data is that I do not want to discuss the northern and western European long mounds before completing the development of the central European sequence. On the other hand, the former are necessary for understanding the latter. I have decided, therefore, to risk confusion that might be caused in the mind of the reader and to use information from north and west Europe where necessary to make my case. It will also be necessary to refer to tombs that vary considerably in date. I wish initially to construct a general argument concerning European megaliths before returning to the central European sequence. Evaluation of the tombs in north and west Europe will be undertaken in chapter 7.

Linear Tombs

In the period after 3300 bc, large parts of the area of Europe considered in chapter 5 develop some variant of the TRB (Trichterrandbecher) or Funnel-Necked Beaker culture (see table 1). In the areas previously occupied by Lengyel (such as Poland and Bohemia) and Rössen (central Germany), TRB groups (such as Sarnowo in Kujavia, Poland) appear as they do also in southern Scandinavia (the Early Neolithic–EN). However, the TRB has itself to be subdivided into, for example, the Baalberg, Salzmünde, Walternienburg-Bernburg sequence in the Elbe–Saale region of central Germany and the regional Altmark, Tiefstich, and Mecklenburg groups in the north European Plain. Distinct regional TRB groups with their own sequences have been established for example in the Polish lowlands, in the Netherlands, and in southern Scandinavia. Groups related to the TRB occur elsewhere in central Europe. In the Rhineland the Michelsberg culture follows the Rössen, and in Switzerland and the Paris Basin are found respectively the Cortaillod and the Chassey (or Chassey-Michelsberg). These latter groups are all linked by, for example, the use of largely undecorated pottery and specific pottery forms.

Regional groupings that emerge within Michelsberg will also be discussed below, as will the development from Chassey to SOM in the Paris Basin. In many areas, the Corded Ware culture takes over in the period around 2300–2200 bc. The phenomena termed TRB, Michelsberg, Cortaillod, and Chassey thus endure for about 1000 years (or 1250 calendar years). They, and the following Corded Ware form the subject matter for this chapter.

Throughout all this area from 3300 to 2300 bc a wide variety of burial rituals was practised. For example, tumuli with pit inhumations, earth graves with crouched inhumations, and skull burials (see below) are found in TRB contexts. The burial rites used in TRB groups also include long or monumental tombs, although the precise method of burial within the tombs varies. My description will first concentrate on the long mounds.

In the Elbe–Saale variant of the TRB (Fischer 1956, Behrens 1973), the Baalberg phase sees the appearance of long barrows (e.g. Latdorf) and grave mounds, often with only one or a very few inhumations in either pit graves or stone chambers. The mounds are often located so as to be conspicuous (Starling 1985b). By the Walternienburg-Bernburg phase, true collective burials are found (Totenhütte), with above-ground timber construction surrounded by rough stone walling (Feustel and Ullrich 1965).

To the south and east within the Danubian province long mounds are less well known, although they are becoming increasingly common. In Bohemia, for example, two barrows (or burial enclosures) have been found at Březno (Pleinerová 1980). They survive as continuous bedding trenches for a wooden 'wall' enclosing the long rectangular mound (figure 6.1). The mounds are oriented west–east, with the entrance and slightly wider end to the east. The longer mound is at least 143.5 m long, the shorter is 24.3 m long. Individual

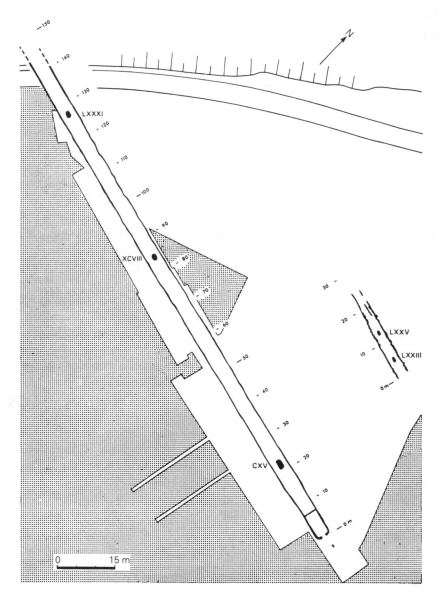

Figure 6.1 Two burial enclosures at Březno. Shaded areas unexcavated.
(Source: Pleinerová 1980)

inhumation burials are placed along the central axis and pottery is generally scanty. The tombs seem isolated from other features. Many of these attributes of the barrows recall the earthen long mounds of northern Europe to be discussed below. It is thus unfortunate that the dating of the Březno tombs is insecure. The C14 dates from the site are not consistent, but the pottery has general early TRB affinities.

In Moravia, long and round barrows from the late TRB are known at Slatinky, Lutotin, and Ohrozim (Houšt'ová 1958). Again placed to be conspicuous, the barrows are grouped into cemeteries. In a few cases (at Slatinky) the barrow contained no grave at all. In other cases one to seven graves were found in each mound, usually containing one cremation deposited in urns which stood mostly upside down. Some graves were surrounded by boulders. This feature joins with other aspects of the burial ritual, apart from the cremation rite, to suggest parallels with the TRB long mounds from Kujavia in Poland.

In the Polish lowlands we have seen the Lengyel developments of villages of trapezoidal long houses such as at Brześć Kujawski. In the following TRB phase, long houses are not found, but cemeteries of trapezoidal long barrows are. The barrows (orientated east–west) are extremely long and almost triangular in shape, and they are contained within a 'wall' of stones. Stones also surround the graves of what are usually single, fully articulated inhumations. Grave goods are rare, but include pottery, ornaments, and a stone mace head. As in Moravia, the tombs are grouped into cemeteries (Midgley 1985). The Kujavian long mounds have a number of attributes in common with earth and wood long barrows (figure 6.2) found across northern Europe, in Scandinavia, and the British Isles (Madsen 1979; Midgley 1985).

A glance at the plans of the long barrows recalls the plans of the rectangular and trapezoidal houses discussed in chapter 5. Indeed, scholars have long noted the resemblance. Daniel (1965, 86) speculated that Oscar Montelius may not have been so wrong in the theory that the European stone passage graves that form part of the same tradition as the earth and wood long barrows may have been lithic funerary versions of wooden dwelling houses. Childe (1949, 135) suggested that 'it is tempting to see in this curious plan [of the northern long burial mounds] an attempt to make the house of the dead approximate to habitations such as are illustrated at Brześć Kujawski.' Sprockhoff (1938) and Glob (1949) also compared the

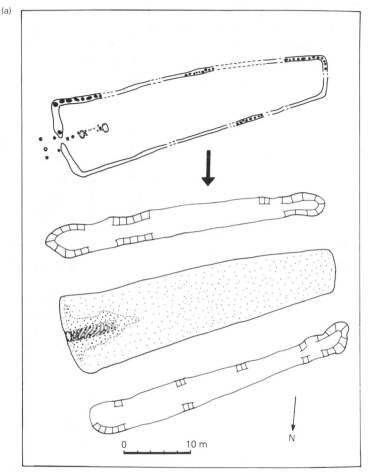

Figure 6.2 Linear mound burial in the British Isles: (a) the structural sequence at Fussell's Lodge;
(Source: Kinnes 1981)

long cairns and barrows of northern and north-central Europe with long houses. The use of Linear Pottery houses as a model for the long mound tradition has been suggested by Case (1969), Ashbee (1970), Whittle (1977a, 221), Kinnes (1981, 85), Powell et al. (1969), Savory (1977), and Piggott (1967). A detailed case has been made by Reed (1974) and Marshall (1981). Clark (1980, 96) noted that the trapezoidal burial mounds of Brittany and Kujavia recall domestic house structures associated with the Lengyel culture, and even the Lepenski Vir houses.

The long houses and long mounds are so similar that it has

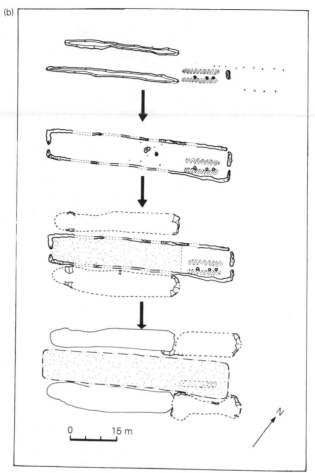

Figure 6.2(b) the structural sequence at Kilham.

sometimes proved difficult to decide which one has been dug up. For example, in Scandinavia Barkaer, long thought to be a site containing long houses, has been convincingly reinterpreted as a site with long burial mounds (Glob 1975; Madsen 1979). However, on the whole, the houses and the tombs occur in different time periods and thus had quite different functions. It is therefore important to be careful about whether there was any possibility of copying one from the other and to be specific about the similarities that are being claimed.

First, is there any chronological overlap between the houses and tombs which would have allowed diffusion? As we shall see, most

TRB houses are not long. So what is the degree of overlap between the late Danubian and the TRB cultures in the period around 3300 bc? How could the diffusion, if any, have occurred? In the Polish lowlands, Midgley (1985) has argued for some degree of overlap in time between Lengyel and TRB. Bogucki (1987), on the other hand, argues convincingly for a developmental sequence. It is true that a date from the Sarnowo barrow of around 3620 bc would put the barrows contemporary with long houses. But this is only a single date from material below the mound. Many of the Kujavian mounds were built in the Pikutkowo phase of the TRB, with dates for this phase ranging from around 3300 to 3000 bc (ibid.). 3300–3200 bc is just about the time that Lengyel settlements disappear. There was thus either no or very little overlap in time. The cultural materials, however, generally show a clear continuity from Lengyel to TRB. For example, the early ceramics from Sarnowo have a number of stylistic similarities to late Lengyel vessels, some of which are highly specific and localized (ibid., 10). It is thus chronologically and culturally possible in the Polish lowlands either for the idea of houses to have diffused to contemporary tombs or for the idea of houses to have been passed down to tombs within an indigenous cultural development.

In central Germany, it is generally assumed (Starling 1983) that the TRB Baalberg group followed on from Rössen around 3300 bc, although in this area it is not clear that the very earliest phases are associated with long mounds. In western Europe there is evidence for continuity or overlap. An important site in this regard is Les Fouaillages in Guernsey, the Channel Islands (Kinnes 1982). This has dates of approximately 3600 bc which fit in well with a series of dates for passage graves and long mounds in north-west France between 3700 and 3000 bc (Hibbs 1983, 285). These sites contain pottery of the Linear Pottery tradition. Les Fouaillages contains pottery linked to the Cerny late Danubian pottery found in the Paris Basin, dated from 3900 to 3600 bc (Ilett 1983), although some C14 dates suggest continuation to a later date (Whittle 1977a, 163). There are Cerny trapezoidal long houses from Marolles and Pontavert in the Paris Basin (Whittle 1977a, 160–1). The mound at Les Fouaillages is trapezoidal with the broader 'entrance' end facing east. There is thus the possibility of chronological overlap or continuity, with evidence of cultural contacts between long house using and long barrow using groups in France. (Further evidence for continuity in France will be discussed in chapter 8.)

Overall, it seems that long burial mounds could have developed from long houses. In general terms it can be argued that the TRB groups may have their origin within, and certainly have affinities with late Danubian groups building long houses. But if the chronological and cultural possibilities exist, are the similarities between the houses and tombs sufficiently close to warrant a derivation of one from the other?

In an earlier publication (Hodder 1984), I argued for eight points of detailed similarity between the houses and the tombs. Here I will reconsider those similarities and discuss the more recent arguments for a relationship between the houses and tombs made by Midgley (1985) and Bogucki (1987).

The first point of similarity concerns the form of the long houses and long mounds. Although round mounds are common, many of the tombs, especially the earthen barrows, are rectangular or trapezoidal in shape. Earthen long barrows are generally trapezoidal in shape in Britain and more triangular in Poland. Trapezoidal barrows are also known from Denmark and north Germany but in these areas rectangular barrows are more common (Madsen 1979, 318). Trapezoidal cairns, limited by a wall or by boulders, are found in Britain in the Severn-Cotswold group, Clyde, Irish Court cairns, and in the Orkney-Cromarty long cairns. There are also examples to parallel the rectangular earth barrows (Ashbee 1970, 90).

Since trapezoidal houses become more common through time in the Danubian sequence, the existence of some rectangular long barrows suggests the continuity of a general tradition or, as I shall argue below, the continuity of certain principles that can be expressed in various forms. In much the same way, it should be emphasized that the formal similarities between the houses and tombs do not imply equivalence of size. Reed (1974, 46) notes that while the lengths of a good many south English long barrows fall comfortably within the range of Linear Pottery and Rössen long houses, most long barrows are about twice the width and length of most long houses, and we have already seen the enormous length reached by a Bohemian barrow from Březno. Marshall (1981) in a detailed quantitative study has shown that the earlier long barrows, the allées couvertes of the Severn-Cotswold group, and those of the Scottish-Irish group are generally larger and wider than the trapezoidal long houses but that the ratio between length and maximum width is similar, especially when comparing the trapezoidal houses and the allées couvertes. Thus the tombs studied are normally larger than the houses but they retain the same shape. Indeed, many of the tombs must have looked very like large houses. The earthen long barrows (see figure 6.2) may have continuous bedding trenches for the walls, or lines of posts, or some mixture of the two, and the same variety is found for the houses. The tradition of tombs looking like houses continues until the end of the third millennium bc.

A second point of similarity between the houses and tombs is that the entrance in the trapezoidal forms is at the broader end. We have already seen the evidence for the houses. In the long tombs, the main burial chamber and entrance facade are also at the broader end although, in certain cases, other burial chambers in barrows can be entered from the side.

Third, both houses and tombs tend to have their long axes aligned west–east or north-west–south-east. Fourth, the entrances generally face east or south-east. The west–east orientation of tombs in the Polish lowlands has been quantified by Midgley (1985). Madsen (1979, 318) notes that in Britain, Poland, north Germany, and Denmark the broader end of the trapezoidal earthen long barrows is to the east. In Britain Hoare noted in 1812 that the earthen long barrows had the broad end pointing to the east. In Brittany the entrances of the passage graves are generally to the south-east especially in the case of the long passaged dolmens (L'Helgouach 1965, 76–9). The entrances of the late Neolithic allées couvertes in the same area are to the east. The Cotswold-Severn tombs mainly face towards the east and in Shetland the entrances face east or south-east, as do the stalled Orkney cairns. Burl (1981) provides other examples of the overall tendency for the broader ends of trapezoidal mounds or the entrances of rectangular or circular passage grave mounds to face east. This is not to say that exceptions do not exist. The Clava passage graves and ring cairns of north-east Scotland generally face south-west and the chambered tombs on Arran show no preferred orientation. However, these exceptions simply emphasize the significance of the overall tendency for long barrows and long houses to face to the east and south-east. A clear choice has been made over a large area and period.

The fifth similarity between the houses and tombs is the emphasis on the entrance – on the foris. In discussing the houses, it appeared that activities and rituals were concentrated in the entrance area, that the entrance area was sometimes marked off by internal partitions and that the trapezoidal shape drew attention to the height and width of the entrance. There was also some evidence to support an increased importance of house entrances through time. This tradition is continued and increased in the long burial mounds, whether or not they are trapezoidal in shape. The long barrows and passage graves frequently have large facades, sometimes with 'horns' pointing forwards from the entrance, forecourts, and antechambers. There is often evidence for rituals and offerings in the forecourt area (figures 7.2 and 7.3), leading to a distinction between the outer, entrance area with many artifacts, and the inner tomb frequently with few artifacts to accompany the skeletal remains. The entrance is often blocked by massive boulders, but may equally be a 'false' entrance, the real entrance being to the side of the mound. Many of these characteristics are found in both stone and earthen barrows. Wooden porches which have been effectively blocked by posts, as at Fussell's Lodge, recall so-called 'false portals' of the Severn-Cotswold laterally-chambered stone barrows (Ashbee 1970, 92). There is a similar emphasis on facades and most of the Scandinavian earthen barrows have a substantial transverse bedding trench in the eastern end holding a timber facade (Madsen 1979).

The sixth point concerns the grading of linear space noted within the Danubian long houses (p. 114). A tripartite division of space is most common, but the lines of posts also divide the house into smaller sections. Cross-lines of posts also occur in Rössen houses (figure 5.6). Internal cross-divisions occur within long barrow mounds and in the graves which they contain. Subdivisions within the mound occur frequently in Britain and Scandinavia, as for example at Barkaer and at Ostergard (Madsen 1979). These subdivisions may have had some role in the construction of the mound. Subdivisions within stone-chambered graves occur widely (e.g. Tilley 1984). Many allées couvertes, including the stalled Orkney cairns, show cross-divisions. In chapter 7 I will discuss further evidence of the grading of space from front to back within the tombs.

Other points of similarity between the houses and tombs that I have noted (Hodder 1984) now seem unconvincing. There seems to be little evidence for the use of decoration in western Danubian houses so it is difficult to make comparisons with the use of decoration within some tombs. Also, it seems difficult to argue for a link between the ditches which flank long houses and long mounds because, as we have seen, the use of elongated pits by the sides of long houses becomes less common through time. There are, however, two additional points of comparison that have been made by Midgley (1985) and Bogucki (1987) which are worth repeating here.

A seventh point of similarity concerns the observation made by Midgley and Bogucki that both the Lengyel houses and the TRB tombs tend to form clustered, village-like patterns. Brześć Kujawski is a good example of the Lengyel long-house village. The tombs in the same area are often clustered in groups of 20 or more. Bogucki (1987, 12) argues that the number of tombs in a cluster approximates the number of houses in use on a large Lengyel settlement at any one time. Looking more widely, Midgley notes that cemeteries of earthen long barrows occur in Kujavia, west Pomerania, and Sachsenwald in north-west Germany. We have seen a similar pattern in Moravia. These are all areas with strong late Danubian influence. Where that influence is weaker, in Denmark, Mecklenburg, and England, the earthen long barrows more often form a diffuse spatial pattern, with barrows located individually or in pairs. It is argued, therefore, that clusters or cemeteries of earthen long barrows refer back to the later Danubian nucleated settlement.

The eighth and final point concerns the relationship between tombs and settlements. The Kujavian long barrows are frequently located on the sites of earlier TRB settlements, as for example at Sarnowo and Gaj. The overall relationship between earthen long barrows and contemporary settlements is unclear, but there are many examples in west Pomerania, Mecklenburg, Lower Saxony, and Denmark of barrows being located directly upon earlier settlements. In Kujavia the mound material frequently includes a range of settlement refuse (ash, animal bones, sherds, flint tools). In many cases there are 'hearth middens' in association with or cut by the graves beneath the barrows. Midgley (1985, 161) suggests that some barrows were built to incorporate earlier settlement structures. Madsen (1979) notes deliberate dumping of domestic rubbish around the graves in Denmark. There is thus strong reason to suppose that at least symbolic ties were created between houses, settlements, and tombs: and it seems that it was not only Danubian housing that was evoked, but TRB housing as well.

In order to argue for the above eight points of similarity, I have had to assume a cultural continuity over the enormous area and period in which long mounds are found. It is of course possible to make the case for indigenous long mound or megalithic burial in separate areas of Europe (Renfrew 1973). I have certainly not made a detailed argument here for why one should consider 'megaliths' as a unified phenomenon. As more of the evidence is unravelled, it will become more evident that although there are regional differences in long tombs, there are also many similarities between for example the earthen long barrows of Scandinavia and England (Madsen 1979). However, it is important to argue for a link between houses and tombs in any one region so that false similarities are not created between unconnected locales. Bogucki and Midgley have completed such a task using the data from the Polish lowlands, and I have argued that a close link exists between houses and tombs in Orkney (Hodder 1984; cf. Sharples 1985).

However, a rather different and perhaps equally valid way to look at the eight points of similarity and at the chronological and broader cultural possibilities for links between the houses and tombs is not to argue for a direct copying or diffusion of the house idea, but to suggest a continuity in the principles by which both houses and tombs were constructed. If there is an underlying domus–foris structure which remains fairly stable but appears on the surface in two different ways, then we need not assume any direct link between houses and tombs.

What might these principles be? The first is monumentality. We saw that the long houses by their sheer size and complexity expressed a strong sense of control over the natural world. Implanted in the forest they dominated and imposed. Later they became the medium for the expression and practice of the productivity and prestige of the competing domestic unit. Some houses became very large. The tombs too are often very large involving large amounts of labour to move earth, wood, and stone, and sometimes extended to imposing lengths, for example at Březno or in Kujavia. The extraordinary lengths of some English barrows will be discussed in chapter 9. It has long been accepted that the tombs were involved in the competition between lineage groups (Renfrew 1973). Even if the tombs were built by a non-lineage group, the practice of construction of a large tomb itself created relations of dependency and competition between social groups. Construction of the tombs, as well as the houses (Startin 1978), would have involved the participation of more than one household unit. Thus in both the house and tombs, group definitions and relations were conducted through the medium of large-scale intervention in nature to produce monumental artifacts.

A second common principle concerns the linear ordering of space, and in particular the bounding or separation of the inside from the outside. In both cases the foris seems important. We have seen that through time, more emphasis is given to the entrances of the long houses. The tombs take the same idea to a further extreme by placing facades across or around the entrance, by depositing goods at the entrance, by blocking or concealing the entrance, or by restricting entry through small 'port holes' (as in the Breton and Paris Basin allées couvertes).

It is possible to derive both long houses and long tombs from these two principles. The two principles are simply applied to two spheres of life (settlement and burial). The tombs may act as the 'house' of the dead and they may refer to houses but not always directly to earlier linear houses. Rather, both types of monument express the domus in terms of a particular form of domestication of the wild. This type of argument seems better able to account for the extraordinarily long time periods over which the houses and tombs were constructed. After all, it becomes difficult to argue that there is any direct link between houses which were rarely constructed after 3300 bc, and tombs which, in the case of the Paris Basin, were constructed after the demise of the Chassey culture in the late third millennium bc. The argument is also better able to account for passage graves in round tombs which look different from linear houses but demonstrate the same emphases on monumentality and linear grading of space.

I have suggested that the principles themselves are intimately linked to a deeper ethic concerning the domestication of nature and society. From this domus ethic and associated principles, long houses and long tombs form a tradition in central (and as we are beginning to see, north-western) Europe which is not found in SE Europe. Megaliths do not occur in SE Europe. The underlying SE European ethic based on the nurturing of nature and society was used to generate different principles and a different historical sequence. Within central Europe there was a different domus ethic and different principles of monumentality and linear grading of space. And people there using these principles generated their own sequences of change.

In central Europe, in many respects the tombs simply continue and extend processes that occurred through time in the construction of houses. Through time some of the houses become longer. Some of the earthen long mounds are even longer. Through time, the entrances to the houses become increasingly emphasized. The earthen and stone chambered long mounds show even further elaboration of the entrance. Through time, the exterior of the house becomes increasingly important, suggesting more of an emphasis on visibility and display. The tombs are often placed in conspicuous, highly visible locations.

Because of these trends and because of the eight-point list of similarities between houses and tombs, it is possible to argue that the long mounds simply continued the processes of the earlier fourth millennium. I suggested in chapter 5 that the decreasing importance of the house towards the end of the Rössen sequence in some areas resulted from a greater emphasis on a larger scale of community production and competition in which individual domestic competition became inappropriate. As we shall see, houses are generally small and simple during the period of construction of long mounds. It is possible to suggest that the emphasis on the community scale of social action was continued in the defended and ritual enclosures (see below). The individual groups who participated in these larger enterprises were able, however, to pursue competitive strategies through the tombs. Individual social units could increase their size and create additional dependencies through competitive display surrounding death. The emphasis remained on monumentality and on the control of access to the tomb. But in many cases the tombs involved larger amounts of joint labour than the earlier houses. Startin and Bradley (1981) have shown that a wood and earth long barrow such as Fussell's Lodge in England might need 6900 construction hours, while the figure for a megalithic long barrow is 15,700 hours. These figures contrast with the 2200 person hours needed for a Linear Pottery house and 3200 hours needed for the longest linear house in the Netherlands (Startin 1978). The very construction of the tombs may therefore have involved creating more numerous or closer relationships and dependencies than in the case of the houses. The processes of inclusion and exclusion could also be extended to all those who could claim links to the ancestors, or who were involved in feasting or gift-giving in the entrance areas of the tombs.

The first people who built linear tombs used existing principles with a beautiful and simple creativity. Entirely unexpected yet altogether expected, the new move grew out of, yet changed, the nature of social relationships. The tombs referred to houses or at least to the principles which had produced them. The move was made possible by the increasing importance and strength of the larger community structures, but it was also a creative act opening up new possibilities for social competition.

As well as deriving inspiration from the domus, the tombs also derived from existing burial practices, subtly linking settlements and burials in a new way. We have seen that Danubian burial included individual inhumation sometimes with grave goods and sometimes in cemeteries. In many of the earthen long barrows of Czechoslovakia, Poland, and Denmark individual burial (normally inhumation) continues, often with grave goods. Cemeteries too continue. In time, multiple or collective burial within monumental tombs becomes more common in central Germany and Scandinavia, as more and more individuals claim access to the ever-expanding social units. It is possible that social units expanded through attempts to include more people and to establish the boundaries of privilege. The Danubian domus, already opposed to but incorporating the burial sphere, was simply expanded in the TRB phase to incorporate burial and death more completely. As a result, the scale of group competition and display could further increase.

I have still refrained from drawing in much of the data about the TRB, Michelsberg, and related groups in this account. As they are gradually incorporated in the following section the limitations of the above interpretation of events will be readily apparent. Perhaps the most unsatisfactory aspect of the account as it now stands, is that I have not fully explained why houses become small and why the domus shifts from the house to the tomb. This change partly results from attempts to define even larger or tighter social entities at the smallest scale, and it partly results from contradictions between the formation of community structures (e.g. enclosures) and individual household interests. But why did the linear house itself not remain as an important social metaphor and why did tombs become important?

Warriors and the Wild

Houses did not of course 'decline' in the late fourth millennium, except in the specific sense that they no longer were the foci of attempts to use the domus in the pursuit of group definition and expansion. Individual household concerns had come to contradict, or at least frustrate, the formation of larger social units. But presumably the household continued to play a role in production, reproduction, and socialization into the domus. And so, although houses become less visible, some of the same principles continued. An example of the interior arrangement of the small rectangular houses

which now become more common is found in the Bernburg phase
at Dölauer Heide (Behrens and Schröter 1980). On a small, steep-
sided promontory outside the defences of the earlier Baalberg enclosure (figure 6.3) was found a high density of storage pits and a house
protected beneath a Corded Ware barrow. In the south-east corner
of the hut (6.6 × 5.5 m) the main concentration of *in situ* finds
occurred in association with an area of burning presumably to be
interpreted as a hearth of a less substantial or well defined type than

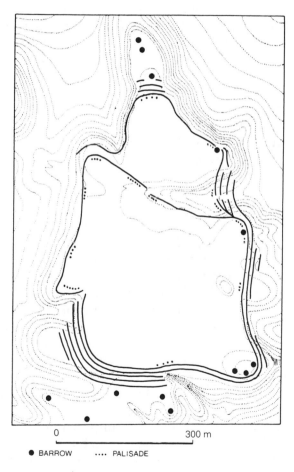

0   300 m

● BARROW   ···· PALISADE

Figure 6.3 Plan of the enclosure at Dölauer Heide/Halle (Saale).
(Source: Whittle 1985)

is found in SE Europe. There are large stones, perhaps for grinding, and also a variety of pots, some of which are complete. It is estimated that about ten pots may originally have stood in this area of the house, including undecorated storage pots and decorated beakers and cups. There are also stone axes and spindle whorls. Overall, the organization of the house recalls the hearth-centred distributions so characteristic of the domus in SE Europe. But there is not the symbolic elaboration of the house either in terms of female representation or in terms of monumentality.

TRB beakers are also found in a possible Altmark hut which contains a hearth (Preuss 1980, 123). In the Polish lowlands at Nowy Młyn, there are poorly defined subsurface features, including a few post-holes suggesting small rectangular structures (Bogucki 1987, 10). In the Michelsberg culture a few small rectangular post-hole structures are known from Urmitz (Lichardus and Lichardus-Itten 1985). To the south, in a zone of secondary Neolithic spread, exceptional preservation of houses has occurred around small lakes in the sub-Alpine region. For example, at Thayngen-Weier, small rectangular structures of varying functions are surrounded by a palisade (Guyan 1967). At Niederwil in the Pfyn culture, there are about 30 one or two-roomed houses with hearths inside or in both rooms (Waterbolk and Van Zeist 1978).

We have already seen that prior to about 3300 bc, houses became increasingly drawn into enclosed settlements. The domus–foris concept was expressed at this new community scale of social production by the emphasis on the grading of space in the monumental 'ritual' enclosures with their multiple circuits and entrances. In the period after 3300 bc, the centripetal (drawing in) uses of the domus–foris principle continue not only at the tomb domus but also at the community scale, in that more and more people are sucked in and entries and exits are more clearly marked. Apart from the development of the tombs themselves, this process is seen in relation to the ditched enclosures. As discussed in chapter 5, such monuments emerge within the Linear Pottery culture and become more common through time. They proliferate, however, in Michelsberg, Chassey (in the Paris Basin), and TRB groups.

There is a great variety of enclosures within the Michelsberg culture (Whittle 1977a). They range in size from small (Miel being about 54 × 60 m) to very large (Urmitz enclosing about 100 ha). Some, such as Michelsberg itself, have continuous encircling ditches and traces of occupation units. Others, such as Urmitz, have interrupted ditches and little evidence of occupation inside. Much of this variation simply continues patterns evident in Linear Pottery and Rössen contexts, although now the frequency of enclosures has increased, as has the emphasis on defence or visibility. Some enclosures are sited on spurs and promontories. In the Paris Basin, too, defence seems to have become an important feature (Burkill 1983b). At Noyen-sur-Seine, for example, interrupted ditches enclosed a river meander and are associated with settlement traces including rubbish dumps, roughly paved areas, and spots where specific activities had been carried out (ibid., 40).

In the Elbe–Saale region of central Germany, hill-top enclosure sites (Höhensiedlungen) again vary from the very large to the very small (Starling 1985b). The major examples date to Baalberg and Salzmünde and went out of use in Bernburg (when collective burials became more common), although the smaller examples continued (ibid.). The impressive hill-top site at Dölauer Heide (figure 6.3) has six ramparts and ditches in some places, and a palisade within. C14 dates for the site range from 3000 to 2600 bc (Preuss 1980). Late TRB and Corded Ware tumuli are associated with the defences of the site and with the edges of the hill-top (figure 6.3). Lichardus and Lichardus-Itten (1985, 429) note that especially large Baalberg tombs with many pots are found near Dölauer Heide, emphasizing the link I have been suggesting between social competition at the tomb and community (enclosure) levels. However, Starling (1985b) finds that the Elbe–Saale enclosures are not evenly spread as a lineage competition model might suggest. In fact they are quite clustered (figure 6.4a) and not closely associated with either unenclosed settlements or graves.

In order to understand the function of these enclosures it would be useful to have some indication of the activities carried out in and around them. Starling (ibid.) refers to communal feasting. Other less tangible activities have also been suggested. For example, in one small excavated portion of the interior of the very large square enclosure at Makotřasy (in central Bohemia) were found numerous potsherds, one stone-packed grave, and some post-holes which do not clearly define a house. TRB in date, several of the pits contain human bones. The authors (Pleslová-Štiková et al. 1980) claim that the enclosure with its single entrance was involved in astronomic observations and alignments to the sun and moon. Some of the camps have 'unusual' deposits of human bones and other occupational material in small ditches (Whittle 1977a). In the Paris Basin,

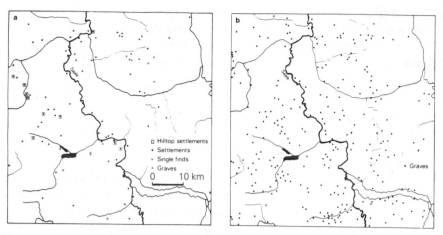

Figure 6.4 (a) Distribution of early third millennium bc settlement in the Saale area of central Germany. (b) Distribution of evidence for the same area during the Corded Ware phase of the later third millennium.
(Source: Shennan 1986, after Starling 1985b)

enclosures are associated with a distinctive assemblage of 'vase supports' and figurines which Burkill (1983b, 54) terms 'ritual'.

Whatever specific activities were carried out at the enclosures, they express most characteristically the two principles found in the tombs and in the houses before them. First, they are monumental, involving large amounts of labour and being highly visible. Second, the encircling ditches and the examples with multiple entrances suggest a concern with controlling space and the exits from and entrances to it. These principles are perhaps seen most clearly in a site about 40 km from Dölauer Heide, called Schalkenberg, by Quenstedt in the Saale region (Behrens 1981). The enclosure is highly visible on a hill spur and consists of five concentric palisades (figure 6.5) which break to form avenues leading into and from the centre. The overall effect is to grade space from outside to inside and to emphasize the drama of coming and going. Two Baalberg inhumation graves were found within the central ring and some Baalberg pottery came from the palisade trenches. Despite some uncertainty about the precise dating of the site (ibid.), it is probably TRB affiliated and recalls the earlier enclosures such as Těšetice-Kyjovice.

Both the tombs and the enclosures of the late fourth and third millennia thus refer to the past. Or at least, they continue the same strategies as were found emerging within the Danubian cultures. The underlying ethic of the domus, by which society is created and controlled through the metaphor of a particular intervention in nature, continues. The principle of monumentality and the domus–foris grading of space produce tombs and continue to produce enclosures. Both tombs and enclosures are larger and more imposing. The defences increase in size and number, and the emphasis on exits and entrances increases in both the tombs and the enclosures. In the case of the interrupted ditch enclosures we see most clearly that the relationship between the individual and the social is the focus of concern. Whatever the specific function of these monuments they place an emphasis on multiple access. But the many entrances and exits lead to and from a common centre. The ditches themselves seem important since it is, according to the domus ethic, movement in and out of delineated space that defines society. Whatever the specific performances that took place, whether highly repeti-

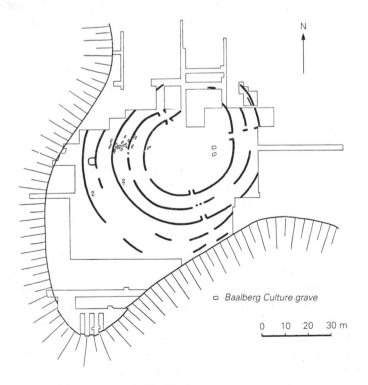

Figure 6.5 Plan of Schalkenburg near Quenstedt.
(Source: Behrens 1981)

tive, economic, or dramatic, the toing and froing created a sense of the social whole out of the individual parts.

I do not wish to mean by this discussion that each enclosure 'controlled' a region of tombs and houses in any simple way. The settlement pattern is organized by a variety of factors in addition to social hierarchy and control. For example, we have seen that tombs are placed on older settlements. Enclosures and tombs are placed in imposing situations in order to enhance their monumentality and in order to emphasize access. We shall see below that they may also be placed in order to have a particular relationship with 'the wild'.

So Starling (1985b) is right to emphasize that the enclosure sites are not always evenly spaced. The clustering and variation in enclosures and tombs result more from the varying success of local groups in 'sucking in' population, prestige, and dependencies. Some groups, for a variety of specific reasons, seem to have been more successful in manipulating the idea of the domus and extending it to new spheres. Any particular local group put the principles together in different ways. In the Paris Basin (see also chapter 8) enclosures are first found (up to the Chassey phase) and only later tombs (in the SOM). In the Michelsberg the emphasis was on enclosures, and in northern Europe small tombs played a major role from early on (see chapter 7). Some local groups emphasized interruptions of the enclosure ditches, others their defensive functions. Some groups placed nucleated settlements within ditched areas, while others separated settlements from the concept of the community as a bounded space. The results of some strategies were more successful than others, although it is difficult to know whether large imposing sites such as Urmitz or Dölauer Heide were ultimately successful or whether they had gone too far. But the overall impression is of a varied and competitive process leading to local variations on a common theme.

In all the ways discussed so far, the domus was reinforced. The centripetal tendencies and the domus–foris principle of inclusion and exclusion were reaffirmed in the bounded enclosures and tombs, as they had been in the houses. But what of the other opposing tendencies within the domus? I argued in chapter 5 that the 'outside' agrios world of death and the wild was relatively undeveloped in central Europe Danubian groups, or at least it was effectively incorporated within the domestication metaphor. Death was, at least in many instances, opposed to the settlement in the provision of a separate cemetery, but on the other hand the cemeteries can be seen as just a reaffirmation of the domus and of the ordered relationship between the individual and the social. However, I wish to argue that defence, warring, and hunting became increasingly important in order to define and create the domus as social groups expanded and competed. These aspects of life worked for the domus. But they also posed a structural threat. Indeed we shall see that they ultimately led to the collapse of the centrality of the domus.

From the logic of the Linear Pottery enclosure boundaries, several implications are gradually realized. I have already referred to the gradually increasing importance of defence and site location on highly visible and defendable positions. It is remarkable that just at the moment when such hill-top sites become more frequent and the linear tombs are constructed – i.e. just at the time when the domus with its philosophy of exclusion reaches its maximum extent in the late fourth and early third millennia – elaborate 'battle axes' appear in the archaeological record in central Europe. Shaft-hole axes and simple 'battle axes' occur from Stroke Linear Pottery and Lengyel times (Zápotocký 1966). Of course we do not know that the later more elaborate forms were used in battle, or even whether the concept 'battle' had any relevance to the period and area being considered. But they are clearly different from domestic axes in that they are large, sometimes decorated as in the Salzmünde examples, and do not have any clear utilitarian function. In Baalberg contexts they often occur in graves, sometimes associated with arrowheads. In Kujavia, the tomb at Rybno contained a grave in which was found a stone mace head (Midgley 1985). The 'battle axes' are best seen as items of prestige, in some way linked to hunting or warfare. In northern Europe there is secure evidence for a link between TRB battle axes and males (see chapter 7).

The importance of the axe in TRB contexts continues the Danubian association between men and axes noted in chapter 5. It is difficult to be sure of the functional interpretation of the perforated axes found in Rössen contexts. In the Rössen cemetery they were closely linked to males (above, p. 110). The TRB battle axes are considerably more elaborate, but they continue out of a tradition in which male prestige is partly based on the symbolism of control and domination inherent within the axe. Whether the 'battle axe' also represented bravery, success in fighting and so on, we cannot as yet know. But the gradually increasing importance of the axe is likely to express the changing role of male representation in relation to the domus through some aspect of defence and warfare.

The latter point is supported by analogy with the increasing importance of hunting and hunting weaponry, such as arrowheads. Once again we are uncertain of the uses of arrowheads in hunting or warfare. They could have had both functions and I shall in any case argue that hunting and warfare were conceptually linked. We saw that projectile points were associated with males in Linear Pottery graves. Arrowheads are, however, relatively uncommon in Linear Pottery contexts except in the Netherlands. Through time, in many areas, they become more common so that, for example, in Baalberg graves triangular arrowheads with good pressure flaking are frequently cited. There is a depiction of a bow and arrow being used in a hunting scene on a Salzmünde sherd (Behrens 1973, 188). After the Chassey in the Paris Basin, the SOM allées couvertes are found. This culture is associated with a very wide range of arrow-heads (Howell 1983, 71). The most characteristic form is barbed and tanged, although tranchet, leaf-shaped, triangular, and lozenge occur frequently, usually as stray finds (i.e. in the 'wild') and in locations suggesting hunting was an important element in the Late Neolithic Paris Basin economy.

The subsistence economy, including the hunting of wild food, is more than economic. It also plays social and symbolic roles that are integrated with subsistence considerations. In the period being considered in this chapter, the importance of the hunting of wild resources increases. In Linear Pottery sites the frequency of wild animals in site faunal assemblages is low. This could either mean that few wild animals were consumed or that they were consumed off sites or so treated (e.g. by burning of the bones) that the bones are not recoverable archaeologically. Either way, the evidence supports the hypothesis of a general relationship with the wild involving boundaries and exclusion. If there was a low economic use of wild animals despite their abundance around the early Linear Pottery sites, that economic strategy was part of the more general social and symbolic strategy of creating the domus by domesticating and controlling nature. The monumental walls and the dirt around the long houses excluded the wild in order to create the cultural within.

That this strategy of excluding the wild was gradually relaxed is clear. Neustupný (1987) has argued that there is a general trend through Lengyel and TRB phases for an increased exploitation of wild resources (although as we have seen the main change may have been to bring the wild resources into the settlement and into archaeologically recoverable contexts). In the Paris Basin, Chassey contexts see an increased proportion of wild animals (Burkill 1983b) and high percentages of wild animals are also found in the following SOM phase (Howell 1983). In the Polish lowlands, Bogucki (1987, 9) notes a markedly higher percentage of wild animals in TRB samples than in Linear Pottery and Lengyel samples. The percentage frequently exceeds 50 and a similar pattern is found in north German sites (ibid.).

Of course it could be said that the increased importance of wild animal bones indicates a real subsistence change linked to other changes in the economy. For example, with increased settlement size and agricultural intensification, perhaps the crops had to be better protected from wild animals. Or with increased intensification, groups were forced to depend on a greater variety of resources, including wild resources. There is probably some truth to all these 'economic' arguments. However a problem remains if we restrict ourselves to such explanations. The adaptational argument has to assume economic changes that are driven in some direction by some process. Through questions of adaptation alone, we could never explain why group size was increasing, and the path towards agglomeration and intensification chosen. The economic changes, including the increased emphasis on or bringing in of wild resources, can themselves be seen as part of changing social and symbolic strategies.

In order to demonstrate that the Neolithic economy of the fourth and third millennia was also social and symbolic it will be necessary to outline the main changes in subsistence and settlement that occurred in this period. In chapter 5 I discussed the Danubian evidence for a dual process of expansion and agglomeration of settlement. In the TRB and related groups, nucleation into defended settlements continues in many areas, and some concentration and retraction of settlement has been noted in the Elbe–Saale area (Starling 1983), although even in Baalberg contexts there are scatters of dispersed settlement between the local clusters. In most areas there is an increased tendency towards dispersed settlements and small ephemeral sites.

In Bohemia, for example, TRB settlements are much smaller than their Danubian counterparts (Neustupný 1987, 16). They are also more evenly distributed than earlier, and most occur in new locations and on new soil types (ibid.). A detailed study by Kruk (1980) in south Poland showed that, in contrast to the valley locations of Linear Pottery and Lengyel sites, TRB sites begin to be placed on the edges of the interfluves as well as in the valleys. Also, rather than forming clusters they are widely dispersed. Kruk sees a change at this time from intensive small-field farming to an extensive slash-and-burn regime. In the Polish lowlands too, the TRB settlement pattern is considerably more dispersed than were the Linear Pottery sites (Bogucki 1982, 113). The sites are more often associated with sandy soils and they appear ephemeral (Bogucki 1987, 9). In a small area in south-east Poland, a detailed study by Milisauskas and Kruk (1984) noted gradual expansion into the uplands even though suitable soils remained in low-lying areas. This more dispersed pattern was associated with the development of a settlement hierarchy amongst the permanently occupied TRB sites. There is some slight evidence of expansion of Michelsberg sites in the Rhineland (Whittle 1977a, 149), but again a clear pattern of dispersal is seen in the late Neolithic (SOM) in the Paris Basin (Howell 1983). The change in overall distribution from the early (Danubian) and middle (Chassey) Neolithic to the late Neolithic (SOM) is striking in the Aisne–Marne area (figure 6.6). It is in the late Neolithic that tombs appear in the second half of the third millennium bc. When analysed in more detail, the different types of late Neolithic sites are seen to concentrate in different landscapes (figure 6.6). There is a change in preferred soil type, and Howell suggests an extensive slash-and-burn economy with a number of small sites, occupied for a short duration, associated with a focal point – the tomb.

In many instances, therefore, and particularly where associated with burial mounds, late fourth and third millennia settlement seems to be more dispersed. It is difficult to see, from the economic evidence discussed in chapter 5, why people would have been forced into this new pattern by external factors. Rather, I would like to suggest that at least two internal processes were at work in relation to the environment. The first concerns the shift in the locus and legitimation of power from the house to the tomb, as described above and in chapter 5. Since social control was now less based on the control of space within houses, the household unit was less constrained in its movements and activities. Second, however, in opposition to the communal domus–foris ethic in the enclosures and tombs, a new relationship with nature and the wild was emerging, less concerned with control through bounding off nature and more concerned with action within the agrios. We have already seen the increased importance of wild animals, hunting, and warring. The dispersed and more fluid settlement pattern, adapting to a wider

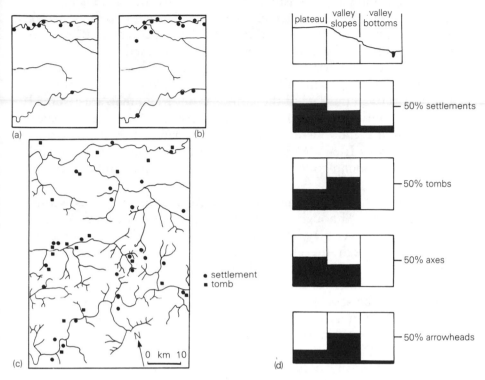

Figure 6.6 The Aisne–Marne area. Comparative distribution of (a) early, (b) middle, and (c) late Neolithic sites, and (d) percentages of different types of SOM sites and finds in different types of location.
(Source: Howell 1983)

range of resources, expressed the same concern to deal with the environment in a new way. The wild environment and scattered settlement contrast with the ordered bounded space within the enclosures and tombs. The new extensive agricultural system allows individual action and decision-making to a greater degree. It allows for individual variation to be created outside the constraints of the dominant ethic. A centrifugal (outwards) movement has countered the centripetal (inwards) tendencies of the domus, through a 'rereading' in terms of the domus–agrios.

This transformation, associated with economic diversification, would in many instances have resulted in new technologies for dealing with the environment. The period from 2700 bc is the main phase of Sherratt's (1981) Secondary Products Revolution.

Ploughing, allowing intensification on already occupied soils and expansion onto a wider range of soils, is evidenced by plough marks under long barrows at Sarnowo in Poland and perhaps at Březno in Bohemia (Pleinerová 1981). Evidence of cattle traction is suggested by double cattle burials. For example three such burials occur in pits at Derenburg in the Elbe–Saale region (Döhle and Stahlhofen 1985). Although the date of these finds is uncertain they are assumed to be Bernburg, in parallel with other Bernburg cattle burials such as the pair at Biendorf associated with a woman and child (Lichardus and Lichardus-Itten 1985). These economic and technological changes correspond to and facilitate the social and symbolic trans- formation.

How was the agrios ethic incorporated into the activities within the household? Although the data are at present inadequate, I think a clue to an answer may lie in the changing assemblages of domestic pottery. Although the changes themselves are easy to see, their meaning is not, mainly because little work has yet been done on pot functions and internal site distributions of potsherds. The period around 3300 bc sees the culmination of a radical transformation of the classes of pottery found in site assemblages. In the Linear Pottery culture, by far the most common form was the simple open bowl (figure 5.9). Early on, however, the neck of the bowl is continued upwards and expanded outwards to form a 'bottle' or 'beaker' shape. In Rössen contexts (figure 5.10) decorated beakers are increasingly common and in the late or post-Rössen sub-groups they are joined by handled jugs and cups. Large numbers of small, handled cups and jugs appear in Michelsberg and related sub-groups (Lichardus 1976). In TRB contexts the main forms include beakers, amphorae, and flasks. In the Baalberg group a similar range occurs including handled beaker forms and very small, presumably individual, pour- ing jugs and spoons or ladles. In Bernburg contexts handled beakers continue, together with small high handled cups.

As in SE Europe, the general decrease in domestic pottery decor- ation around 3300 bc can be related to the decline in the social and symbolic importance of the household at this time. I suggested in chapter 5 that prior to 3300 bc in central Europe decoration played an increasingly important role in relating the household to the outer world. For example, it may have been involved in competitive displays of food and drink involving feasting, the bringing in of others, the definition of social groups and foreigners. Pottery decor- ation became more complex as the front ends of houses became more emphasized. It was most elaborate when the foris was emphasized in the domestic context. But after 3300 bc the main context in which the foris and agrios are manipulated shifts from houses to tombs. As a result, after 3300 bc, domestic pottery decoration declines. (The situation in Scandinavia is rather different and will be discussed in chapter 7.) But it is now clear that this change in decoration is associated with a gradually increasing importance of small drinking or pouring vessels. A similar development was noted in SE Europe (chapter 4). Unfortunately we do not know what liquids were involved. The beakers are found in houses (for example, in the Bernburg house at Dölauer Heide) and in graves. Whatever their specific use and meaning, there appears to be a trend through time which draws boundaries around and attention towards more individualistic consumption, probably of liquids. Of course, the beakers and handled cups have a common style and they may have been used in communal events. But they nevertheless draw attention to the individual in relation to the social. As more data become available on pottery usage it will be possible to examine whether the changes in the common functional classes of pottery do relate to the more widely found process of an increasing emphasis on the individual in relation to the social.

Thus the period after 3300 bc sees two processes at work. On the one hand, tombs and enclosures reinforce the strategy of forming social relationships and dependencies through the domus–foris principles. On the other hand, battle axes, hunting, and dispersed settlement become increasingly important. At one level the latter renewed emphasis on the agrios reinforces the domus. By controlling, domesticating the wild, the domus maintained its centrality. Elaboration of the domus–agrios opposition served to add fuel to the domus–foris. Indeed, I will argue below that the tombs and enclosures themselves do incorporate and manipulate the agrios in order to emphasize the domus. But at another level the emphasis on the agrios begins to diminish and transform the domus. In order to understand the changing relationship between the domus and the agrios it is necessary to consider further aspects of these two concepts.

Linear Houses, Linear Tombs and the Gods

How were the domus structures of symbolic meaning manipulated so as to have dramatic and social effect? I have suggested that the underlying domus ethic, expressed through monumentality and the organization of space, concerned the creation of boundaries between culture and nature. Such a strategy, clearly understandable in terms of the early Neolithic house lost within a central European untamed woodland, continued to have force in later years. But why was it accepted?

One possible answer can be reached by asking why the Danubian long houses were long. Linear space allows a clear grading of space between different functions. But the 'longness' of the house also creates a directionality. Activities, such as the digging of pits for daub, are stretched out along the sides of the house. In moving along the outside or inside of the house one is channelled into a certain direction. In the same way that 'longness' of houses is not emphasized in SE Europe, the direction faced by the doors of houses in that area is varied, linked more closely to the exigencies of packing within settlements. In contrast a distinctive attribute of the Danubian long houses is that, with few exceptions, they face in the same direction. The doors face somewhere in the 90° arc between east and south.

It is to be assumed that location of the doors of long houses at the south-eastern end protected them from prevailing north-westerly winds and minimized direct battering from such winds against the exposed long side of the house. But if this was the only reason for placing the door to the south-east, the degree of variation in Danubian house orientation is remarkably slight (see Marshall 1981 for quantitative data). If the direction of the wind or warmth from the sun were of concern, one might have expected other local factors, including local wind variations, the locations of other houses and water sources, and localized aspects of terrain to cause some considerable variation. That the variation is controlled implies that some other factors, perhaps in addition to protection from the wind, played a role. In any case, Lüning (1982, 10) shows that the prevailing winds on the Aldenhoven Plateau are not, at least today, in line with Linear Pottery house direction.

That orientation was conceptually significant is supported by looking to other cultural spheres in Danubian society. Although the orientation of graves in cemeteries is variable, there is often a common direction in which the long axis of the grave is dug in any one cemetery. In a general review of Linear Pottery cemeteries, Lichardus and Lichardus-Itten (1985, 281) note a tendency towards a west–east orientation. Alignment is also important with regard to some of the early ditched enclosures. In the more formal examples shown in figure 5.5, the four opposed entrances are organized to face north, south, east, and west. In the later example at Schalkenberg a similar pattern occurs (figure 6.5).

The concentric circles of these ditched enclosures mark space from centre to periphery. As in the long house, one has to move in a linear sequence through graded space. But we have now seen that the gradation, in houses and enclosures, is linked to a more distant focus. It is aligned to something beyond itself.

Much the same can be said for the long tombs. I have shown above how the long tombs are clearly oriented in specific directions. Here it is still less obvious that wind direction played much of a role although it may have been relevant to the frequent use of fire in the burial rituals. All the communal monuments that have been discussed thus far seem to be frequently oriented in relation to something external to them. It is uncertain what this external focus might be – a point in the movement of the sun, moon, stars, an ancestral home, or the wind itself. We are unlikely to be able to resolve this specific issue. But we can begin to see a pattern. The central European long houses and tombs are linked into a structure higher than and external to them. Whatever this specific meaning of the orientation of the monuments, it implies a higher order. The grading of space 'on the ground' now has a higher motive and a higher justification.

If I am right in arguing that monumentality and the ordering of space in central Europe had a higher authority, the transfer of the domus, which embodied and generated those principles, to the domain of burial and death was both simple and powerful. The domus itself referred to a higher domain. The tomb contained the ancestors. Thus two higher authorities were linked. The powers of the domus and of the social group linked to the tomb were magnified by this doubling of higher authorities. The tomb monument not only created society and social dependencies through the control of space, but also through being oriented in relation to a higher realm. The ancestors of the social unit that constructed and used the tombs also became linked to this higher domain, thus elevating the social unit, taking it closer to 'the gods'. By these various linkages, the transformation of the domus (see figure 6.7) is both legitimated and given further power.

Some of the complexity and multivalence of the tombs is becoming apparent and will be followed further in chapter 7. So far, they

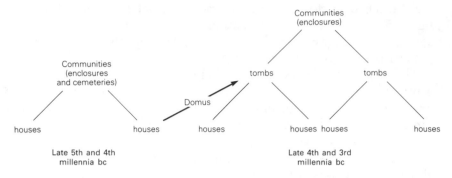

Figure 6.7 The shift of the domus from houses to tombs through time.

represent the domus, monumentality, and the control of space in relation to higher authorities. We have also seen that they act as fixed points in a fluid and dispersed settlement pattern. Indeed, their role as 'houses' of the ancestors is particularly appropriate within a more fragmented 'homeless' pattern of social and economic behaviour. But it is also likely that there is yet another side to the long tombs, more akin to the agrios that increasingly dominates the evidence.

After all, the tombs emphasize disaggregation in relation to the ditched enclosures. They are themselves widely dispersed and often particularly associated with non-settlement areas (see figure 6.6). We have seen (p. 163) that they can be associated with hunting and warfare. Many of the long mounds in central Europe contain single burials, sometimes with artifacts associated with the body in the grave. In Kujavia, graves in the long tombs contain mace-heads and are particularly associated with men. Of the sexed burials known in this area twelve are male, three female. Twenty-four are adults and only three 'children' (Midgley 1985). The gender affiliations in the long mounds will be discussed more fully in chapter 7. For the moment it is of interest that the long tombs both reaffirm the communality of the domus (in the communal construction of monumental forms) and they are involved in the strategies which contest the domus.

We might expect that some people and some groups would be more successful than others in conducting these various strategies. Indeed, at this time, in the late fourth and third millennia bc, a wide range of burial practices proliferated. There are many local differences in the presence and absence of tombs and of different types of tomb. Some groups linked the tombs closely to the communal ethic of the domus. Others emphasized individual attainment.

But the variation was not random. It concerned varying abilities to mobilize labour and conceptual schemes in order to further the power of local social groups. In the Baalberg area in the Elbe–Saale region there are tumuli with either simple pit inhumations or stone chambers. There are also collective inhumations in pits, skull burials, and earth graves with crouched inhumations (Lichardus and Lichardus-Itten 1985). A similar variety of burial rites is encountered in the following Salzmünde and Bernburg phases. By the end of the latter, this variety ranges from single graves to large collective graves. The single graves may form cemeteries of up to 20 graves. There are also collective inhumations in subterranean rectangular cists. In Nordhausen, for example, the bodies were arranged in three rows and the bone morphology suggests that this was a family tomb (Feustel and Ullrich 1965). In other regions, such as the Paris Basin SOM, there are non-megalithic pit burials in addition to the allées couvertes. Some groups placed their tombs most clearly in relation to the communal ethic. For example, right at the end of the period being considered a tomb was built on Dölauer Heide. And in some cases the tombs emphasized communal access. In other cases the tombs contained individual graves and were placed away from defended hilltop sites. The various strands could be brought into play differently.

It seems that the importance of the long mound lay in the multiplicity of social meanings which it was able to bring together. On the one hand, it brought together all the essential components of the domus and the domus–foris opposition. It incorporated the monumental, the bounding and grading of space, inclusion and exclusion, and the higher authorities of the ancestors and perhaps the gods and cosmos. It allowed the expansion or tightening of the scale of local dependencies and relationships, and of the size and status of small-scale social units. On the other hand, the long mound obtained part of its meaning through its associations with attributes of the agrios, such as the fragmentation of small settlement units, their dispersal across the landscape, their use of a wider variety of resources including wild resources, and their involvement in hunting and warfare. Linear tombs such as those in Kujavia incorporated both the communal (in their size and linear ordering of space) and the individual (in their individual burials).

A similar process is evident in relation to the enclosures. On the one hand, they emphasize the domus–foris opposition in the use of boundaries and entrances, and in their communal construction and communal activities. On the other hand, the bounding of space is closely linked to the protection and defence of space. Some enclosures have banks and ditches which are defensive in nature, even if only symbolically. Some enclosures are unoccupied and not intended for domestic functions.

The very idea of the domus involves incorporating the agrios in order to control and domesticate. It is thus not surprising that aspects of the agrios are increasingly evident in the archaeological record. But initially, in the linear house, the emphasis had been on separating off and excluding the wild. The increasing use of the metaphor of domestication in social life created a potential for manipulating the agrios at the expense of the domus. The dispersal of settlement and the emphasis on hunting and warring are therefore not passive results of the use of the domus in maintaining authority structures. Rather they can be seen as active forces – creating new strategies of power, based on the agrios, in relation to the tombs and enclosures.

The latter monuments themselves play actively on the relationship between domus and agrios. In contrast to the Danubian house, the linear tomb does more than emphasize monumentality, inclusion, and exclusion. It also incorporates aspects of the agrios. In doing so it can be used to begin a break with traditional structures of power, allowing wider or closer dependencies and larger scales of domination. The same can be said of the enclosures. Later, however, the increased conceptual dependence of the domus on the agrios allowed individual groups further to transform the domus in order to define new dimensions of power.

Conclusion: the Corded Ware

A further transformation of the domus in central Europe created the Corded Ware and Bell Beaker cultures, in many areas via the Globular Amphora culture, and an idiom that was to have long duration but which goes beyond the confines of this book. Dated from about 2400 bc to beyond the turn of the millennium, the Corded Ware sees the final 'disappearance' of settlement. Certainly small ephemeral habitation sites are known, with small rectangular houses. But they seem slight, associated with a still more widespread dispersal across the landscape (e.g. Kruk 1980 and see figure 6.4), and evidence of forest clearance. Enclosed settlements disappear, and we arrive at an almost purely burial archaeology.

There is a wide variety of Corded Ware burial rites including cremation and inhumation in earth or stone-lined pits (Fischer 1958, Buchvaldek 1966, Sherratt 1986b). In some instances no mound seems to have been raised over the grave, but there is often a round tumulus, up to 2 m in height, and 8–15 m in diameter (Lichardus and Lichardus-Itten 1985). So, rather than a large long mound concerned with exits and entrances and the ordering of space, the Corded Ware mounds are simply heaped over an individual. The highest point of the mound marks and draws attention to the grave. The individuality of the deceased is expressed in other ways too, especially by the placing of artifacts with the body. Women, some-times lying crouched and east–west, are associated with ornaments such as necklaces of perforated animal teeth and shell or bone beads. Men, lying crouched and west–east, are associated with battle axes and bone pins. Graves are also characteristically furnished with beakers, amphorae, but bowls, jugs, flint axes, and arrowheads also occur.

The overall dispersed distribution of the tombs (although in some areas flat graves occur in cemeteries), the individualism of the burial rite, and the importance of battle axes and beakers (as well as the daggers and arrowheads that become important in Bell Beaker graves) all evoke the alternative discourse of power that we have seen gradually rise in influence in opposition to the domus. The idiom of social debate is now warring, hunting, and drinking. Social compe-tition continues as seen in the slight differences in grave assemblages and perhaps in the differences in some areas between those buried under tumuli and those buried in flat graves or as 'secondaries' in tumuli. The domus ethic allowed but constrained this social competition. Released by the idiom of individual action in the wild, the competition expanded into the Bell Beaker and early Bronze Age, perpetuating the new ethic as it did so. A distinctive aspect of Corded Ware and Bell Beaker is the widespread cultural uniformity. It is possible that we are witnessing here some form of legitimation by reference to the long range, the external, the foreign, the agrios. Rather than seeing invasions at this time, widespread cultural uni-formities may be produced by the rise to dominance of a new idiom of power based on, for example, the idea of conquest from abroad.

But the old expressions of the domus did not become irrelevant monuments on the landscape. The Corded Ware burials seem to create the new by transforming the old. After all, the burial mounds are still, although rather feebly, monumental. There is still an east–west axis for the graves and there are repeated burials within the same mound as secondary burials are added in much the same way that bodies were sometimes added to the more communal long tombs. Corded Ware burials also occur as secondaries in long mounds, perhaps as a deliberate attempt to convert some of the older status of the long tombs into a new meaning. At Dölauer Heide, Tumulus 6 begins as a TRB burial in a small mound and goes through a series of phases of remodelling into the Corded Ware, including the construction of a small familiar trapezoidal barrow with a decorated stone chamber at the eastern end (Behrens and Schröter 1980). At the same site a Corded Ware tumulus is built over the Bernburg house discussed earlier. In addition the Corded Ware pottery decoration at this site, and the decoration used in the stone burial chamber in Tumulus 6, clearly recall the distinctive zigzag decoration on earlier Bernburg beakers from the same location. The overall impression is of an attempt to create the new idiom out of the old – to establish new powers according to an alternative scheme, but by incorporating some aspects of the status and power of the domus ethic.

Because the domus–foris–agrios set of principles is organized by oppositional principles and is patterned in coherent ways, the evolution of culture appears patterned when the principles are articulated in social action. The cultural sequences through time have a logic because social action has to make sense in cultural terms. As a result, for example, there appear to be resemblances between the unfolding of structures in SE Europe and in central Europe. In both regions the domus has gradually given way to an increased emphasis on death and the wild. Of course the two areas were presumably in continual contact, and historically one cultural sequence derived from the other. Thus it is hardly surprising, perhaps, that the two regional sequences end up looking so similar. On the other hand, the domus concept is appreciably different in the two areas, and as it unfolds it has rather different results. It is because of different logics that megalithic long tombs and large 'ritual' enclosures do not develop in SE Europe. And yet individual burials, warring, and hunting end up being important in both areas. In central Europe an emphasis on the foris defines the domus in a unique way, but out of existing ideas within the domus. In the particular context of central Europe a creative move is made. Through the domus–foris opposition there is a move towards communal fora (the enclosures) and towards strategies of inclusion and exclusion in linear houses and linear tombs. Ultimately, however, tensions within the domus in central Europe have a similar result to that in SE Europe. In both areas agrios principles become dominant.

This similar end position, reached via rather different paths, results in my view from the overarching importance of the basic domus–agrios opposition – that is the basic idea of the creation of society through the domestication of the wild. Initially the domus is of central importance. But as the concept is extended as a social metaphor to incorporate more and more of the wild (such as death, secondary animal products, upland resources, wild animals), the agrios increasingly and 'logically' becomes central. Whatever the specific lower-level principles involved, the domus becomes increasingly contradicted by, for example, defence or settlement dispersal. Even if these contradictory trends had initially been generated by using the metaphor of domesticating the agrios, their increasing centrality led ultimately to the use of the agrios as a major axis of social life. The constraints on individual action were too easily thwarted by reference to the agrios. That there are logical conceptual links through the European Neolithic in central and SE Europe does not necessarily imply predetermined evolutionary sequences. The practical effects of using particular structuring principles are 'read' according to existing schemes, and transformations therefore appear 'channelled'.

I have so far outlined the process by which the domus is transformed in two regions in Europe. I have been considering enormous areas with scant regard to detail. It is time now to evaluate a slightly smaller region. The south Scandinavian sequence will also allow a fuller discussion of megalithic burial practices. The fuller detail available from this area allows the transformation of the domus in the burial context to be better understood.

7

Domes of Rock: the Neolithic in Southern Scandinavia

Setting the Stage: the Ertebølle

Towards the end of the fifth millennium bc, during the period of early agricultural development and village and cemetery formation in the central European area to the south, southern Scandinavia witnessed the appearance of the Ertebølle culture.

At the outset it has to be confessed that the date for the beginning of Ertebølle is partly a matter of definition since many flint types demonstrate a long period of gradual change from Maglemosean groups, via a series of intermediaries, to the full (but still changing) Ertebølle assemblage. Certainly by 4100 bc the term Ertebølle is used to describe flint assemblages (Albrethsen and Petersen 1976) and an earlier date is implied by Jensen (1982).

Prior to the Ertebølle there is evidence for gradually increasing population and site complexity (Clark 1975). Paludan-Müller (1978) and Rowley-Conwy (1980) have shown that Ertebølle sites include permanent bases and temporarily used special purpose camps for the exploitation of seasonal resources. Although terrestrial inland resources are used, estuarine and marine resources are an important economic focus. Rowley-Conwy suggests that 45 to 240 individuals inhabited Ertebølle settlements. The slightly decorated, pointed-base pottery may have played a role in storage and food preparation (Clark 1975). Traces of small, probably single-celled houses have been recovered associated with pits, forming settlements with cemeteries (Albrethsen and Petersen 1976; Larsson 1984).

So the general structure and trajectory of the data are reminiscent of the contemporary evidence for agriculturalists in central Europe. In the latter area in the late fifth and early fourth millennia bc, there is evidence of increasing agglomeration of settlement, and the formation of cemeteries. The more intensive (agricultural) use of the environment is perhaps equivalent to the more intensive use of estuarine and other resources in the Ertebølle. In Woodburn's (1980) terms, in both areas there is increasing emphasis on an economic system with 'delayed returns'. Through time, both areas see increasing regional diversity. In the Ertebølle this is seen in types of axes, combs, bird-bone points, harpoons, bone rings, and pottery (Jennbert 1985). In the Danubian area, I have noted the increasing regionalization of pottery styles. By the middle of the fourth millennium Danubian shaft-hole axes, of the types found in Stroke Linear Pottery and Rössen contexts, are being exchanged into Denmark, appearing in Ertebølle contexts (Fischer 1982).

If there was contact between southern Scandinavia and the Danubian area, and if both were going through processes of economic intensification, why did groups in southern Scandinavia not adopt agriculture? Perhaps the reason was partly climatic (Clark 1975; Larsson 1986). After all, the post-glacial climate changed markedly but gradually, and sea-level changes had considerable effects on the availability of marine and estuarine resources. However, by 5000 bc, a full mixed oak forest had developed, and Rowley-Conwy (1980) argues that there were many soils, similar to the Danubian loess, available for agricultural use. It was not the lack of soils which prevented the adoption of agriculture contemporary with developments in central Europe.

Agriculture was adopted in southern Scandinavia around 3200–3100 bc. Since we know that Danubian sites began their occupation of the adjacent loess areas by 4400 bc, it is necessary to explain the lack of adoption of agriculture in southern Scandinavia over a period of at least 1300 years, despite evidence of exchange and contact between Denmark and Danubian sites. Certainly an important part of the answer (Rowley-Conwy 1980) is that the hunting, gathering, and fishing adaptation in southern Scandinavia was successful and well established, with high population densities in comparison to the low frequencies of fifth-millennium bc Mesolithic sites in the loess areas of central Europe (Clarke 1976b). In Denmark there was simply no need to change to agriculture, which might well have involved greater labour input. Ertebølle settlements are especially located in areas (e.g. estuaries) with high degrees of resource productivity and diversity (Paludan-Müller 1978). The use of seasonal resources from temporary or seasonal camps added to the amount and variety of resources that could be tapped.

The difficulty with this type of adaptational argument is that we cannot, in any absolute sense, determine whether the inhabitants of Ertebølle settlements were or were not experiencing any 'stress' in relation to their environment. Certainly we can work out the amount of calories obtainable from resource x for each hour of labour input. But we do not know how that labour input was partitioned (between men and women, elders and juniors for example) or what degrees of labour input or of diminishing returns from that input were considered unacceptable. It is extremely difficult to demonstrate stress or lack of stress in the relationship between economy and society, despite claims to the contrary (Cohen 1977). As we have seen, the economic is closely bound to the social and cultural, and the retention of a hunting-gathering-fishing economy is actually the retention of a whole way of life that has social and cultural components. This is evidenced in the Ertebølle case by the selective way in which Danubian traits are adopted. Danubian shaft-hole axes were incorporated into Ertebølle contexts. But long houses were not adopted, and neither was the elaborately decorated Danubian pottery. I shall argue that the rejection of agriculture was systematically linked to the Ertebølle way of life.

Despite the abundance of evidence for Ertebølle sites, it is difficult to find any traces of the domus. Further excavation may change the picture, but houses seem small and uncomplicated. There is no evidence of any symbolic elaboration within the house, or in relation to the female role within the house. The domus does not seem to be present either in its nurturing or in its monumental, boundary-controlling form. Indeed my inability to identify any component of the domus in pre-agricultural contexts in southern Scandinavia gives some confidence to my identification of the domus in early sites elsewhere. I do not seem to 'see' the domus everywhere, in all data I examine.

The focus of symbolic elaboration in Ertebølle contexts seems not to be the household or home at all, but in different domains. S. H. Anderson (1980) notes that most Ertebølle 'art' occurs off sites as stray finds rather than in domestic contexts. Continuing Maglemosean traditions, a range of geometric, abstract designs occurs on bone, antler, amber, and stone. Only a limited range of artifacts is decorated, and in particular antler axes and shafts. The latter sometimes occur in burial contexts. For example, at Skateholm in Sweden, an ornate antler axe was found in a male burial (Larsson 1984). At the latter cemetery, there are differences in the way in which the bodies of men and women are laid out, and men are associated with arrowheads and blades, while women are found with jewellery and a range of bone implements. At the Vedbaek cemetery in Denmark, knives, blades, and antler axes are again associated with men (Albrethsen and Petersen 1976). So we can say that one major focus of symbolic interest centres around male axes.

Another important focus of decoration is seen in the impressed and coloured oar blades from Tybrind Vig (Andersen 1980 and 1983). The decoration of these oars is extremely detailed and rich and rather different from that found on antler and bone (Andersen 1983). We cannot link these oars to any particular social group, but it seems that they and the boats found at Tybrind Vig were used in fishing and/or exchange activities. In either case, they have a non-domestic focus.

The evidence is as yet scanty, but a picture appears to be emerging in which Ertebølle symbolic activity creates links between the non-domestic, the male, killing, cutting down, hunting, and perhaps trading. Symbolic elaboration was not, therefore, linked to the house or to any concept equivalent to the domus. Rather it was more associated with what I have termed, in the central European context, the agrios.

It is thus of interest that it is items linked to the agrios in central Europe that are adopted in southern Scandinavia. As we have seen Danubian shaft-hole axes diffuse into Denmark. They could find an easy place within the dominant Ertebølle ethic, itself already incorporating axes. But the elaborately decorated Danubian pottery styles are not copied. Danubian long house construction is not adopted. It is thus possible to argue that aspects of the Danubian agrios could be incorporated in Ertebølle contexts, but that the domus principle itself was antithetical to existing principles of power in southern Scandinavia.

We have seen in central and SE Europe that there is some evidence to link the domus with at least some stages of agricultural production (see p. 90). It is possible that the long period of non-adoption of agriculture in southern Scandinavia may be linked to a more general rejection of the Danubian domus in that area. Agriculture, linked to the domus in central Europe was simply incompatible with the principles of power as they had developed in southern Scandinavia. I do not deny that other environmental, technological, and economic factors may have been involved. But a full explanation of the non-adoption of agriculture by Ertebølle groups needs to take into account the wider evidence of other cultural traits that are adopted or rejected.

In my view, the argument above is strongly supported by a further piece of evidence. While the domus dominates in central Europe, agriculture, houses, and pottery styles are not adopted in southern Scandinavia. But in central Europe the domus shifts in locus around 3300 bc. Houses decline in importance, pottery is no longer elaborately decorated and burial ritual becomes of greater centrality as the new domain for the playing out of the principles of the domus. I have argued that this shift allowed or was associated with a changed social and economic system in which dispersed settlement, exchange, defence, and warring increasingly formed the basis of authority structures and in which the agrios could increasingly be used to play a central role. Soon after this transformation in central Europe, agriculture is adopted in southern Scandinavia. It is as if the inhabitants of Ertebølle sites were unable to adopt agriculture until transformations had taken place within central European society which made agriculture more compatible with Ertebølle principles. The main product of that transformation in central Europe was the development of the TRB culture by 3300 bc. By 3200–3100 bc, a branch of the TRB grew out of the Ertebølle culture.

There are certainly many other factors involved in the adoption of agriculture in southern Scandinavia (for recent reviews see Madsen 1986, Nielsen 1986, Larsson 1986). The continuing changes in climate and sea-level certainly had some effect. For example, Rowley-Conwy (1980) argues that sea-level and related changes resulted in oysters, which had played an important role in the seasonal Ertebølle economic cycle, being no longer available. Because the scheduling of the whole economic system was linked to the oyster, its disappearance necessitated overall change and influenced the adoption of agriculture. Another factor may well have been population increase. Paludan-Müller (1978) suggests that the sedentism evident in Ertebølle sites, coupled with the richness of estuarine resources, would have led to a breakdown in population control and massive population increase. There would then have been budding off of population to exploit more marginal environments. The latter would have included inland locations well suited to the adoption of agriculture. Jennbert (1985) argues for mixing and continuity between Ertebølle and TRB assemblages in southern Sweden but prefers a social explanation for the change, suggesting that agriculture was adopted as a 'prestige item' in competitive exchange.

Thus the adoption of agriculture in southern Scandinavia has been subjected to the whole gamut of stock answers that archaeologists routinely trot out in order to explain the origins of agriculture wherever it occurs in any part of the world. The main ideas in all such debates concern changes in resource availability, population increase, and social competition. Indeed these same ideas are used for most later (and earlier) evolutionary developments from the Secondary Products Revolution, to the growth of chiefdoms, states, and urbanism (and even the change to the Upper Palaeolithic). While I would agree that population levels, resource availability, and social competition constrain and play a part in evolutionary change, it often seems as if these answers are too easily applied and that too much is left unaccounted for. For the Near East I tried in chapter 2 to suggest an historical interpretation that dealt with the full richness of the specific data for the adoption of agriculture. In southern Scandinavia I have tried to address specific questions such as 'why did Ertebølle groups adopt certain Danubian items but not others?' I am sure that technological, population, and economic factors are involved here. For example it is possible that ploughs were not available in Europe prior to the TRB, and that the technology of ploughing facilitated the spread of agriculture into Scandinavia. Even if the evidence was strong on this point (which it is not – the precise date of the adoption of ploughing in Europe remains uncertain), groups adopted much more than the plough, including new ways of decorating pottery and new burial rites. In order for our explanations to account for the full range of data, it is necessary to undertake an historical account of the specific sequence of events.

TRB – the Early Neolithic

The TRB in Scandinavia appears to develop rather later than in Poland and than the development of Baalberg in central Germany (see chapter 6). The Early Neolithic (EN) phase begins around 3100 bc and ends around 2700–2600 bc. Traditionally the Early Neolithic was divided into EN A, B, and C, the latter also divided into a megalithic and non-megalithic group. It is now realized that a number of regional groups can be identified in the earlier Neolithic, including the Svaleklint and Oxie groups concentrated in the eastern part of southern Scandinavia and the westerly Volling group, whereas megalithic C is later within the Early Neolithic (perhaps 2800–2600 bc), but again with regional groups such as Virum and Fuchsberg

(Madsen and Petersen 1983; Andersen and Madsen 1977; Madsen 1986). The Middle Neolithic (MN) begins by about 2600 bc and is divided into subphases (MNI–V) some of which may again be regional subgroups. The later Middle Neolithic in southern Scandinavia is represented by the Corded Ware/Battle Axe culture, with the Single Grave variant in Denmark and the Boat Axe variant in Sweden. It lasts from about 2300 to the early second millennium bc, and is followed by the southern Scandinavian Late Neolithic which I will not consider here since it is part of cultural developments which go beyond the subject of this book. In this chapter I am thus mainly considering the third millennium bc, and I wish to start with the Early Neolithic.

As elsewhere in Europe in the third millennium, the Scandinavian EN domestic unit is neither elaborate nor monumental. A number of EN houses have been excavated, although Madsen (Madsen and Jensen 1982; Eriksen and Madsen 1984) has suggested there is reason to doubt many of them. Those that have been excavated with modern methods include Mosegården and Lindebjerg (ibid.). Most EN (and MN) houses were small, slight, perhaps short-term (3–6 years) and left little trace. At Mosegården the settlement was preserved beneath a barrow and consisted of a dwelling area with post-holes perhaps forming a hut of about 20 m², a primary activity area with hearths, the highest density of pottery and a fairly high density of waste flint flakes, secondary and marginal activity areas, and a dump area with much pottery waste.

Such houses do not seem to have been grouped into large settlements throughout most of the EN phase. In east Jutland, Madsen (1982) was able to identify two types of site: catching sites in coastal or aquatic locations, containing an Ertebølle-type use of the environment, and residential sites consisting of small, short-term sites on low-lying sandy soils. Similarly, in south-west Scania, Larsson (1984) found an EN pattern of small, scattered, detached farms, each with one or two families, situated by watercourses in diverse environments. The economy, including domesticated crops and cattle, included a considerable amount of hunting, gathering, and fishing. By the end of the EN in this area, larger residential 'camp' sites appeared (see below), in addition to specific function and hunting, gathering, and fishing sites.

Most archaeologists have assumed a slash-and-burn economy for the EN (see Rowley-Conwy 1980 for a different view). Pollen evidence suggests that impact on the well-forested environment was usually of limited extent, although at Lindebjerg (Liversage 1980) some more extensive clearance is implied. There is some evidence for a concentration of settlement on more productive soils (Randsborg 1975), and plough-marks have been identified. The over-all impression gained is of a varied adaptation to the environment, but with many sites being relatively impermanent and with a con-siderable reliance on wild resources.

Much of the EN evidence, continuing from the Ertebølle, suggests an emphasis on the symbolic elaboration of non-domestic contexts. EN settlement pottery differs considerably from Ertebølle styles, but it remains largely undecorated until the end of the phase. On the other hand, within the Volling and Svaleklint groups heavily decorated lugged beakers and lugged jars occur, very often in connec-tion with burials and with a clear ritual significance (Madsen, pers. comm.). Battle axes and mace-heads are found as stray finds and in burial contexts. Such aspects are emphasized at the expense of the domestic context which remains largely 'invisible'. We have seen this agrios ethic grow in central Europe. The ethic is well suited to the pre-existing Ertebølle groups in southern Scandinavia, facilitating the adoption of the TRB in this area.

Even burial rites continue the Ertebølle tradition in that simple earth graves, similar to those at Vedbaek, are found with usually individual inhumation, often covered with red ochre, and containing grave goods such as amber beads, pottery, and axes, including battle axes. But in addition, there are dolmens and earthen barrows in which a similar range of goods is deposited with usually individual inhumations. We see here evidence of a different tradition.

For central Europe, I argued that the fuller use of a wide variety of resources in the TRB came about as part of a redefinition of the domus. There was a shift in the domus to the burial context, and a transformation of its meaning in order to incorporate a greater flexibility of individual action by the domestic group. At the same time the domus in the burial context also allowed the creation of social prestige through a renewal of the idea of domesticating the wild in monumental works and in the control of exits and entrances. How this was achieved can be more fully understood by reference to the long mounds that were constructed in southern Scandinavia.

The Scandinavian long mounds contain either wooden or stone 'chambers' which also seem to exist without mounds (Madsen 1979). The wooden chambers are either tent-shaped or rectangular, and it is the latter form which is also constructed in large stones forming either a rectangle or a horseshoe-shaped cell. The floors of the chamber are often well prepared, and often contain several fully articulated inhumation burials, and grave goods including pottery. There is normally evidence of burning or firing of the wooden chambers, leading to burning or scorching of the bodies and burial gifts.

It is important to recognize that the burial goods associated with graves within long mounds are no richer, more numerous or more varied than those in the simple earth graves or in chambers without mounds. The importance of the long mounds does not appear to lie in any simple expression of individual social status. Rather, the construction of a long mound seems to be aimed at creating and representing social entities, through the exercise of the principles of the domus.

First, the tombs are clearly monumental. Some are over 100 m long. They may have palisades or stone kerbs around them. And in some instances the chambers and dolmens are constructed in large stones. Second, there is an important emphasis on linearity. The graves and mortuary structures are arranged in linear sequences within the mound. For example, at Lindebjerg in Zealand, not only are several barrows arranged on a linear axis, but within the excavated long mound there is, moving from west to east, a trapeziform chamber, a mortuary structure, a bank associated with burnt timbers and deposits of pottery, and an entrance facade (Liversage 1980). In many examples, there are internal divisions along the mound associated with separate graves (figure 7.1). In particular, there is often a wooden facade or screen at the eastern end. Even though no entrances have been found in the eastern ends, pottery deposits are normally found here, reminiscent of the importance of the eastern end of the Danubian long houses.

There are chronological difficulties in arguing for any direct copying in southern Scandinavia of Danubian long houses. We have no dates for the latter which would take us near the early dates for Scandinavian long barrows, right at the beginning of the third millennium bc, and the closest parallels for the Scandinavian examples are British tombs (Madsen 1979). However, the Scandinavian long mounds do continue the general tradition of TRB long mounds found in central Europe. By the time we get to Scandinavia, the principles of monumentality and sequence are still strongly expressed, even if direct contact with the earlier expression of those principles (the Danubian house) is impossible. But there is also clear

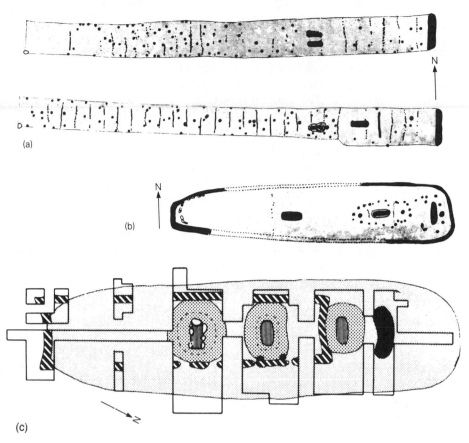

Figure 7.1 Scandinavian earthen linear barrows: (a) Barkaer; (b) Bygholm Nørre-
mark; (c) Sjørup Plantage.
(Source: Madsen 1979)

evidence that the long mounds were nevertheless seen as houses. They
are frequently, if not always, placed on settlement sites, sometimes
with the burial chamber placed directly over earlier dwellings. At
Mosegården, the two megalithic tombs (dolmens) within the long
barrow were situated to be directly over the main dwelling part of
the settlement site (Madsen and Petersen 1983). At Lindebjerg, there
is evidence in the pottery styles of only a short period of time
between the pre-mound settlement and the graves placed on it. In
other cases, the material from within and around the graves is so

similar in date that Madsen (1979) has suggested that settlement material was built up around the grave as part of the mortuary ritual.

The long mounds thus clearly represent the main components of the central European domus. As well as referring to and deriving from the domestic context, they express monumentality and the controlled linear ordering of space, particularly in relation to the residual entrances. The long mounds are again oriented west–east, with the facade, 'entrance' end towards the east. As was suggested more widely in chapter 6, it seems likely that orientation in relation to an external logic placed the earthly human ordering within a higher domain. The burial ritual involved placing of the deceased within his or her 'house'. But the 'house' was made permanent, visible, and very 'present'. The ground was deturfed, at Lindebjerg for example (Liversage 1980), and the graves and mortuary structures constructed in large stone or large oak planks. Once covered with a long mound, the tomb represented a massive transformation of nature. The very practice of its construction involved the creation of social ties and dependencies. And once the tomb was constructed, the social ties were re-formed in the addition of secondary graves and in the deposition of pots at the eastern end of the tomb. The use of the tomb created social entities and relationships that may also have played a part in joint agricultural and exchange activities. The very monumentality of the tomb created the meaning and drama for the social dependencies, but the power of the drama was enhanced by links to a higher sacred authority.

The mounds placed over the graves are often long, although some round examples occur. The concern was not simply to mark the tomb with a large mound. It was also to control access to the tomb, and to create relations of asymmetry and dominance within the tomb-using group. The facades seem to 'hide' or at least separate off the activities within the tomb. Certain activities such as the deposition of considerable numbers of large (storage) pots are carried out at the front of the tomb. It is as if access and ritual knowledge are carefully being controlled through the construction of the tomb and through the domus–foris opposition. The nature of the relations of domination within the tombs will be discussed more fully in the following section.

In the EN in southern Scandinavia, we see the domus as expressed in the long mound as the main focus for the creation of centripetal (group formation) forces through the manipulation of historically generated principles concerning the transformation and control of nature. At the same time, centrifugal (dispersion) forces and principles connected with involvement in the wild are encouraged precisely because the long mounds are not living but abandoned 'houses'. The practices of daily life of members of tomb-using groups included flexibility, individual mobility, hunting, warfare, and the use of wild resources.

Fuchsberg to MN II

In early MN, the principles and practices of EN are elaborated to reach their full extent. Pottery becomes richly decorated, tombs are numerous, and mortuary rituals become multifaceted and complex, causewayed camps are built, and votive deposits in bogs continue. The richer evidence allows a better understanding of the principles and practices themselves, although of course my prior knowledge of the MN material influenced my account of the EN data in the previous section.

The great dolmens and passage graves which develop out of the EN burial forms gradually develop a permanent passage linking the grave chamber to the outside world (figure 7.2). There is an increasing emphasis on going in and coming out of the chamber within what is now frequently a round burial mound. This stress on entrances is by now a familiar pattern within the domus control of space.

The separation of the inside from the outside, in a linear sequence, is seen clearly in the depositional patterns associated with the use of the tombs. Frequently pottery is mainly placed outside the tomb and stone tools inside. There is much regional and temporal variation, and different activities were carried out at the same tomb through time. A major difficulty is that many of the tombs seem to have been cleared out, perhaps in some cases after the early MN phase, resulting in deposits in front of the tomb which are a mixture of primary pottery votive offerings and materials cleared out from the stone chamber. In some cases, however, it has been possible to separate stratigraphically the lower pottery deposits and the overlying clearings of axes, arrowheads, amber beads, and a few pots. A clear result of these processes of deposition and clearing is seen in figure 7.3. Large amounts of pottery were placed in front of this MNI tomb, and in some cases the pottery was placed on the kerbstones (Ebbesen 1979). All the pottery was deposited slightly to the right of the entrance to the tomb. Within the stone chamber pottery

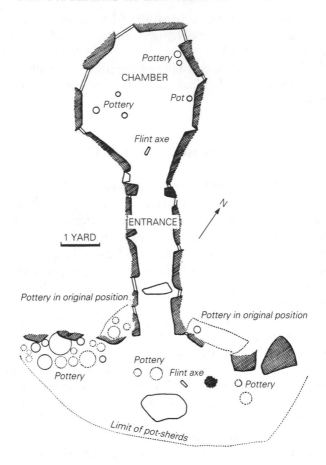

Figure 7.2 The Grønhøj tomb.
(Source: Klindt-Jensen 1957)

is extremely rare, but there are stone tools, axes, and amber beads, some of which have the form of battle axes. The same range of material as found within the tomb is also found immediately in front of the passageway entrance (figure 7.3b), and Ebbesen interprets the material in front as clearings from the chamber.

Undoubtedly, pottery is sometimes placed within the burial chamber as well as in front of the tomb, for example at Himmelev in Zealand (Skaarup 1982) and Ramshög in southern Sweden (Strömberg 1971). Nevertheless, pottery is often concentrated outside the tombs. In southern Sweden, 50,000 sherds of pottery were

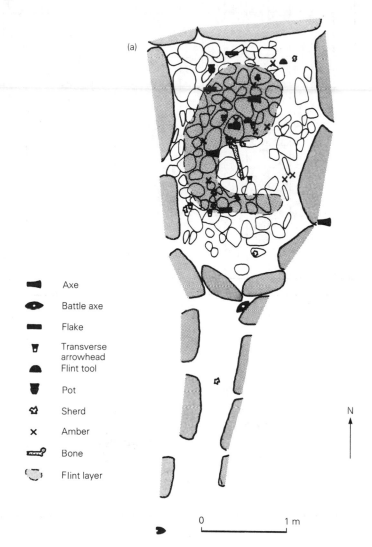

(a)

Axe

Battle axe

Flake

Transverse
arrowhead

Flint tool

Pot

Sherd

Amber

Bone

Flint layer

N

0   1 m

Figure 7.3 Vedsted (this page and overleaf). The distribution of finds (a) inside and (b) outside the tomb, and (c) a typical distribution of a pottery type outside the tomb.

(Source: Ebbesen 1979)

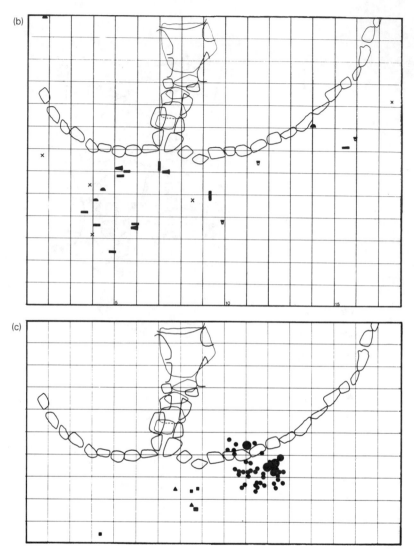

Figure 7.3(b) and (c)

found by the facade of a tomb, representing the remains of more than 1000 pots. In Jutland, 50–100 pots are more usual (Kjaerum 1967). The detailed evidence from Vedsted suggests that the pottery offerings result from successive votive ceremonies unconnected with, or at least in addition to, burial (Ebbesen 1979, 106), whereas other evidence suggests discrete placings of pots on megalith facades in conjunction with burial (Madsen 1979, 317).

The placing of pottery in front of the tomb recalls the deposits of larger numbers of larger pots at the eastern ends of the EN tombs than are found inside (above p. 186), and the opposition between stone tools and axes inside and pottery at the front is reminiscent of the Danubian long house pattern shown in figure 5.3. In the contexts of the bog deposits in EN and early MN southern Scandinavia, there is a similar separation of pots and stone tools. These votive deposits consist either of pots or axes. Of the 150 pottery deposits known to Becker (1947), only 17 had axes associated with them. There is also a detailed difference in the location of deposition of pots and axes within wet areas. Bennike and Ebbesen (1986) note that pots are generally found below 1.5 m under the modern bog surface, whereas axes are generally found only within 1 m of the surface. Pots seem to have been deposited in what was at the time open water, while the flint axe hoards were placed on the water's edge. It is tempting to suggest an overall distinction between wet and dry, pottery and axes, linked to the distinction between outside or front (wet and living flesh) and inside or back (dry bones). Bennike and Ebbesen (1986, 99) draw parallels between the votive offerings of pottery of early and middle Neolithic date in wet areas and those in front of the entrances of large dolmens and passage graves, even though the types and sizes of the pottery deposited in the two contexts differ to some degree. They also note (ibid., 96) cases in which votive offerings took place in wet areas, settlement on the edge of this, and the graves on dry land further back, towards the bottom of the slope.

Fuller understanding of the depositional practices can be gained by considering other aspects of the bog deposits. The votive deposits are sometimes associated with platforms that may have been returned to several times (Becker 1947). The pots are normally empty, but one contained bones of fish, duck, beaver, and eggshell. Birds and domesticated animal bones are found with the pots. The provision of food associated with the pottery could be identified as a characteristically domestic function. On the other hand, there is never flint waste nor normal settlement debris associated with the deposits. The pots are sometimes associated with human bones, and the early Neolithic pottery deposit at Sigersdal Mose was associated with the skeletons of two young people, one with a cord round its neck (Bennike and Ebbesen 1986). Thus the domestic context is implicated in the pottery deposits, in the provision of food, but the depositional event is also concerned with feasting or sacrifice.

Although a number of Ertebølle vessels recovered from wet areas are probably to be regarded as precursors of the Neolithic pottery deposits (ibid.), most pottery deposits occur in ENC and MNI (see figure 7.4). In the early MN, the opposition between pottery and axes is further clarified by the contents of the so-called 'cult houses', which are outside the tombs and which mainly contain pottery rather than tools and axes. The types and shapes of pottery found in the cult houses are very similar to those found on the facades of the tombs.

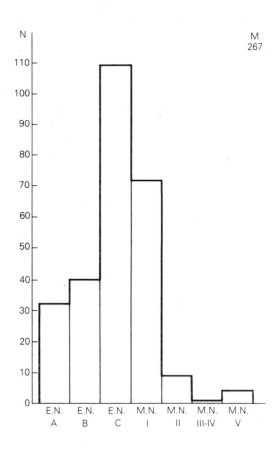

Figure 7.4 The quantity and date of the bog vessels of the TRB in Denmark.
(Source: Bennike and Ebbesen 1986)

The cult houses are often located so as to be central to a small group of MN dolmens and passage graves (for example, at Tustrup (Kjaerum 1955) and Ferslev (Marseen 1960)). The link between the cult houses and mortuary practices is clear not only in the spatial positioning of the cult houses and in the shared types of pottery, but also in the construction of the houses themselves. The 'hearth' in the Ferslev cult house recalls the stone-lined cists with floors of burned flint often found in the chambers of passage graves (Kjaerum 1967). The cult house at Sejerø (Liversage 1982) has a form reminiscent of one of the mortuary structures beneath the nearby EN mound at Lindebjerg (Liversage 1980). And the two opposing pits or post-holes in the Engedal cult house (Faber 1977) and at Herrup (Becker 1973) are similar to the arrangement of single opposed posts in the EN tent-like mortuary structures (Madsen 1979).

The cult houses do not contain stone tools and normal settlement flint waste. And the pottery in them differs from that found in domestic contexts in that, as in the case of the deposits in front of the tombs, there is a higher frequency of decorated sherds and a higher frequency of special pottery forms including pedestalled bowls and 'ladles'. So the cult houses, although made at least partly of wood and perhaps looking rather like domestic houses, have different assemblages which tie them more clearly to mortuary practices. On the other hand, there is an absence of the type of material found within the chambers of the tombs. There are no human bones and no axes, tools, and beads. Quite unlike the tombs, pottery is concentrated well within the interiors of the cult houses. This inversion of the tomb practices emphasizes the opposition between the inside and the outside of the tomb. But it is important to note that the tombs are sometimes concentrated around the cult houses, and that the cult houses may have played a necessary part in the progression from the outside domestic world to the inner sanctum of the stone passage grave chamber. Decorated pottery, pottery deposits in bogs, the fronts of tombs, and the cult houses are all linked to domestic activity but they have specific connotations of entrances and exits, public rituals and sacrifices. This is the world of neither the domus nor the agrios, but the foris. In the evidence I have discussed so far, the foris (the entrance to the domus) is opposed to an inner area associated with axes.

What occurred in the inner sanctum of the tomb? We have seen that in the chamber, artifacts include flint tools, flint axes and amber beads, at least some of which have a battle axe form, and small numbers of small pottery vessels. It is also in the chamber that human remains are found. In the early tombs most burials were of individuals. But there is clear evidence in many tombs that as more individuals were added not all body parts were included. Shanks and Tilley (1982) have suggested that the patterning in the presence and absence of human bones is not the result simply of differential survival of different parts of the human skeleton. It is uncertain exactly what the absence of skeletal parts means. Jensen (1982) suggests that the flesh was removed from bodies prior to placing some of the bones in the tomb, and Kaelas (1981) too notes that skeletal remains may have been placed in the burial chambers only after the bodies had lain for some time in another place. Human bones are found amongst refuse on settlement sites, as at Fannerup (Eriksen 1984) and in the interrupted ditch enclosures which appear at this time (see below). We know from later MN contexts that human bones on settlement sites may show evidence of burning and gnawing (Davidsen 1978). It is quite possible that the passage graves only received certain human bones at a late stage in the mortuary process. But another possibility is that much of the mixing and resorting of bones that is evident inside the chambers of some of the tombs results from reorganization of the bones after the flesh had rotted off within the tomb. However we look at the evidence, it is clear that one of the major activities that took place inside the chamber involved selection and sorting of human bones, and that these activities increased through time.

In a study of two tombs in southern Sweden, Shanks and Tilley (1982) have argued that the reordering of the human body in the tomb was extremely complex. As well as specific practices such as the arrangement of ribs, vertebrae, or femora, or the placing of skulls on both the upper and lower long bones, there was evidence of a differentiation between adult and immature remains and between left and right parts of the body. At the later tomb of Carlshögen in Sweden, this ordering of the bones is emphasized by the provision of stone boundaries within the chamber dividing the chamber and the bones into separate groups. Similar, if rather simpler, divisions also occur with Danish tombs.

There are a number of implications of the type of bone treatment observed in the inner sanctum of the tombs. Many of the megalithic graves were initially built for the burial of one person (e.g. Ebbesen 1979, 100). But through time, continuing into the later MN, more bodies were added and the communal became stressed over the individual. The individually identifiable flesh was allowed to rot off, and the bone was then reordered according to cultural rules. The end result was that the individual was lost within an impersonal cultural code. The inner sanctum, then, expressed the communal and the social in the same way that the construction of a large mound containing large stones must have involved communal labour by the social group.

The resorting of the bones was not only complex but it was also hidden. We have already seen the evidence of marking off, 'hiding' the activities of the tomb behind a facade in the EN long mounds. The MN passage graves also distance the inside from the outside and we have seen that certain mortuary practices (such as pot deposition) are frequently kept out of the tomb chamber. It is reasonable to argue, therefore, that there was a special domain of knowledge within the tomb. This esoteric knowledge concerned the relationships between the individual and society, the dead ancestors, and presumably the gods.

There is some evidence, although as yet it is slight, that this control of esoteric knowledge was associated particularly with the male. There is no difference in the 'richness' and variety of the artifacts placed in the passage graves and in contemporary flat graves. But Jensen (1982, 111) notes a heavy overrepresentation of men as opposed to women, and Randsborg (1986) has noted a similar pattern. In Zealand, Gibbs (1987) has noted a symbolic association between males, hide and wood-working, and agriculture through artifact associations. We have seen the inclusion of tools for such tasks within the chambers of the tombs. The battle axe beads within the chamber can be linked to men because of the close associations between battle axes and men that we have seen in Europe and will see later in Scandinavia. We have also seen the absence of male-associated tools from the votive deposits in front of the tombs and in the cult houses. Shanks and Tilley (1982) could not identify male/female differentiation in two southern Swedish tombs. It is possible that male bones often appear as overrepresented in tombs because female bones are less easy to distinguish from unsexed 'immature' bones.

We shall see below that the production of southern Scandinavian Corded Ware pots can be linked to women. We have also seen that in the Danubian tradition from which TRB pots derive, women are often linked symbolically to pottery. It is thus attractive to argue that the separation of tools from pots in the tombs represents a symbolic opposition between the male control of ancestors and esoteric knowledge (in the domus) and female control of the entrance to that knowledge (in the foris). If this structure is supported as further evidence is amassed, it will be apparent that the symbolic opposition does not imply a simplistic separation of gender activities. 'Male opposed to female' (cultural categories) does not equate with 'men opposed to women' (biological categories). Thus the bones of women do occur in the stone chambers. Women were clearly buried there and some of the tools and ornaments found in the chambers may have been deposited with women. Women may have played a role in the rites of the inner sanctum, and equally men may have taken a part in the rites of the cult house and tomb facade. Nevertheless the cultural categories (male/female) could be used socially and metaphorically in the control of inner space and of the entrances to that space. Although the male (back) and female (front) opposition will be supported by evidence that I shall consider in chapters 8 and 9, it should be emphasized that for southern Scandinavia, as for the Danubian province as a whole, there is as yet not enough evidence to support such an opposition strongly. It is nevertheless of interest to refer back to the evidence of central Europe where pottery could in one case be linked to the front of linear houses and where the elaboration of both decorated pottery and house entrances increased in tandem (pp. 105 and 135). Decorated pottery seems especially associated in central and northern Europe with the foris. And there is some evidence in southern Scandinavia that this front part of the domus might be more closely associated with the female than with the male. The more detailed Scandinavian evidence hints at what might have been expected in central Europe – that in contrast with SE Europe, the inner part of the house or tomb is associated metaphorically not with the female and elaborate pottery, but with the male. It is the foris (entrances and exits and the presentation of food in feasts and rituals) that is the focus of pottery decoration in central and northern Europe. It may also be relevant to refer back to the evidence from the Near East, where pottery decoration became more frequent when relationships between, rather than within, domestic units were stressed (chapters 1 and 2).

It would be nice also to have fuller evidence of other oppositions in Scandinavia which are weakly suggested by the existing data. It seems to me that the opposition between stone tools inside the chamber and pottery outside might be linked to an opposition between inner stone chamber and the earth mound around it (between stone and earth, axe and clay), or between inner stone burial chamber and outer wooden cult or domestic houses (between stone and wood). I have also discussed the possibility of making an opposition between dry bones inside the tomb and the wet flesh and bog deposits outside the tomb. We may also be able to begin to discuss the relationships between the placing of tombs below the ground (beneath a mound) and their orientation in relation to the sky, and between the dark inside and light outside. Thus we might have

inside(back)   male   axe   stone stone dry bones below dark
outside(front) female pottery earth wood wet flesh above light.

I mention the possibility of these additional meanings of the passage graves in order to intimate the potential richness of allusions and evocations that may lie within these monuments and in order to point to the need for further work in these domains. Although we cannot yet grasp the full significance of the tombs, it is likely that they meant many different things at one and the same time. Use of the tombs would have played upon and been empowered by the multivalent and ambiguous meanings. The dramas that were enacted there would have been evocative and many-layered.

Another aspect of the meanings of the tombs is a particular transformation of nature into culture – the central theme of the domus as expressed in central Europe. We have already seen that the natural flesh-covered body was transformed into a cultural product through the ordering and categorization of the human bones. The very practice of the construction of the tomb out of large rocks and soil represents a massive transformation of natural objects into a culturally ordered environment. Many of the tombs have evidence of burning, and this is a pattern that continues from the EN and which is repeated in the cult houses. Strömberg (1971) notes a number of tombs in Denmark and Sweden with charcoal layers at the front, although these may again be the result of clearing out from the chamber. The burning may have been involved in some cases in the removal of flesh from the bones. The use of fire to transform may well have played some role in the burial rites, adding to the drama. If we look at where else fire was used in Neolithic Scandinavia we see that it often involved transforming a natural into a cultural product – raw food into cooked food at the hearth, natural clay into ceramic product, and natural woodland into agricultural fields. The use of fire in the transformation of life into death has powerful evocative qualities, concerned with the transformation and cultural control of nature. It is even possible that some of the ard marks that are frequently found beneath MN barrows had a similar significance. It is often thought that the barrows were sometimes placed on disused agricultural fields, but careful stratigraphic excavation of a passage grave at Lundehøj (Ørsnes 1956) showed that the ard marks in the chamber, which ran in two directions, had been cut into a laid clay floor within the chamber. The marks had thus been made after the construction of the chamber and after the laying of the chamber floor. Due to the lack of space within the chamber the marks could not have been made with an animal-drawn plough. The scoring of the clay floor could have been part of the clearing out of this tomb, and further detailed study of other ard marks beneath tombs will demonstrate whether they really are ard marks and whether they have some ritual purpose (Rowley-Conwy 1987) in either preparing or leaving the tomb. Since in some cases the marks occur beneath the mound itself they may be related to the preparation of the tomb for use or to the construction of the mound (ibid.). If such marks can be shown to represent ploughing with an ard or another form of breaking the ground, the symbolism involves a particular transformation of nature into culture, perhaps allied with ideas concerning renewal.

Much of the above evidence is uncertain, but we can at least say that the linear monumentality of the tomb expresses a particular transformation of nature into a culturally controlled product. The large stones and mounds and the internal ordering of space and bones are enough to allow this assertion. The tombs thus recreate the central concept of the domus, in its central European form. The domus expresses the formation of social groups as a triumph of the cultural over the natural. The sheer size and permanence of the tombs, never mind all the other 'awesome' attributes that we have seen may have been associated with them, demonstrate the power of the social and the cultural over the wild and non-social. But the tomb does not only create society conceptually. It also creates social units and dependencies in its very construction, in the repeated votive deposit, and in the decision as to which bodies to include or exclude. In all these practices, the tomb-using group reforms itself and reforms more general principles which can be brought into play in other contexts.

One other context which is clearly drawn into the same web of meanings is provided by the ditched enclosures (e.g. figure 7.5)

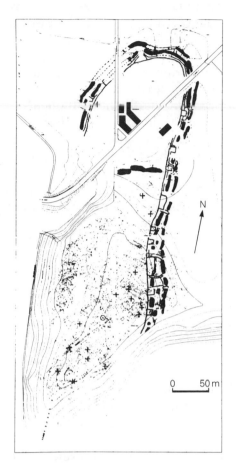

Figure 7.5 The causewayed enclosure at Sarup, Denmark. The phase 1 ditches are shown in black and phase 1 construction traces are shown as black dots. The smaller, phase 2 enclosure ditches are just visible, cutting off the southern part of the promontory.
(Source: N. Andersen 1988a)

which are mostly built in this same period (Madsen 1988). It is apparent that the tombs themselves formed larger groupings than the tomb-using group. Kaelas (1981) has provided instances of their clustered and particularly their linear arrangement in the landscape. As occurs within the tomb itself, the linear ordering of space creates social entities through the framework of the domus and the domus–foris relationship. But individual entities were also brought into larger groupings by participating in the construction and use of the enclosures with interrupted ditches (causewayed camps). The digging and/or toing and froing between these ditches created a unity out of separate parts. Most of the cultural material in the double ring of ditches at the Toftum site was found in the inner ditches (Madsen 1977). Some of the camps have palisades, and many are on promontories and have at least a symbolically defensive character.

Human bones occur in the ditches although not in the form of entire skeletons. It is possible, therefore, that the enclosures played some role in the sequence of mortuary practices. There is also evidence of large fires in the ditches, again recalling mortuary contexts, and deposits of whole pots (which also occur within the enclosures). Whole intact animal skeletons, or partially intact skeletons occur in the ditches and this pattern does not suggest normal domestic consumption. Feasting activity is often supposed. The interiors of the enclosures do not provide evidence of major occupational use contemporary with the ditches. The ditches often seem to have been deliberately backfilled after a short period of use, and this practice of backfilling, packing, or blocking is also found in relation to the tombs (e.g. Ørsnes 1956).

Both the tombs and the enclosures, at different scales, are concerned with the control of space, with exits and entrances, with the participation of individual units in monumental works, and at least in the former case with linear ordering. Both embody the ideas of the domus and the foris. Both attempt to create domination through strategies of inclusion and exclusion couched within the notion of the transformation of nature into culture. Not everyone was buried in a passage grave, since earth graves continue, and it is possible that not everyone had access to a causewayed enclosure. These monuments were probably constructed actively and competitively in order to attract and impress dispersed individual farmsteads, and to cement social relations of dependence and domination within the practices of construction and use of the tombs and camps. Madsen (1988) has noted that the enclosures often form the foci for later Middle Neolithic settlements. It is possible to argue, therefore, that the 'ritual' monument founded on the domus–foris opposition created the possibility for substantial settlement agglomeration (Hodder 1988). In other words, the idea of agglomeration was first generated or 'written' using existing structural principles (such as the domus–foris opposition). But the possibility of this 'writing' also depended on changing social and economic conditions.

This last point can be recognized in the early Middle Neolithic.

Houses remain relatively insubstantial. No house structures could be identified at Fannerup (Eriksen 1984), but a probable stationary settlement at Runegard East contained a 6 × 6 m house with post construction (Kempfner-Jørgensen and Watt 1985) and there is a small, possibly D-shaped hut from Hanstedgard (Eriksen and Madsen 1984). Many sites still do not comprise stable settlements, but in southern Sweden there appears to be some clustering of individual homesteads within a few kilometres of a tomb (Tilley 1984, 117). The appearance of interrupted enclosures in early MN is associated with more permanent settlement occupation and thicker occupation levels, and an increase in the size and number of settlements (Madsen 1982). Thus, the elaboration of the domus–foris seen in tombs, bog deposits, cult houses, pottery decoration, and causewayed enclosures is dialectically related to greater aggregation, greater social constraint, and also economic intensification. There is a gradual increase in the proportion of barley in botanical remains, and cattle increases in several assemblages at the expense of pig. The cattle may have been used for meat rather than dairying (Rowley-Conwy 1984). The overall result of this mixed and more intensive agricultural economy is that at least initially in MN Denmark there is evidence of deforestation in pollen diagrams (Madsen 1982). More stable and larger settlement aggregations become possible. The economic domain may have been linked to social strategies through the principles of the domus. Although hunting camps continue in Denmark (Madsen 1981), the amount of wild bones on most sites is relatively low. The emphasis is on the transformation of the natural into the cultural. The changing economic practices may thus take their place within a social and cultural strategy. The formation of social groups through the practice and drama of the tombs and enclosures grew out of and manipulated the practice and meaning of an economic culture. Again, the domus and domestication are connected.

Nevertheless, the important shift of the domus from the domestic context to the tomb, a shift for which the development of agriculture in southern Scandinavia had had to wait, allowed a relative independence to small settlement units. I have suggested that in Europe as a whole a decline in the symbolic elaboration of the house was linked to a shift of the domus away from the domestic unit. The house-using group was perhaps becoming contradictory to the strategies of the larger social units. But elsewhere in Europe, the decline of the importance of the house was associated with a decline in the

Figure 7.6 Early MN TRB bowls and ladles from the cult house at Tustrup.
(Source: Kjaerum 1955)

symbolic elaboration of pottery. I have so far avoided the fact that
Scandinavian early MN pottery is one of the most richly decorated
pottery forms in the European Neolithic (figure 7.6). Why was it
so elaborate when the domestic houses with which it is associated
were so simple?

It is often forgotten by archaeologists, absorbed in their typological arguments about the decoration on the outsides of the pots, that
the primary purpose of pottery is usually for food and drink. Indeed,
one of the major limitations I have found with the data in writing
this book is that so little work has been done on food residues in
European Neolithic pots that contextual interpretation is severely
hampered. Nevertheless, in the Scandinavian early MN, we are
drawn to the link between pottery and food by the frequent associations of pots with evidence for feasting. We have seen such a link
in the bog deposits of the EN and early MN and in the ditches of
the enclosures. The non-domestic contexts of cult houses and passage
grave facades are particularly linked by their high frequencies of

'ladles' and pedestalled bowls with especially elaborate decoration. Whatever the specific functions of the ladles, it is likely that they were used for some type of presenting, mixing, or formalized preparing of food. The two types are not common in settlement contexts. Rather they, and other especially well decorated forms are associated with public rituals including feasting and with the entrances and exits of public monuments. Tilley (1984) and Ebbesen (1975) provide good quantitative evidence in Sweden and Denmark respectively for a concentration of decoration outside the domestic context, in relation to the monuments. So it is not so much the domestic context which is being elaborated in the pottery decoration. Rather, the emphasis is on the drama of the presentation of food at the entrances to communal rituals. Certainly the domus was contributed to by the domestic unit. Decorated pottery does occur in settlements and domesticated plants and animals were presumably cared for there in preparation for the public feasts. But pottery became especially elaborate when it was linked to the foris in a non-domestic public arena, where emphasis was on the entrances to ceremonial structures, and on the welcoming and drawing in of individuals through the metaphor and practice of providing and sharing food.

Similar practices were probably associated with ditched enclosures and long mounds elsewhere in Europe. Why was southern Scandinavian pottery so particularly decorated and elaborate? Part of the answer is simply that pottery decoration there had not been linked historically to the domestic context as strongly as it had been in central Europe. We saw in Ertebølle contexts that it was in the non-domestic world that symbolism was heightened by decorating objects. Yet the specific link of decoration and the foris is not obvious in Ertebølle contexts. Earlier in Europe we have seen decoration linked to the foris in both the domestic context and in communal enclosures. In Scandinavia this general idea is transferred specifically to the arena of public rituals. Ultimately it is not possible to explain the Scandinavian TRB decoration by reference to a set of conditions or causes. The elaborate decoration in Scandinavia was a creative, interpretive act – a transfer to a particular context of commonly found European ideas. All we can do is identify the conditions which made and make the act understandable. Thus the emphasis on pottery decoration in public feasts makes sense in a context in which groups are involved in competitive food offerings, in a context in which food giving is linked to a concept such as the foris, in a context in which the foris is linked to the public, non-domestic sphere, and in a local context in which pottery decoration has not been strongly linked historically to the domestic world.

So far I have suggested that agriculture was adopted in southern Scandinavia as part of a larger cultural and social package permeated by the domus principle. Social dependencies could be formed in the construction and use of tombs which expressed the imposition of a cultural order in contrast to dispersed individual settlements. In the early MN the domus–foris ordering and controlling was increasingly evident in the back–front organization of tomb activities, in the decorated pottery, cult houses, and enclosures. Wet areas too were enmeshed within the same set of ordered principles. From tomb practices to economic organization, an intensified 'culturing' of nature can be seen. That this was primarily a social process is suggested by the gradual appearance of more stable and village-like occupation. Both at the level of the tombs and the enclosures larger social units could be 'domesticated' through an elaboration of the domus–foris–agrios ideas.

Certain local groups were more competent than others in their manipulation of the principles of the domus. In some areas there are ditched enclosures and dense clusters of tombs, while in other areas enclosures and tombs may be absent or scarce. The whole process is a competitive one. Any attempt to increase group size must involve attempts to control access to people and resources. We have seen the evidence for agricultural intensification, and it is important to note that causewayed enclosures frequently have a defensive appearance. Skeletal evidence for warring or fighting is discussed by Randsborg (1986).

I have argued in this book that the need to defend the domus and the general idea of domesticating the agrios created or sustained forces that must ultimately erode the domus. In the rest of this chapter I wish to consider the rather fuller data on this transformation that are found in Scandinavia. We have seen that from the Scandinavian EN, battle axes are found, and in the MN these continue (figure 7.7). It should be emphasized that the stone battle axes with shaft-holes have little to do with the flat flint axes of the same period. The latter have woodcutting and ceremonial functions linked closely to the range of activities and monuments that I have so far been considering. The battle axes, on the other hand, do not have clear utilitarian functions and it is extremely difficult to allocate them a place within either the domestic context or the domus. Ebbesen (1975) has classified the battle axes into types which have the chrono-

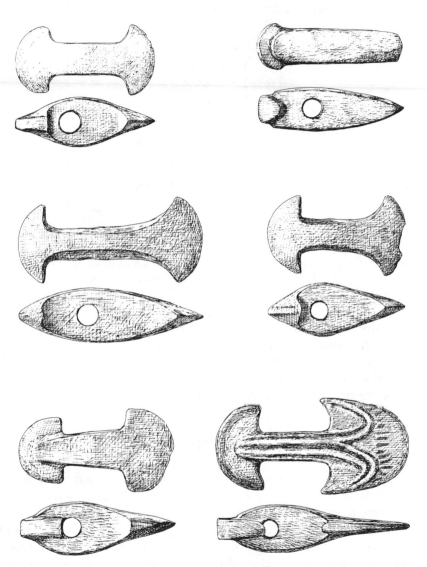

Figure 7.7 Examples of Scandinavian TRB MN battle axes.
(Source: Ebbesen 1975)

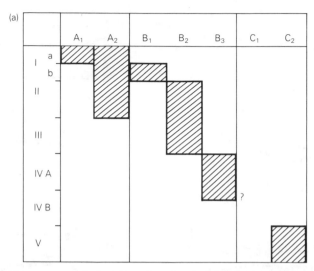

Figure 7.8 (this page and facing) Scandinavian double-edged battle axes: (a) chronological distribution (I–V) of the types (A1 to C2);

logical distribution shown in figure 7.8. In MN I–II it is clear from
this that the battle axes in Denmark are mainly found as stray objects
or in bogs. They are not common in tombs or settlements. Through
time, however, it is clear that the pattern changes, and battle axes
are increasingly deposited at the tomb.

MN III–V

Pottery ceases to be deposited outside the tombs, and it becomes
less decorated. This correlation between the disappearance of pottery
from formalized public dramas (since, as we shall see, bog deposits
and causewayed camps have also largely ceased by this time) and
the decrease in pottery decoration, supports the assertion made
earlier that the decoration of the Scandinavian pottery is linked to
its role in public rituals.

In place of pots at the tombs we find flint axes and battle axes.
Thick butted flint axes are often found outside Scandinavian megaliths (Liversage 1980), and as is clear from figure 7.8, battle axes are
increasingly deposited in megaliths even though megaliths cease to be

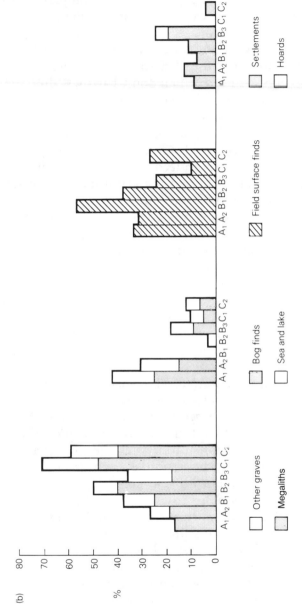

(b)

Figure 7.8(b) percentage distribution of the battle axe types in different find contexts.
(Source: Ebbesen 1975)

constructed. Through time, too, the battle axes become increasingly elaborate as the pottery decreases in stylistic complexity. Overall, the foris food-providing and feasting component in the tomb is being replaced by an increased emphasis on warring and fighting symbols of the agrios and heavy cutting tools. (If there is any validity to the stone–wood opposition noted earlier (p. 199), the decline in the use of timber chambers within earthen long barrows after the Early Neolithic and the more general use of stone chambers may prefigure the increased association of stone axes with the tombs.)

Bog offerings cease by the beginning of this period and causewayed camps are no longer constructed. Cult houses of the type found in MNI–II largely go out of use. Indeed, the concurrent disappearance of camps, bog offerings, elaborate pottery decoration, offerings in front of tombs, and cult houses, reinforces the evidence already discussed that a set of principles existed between all these monuments and activities. In contrast, during this later MN period the ordering of bones inside the tombs into categories and oppositions continues and increases in importance (e.g. Tilley 1984). The taking of further bodies through the passage into the tomb, removing the flesh, and reordering the individual bones into an impersonal code, establishes the centrality of the domus, but in a changing idiom. The domus remains and is re-emphasized at the core but, to put it oversimplistically and uncautiously, domus–foris is increasingly being replaced by domus–agrios.

Further insight into the way in which aspects of the non-domus begin to take over the domus is provided by the 'stone-packing graves' (Becker 1959) which are found in this phase (MNIII–V). This type of grave, more found in western Denmark rather than in eastern Denmark where more of the passage graves are located, consists of what appears to be a simple earth grave covered by a heap or layer of stones but with few bones surviving. The graves frequently occur in pairs or in rows (figure 7.9). Associated with each pair is usually a small mortuary house, itself constructed from a pair of uprights and covered with stones. There may, however, be up to six graves with one mortuary house.

The stone-packing graves have some strong affinities with passage graves and the principles of the domus. They are often arranged in long linear patterns, and at Vroue Hede they are aligned in relation to a passage grave (figure 7.9). In addition, the mortuary houses seem to have fulfilled a similar function to the earlier cult houses. Like the cult houses they are spatially close to graves. In Davidsen's

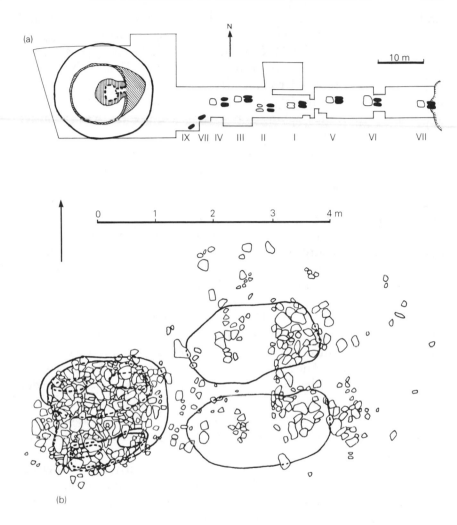

Figure 7.9 Stone packing graves (a) aligned outside the entrance to a tomb at Vroue
Hede, Jutland
(Source: Kaelas 1981)
and (b) as in this example from Fjelsø.
(Source: Madsen 1975)

(1978) survey of MNV in Denmark, he found that pottery associated
with stone-packing graves is rare but is most commonly found in
the mortuary house (six finds) although it does also occur in the
graves (two finds) or outside the mortuary house and grave (two

finds). If this preferred association between mortuary houses and pottery is supported in more adequately-sized samples, it suggests a continuity from earlier MN practices in which pottery was associated with cult houses and the outsides of tombs. That such a continuity will be confirmed by the data is strongly suggested by the information from Engedal in Denmark, where the mortuary house associated with stone-packing graves is placed directly over an earlier cult house (Faber 1977).

In the above ways, the stone-packing graves continue the earlier traditions of the domus–foris. A collective social entity is created through the linear ordering of space. The ordering is sometimes aligned in relation to a higher authority, such as the ancestors within an earlier passage grave (figure 7.9). Like the later use of the passage graves, the stone-packing graves contain large numbers of axes in contrast to the relatively rare pottery (Becker 1959). Indeed, the stone-packing graves, in addition to continuing the earlier passage grave tradition, also express quite a different concept. As Becker (ibid.) notes, the idea of packing a grave with stones is found in earth graves of the earlier MN and in the EN. We have also seen the placing of stones in a male grave in an Ertebølle context. Single earth graves continued throughout the construction and use of megalithic monuments. They represent a more individualistic practice which we will find developing more fully in the following Corded Ware period, where again single graves filled with stones occur (e.g. Randsborg 1986). In the later TRB MN, however, an increased importance for this individualistic type of grave was created through existing principles.

So far we have seen that in certain spheres the early MN principles of the domus were continued, if given a new significance, in the later MN. The main developments which occur as part of the transformation are the collapse of many aspects of the domus–foris ritual, the increased elaboration and incorporation of battle axes, and an increase in individual burial alongside the complex communal ordering within the chambers of the passage graves. This same opposition between a continuation of the domus and increasing evidence of its demise is seen in the settlement and economic evidence. On the one hand, barley and cattle continue to increase and this more intensive economy is associated with larger and richer settlement sites (Madsen 1981). As was suggested in relation to the earlier MN, the occurrence of later settlements within ditched enclosures as at Sarup, implies the ability of the drama of the domus to be used to form economic and settlement groupings. At the household level, small slight houses continue so that often they escape archaeological recovery (e.g. Larsson 1983). At Grødby, Bornholm, two rectangular houses were found, one of which was clearly 7 × 13 m and had a central row of main posts plus two slighter side rows (Kempfner-Jørgensen and Watt 1985). The impression gained here of a will to create some larger and more substantial houses is reinforced by evidence from another Bornholm house at Limensgard (Nielsen and Nielsen 1985). Here a similar arrangement of central posts is associated with a house which is at least 6 × 18–19 m. Some aspects of the domus were clearly continuing. On the other hand, the late MN settlement pattern became increasingly diversified in some areas. Although Davidsen (1978) argues that there is no evidence for population increase at this time, he identifies six types of MNV site: home bases with mainly domestic animals, settlements with a mixed economy including the use of wild resources, shell middens, manufacturing sites (for example, for axes or stone tools), transit sites, and kill sites with mainly wild animal bones (for example, related to the killing of the grey seal during its breeding season). Madsen (1988) suggests that during the MN the fishing, hunting, and gathering special activity camps typical of the EN gradually disappear to be replaced by less specialized sites.

I have characterized the domus in central Europe and southern Scandinavia as fundamentally concerned with a particular way of separating the cultural from the natural, domesticating the wild. After the time when the megalithic tombs, the main vestiges of the domus ethic, have ceased to be constructed (in MNII), the Pitted Ware culture appears (probably in MNIV–V, see Rasmussen 1984) with sites heavily dependent on wild resources. The Pitted Ware is part of a wider Baltic phenomenon, and in the Netherlands a related development is termed the Vlaardingen culture (e.g. Bakker 1982). In Scandinavia, the Pitted Ware (Becker 1950) is distinctively associated with coastal resources. Pottery is pointed based with an angular profile and decorated with pits and comb impressions. While the Pitted Ware sites, which continue and are also contemporary with the early Corded Ware sites (see below), are clearly linked to the use of wild resources, the status of these sites in relation to the later MN sites is unclear (Nielsen 1979; Rasmussen 1984). Certainly there is much evidence of interaction between Pitted Ware and later MN sites (Larsson 1982 and 1983; Nielsen and Nielsen 1985). In relation to the Corded Ware, Tilley (1982) argues for an ethnic distinction. In relation to the TRB MN, however, the nature of the difference between agricultural and Pitted Ware hunter-gatherer-fisher sites is uncertain. Were the Pitted Ware sites seasonally occupied by the inhabitants of TRB sites, or were the two types of site occupied concurrently by different groups? Whatever further evidence shows to be the answers to these questions, Pitted Ware sites such as Kainsbakke (Rasmussen 1984) have an undoubted mixed economy in which rigid culture–nature distinctions are not easily found.

Overall then, if we consider the later southern Scandinavian TRB as a whole, including its many regional manifestations, I have shown an increasing centrality of aspects related to warring and the wild. The social and symbolic power of the domus in the EN and early MN depended on the idea and practice of monumental intervention in nature and the control of exits and entrances. But already the power of the domus idea depended on metaphorical references to the outside and the wild (the agrios) as seen in the emphasis on bounding or (symbolic) defence in the enclosures and in the occurrence of battle axe amber beads in the tombs. The domus and the domus–foris are redefined in Scandinavia in relation to the agrios and to a more dispersed settlement pattern and associated economic system. The more that the domus was used to create social prestige, more intensive economies, and larger and more stable settlements, the more did the agrios have to be referred to and opposed in establishing authority through the domus and the more could the agrios come to be used as an alternative metaphor for social control. In any case the economic system in southern Scandinavia had historically tended to incorporate extensive use of a wide range of environments. Thus, on the one hand there is increasing emphasis on the use of the tomb chambers as ossuaries in the later MN. On the other hand, this emphasis on the domus, the communal, the culturally ordered, is increasingly associated with battle axes. The stone-packing graves also demonstrate the transition well since the old scheme of the linear ordering of space is used but is associated with individual burial outside the context of monumental, communally constructed tombs. In one region, the Pitted Ware shows the full incorporation of aspects of the agrios in the patterning of its subsistence remains and an incorporation of the wild in the domestic domain may occur elsewhere.

As the domus–agrios increasingly replaced the domus–foris, and as the agrios became increasingly the central idiom of social power, the material symbols of the older system were rejected. The causewayed camps were dismantled and the communal feasting stopped. Tombs were no longer constructed but they continued to be used. Like the ditches of the big enclosures before them, the tombs were in the later MN, Corded Ware, and late Neolithic phases cleared out, or blocked and packed with earth (e.g. Ørsnes 1956).

Corded Ware

Even when the Corded Ware battle axe material is considered, some traces of the old domus principles can be found. After all, mounds are still constructed even though they are less monumental and constructed over dead individuals rather than over chambers that can repeatedly be visited and added to (Kristiansen 1982, 1984). There is less the idea of sequence through time or linear sequence from front to back. However, temporal sequence is retained in the construction of series of graves, from the bottom upwards, in the round mounds (figure 7.10), and in the addition of secondary graves into the mounds. Corded Ware material (termed Single Grave in Denmark) is also found within the chambers of older passage graves, as for example at Vedsted (Ebbesen 1979), even though the blocking or closing of passage graves may sometimes be linked to Corded Ware activities (ibid.). Thus despite the increased emphasis on the burial of individuals associated with a personal array of artifacts, the

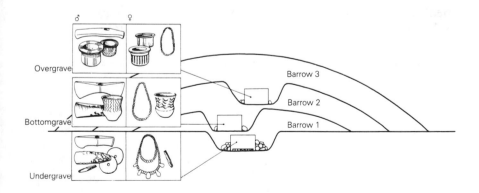

Figure 7.10 Cross-section of a typical Single Grave barrow.
(Source: Kristiansen 1984)

organization of the burial rite still refers back to the monumental, the collective and the sequential. The barrows are often arranged in long lines, thus reasserting the linearity concept. There is also a possibility that the Corded Ware tombs still refer to houses, since several of the circular mounds are placed on MNV settlements. Stones (non-megalithic) are often still packed into the graves. At least we can say that overall, there is a strong emphasis in Corded Ware burial on legitimating new social strategies within older structures.

The new strategies also involve bringing an end to old ideas. As already noted, passage graves may be closed or cleared out (Kjaerum 1967) at this time. Indeed the emphasis on the control of esoteric knowledge about the ordering of human bones within the inner sanctum of tombs disappears. There is little emphasis on the transformation of the natural into the cultural. Rather, the body is placed, without the removal of flesh, in a simple grave associated with artifacts which directly express the social standing of the deceased.

It is particularly gender distinctions that can be identified. Male graves are associated with weapons and female graves with jewellery but also with small polished working axes (Randsborg 1986). More specifically, men are often found in the graves with a battle axe by the face, a beaker presumably containing some form of liquor, a flint axe, and amber. Women are buried, sometimes with hundreds of amber beads, and a beaker (Kristiansen 1984). Men are normally placed on their right and women on their left, both looking south (ibid.). In southern Sweden, there is limited physical anthropological evidence which suggests that battle axes and horn daggers mark men's graves, and amber pendants women's graves (Tilley 1982, 21). A large-scale quantitative study of Corded Ware graves there has shown a general distinction between graves with pottery and flint blades and graves with battle axes and thick-bladed axes (ibid., 22). Although such a distinction may be partly related to social differences other than gender, it is of interest that the Swedish Corded Ware allows us to make a rare link between gender and pottery decoration. An unusually rich and varied grave from Bedinge contained two young adult women, with four fine ceramic vessels, two polished flint work axes, four flint blades, three bodkins of bone, a copper ear ornament, more than 100 amber beads, and a few bones of sheep. In addition there was a small comb-shaped instrument which was probably used for making the comb impressions on the pottery (Randsborg 1986).

Male associations appear to dominate the burial evidence. For the Corded Ware culture in Denmark, Jensen (1982, 169) notes that 75 per cent of the approximately 500 graves known are male graves, on the basis of the grave goods. Randsborg (1986) suggests that women appear less frequently in graves in the Corded Ware than in earlier phases. Even if many of these 'male' graves actually contain women, it seems as if warring has become a dominant ethic in burial ritual, continuing the increased prevalence of battle axes found in the TRB MN burials. There is also evidence from Sweden of an associated emphasis on hunting and the wild. Of the animal bones (often artifacts) in the Corded Ware graves, over 50 per cent represent wild animals, roe and red deer predominating (Tilley 1984, 120). The domestic species represented are pig and sheep or goat.

This evidence for a high percentage of wild animal bones in Corded Ware burials provides an unreliable indicator of the overall Corded Ware economy in Sweden and Denmark. Ard marks occur under barrows, and in Sweden barrows and probably associated settlements are limited to high-quality, tractable, arable soils (ibid., 121), even though there is some evidence for inland expansion. There is some doubt about whether the pollen evidence for increased clearance at this time in southern Sweden and Denmark can be directly tied to Corded Ware activities (Larsson 1983). At what may have been a temporary grazing station at Kalvø, the small faunal assemblage supports Rowley-Conwy's (1985) assertion that cattle continued to be produced for meat rather than as part of a dairy economy.

There is quite a high proportion of red deer and other wild animals at Kalvø. In general the Corded Ware settlement pattern sees the disappearance of the larger settlements found in later MN. Little groups of three to four small rectangular houses were increasingly scattered across a more open landscape, and in Denmark there was a more western, inland focus than had been associated with the MN passage graves. The continuation of the Pitted Ware sites in coastal regions allowed further early Corded Ware involvement in wild resources, either through exchange or direct exploitation.

By the time the Corded Ware phase is reached in Scandinavia, most of the attributes of the domus have moved off the centre of the archaeological stage. Houses are slight, small, and internally simple (Simonsen 1986). Larger settlements, either bounded or unbounded, have disappeared. Large mounds, megalithic, and monumental architecture have disappeared or declined. The linear control of space between back and front has largely ceased. The transformation of culture into nature seems less important. Battle axes, warring, and the wild seem to play a more central role. In certain respects, the Corded Ware rites continue the non-megalithic practices that had always existed side by side with the megalithic tombs and monumental architecture. This antithesis now turned thesis, involved individual burial and ultimately the model of the warrior or hunter.

I have suggested that many aspects of the Corded Ware burial rites incorporate the dominant earlier traditions of the domus. The stronger life-taking ethic is legitimated through and partly derives from the domus itself. Some aspects of the older emphasis on linear sequences, monumentalism, and the domestic arena are retained in the new burial rites. Pottery decoration plays a renewed role in ritual contexts and it seems likely that it was produced by or closely linked to women. Decorated pottery is also found on settlement sites. We have seen the general absence of the 'female' in the burial context, but it seems that, as in the TRB, the 'female' and the 'domestic' continued to contribute an important, if increasingly subsidiary role in public ritual. The importance of decoration and ornament in the non-domestic sphere is a theme that has continued in southern Scandinavia since the Ertebølle. Equally, axes have always been linked to male prestige, and we have often found axes opposed to pottery. It is as if there is really nothing new in the Scandinavian Corded Ware. All the cultural principles are old ones. The Corded Ware is new but the old antitheses remain.

Overall, and oversimplistically, in southern Scandinavia I have argued for dialectical movements between domus and agrios and between these conceptual structures and their social and economic equivalents. Initially the spread of agriculture into Scandinavia is enabled by a shift in the meaning of the domus in central Europe which allows a greater role to the agrios. In the EN in Scandinavia this shift allows disaggregated social and economic strategies. But it also allows the domus to be introduced and to be used as the basis for group formation and competitive strategies. As a result, in the early MN, the domus and domus–foris are reasserted over the agrios. Aggregation and intensification occur as components in the attempts made by dominant groups to increase production and success in feasting and exchange. These processes ultimately lead to a wider use of environments, defence, warring, and an opportunity for the pursuit of new social strategies based on the idiom of the agrios. Each synthesis appears only to reformulate the relationship between thesis and antithesis.

8

Dames and Axes: Parallel Lines of Development in Northern France

I have so far suggested that the metaphor of the house was used to create two rather different social themes in south-east and central Europe, both of which I have termed domus. I have shown how the central European version of the domus was transformed still further in northern Europe. The purpose of this and the following chapter is to interpret the transformations that took place in northern France and England parallel to the Scandinavian sequence.

It has become commonplace in European prehistory to note similarities between Neolithic cultural material in Scandinavia, France, England, and elsewhere along the Atlantic facade. A debate has continued concerning the unity of the megalithic phenomenon in these areas and the nature of the contact between them. The main question has been 'do the megalithic burials from each region arise independently or as a result of diffusion?' Probably the safest contemporary answer to this question is 'a bit of both'. Certainly, early dates from Ireland, Brittany, and Iberia and the evidence of local developments in all regions suggest the possibility of independent origins, while the similarities in the burial rites between, for example, Scandinavia and Britain speak no less eloquently of the diffusion of ideas.

The approach taken in this chapter is rather different. In chapters 5 and 6 I described the main characteristics of the central European domus as monumentality, linear grading of space, the control of entrances and exits, and orientation. All these characteristics are present in the Danubian long house, but they are gradually extended to the burial domain. In the extension of farming to northern France and England, I will argue that the domus is again used as a medium for action. The domus provides the currency in which different problems are perceived and dealt with. Since the underlying logic does not determine action, the results of social endeavour are never precisely equivalent. Different answers are found to the same problems. But the underlying scheme by which those answers are found can still be recognized. It surfaces in different ways in different areas. We shall see that the domus is expressed differently in the Paris Basin, Brittany, and England. Even within one region there is considerable variety. Yet despite this contextual variation there is clear evidence that the central European domus, gradually changing itself, provides the common underlying scheme of things.

Thus the similarities between the megalithic and collective monuments found in northern and western Europe do not so much result from diffusion along the Atlantic facade as from a common cultural background. And the differences between the different regions do not so much result from independent origins as they do from the inherent non-determining nature of cultural logics. The aim of including parts of France and Britain in this book is thus to explore these ideas. But there are other reasons for including additional areas. For example, since the underlying structures 'surface' differently in different areas, the more data that can be considered, the more can the generating structures be understood. The Paris Basin material is important in supporting the hesitant attempts I have made so far to understand male–female oppositions within the domus. Another reason for including France and Britain is that without them my story remains unfinished. We shall see the domus rising beyond burial to still further heights of abstraction and collective ritual.

For many parts of the French and British sequences, detailed chronologies remain imperfectly understood. The data are often dogged by survival problems. For example, human bones have not survived well in the Breton tombs because of soil conditions. Settlements associated with the SOM in the Paris Basin have scarcely been investigated, and the same is generally true of all phases in Brittany. In England, too, the study of settlement organization is based on little secure foundation, and many burial monuments were excavated prior to the development of adequate recording standards. Much of the discussion provided below will thus be particularly provisional.

The Paris Basin and Adjacent Areas

The first phase of the Neolithic in the Paris Basin is Danubian in character and some of the data has already been discussed in chapters

5 and 6. Linear houses and late Linear Pottery occur from 4100 bc and there is gradual cultural change through Rössen-related groups such as Cerny to Late Rössen assemblages as, for example, at Berry-au-Bac. This local Danubian sequence (see table 1) ends around 3300 bc (Ilett 1983; Bailloud 1979).

The overall Danubian sequence in the Paris Basin is similar to that found in central Europe. The Linear Pottery site at Cuiry-les-Chaudardes has already been discussed (figure 5.7). The lack of overlap between houses at this site and the overall coherence of the site plan perhaps result from the late start to the Linear Pottery culture in this area and a resulting shorter period of occupation than in some central European sites (Ilett et al. 1986). Two-fifths of all the artifact material from this site derives from three big houses (ibid.), so indicating the differentiation between houses noted elsewhere. But the dominant patterning on the site is linear, as seen both in the linear houses themselves and their adjacent linear pits, and in the rows of houses within the settlement. The principles of the domus are clearly being used to define and order social groups.

Through time, there is increased emphasis on the definition and defence of larger social groupings. An interrupted ditch enclosure has been discovered at Menneville with a Linear Pottery date (Ilett et al. 1986, 133) and defended sites occur in Cerny and in Late Rössen contexts (Bailloud 1979), as at Berry-au-Bac (figure 5.8). As elsewhere, therefore, the larger social entities are formed out of a desire to control entrances and exits as is found in the linear ordering of space within houses. However, larger community production increasingly conflicts with the cultural emphasis on the household. Through time, the centrality of the house declines. Through Cerny and into Late Rössen, houses decrease in size and elaboration until at Berry-au-Bac they are simple two-roomed affairs. Domestic pottery is typically well decorated, but at the end of the Danubian sequence, around 3300 bc, domestic pottery becomes largely undecorated (see below).

There is some remarkable evidence from an area adjacent to the Paris Basin which further demonstrates the extension of the domus away from the house to other domains – in this case to burial. Over recent years, air photography over the Yonne area in Burgundy has revealed what initially appeared to be enigmatic linear marks (figure 8.1). Given the emphasis on linearity that I have read into the European Neolithic in this book, it would have been a good guess that these monuments were Neolithic and Danubian-influenced. Indeed, excavations have shown that the monuments at Passy are funerary in character and that they have a late Danubian, especially Cerny date (Thevenot 1985; Duhamal and Presteau 1987).

Adjacent to the 25 linear monuments is an occupation site with small rectangular houses and post-Linear Pottery including Cerny material. It is possible, however, to argue, as I have done in chapter 6, that the Passy linear tombs continue the principles found in earlier houses. The Passy monuments are long (20–250 m). They expand towards one end, which is always towards the east. Burials occur along the central axis, particularly at the eastern end. While the similarities with long houses are again clear, it was found elsewhere in Europe that the Danubian contribution to the construction of linear mounds remained conjectural. At Passy, however, the Danubian influence is evident in the associated material culture and in the continued use of the Danubian practice of individual burial, with the body often laid out in a typically Danubian style (Thevenot 1985). The evidence thus suggests that the extension of the domus into the burial domain was an internally generated process.

The Passy evidence also resolves another problem concerning the extension of the domus. I argued in earlier chapters that the same underlying principles generated both rectilinear forms (linear houses and long mounds) and circular enclosures. The reasoning behind this rather unlikely conjuncture was that the approach towards the centre of a multiple or single ditched enclosure with multiple entrances involved linear movement from outside to inside. In addition, both types of site are monumental and there is a similar emphasis on exits and entrances. The separate circular enclosures to the east of the long enclosures at Passy, seen in figure 8.1, are of Bronze Age and Iron Age date. But at the eastern end of several of the long enclosures themselves, circular enclosures close in date to the long enclosures are found. Indeed, some of these circular enclosures seem to be integral to the long enclosures. Some have interrupted ditches. The Passy evidence thus supports the idea that very different shapes of monument (linear or round) can be produced by the same underlying logic. We shall see more of this in Brittany. But for the moment it should be emphasized that the underlying principles are not simply dry and logical. They are also dramatic in nature. The linear monuments at Passy, expanding towards the eastern end, draw attention to that end and to the burials placed there. The linearity of the monument grades space and limits access sequentially. The circular monuments act as the foci of that sequential movement and add to the drama of enclosure and control. It is through that drama that

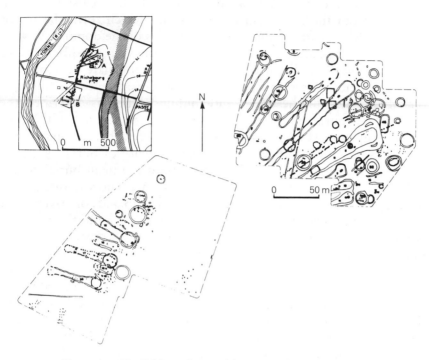

Figure 8.1 Neolithic and protohistoric enclosures at Passy.
(Source: Thevenot 1985)

the domus–foris principles are used to create social groupings and dependencies beyond those centred on the household. Burial monuments are used to extend the domestication metaphor to death and the ancestors. The domestication of death is a metaphor for the domestication of society. Renewed and enhanced in the drama of death and burial, the domus–foris ideas provide the framework of meaning within which larger or closer social groupings can be formed and linked over the longer term to the lineal ancestors. Through time, as groups compete in production, reproduction, and exchange and in feasting and funerary ceremonies couched in domus–foris terms, the monuments are reused and enlarged. At Passy there is evidence of the drama, linearity, and monumentality of the tombs being increased as extensions are added to the back, western ends (Duhamal and Presteau 1987).

In the Chassey-Michelsberg sites in the Paris Basin which develop from the Danubian cultures in the late fourth and early third millennia bc, it is the defended or interrupted ditch enclosures which continue from the Danubian examples and which form the major focus for the transformation of the principles of the domus. As with the Michelsberg culture in the Rhineland, the Chassey-Michelsberg culture in the Paris Basin does not see an immediate development of linear tombs. A recent survey of the sparse evidence for burial in the Michelsberg of the upper and middle Rhine has described the evidence for burial within pits and ditches in association with domestic occupation (Lichardus 1986). Similar evidence occurs in the Paris Basin (Bailloud 1979). The overall paucity of burials suggests that some form of exposure may have been the main burial rite.

On the other hand, substantial 'camps' are known, often with interrupted ditches and palisades, and in upland or river spur locations appropriate for defence. As well as domestic activities carried out at these sites, there is some evidence of special activities in that the high camps provide the main find-spots in the Paris Basin for the so-called vase-supports. These ceramic objects are of special interest for a number of reasons. First, they were probably not used as vase-supports since traces of burning indicate some function to do with lamps or incense burners. Second, in Brittany they came largely from funerary monuments or stone circles indicating a ritual use. Third, they are heavily decorated in contrast to all other types of Paris Basin Chassey-Michelsberg pottery. It is perhaps also relevant that the few stylized female figurines from this period in the Paris Basin are also undecorated. Whatever the full range of activities carried out at the camps, they appear also to have been foci of non-domestic specialized rituals. Decoration has shifted from domestic pottery (in Danubian phases) to a ceramic type used in specialized rituals within larger monuments. These camps draw together larger groups, and emphasize exits and entrances to those groups. As part of this new process, houses become slight and there is little evidence of elaboration of the domestic context.

As we have seen elsewhere in Europe, the camps themselves introduce subtle changes to the domus. Not only does the role of domestic symbolism decline, but also the emphasis on defence leads to a new relationship with the non-domus 'other'. Prowess *in* the wild as opposed to control *over* nature takes on a renewed significance. The roles of the warrior and hunter and the idiom of the agrios become revalued, placed at the centre of social discourse. In the Chassey-Michelsberg phase, sites are found over an increasingly wide range of environments, but there is only slight evidence of an increased use of wild resources (Bailloud 1979; Burkill 1983a). Pollen evidence does not indicate massive forest clearance at this time (Burkill 1983a, 47). It is in the following SOM (Seine-Oise-Marne) phase, that there is good evidence of extensive clearance, a major expansion and dispersal of settlement, and an increased importance of hunting (Howell 1983). SOM assemblages are characterized by large numbers of finely worked arrowheads, while carefully produced flint daggers also occur. One of the distinctive symbols found in the art at this period is the antler-hafted axe, and the antler hafts themselves are found as perhaps the most distinctive cultural indicators of the SOM.

Given the new centrality of the agrios found in the SOM at the end of the third millennium bc, it is as expected that not only do houses remain slight and difficult to identify but also the camps cease to be constructed. But, as we have seen elsewhere, the domus is not abandoned. It is used as the medium for creating the new sense of order. Indeed, although the older form of the domus has lost much of its real power by the time of the SOM, the domus retains an important symbolic role in creating the new, 'more individualistic, closer relationship with the wild. In other words, although strategies of inclusion and exclusion have lost much of their central social focus by the end of the third millennium bc, the new idiom is itself made possible through continuation of these earlier principles.

I hope to demonstrate this complex relationship between continuity and change, between the reversal and retention of older structures, by considering the allées couvertes of the SOM in the Paris Basin, and to some extent in adjacent areas. Indeed, consideration of these graves in France allows further insight into some aspects of the domus in other parts of Europe that have only been hinted to us so far. In particular it will be possible to evaluate the possible separation and linking of male and female symbolism. The northern French allées couvertes present a particular 'surfacing' of the underlying principles of the domus.

Some examples of the allées couvertes and rock-cut hypogées of the Paris Basin are shown in figure 8.2. A first point to make about these tombs is that they are hidden from view in the landscape. Unlike the long mounds that I have been considering elsewhere in Europe, and unlike the allées couvertes of Brittany, the Paris Basin allées couvertes are dug into the ground as are the hypogées. They cannot therefore be claimed to be overt symbols of local rights to

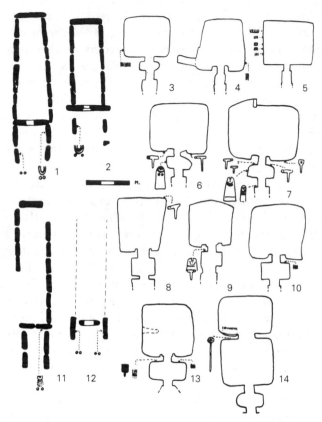

Figure 8.2 Carvings and drawings in the Paris Basin allées couvertes and rock-cut tombs.
(Source: Bailloud 1979)
1 La Bellée, Boury (Oise); 2 Aveny, Dampmesnil (Eure); 3 Razet 19, Coizard (Marne); 4 Razet 22, Coizard (Marne); 5 Razet 28, Coizard (Marne); 6 Razet 23, Coizard (Marne); 7 Razet 24, Coizard (Marne); 8 Vignes-Jaunes, Courjeonnet (Marne); 9 Houyottes 2, Courjeonnet (Marne); 10 Houyottes 5, Courjeonnet (Marne); 11 Trou-aux-Anglais, Epone (Seine-et-Oise); 12 Guiry (Seine-et-Oise); 13 Ronces 21, Villevenard (Marne); 14 Saran 7, Chouilly (Marne).

land or group allegiance. Rather, the hidden, invisible nature of the communal tombs does not overtly contradict the settlement and economic emphasis on dispersal, and flexible individual action. In addition, the esoteric knowledge associated with the chambers is deeply hidden. The tombs are distinctive in that very large numbers of individuals are placed in them. The numbers of inhumations in the tombs vary from 3 to 8 in the cists, from 2 to 60 in the hypogées, and from 20 to 200 in the allées couvertes (Bailloud 1979), although about 350 individuals were found in the Chaussée-Tirancourt allée couverte (Masset 1971). There is evidence of compartmentalization within the graves and organization of the bones into 'boxes' (ibid.), but much of the patterning of articulated and disarticulated remains within the tombs seems to have been the result of the moving aside of earlier skeletons in order to make way for later interments (Bailloud 1979). The ornaments, weapons, and tools found with the bodies in the graves show little evidence of in-group differentiation. Overall, the tombs express an ordered communal ethic.

The individual prowess of the hunter and the warrior was itself created and made possible through reference to the boundary forming principles of the domus. Howell (1983) suggests that the tombs in the Paris Basin tend to be found away from the main settlement areas – away from the domestic context (see above p. 167). They contain large numbers of arrowheads and flint daggers, and their construction and use do much to enhance the playing out of the principles of the agrios. Indeed, Scarre (1983) has argued more generally that megalithic tombs in France are opposed spatially and temporally to evidence for substantial enduring settlement. But the new emphasis on the agrios is created through the medium of the domus.

Although the Paris Basin tombs do not appear to be oriented in any particular direction, a glance at figure 8.2 shows the familiar form of a linear arrangement of space and the separation of an entrance vestibule. The means used to draw attention to the vestibule and separate it from the main burial chamber in which bodies were placed include closing off the vestibule from the chamber by large transversal stones. In both the allées couvertes and hypogées, entrance to the inner chamber is sometimes restricted to movement through a port-hole, usually 50–60 cm in diameter, which is often round in shape but may be oval, square, or rectangular.

The entrance vestibule was also separated from the inner chamber by the depositional practices associated with the tomb. Human bones were deposited in the inner chamber, but rarely, if at all, in the entrance area. Artifact deposition also differentiates inside from outside. In general terms pottery is rarely found in the Paris Basin graves, and when it does occur it often seems to be associated with deposits near the entrance or in the entrance vestibule (Bailloud 1979). Unfortunately specific examples can rarely be given as a result

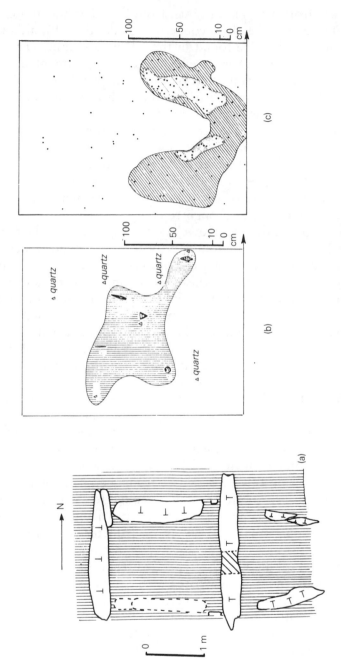

Figure 8.3 The distribution of artifacts within the Aillevans 2 tomb: (a) layout of the tomb; (b) distribution of archaeological finds; (c) distribution of pottery sherds.
(Source: Pétrequin and Piningre 1976)

of the paucity of recent careful excavation and recording. In the Haute-Saône site of Aillevans 2 (figure 8.3), a small east–west oriented tomb, with the entrance facing east, seems to have been set in a trapezoidal area of paving which is badly understood. Before use of the chamber, a small fire was lit in the chamber near the entrance, recalling the frequent association of fires with entrances in the Paris Basin (Bailloud 1979). When the fire had gone out an arrowhead was placed on it and a paving placed over the floor of the chamber. Disarticulated bodies (from at least 33 adults and 8 children) placed on the paved floor had been pushed aside to the east and west so that stone tools including arrowheads and a flint dagger could be placed in the centre of the chamber. As figure 8.3 shows, undecorated sherds of a type often associated in this area with Bell Beakers, were found mainly at the east of the chamber towards the entrance. Putting the sherds back together, it seemed as if three pots had been placed just inside the entrance. The Aillevans 2 evidence thus suggests a separation of pottery towards the entrance and stone tools towards the interior.

The same pattern is found in the Paris Basin in the Vers-sur-Selle allée couverte (Piningre and Bréart 1985). The grave is oriented north–south, with many of the stones having been removed. The linearity of the arrangement of bones and artifacts emphasizes the domus principles (figure 8.4). The entrance antechamber occurs to

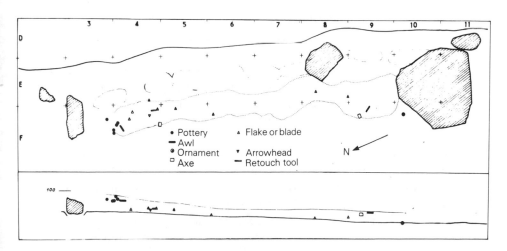

Figure 8.4 Vers-sur-Selle. Distribution of artifacts in the main chamber. The denser distribution of artifacts in the antechamber, to the left in the plan, is not shown. (Source: Piningre and Bréart 1985)

the left in the figure, and it is from this area of the tomb that 90 per cent of all the artifacts derive. There is a primary ritual deposit of a pot and an axe haft, the latter set vertically in the ground. Pottery, bone points, arrowheads, and flint blades and scrapers occur more generally in the antechamber, but there is little human bone. The pairing of antler axe haft and pot in the antechamber deposit is turned into an opposition within the sparser artifacts placed within the main chamber. Towards the front of the chamber, where bones of children are particularly found, pottery sherds occur, whereas in the central and back parts of the main chamber there are adult bones, no pottery, and flint blades, axes, arrowheads, and one ornament (figure 8.4).

At La Chaussée-Tirancourt also, there is a deposit of a SOM pottery vase, three antler axe hafts, and two ornaments in the antechamber (Masset 1971). Overall, the evidence suggests a pairing of and opposition between pottery on the one hand and axe hafts, arrowheads, and daggers on the other, with pottery being found more towards the entrance than towards the interior of the tombs where axes and weapons dominate. In one case, the pottery towards the front is associated with the bones of children, and more generally bones are found more inside, associated with axes and weapons. It should also be noted that many of the ornaments within the tombs are small perforated axeheads. Another pottery deposit in the allée couverte antechambers draws attention to a further set of oppositions. At the allée couverte of La Bellée at Boury (Oise) an entire pot was found in the entrance at the feet of a depiction on the wall of a woman.

Clear representations of women and hafted axes are found in a number of Paris Basin allées couvertes and hypogées. Some examples of the placing of these depictions are shown in figure 8.2. The breasts of women only occur in the antechamber. Where axes occur, they are usually found further in towards the main chamber, or in the main chamber itself. Women, like pottery, are not closely associated with the inner reaches of the tombs. Axes, whether as depictions, ornaments or as tomb deposits, do occur within the main chamber as do deposits of arrowheads and daggers.

It is difficult to know how secure and widespread this patterning might be in the Paris Basin, since so few well-excavated sites have been recovered. Certainly in the allée couverte of L'Usine Vivez at Argenteuil (Val-d'Oise), the distributions of artifacts, reconstructed from old excavation notes, suggest that pottery was abundant inside the chamber although it was more clustered and localized than the flint axes, arrowheads, and ornaments (Maudit 1977). Variation and reinterpretation will occur in the application of underlying principles in concrete situations so that in actions recovered by archaeologists the principles are often difficult to see. Nevertheless the pattern suggested by the depictions in the tombs shown in figure 8.2 does seem clear and it correlates well with much of the depositional distinctions that I have been discussing.

In order to understand the implications of the Paris Basin depictions it would be useful to be able to identify whether axes were symbolically linked to the concept male. It is of interest that in the one case in which axes and persons are directly linked in the depictions, the person does not have breasts (figure 8.2, no. 9). Of course, it would be possible to rest a case for the link between axes and males simply on the widespread European evidence throughout the Neolithic for an association between axes and male graves. However, this is not a universal relationship as finds of work axes in female graves in the Scandinavian Corded Ware attest (see above, p. 216). In northern France, however, a more particular case can be made for linking axes with males by considering a wider range of anthropomorphic representations.

In a useful review, Kinnes (1980) considers anthropomorphic carvings from the Paris Basin, Brittany, and the Channel Islands which are all clearly of a related tradition. He provides an example, from Le Déhus, of a figure without breasts but with a bow. He also provides examples of tombs in which figures with breasts are placed facing or opposed to or hidden from axes. Kinnes suggests the possibility that the male principle was expressed by the axes (ibid., 15). Hunting equipment could have played a similar if secondary role.

We are left, then, with some intriguing possibilities which only a larger sample of carefully excavated tombs in the Paris Basin will clarify. The minimal evidence from central European and Scandinavian representations of the domus for an opposition between female at the entrance and male in the interior seems to be repeated in the Paris Basin and adjacent areas. As one approached the entrance (the foris) to the allées couvertes, one would in many cases have been met by depictions of women. Their breasts dominate the entrance. To the outside world the tomb as a whole appears female and it is towards the entrance that domestic pottery is deposited and, at Vers-sur-Selle, children are buried. But as one moves into the interior, male symbols, including items used in hunting and warring, come to predominate. The placing and organization of the ancestral bones at the heart of the domus form a male domain.

It is too easy, however, to draw simple oppositions between male and female, inside and outside, axes and pottery. In the examples provided above, axes do occur together with pots at the entrances to the tombs, depictions of women and axes are as much associated at the entrances as they are opposed, and from different points of view the entire tomb is both female (associated at the outset with the whole tomb) and male (associated with the inner core). The ambiguity of the link between women and axes at the tomb entrances is reminiscent of the Çatal Hüyük female figures associated with leopards or the SE European figurines associated in houses with bucrania. The material culture symbolism dramatizes problems and the unity of opposites as much as it tries to resolve and separate them. We will never know all the ways in which the Paris Basin symbolism could have been read by different individuals. I find it hard to imagine, for example, that the passing of a body through a narrow port-hole entrance into a long dark cool tomb did not have sexual allusions at one level or another. I doubt, indeed, whether the tomb symbolism did have clear unambiguous meanings, or messages that all members of society could agree upon. Rather, the depictions and the rituals awake basic emotions and fears in a dramatic context. As people participate in these public dramas, they seek to provide solutions which resonate with their wider experiences.

In terms of my wider model concerning European social change through the discourse of the domus, the Paris Basin allées couvertes demonstrate once again the creative artistry within the dramas and strategies of cultural life. In short, in the graves, the domus is manipulated in order to allow new social strategies incorporating the agrios. New strategies based on settlement and group dispersal, a greater use of a wider range of resources, and a new emphasis on prowess in warring and hunting are played out in relation to the tomb rituals. But at the same time, the inner chamber of the tomb continues to define the social unit through the deposition there of the bones of the ancestors. The tomb rituals as a whole reassert the domus–foris principles of inclusion and exclusion. By following strategies such as excluding female depictions, domestic pottery, and children's bodies from the tomb interior, the world represented by male depictions and axes is emphasized at the 'inside'. Equally, in the practices of daily life, the domestic world (as seen in pottery, houses, and settlements) was not elaborated. But the symbolic power of the ordering, controlling, domesticating idea was enhanced by its closer association with, for example, arrowheads, daggers, and non-settlement areas. As a result of this symbolic dependence on the agrios, and as a result of social disaggregation and of changes in the economy, the agrios attains a new centrality. The results of this transformation in Europe have already been examined. In the Paris Basin, however, Bell Beakers have little impact and so to watch the further unfolding of the Paris Basin story would take us outside the frame of this book. Instead, I wish to examine a parallel sequence in Brittany.

Before doing so, however, I wish to emphasize again that to talk in a provisional and preliminary way about male and female principles, which the Paris Basin data have allowed me to do, is not to make assumptions about the roles of men and women. While I feel that there is some justification for discussing male and female symbolism, I would not feel justified in making any claims about the relative position of women and men through time in the Paris Basin. The elaboration and symbolic centrality of the female might imply either abject domination of women or a relative degree of independent power. Similarly, domination of male symbolism to do with axes, hunting, and warring might imply either male control of the domus or simply the representation of a certain type of power (male and female) through male symbols. It might be assumed that throughout the Neolithic men dominated. Whether they did so through female-centred symbolic principles (as shown in the study by Meeker et al. 1986) or through warring and hunting does not seem to me to have necessary implications for the day-to-day experience of that domination. Indeed, it is quite possible that men, at least in many aspects of life, did not dominate. While I have been able in this book to talk about the cultural principles through which social strategies were negotiated, I have not found it easy to talk effectively about those strategies themselves.

Breton Megaliths and Stone Alignments

The evidence from Brittany allows me to discuss, as in Scandinavia, the subtle interlacing of indigenous principles and the Danubian principles of social domination centred on the dramatic idea of linear monumentality. Of course, it is an assumption that the domus was introduced into Europe with the Neolithic. I have not so far sought to investigate in this book the alternative plea (see chapter 10) that the principles of the domus were prefigured in, and grew out of, Mesolithic Europe. Nevertheless, in Brittany it is possible to identify a particular manifestation of more general processes and thus, as in the Paris Basin and Scandinavia, to achieve a better and fuller understanding of those general principles.

Megalithic tombs occur in Brittany from 3800–3700 bc onwards, associated with full agricultural assemblages. But the indigenous tradition within which these developments took place can be glimpsed in the mid fifth millennium bc. The Mesolithic site at Hoedic (Pequart 1954), closely associated with Teviec (Pequart et al. 1937), has a date of about 4600 bc (Hibbs 1985). At the larger site of Teviec there is a mixture of hearth types, some of which are closely associated with or placed above burials, themselves frequently stone-lined and stone-covered. The tombs themselves contain up to six inhumations. In addition to flint and antler artifacts found with the bodies, there is an emphasis on body ornament using shells (Taborin 1974). There is a clear tendency for men to be found with *Trivia europea* and women with *Littorina obtusata*. These two types of shell are small, common, and quite similar species occurring in local marine contexts. There are also slight gender differences in the way the shells are worn. Both occur commonly as necklaces, but men more frequently wear them also as bracelets than do women. The shells also occur across the forehead as 'diadems'. Graves containing bodies with diadems tend to have more other beads than are found in most graves. They may also be otherwise distinctive. For example, they may have large amounts of deer antler or a stone cist (ibid.). Part of this latter variation may relate to age, since decoration is generally concentrated in the 14–30-year age group. But there also appears to be some evidence that certain individuals were given higher 'status' in burial contexts.

The Teviec and Hoedic evidence presages later developments in a number of ways. First, the burial ritual involves stone 'chambers', multiple inhumations, and small tumuli at Teviec. Second, the importance of necklace decoration becomes a leitmotiv for the northern French Neolithic, as we have already seen in the anthropomorphic depictions from the SOM group. Third, the overt display of status differentiation is a strategy that recurs frequently in the Neolithic of Brittany, as opposed to many areas of Europe discussed so far.

There is little evidence of an emphasis on orientation, linearity, or monumentality in the Teviec and Hoedic tombs. These attributes were, however, associated with Danubian influence in north-west France and with the adoption of agriculture. Several early Neolithic tombs were built on open, already cleared, areas (Hibbs 1983, 275). And when the tombs were built, it was in a milieu influenced by or in contact with Danubian groups in the Paris Basin constructing linear houses. Adjacent to Brittany, in Normandy there is Danubian-influenced pottery, dated to just before 4000 bc on typological grounds, found beneath a cairn dated to about 3600 bc (Verron 1986; see also Giot et al. 1979, 198).

But perhaps the clearest example of Danubian influence comes from Les Fouaillages in Guernsey (Kinnes 1982). The trapezoid tomb (figure 8.5) has dates ranging from about 3600 to 3300 bc. Beneath and within the mound there is pottery, much of it decorated, of ultimate Linear Pottery (Cerny) tradition. The Danubian influence might also be seen in the orientation of the mound, its wider end facing east, and in its trapezoidal form. Also distinctive is the linear arrangement of features on the central axis. From west to east, these are a circular paved area, a cairn and menhir of generalized anthropomorphic form, an unroofed double chamber, and a roofed chamber. Since linear and trapezoidal houses exist in the Paris Basin Danubian tradition, it is easy to agree with Kinnes's claim (1982 27), argued mainly from ceramic evidence, that 'the mound was therefore used and constructed by groups of direct Bandkeramik

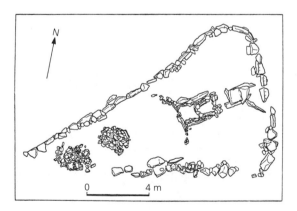

Figure 8.5 Les Fouaillages. The initial monument.
(Source: Kinnes 1982)

ancestry', although, as noted earlier, the nature of that ancestry is uncertain.

Some of the earliest passage graves in Brittany retain the same emphases on a trapezoidal mound facing east and on a linear sequence of burial functions along the central axis (L'Helgouach 1965). For example at the cairn III of Ile Guennoc at Landeda, there are initially four chambers on the central axis of a trapezoidal mound. The broader end of the mound faces south-east. There are crude anthropomorphic stele to the left of the entrance of three of the chambers. It is important to note that the concept of linearity can be both spatial and temporal. At Ile Guennoc, the south-east end is later extended and two further passage graves added. A similar process is found at the very large, imposing tomb of Barnenez (figure 8.6). The first phase consists of the south-eastern end containing five chambers. The central grave (H) is clearly distinctive and a privileged function is suggested. It is bigger, has a double chamber, has megalithic (not dry stone) construction, and has a greater concentration of art. Giot et al. (1979) suggest that six more dolmens were added to the first five about 200–300 years later, thus extending the linear sequence of tombs to 11 in all.

Even though most Breton passage graves are in round mounds, the emphasis on linearity remains clear in the long passages leading from the exterior into the chamber. As L'Helgouach (1965) demonstrates, the entrances face to the south-east in the great majority of cases. Temporal sequence is central to the placing of bodies within

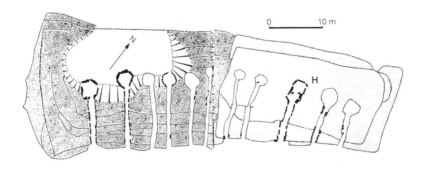

Figure 8.6 Breton passage graves. Barnenez, showing the addition of the western portion.
(Source: Giot et al. 1979)

the passage graves. Although soil conditions in Brittany have destroyed most of the bones in the tombs, there is some evidence of the separation and organization of bones from multiple interments (ibid.). On the other hand, the mixing of bones may be the result of adding in later bodies and pushing aside earlier ones. The artifacts placed within the tombs often cover long periods of time, suggesting sequential rituals and burials at individual passage graves over many centuries.

Through time, into the first half of the third millennium bc, the forms of passage graves change. In particular the chamber becomes longer and rectangular, while the passage diminishes. Indeed it could be argued that the overall development is towards the allée couverte form, and the inner 'domus' zone is increasingly emphasized. Also in Brittany, there is increased evidence through time of larger social groupings, as indicated by the increased frequency of fortified 'camps' with Chassey related pottery. For example, at Lizo (Le Rouzic 1933) there is a river promontory site, surrounded by stone banks, and containing hearths and possible huts inside.

I argued earlier that increased emphasis on the domus–foris provided the mechanism for the formation of larger social entities. The relevance of these ideas for Brittany is strengthened by the evidence of the 'tertres tumulaires', as at Manio. The latter is trapezoidal, with the broader end towards the east. It measures 35 × 11–16 m. There are rows of cists inside. At the centre, one large cist was recovered. But the major finds are at the eastern end of the monument. Here there is a menhir 4 m high, decorated at its base. At the foot of the menhir five axes were found. Nearby there is a carving of a handled axe. It is easy to see why early French antiquarians were attracted to a psychoanalytical perspective on these mounds and menhirs. As Flaubert suggested in 1858, 'le tumulus symbolise l'organe femelle, comme la pièce levée est l'organe mâle' (quoted in Giot et al. 1979, 408). Whether interpretations of, for example, Manio in these precise terms are warranted is debatable. It is my thesis, however, that the cultural construction of gender relations played an important role in the definition and formation of larger social entities.

The rich art of the Breton passage graves is less easy to interpret than in the SOM grouping. Twohig (1981) has divided the art into two phases, the first (3700–3000 bc) including the axe, buckler (or écusson), and other wavy-line motifs, and the second (3000–2500) including deep-carved and relief techniques used to produce bigger and more elaborate motifs incorporating both axes, bucklers, and meandering lines which might now cover the whole surface of a stone (figure 8.7). It is often suggested that the buckler–écusson motif represents women because in some cases the concentric arcs appear to have a humanoid form, because of the tradition of human representation in the Breton passage grave stele (see above), and because of the clear SOM representations of women. Certainly Crawford (1957, 79) made a good case for linking the related depictions on the late, angled passage graves to the SOM females. His argument was based on a detailed comparison of the attributes of the different depictions. But for most of the Breton art it is not possible convincingly to associate women with any particular motif. It is also difficult to see any evidence of the spatial separation between front and back seen in the SOM evidence. Much of the placing of the Breton passage grave art seems chaotic. L'Helgouach (1965, 84) suggests that much of the art was placed in order to appear spectacular and to have most dramatic effect. Giot et al. (1979) argue that the placing of the symbols was regulated by precise laws associating axes with the concentric curve motif (which they

Figure 8.7 Axe, buckler, and other motifs in the Breton passage grave art. Examples from Gavrinis.
(Source: Twohig 1981)

term the 'idol'). But there is no good quantitative evidence to substantiate these claims. All we can say with certainty is that axes are found throughout the tombs. It is less easy to say anything about the presence or placing of female symbols. But the apparent mixing of different types of motif in the Breton passage graves is similar to the evidence from the later Breton allées couvertes where unambiguous depictions of female breasts occur throughout the tombs. In the Breton tombs overall, if male and female are opposed, spatial distinctions are not used.

That the domus–foris principles used in the passage graves were also used to form larger entities is, in my view, especially clear in Brittany because of the stone alignments and circles that are so characteristic of the landscape in this part of Europe (figure 8.8). In some cases these larger-scale monuments are directly associated with tertres tumulaires or passage graves. For example, a stone alignment is associated with Manio, and there is a stone circle around a passage grave at Kercado, Carnac (L'Helgouach 1965, 28). More significant, however, is the evidence that the stone alignments lead up to stone circles or enclosures (see figure 8.8). Indeed, as one approaches the stone circles at either end of the Menec alignment the stones get bigger. This is a strategy used in the passage grave, where the height of the passage often increases as one approaches the chamber. In both types of monument there is linear access to round or rectangular enclosures. The multiple parallel entrances perhaps recall Barnenez and Ile Guennoc.

The alignments and circles thus take the principles of the domus to an extreme. The emphasis on monumentality and linearity are simplified and exaggerated. In Brittany as a whole there are about 100 simple or complex alignments (Giot et al. 1979). Quite common are series of 5–7 lines of 50–70 stones. At La Madeleine in the last century there were 4 rows extending for about 1 km, incorporating 500–600 stones. But there are still bigger examples. At Kerzerho 1130 menhirs occur in 10 lines over a distance 2 km long and 64 m wide. At Menec (figure 8.8) there are 1099 stones in 11 lines, covering an area 1165 m long by 100 m wide. These stark figures express only part of the drama of these monuments. The long lines of approach lead upwards towards a focal point, a 'centre'. Everything is channelled into a long slow entry. Both the construction and use of these monuments formed large social entities through the linear ordering of space and through the domination and control of nature. The natural landscape has been transformed through massive, direct cultural intervention.

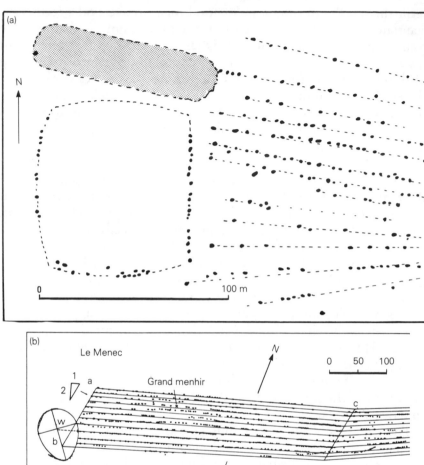

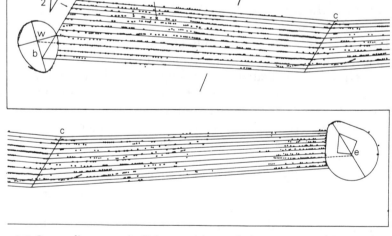

Figure 8.8 Stone alignments in Brittany: (a) cromlech, tertre tumulaire, and stone
rows at Kerlescan West
(Source: Burl 1985);
(b) stone circles and alignments at Menec, Carnac
(Source: Giot et al. 1979)

The extent to which the earthly ordering was linked to a higher authority is unclear. The main alignments in Brittany tend to take a familiar east–west orientation. But much more ambitious claims have been made (Thom 1978). For many archaeologists, the details of these claims are unconvincing. There are many uncertainties in the associations made between stone alignments and the movements of the sun, moon, and stars.

As might be expected, the great elaboration of the domus seen in Brittany is associated with an increased limitation of wealth, and thus perhaps power, to restricted groups. After all, the emphasis in the linear grading of space, in the elaboration of entrances, and in the drama of approach and seclusion is on social ordering in relation to a centre. Of course, the overt expression of status differences has been a continuing theme in Brittany, as seen at Teviec, Barnenez, and Manio. But the 'Grands Tumulus' of the Carnac region take this differentiation still further. The mounds are often rectangular and sometimes circular, and they are large. The Tumulus Saint-Michel, for example, is 98 × 10 m and contains a central trapezoidal cist surrounded by 15 smaller cists. Although there is little pottery in these tombs, the collections of axes and beads are extremely rich. For example in three tombs discussed by Giot et al. (1979, 222) the numbers of axes are 106, 30, and 39, and the numbers of beads 49, 249, and 136 respectively.

In contrast to the passage graves, circles, and alignments which tend to have a coastal distribution in Brittany, the allées couvertes of the second half of the third millennium bc are spread across the whole of the landscape and they are associated with pollen evidence of the first large-scale forest clearance (Hibbs 1983). In many ways these developments are new. There is a dispersed pattern of land use. There are new exchange networks linking the Breton and Paris Basin allées couvertes, and daggers of Grand Pressigny flint appear in the tombs (Giot et al. 1979). Battle axes had occurred in a few passage graves (L'Helgouach 1965, 114). But most are found outside structures 'dans les champs' (Giot et al. 1979, 285). Giot et al. (ibid.) may be correct in arguing that the battle axes found in agricultural fields are the result of the destruction of flat graves. By the time of the allées couvertes, however, when the use of battle axes may have declined, daggers are found in the tombs.

The Breton allées couvertes, although being above ground, are similar in form to the Paris Basin examples. The entrance vestibule tends to face south-east and there is a 'port-hole' leading into the main chamber. Thus it is possible to argue that the principles of the domus do continue. Indeed, Giot et al. (1979, 380) point out that the 'tertre de construction' surrounding the allées couvertes often looks rather like the 'tertres tumulaires'. And I have argued above that the Breton allées couvertes can be seen as a logical outcome of the gradual changes seen in the development of the passage graves.

The principles of the domus provide the medium for a radical change in which warring and the wild play a more central role. In so far as the domus–agrios opposition can be linked to life-giving versus life-taking principles, the limited art found in four of the Breton allées couvertes provides some slight evidence. There are two main motifs used: breasts sometimes with necklaces, and tanged daggers. As L'Helgouach (1965, 282) notes, in two cases the breasts are placed to the upper left on the stone and the daggers or lance-

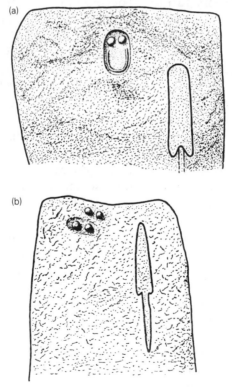

Figure 8.9 The placing of weapon and breast motifs on stones in Breton allées couvertes: (a) Prajou-Menhir; (b) Mougau-Bian.
(After L'Helgouach 1965)

points to the bottom right (figure 8.9). Once again, in a small way, it is possible to argue for both association and opposition between the domus and the agrios.

In Brittany as a whole I have suggested that the opposition between the domus and the agrios begins to take a regional spatial form. While the principles of the domus are taken to their extreme in coastal regions historically associated with passage graves, settlement expands in interior regions and societies there both continue the domus and begin to oppose it. One way in which domination and the restraints of the domus can be countered is simply to form new social entities on the peripheries of the old, created through but in opposition to those older principles.

9

Taming the Landscape: Changing Idioms of Power in the Neolithic of Lowland Britain

The Neolithic sequence in lowland Britain can be read to show once again the 'surfacing' of the principles of the domus identified elsewhere in Europe. The particular form in which the principles are expressed is again different. In addition, there are important differences within lowland Britain between the Neolithic cultural sequences in, for example, Wessex, Dorset, the Upper Thames, and East Anglia. Because of these substantial differences it is difficult to talk of lowland Britain as a whole. However, a general account is partly forced on me by the paucity of reliable modern excavations, and it is partly created by me. Although the regional variations are undeniable, change and variation may occur through the medium of common principles. That principles of the latter form exist in the British Neolithic has been argued by, for example, Kinnes (1979) and will be further argued here.

Study of the British Neolithic is dogged by poor survival of settlement evidence, by a lack of good associations and dating, and by a predominance of poor, early excavations. It is the paucity of settlement evidence which is particularly frustrating in the context of this volume. To some extent this paucity is real. Although some small houses and a few longer examples have been found, the monumental forms of Danubian houses do not occur in Britain. The lack of emphasis on settlements is part of the general weakening of the link between house and domus throughout Europe in the later fourth and third millennia bc. Where houses have been found in Britain, they are often small and dispersed. Nevertheless, fieldwork has contributed little to our understanding of the organization of such domestic contexts.

Burial Traditions

It is natural to focus, therefore, on the burials and monuments of the British Neolithic. After possible small-scale forest clearance in the first half of the fourth millennium bc, burial monuments begin to be constructed by 3300 bc (Bradley 1978 and 1984). The construction of megalithic and non-megalithic long mounds in lowland England is concentrated in the earlier Neolithic, up to approximately 2500 bc.

There are in fact both long mounds (Ashbee 1970) and round barrows (Kinnes 1979) in the earlier Neolithic non-megalithic tradition in Britain, but in both an emphasis on a linear or axial arrangement of space is evident. The non-megalithic chamber in both the long and round barrows consists of an embanked linear zone, sometimes defined or subdivided along the linear axis by pits or posts. The linear zone is up to 1 m wide, up to 10 m long, and sometimes paved (Kinnes 1979). Additional features or enclosures often follow the same linear axis, as at Street House (Vyner 1984). The megalithic chambers in the Cotswold–Severn area have a similar linear ordering, although often with the addition of side-chambers (Darvill 1982). The mounds of the non-megalithic tombs are themselves constructed in such a way as to emphasize a linear ordering. In a number of cases (e.g. Beckhampton Road and South Street, Ashbee et al. 1979) the mound has been constructed along a central wattle fence with secondary 'bays' formed by cross-fences. At South Street the two halves of the mound, divided by the east–west axial fence, consisted of different material which had been quarried using different digging techniques, emphasizing the primary importance of the central axis.

At South Street the very construction of the mound involves organizing the community on a linear axis. I have already referred to the linear grading of space achieved by the placing of pits and posts along the non-megalithic mortuary chambers. What social distinctions were being created by this linear grading? While detailed contextual information is scarce, we can begin to identify some of the social meanings involved.

For example, human bones more frequently occur inside the chambers than outside, and they frequently show evidence of disarticulation and perhaps the removal of flesh as part of the treatment of the corpse. In the Cotswold–Severn tombs the numbers of bodies vary from 2 to greater than 45. The bones are usually disarticulated and there is some slight evidence for excarnation (Darvill 1982). Non-megalithic linear barrows contain bones from up to 55 individuals (Ashbee 1970), and disarticulation is common. Much of the observed disarticulation could have been produced by later disturbance of skeletons which were originally placed in the tombs fully fleshed. However, this later 'disturbance' often involved reordering of the human bones (Shanks and Tilley 1982). The reorganization often concerns an opposition between articulated individuals and disarticulated collections of bones. Amongst the non-megalithic barrows, articulated and disarticulated bones are separated within the chambers at Fussell's Lodge, Wor Barrow, Wayland's Smithy, and Nutbane (Ashbee 1970). Amongst the megalithic Cotswold–Severn tombs, Ascott-under-Wychwood contains bones from different individuals which were articulated together to form a 'fake' individual as a last event in the use of the chamber (Chesterman 1977). At Hazleton North, the bones may have been left to decompose in the entrance before being taken through to the interior (Saville 1984).

The restructuring of the individual into a social order within the tomb is the major social theme of the domus – dominating individuals through the metaphor and practice of domesticating the wild, the agrios, including death. The same idea in the British earlier Neolithic is seen in other ways too. For example, certain bones seem either to have been removed from the tombs or selected for placing within the tombs. It has often been noted that the relative numbers of human skull and long bones in long barrows differ from those in approximately contemporary causewayed camps, although the precise nature of this difference seems to vary regionally (Bradley 1984; Thomas 1987a; Ashbee 1970). Thorpe (1984) has provided some evidence which suggests that in Wessex, if the body parts from incomplete skeletons are counted, long bones are more evident in long barrows, whereas skulls predominate in causewayed camps (figure 9.1). Within the tombs also there is clear evidence from a number of sites of long bones being grouped separately from skulls, with the long bones sometimes bundled together as if tied (Ashbee 1970, 63).

Many tombs, particularly in Yorkshire, have evidence of burning in the chambers, especially towards the entrance. In many cases the burning may have been a final act in the closing of the tomb, to be

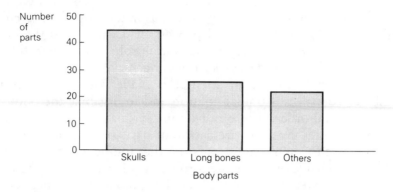

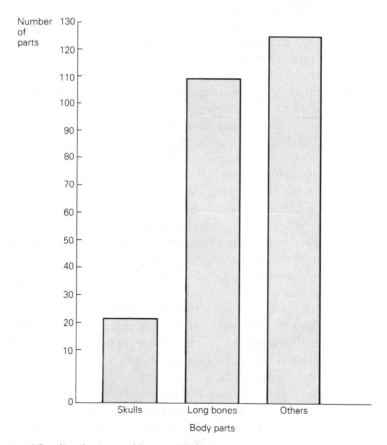

Figure 9.1 The distributions of human body parts in Wessex monuments. Above, causewayed enclosures. Below, long barrows.
(Source: Thorpe 1984)

discussed below. But in some cases fire may have been used in the transformation of flesh into dry bones, as in the Yorkshire 'crematoria' (Manby 1970). The natural process of decay moves the human body away from the identifiable social role that it has filled in society. As the body decays so does the social life in which it has played a part. And yet an attempt is made within the Neolithic tombs to control this transformation and to organize the body into a new cultural order. There is a drama in this reordering. Whether the specific rites involved circulation of parts of the bodies amongst the dispersed communities outside the tombs (Thomas 1987a), defleshing outside or inside the tombs, or other activities, the rituals imply emotive relationships between flesh, blood, and bone, between the individual and society, and between the individual and his or her place in relation to the ancestors or to the ancestral line. The rites play on the natural, and perhaps naturally fearful, process of decay and death so as to create a cultural and social order. The individual is transformed and 'reassembled' so as to embody an artificial system.

In whose interests is this drama played out? It has often been suggested that there are many more males in long barrows than females, especially in the later parts of the earlier Neolithic (Bradley et al. 1984). The bias towards males may occur because the bones of females are more difficult to differentiate from the bones of adolescents or children, thus distorting the proportions of male and female bones in the favour of males. It should also be borne in mind that many of the relevant excavations took place in the nineteenth century. However, at times the size of the difference is so great as to suggest an originally higher frequency of male bones. For example in Wessex long barrows there are approximately 120 disarticulated males and less than 60 females (Thorpe 1984). There is also some slight evidence that males are more closely associated with the inner parts of tombs, as has been noted for France. Reanalysis of the detailed processes of deposition at West Kennet has emphasized the previously identified pattern at this site in which primary deposits are differentiated between adult male bones in the inner, western chamber and mixed sex groups including young individuals in the other outer chambers (Thomas and Whittle 1986). A similar pattern has been identified at Notgrove (Thomas 1988, and see figure 9.2). An overall preference for adult skeletons in the Wessex long barrows is clear in figure 9.5 (Thorpe 1984).

It is unlikely that the male–female/inner–outer pattern will be found in all tombs. Many local and contextual factors will have

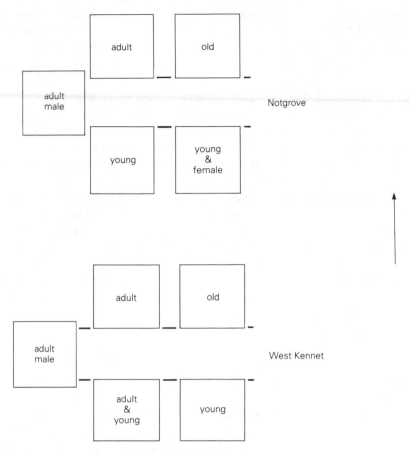

Figure 9.2 The representation of different ages and sexes in the chambers of two
tombs.
(Source: Thomas 1988)

transformed any underlying principles. But through time, as we shall
see, monumental tombs become increasingly associated with adult
males. It seems reasonable to accept the evidence that even in the
early tombs discussed so far, there was a tendency for the ordering
of the bones within the chambers to be linked to adult men. Social
power within the community may partly or largely have depended
on a 'male' idiom of cultural control and on the creation of a
discipline within the drama of death.

But the order with which the male was particularly associated was
not restricted to the use of the tomb and the social map provided by

the human body. It resonated outwards, implicating other domains within which individuals participated. For example, the deposition of animal bones within the tombs also expressed cultural ordering, thus incorporating economic practices in the male-centred rituals within the tombs. There is often a placing of ox skulls or pig jaws within the burial chambers, and 'head and hoof' deposits also occur (Thomas 1987a). But it is particularly cattle bones which are associated with the chambers. For example, Bradley (1984, 24) suggests a predominance of cattle bones within burial chambers, with pig bones and feasting occurring in the facade or forecourt areas in front of the tombs. This pattern has been documented for the Cotswold–Severn tombs by Thomas (1988, cf. figure 9.3), who also notes that cattle bones seem to have been given the same treatment as humans, burnt where human bones are burnt, articulated where human bones are articulated, and disarticulated where human bones are disarticulated. The ability of cattle to 'stand for' humans is shown at the Beckhampton Road long barrow which had no evidence of human burial. Placed along the long axial fence of the mound were found three skulls of domestic ox (Ashbee et al. 1979). Here the central axis of the tomb is clearly associated with cattle.

It is possible that the higher frequencies of pig outside the tombs are associated with later activity concentrated around the tomb entrances and a later economy linked more closely to pig. Consideration of this problem (e.g. Thomas 1987a) has tended to emphasize the partial contemporaneity between the deposits inside and outside the chambers. Even if a chronological factor is involved in the inside–outside/cattle–pig pattern, we know that pig was available to tomb-users in the early Neolithic but that cattle were often placed in significant locations within the tombs. There are also patterns in the body parts represented in the tombs and perhaps in the relative proportions of wild animals. In highland Britain, outside the area being considered here, the bones of wild pig are more frequent in chambered tombs than domesticated pig. An opposite pattern is found in the settlements (Bradley 1978, 73).

Since it is generally assumed that the main use of pigs was for meat consumption, the concentrations of pig bones at the front of tombs has been interpreted in terms of feasting activity (Bradley 1984, 24). This hypothesis is perhaps supported by the placing of pots in the facade area at the Haddenham long barrow (Hodder and Shand 1988). At Street House too, most of the pottery finds came from the infill of the central section of the facade trench and from

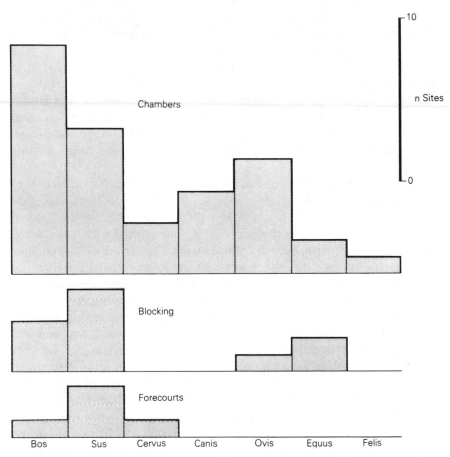

Figure 9.3 Animal species present in different parts of Cotswold–Severn tombs. (Source: Thomas 1988)

the area in front of the tomb (Vyner 1984). Inside the chambers, grave goods are often absent (Manby 1970; Hodder and Shand 1988) or scarce (Ashbee 1970, 71), although pottery and flint do sometimes occur with the bones (Bradley 1984, 29).

There is therefore a slight tendency in lowland Britain towards a pattern seen elsewhere in Europe in which pottery and feasting are associated with the fronts of tombs rather than with the inside chambers. The linear axis of the tombs is used as a 'map' on which to overlay a number of different dimensions. For example, there are differentiations between parts of the human body, between categories of domestic animals and their bodies, and between types of artifact. There is even a resonance outwards to the orientation of the heavenly bodies. In many, although not all cases, the forecourts of the tombs face towards the east (e.g. Darvill 1982, 10; Manby 1970). It is thus clear that the burial practices in the tombs linked together these different dimensions within the framework of a powerful and emotive drama. The social dimensions implicated in this deep cultural overlay seem to have concerned the social control of the individual and perhaps also the relations between adult men and other groups in society.

I have suggested earlier in this book that oppositions or differences are rarely equal and balanced. From different perspectives, one side of an opposition can be made dominant, or 'centred'. In the case of the tombs, the activity at the inner core is associated with adult men, with cattle, and with non-domestic items. 'Inner' is of course not necessarily 'better'. But there is other evidence to suggest that the ordering of bones within the tombs involved esoteric knowledge of cultural codes to which access was restricted. Entrance to the tombs is increasingly difficult, hidden or blocked. The non-megalithic chambers frequently have large proximal posts which would have hindered access from the 'front' of the tomb, and at Haddenham the wooden facade prevented access from the 'front' even though an 'entrance' passageway led towards the chamber and pots were placed at the 'front' (Hodder and Shand 1988). 'False entrances' are found in the megalithic tombs of the Cotswold–Severn region, with the eastern end blocked as if it was a real entrance (Darvill 1982). For the same region, Darvill (ibid., 48) discusses all the evidence for constricted access to the tombs or to the chambers within the tombs. These mechanisms include the placing of stones to constrict the aperture or make the entrance smaller, and there are also examples of 'portholes'. The filling of passages and chambers and the blocking of the front entrance and facade (ibid., 55) are perhaps comparable processes. In some cases, as at West Kennet, the filling seems to have involved ritual deposits over a long period of time (Thomas and Whittle 1986). In many cases, the purpose of the filling is clearly to seal off the tomb and to block access, even though the tomb mound itself may continue to be used for later secondary burials.

However we interpret the final act of blocking, the abstract knowledge about the contents of the tombs and their cultural ordering seems to have been associated with attempts to hide, mask, or restrict that knowledge. The potential importance of this observation is considerable. If the tomb practices link together or resonate through many domains of life (the human body, the domestic world, wild and domestic animals, orientation in relation to a higher authority, etc.), any attempt to control knowledge of the use of the tomb creates a social and cultural control which also resonates through society at large. Fragments of life are put together in the tomb. Access to the tomb is restricted. An imbalance is created. Those associated with the inside become the centre. They provide the origin or legitimation of the social order.

It is not easy to throw light on the specific social strategies which were involved in the construction and use of the tombs. Some early Neolithic flat graves are known (Bradley 1984, 22; Thorpe 1984) and the presence of human skeletons in a wide range of sites suggests that not everyone was buried in linear or round mounds. Only certain local groups may have had access to a tomb. Thus the emphasis on the control of social order within the tomb may have been intended not only to create the dominance of subsections within the tomb-using group, but also to establish the dominance of the tomb-constructing and tomb-using group as a whole. The drama of the tomb rituals and the restrictions of access thus act competitively and strategically in the relations of dominance within and between groups. Individuals are brought to the tomb. The feasting and ritual deposits at the front of the tomb bring people together. But the tomb itself divides and restricts, creating 'centres' and imbalances.

I have suggested that much of the tomb ritual is about creating a cultural order through the natural process of bodily decay and then linking that order to other domains. The idea of creating social control through a particular 'culturing' of nature is the central aspect of the domus in central, north, and western Europe. In lowland Britain, the tombs are again monumental and even the early round mounds incorporate an emphasis on a linear axis. The large tombs and the linear grading and restricting of space with which they are associated, themselves constitute a massive attempt to insert the cultural into the natural. In this they replicate the rituals which take place inside them. But there is yet another way in which the 'culturing' of nature inside the tomb resonates outwards to other domains.

The tombs are sometimes located on domestic sites, but many are away from settlement (identified by flint scatters) or on the margins of cleared areas (Bradley 1984, 17; Thomas 1987a; Bradley et al.

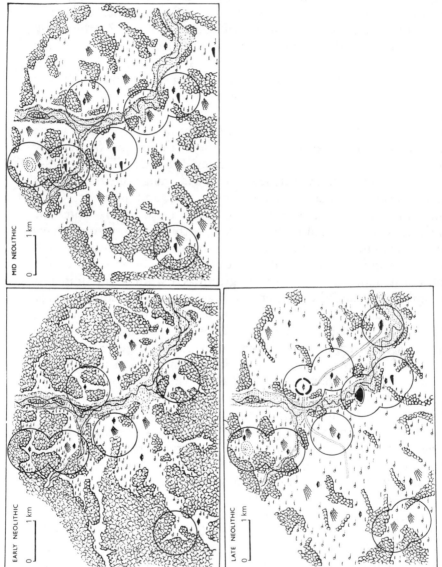

Figure 9.4 The transformation of the Avebury landscape through time.
(Source: Smith 1984)

1984; Richards 1984). For example, at South Street, the environment immediately preceding the construction of the long barrow consisted of pasture land with an open vegetation of grass maintained by grazing stock (Ashbee et al. 1979). The reasons for the locations of the tombs will have been multiple, including visibility. But one recurring factor in some areas seems to have been distance from concentrations of habitation. The drama of the control of nature would thus be enhanced by the very construction of the tomb in more distant or marginal places.

As noted elsewhere in north and west Europe, the tombs in England show the gradual extension of the domus away from the domestic sphere. The tombs are associated with death and the non-domestic sphere. They thus provide the channel for transforming the domus into the agrios. This process can be seen especially clearly in lowland Britain if one looks at the changing uses of burial mounds through time. Two general trends can be identified. First, the process of monumentalization proceeds such that the axial organization of space comes to overlay the entire landscape. Multi-period long barrows often become more monumental in that the ratio of mound area to tomb area increases over time (Bradley 1984, 24–5; Hodder and Shand 1988). Facades and forecourts may also increase in importance (Bradley 1984; Thomas 1987a). The few dates available for bank barrows and cursus monuments suggest that they were constructed between 2800 and 2500 bc and perhaps down to 2200 bc (Thomas 1987a; Bradley 1984; Richards 1984). Both these types of site can be seen as developments from long barrows and long mortuary enclosures. The bank barrow at Maiden Castle is 18 × 546 m (Wheeler 1943). It is flanked on either side by ditches. The western end was destroyed in the Iron Age, but the eastern end has a concave revetment, recalling long barrows. On the central axis within the eastern end was a pit containing pottery, shells, and animal bone. The linear cursus monuments cover even greater distances but can again be seen to be affiliated to the long mounds. The Stonehenge cursus is aligned against a long barrow built across its east terminal (Christie 1963) and at Dorchester-on-Thames the cursus is associated with an alignment of monuments including a mortuary enclosure. Cursus monuments tend to be located between areas of settlement (as at Stonehenge). In the late Neolithic, dense extensive occupation occurs away from the Dorset cursus (Bradley et al. 1984). It is perhaps not too fanciful to see the stone avenues of the latest Neolithic as continuing still further the linear principle. As is suggested by the reconstructions in figure 9.4, the domus increasingly incorporates and integrates the entire landscape.

However, the second general trend through time that can be observed is that the domus is transformed from within. As I have argued elsewhere in Europe, the process is smooth and subtle in its execution. Gradually the basis of social domination is changed from the maintenance of an abstract cultural order to the expression of personal prowess. In the tombs of the early Neolithic a concern with the relationship between the individual and the social collective has already been seen. At times it became possible for an individual body to be assembled out of different individuals and thus for the individual to 'stand for' the collective or the idealized ancestors. This 'individualization' is more directly shown by the decreasing frequency of disarticulated burial and the increasing frequency of male articulated burials associated with grave goods (see however Thomas and Whittle 1986). This sequence has been suggested for Wessex (Thorpe 1984) and Cranborne Chase (Bradley et al. 1984). The appearance of oval mounds in association with articulated male burials has also been discussed (Bradley 1984). The greater emphasis on individual burial has often been linked by British archaeologists to smaller and particularly to round barrows. Certainly less labour was involved in many of the round barrows than in the long barrows. However, as already noted, round barrows already existed in the earlier Neolithic associated with disarticulated burial and linear burial zones (Kinnes 1979). The emergence within round mounds of single burials with individual grave goods is associated with a general decline in structural provisions as the mounds become simpler (ibid., 48–9). Individual burial in round barrows in the late Neolithic is thus 'prefigured' in the earlier round mounds and in the earlier concern with the relationship between the individual and society.

Emerging individual burial is concealed within existing round and long barrows. The outsides of both these types of monument remained similar despite the fact that on the insides the individual had come to usurp the place of and perhaps to stand for the social. There were additional ways in which individual burial grew out of the older tradition in the period after about 2500 bc. Even though few long mounds were constructed after this date, individual burials were often placed in older mounds. At Haddenham it could be argued that an extensive round barrow cemetery was aligned in relation to a long mound (Hodder and Shand 1988). It should also be noted that although single burial increases in frequency into the later Neolithic, enclosed cemeteries (as at Dorchester-on-Thames) also appear (Kinnes 1979). These cemeteries of individual cremations associated with circular arrangements of segmented ditches recall earlier causewayed camps (ibid., 68) and earlier more communal burial practices. Once again, then, the new is created through the old.

The artifacts associated with the individual and frequently male burials in the later Neolithic demonstrate the nature of the new burial ideology that came to be associated with the round barrows. Distinctive finds include edge-polished axes, antler mace-heads, arrowheads, boar-tusk blades, and beaver incisors (Kinnes 1979, 64–5; Thorpe and Richards 1984). This new range of items is legitimated through existing structures, not only by being placed within apparently traditional forms of tomb, but also by association with the major landscape monuments. For example, although later Neolithic flint occupational debris is not concentrated around the Dorset cursus (Bradley et al. 1984), the cursus is associated with smaller clusters of a less wide range of tools, dominated by high-quality artifacts such as polished tools, plano-convex knives, imported stone axes, and mace-heads.

Through time, therefore, the domus extended beyond the individual tomb to act as the focus for large tracts of landscape and presumably for ever larger social units. The coherence provided by the overlay or fitting together of different aspects of life within the tomb gradually reached outwards. The force of this constructed coherence derived partly from a dramatic setting involving control of the wild, death, and nature. But as the domus expanded it seems to have continued an internal transformation, as it became increasingly dependent on reference to the agrios. In the early Neolithic the male skeleton, placed as part of a structured use of space within the tomb, was centred within that structure. But gradually the male skeleton came to be placed alone in the tomb associated less with esoteric knowledge concerning structural elaboration and more with symbols of warring, fighting, and personal prestige. The later Neolithic round mounds and individual burials may still have represented collective social units. Indeed they seem to have emerged in close association with large monuments involving communal labour. The whole process unfolds gradually. At times it appears as if much of the cultural patterning in the later Neolithic was prefigured. In order to understand this process more fully it will be necessary to examine the causewayed enclosures contemporary with the long mounds, and their transformation into the henges of the later Neolithic.

Turning Things Inside Out

There are a number of ways in which long barrows and causewayed camps are linked, apart from their general contemporaneity in the earlier Neolithic. For example, they are often spatially associated as at Hambledon Hill (Mercer 1980) and Haddenham (Hodder and Shand 1988), and at Maiden Castle the bank barrow was built over the causewayed camp circuit (Wheeler 1943). More clearly than the long barrows, the causewayed enclosures are frequently sited in peripheral or marginal environments (Richards 1984; Gardiner 1984; Smith 1984).

There is evidence for 'segmentary' divisions within both long barrow mounds and ditches and in the construction of the interrupted ditches of the causewayed enclosures. At Hambledon Hill the fill of the long barrow ditch demonstrated a sequence very similar to that of the causewayed enclosure ditches (Mercer 1980). Another similarity concerns the emphasis on placed deposits in the causewayed camp ditches (Pryor 1987) and interior (Mercer 1980). These are reminiscent of the placed deposits of pottery in front of some tombs and in some long barrow ditches. Indeed an overall 'ritual' interpretation has generally been associated with both types of monument. An important aspect of this similarity in ritual use is the frequent occurrence of human skeletal material in the enclosures. While both types of site are used in burial ritual, figures 9.1 and 9.5 demonstrate that at least in Wessex there is a complementarity of skeletal material, with skulls more common in the enclosures than long bones, and children more common than adults. At Etton, human skulls or, it is suggested (Pryor 1987), an inverted vessel or round fossil representing skulls, were placed in the ditches of the causewayed enclosure.

Another similarity between the long barrows and causewayed enclosures concerns the foris emphasis on feasting and consumption. Legge (1981, 179) has suggested that 'the majority of cattle killed at the causewayed camps were female, and that these animals represent the surplus available from economies based at lowland (and undiscovered) Neolithic sites'. Other evidence of consumption is suggested by a predominance of consumption rather than storage pottery vessels in causewayed camps (Thomas 1987a), and by the concentration of meat-bearing parts of cattle in the inner ditches at Windmill Hill as opposed to the exclusively 'waste' dumps in the

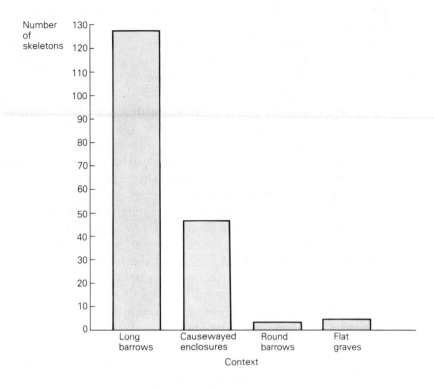

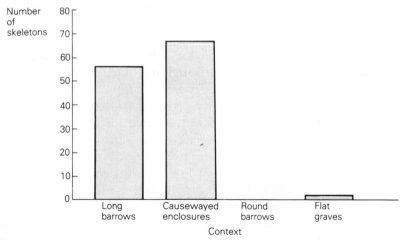

Figure 9.5 The distributions of adult and child skeletons in different types of monument in Wessex. Above, adult skeletons. Below, child skeletons.
(Source: Thorpe 1984)

outer ditch (ibid.). We have already seen that suggestions have been made for feasting activity at the fronts of tombs.

As was found in central Europe, the English enclosures seem to have associations with the domus. Like the long barrows, the enclosures are located such as to emphasize a monumental intervention in nature. In both the causewayed camps and long barrows there is evidence of segmentation, participation, feasting, ritual, and burial. Individuals are brought in across the causeways between the ditches. At Windmill Hill people are brought through the outer ditches to the central area of meat feasting. The enclosures are fewer, larger, and more widely spaced than the barrows. They aggregate at a higher level. But the principle of defining and segregating a community is found in both. At a conceptual level, the linearity principle in the tombs 'leads to' the higher level of community aggregation.

The precise functions of the causewayed enclosures remain enigmatic but may have varied across space and time. Several show little sign of occupation within the circuits of ditches. The interior at Etton did not contain houses (Pryor 1987) and there are low densities of artifacts within the Haddenham enclosure (Evans and Hodder 1988). Elsewhere too it seems as if the insides of the enclosures were kept relatively clean with perhaps later Neolithic settlement occurring outside them (Bradley 1984, 79). Half of the enclosure at Etton seems to have had a funerary function (Pryor 1987) and it has been suggested that the interior at Hambledon Hill was used for the exposure of corpses (Mercer 1980).

On the other hand flint scrapers, perhaps indicating settlement occupation, and houses do occur at a number of the causewayed enclosures (Bradley 1984, 26), although it is possible that at Crickley Hill, for example, the primary purpose was non-domestic with only later use focusing on settlement activities (Dixon 1981; Thomas 1987a). The enclosures are often well located for defensive purposes and the banks inside the ditches are often substantial. The overall evidence for a defensive function for some of the camps is good (Bradley 1984, 35), and at least in some cases the emphasis on defence increases through time (Crickley Hill and perhaps Haddenham).

At first, then, the enclosures help to define the wider community of the domus–foris (that is, a community based on the principles of 'culturing' nature, controlling space, and restricting entrances). But the definition of a community boundary leads to the implication of a need to defend that boundary. As a result, new principles of social life are engendered, based less on community structure and more on warring and hunting in the wild. At the same time, the conceptual dependence of the domus–foris on the domus–agrios means that the symbolic power of the domus–foris has continually to be reproduced either by increasingly monumental works, or by closer association with and reference to the agrios.

This is a transformation I have discussed for other parts of Europe. But in England the process is particularly absorbing. The overall evidence for an increase in the frequencies and centrality of polished axes, arrowheads, and symbols of warring and hunting into the later Neolithic is good. I have already described the increasing dominance of male burials and of burial assemblages with axes, mace-heads, arrowheads, boar-tusk blades, and the like in the later Neolithic. The percentage of arrowheads at Windmill Hill rose from 7 in the causewayed camp to 15 in late Neolithic contexts, while 19 per cent was found at the late Neolithic Durrington Walls henge (Bradley 1978, 80). Green (1980) has demonstrated a not exclusive but clear link in burials between males and arrowheads. At a number of sites of different dates arrows have been found embedded in human bones (Edmonds and Thomas 1987) and there are a few, perhaps later, cases of arrowheads embedded in animals (horse and wolf) (Green 1980).

This new emphasis on individuals, males, warring, and hunting, although in principle opposed to the domus, begins to emerge from its very centre. In the earlier Neolithic the domus has already been removed from the domestic context and is most visible in burials. This outwards movement itself allows the agrios to be manipulated to attain a new centrality. The new individual burials occur within tombs which recall earlier forms and the new artifacts occur concentrated round the Dorset cursus, linked to massive expressions of the domus. In Yorkshire the 'richer' male burials are most often at the centre of the more 'monumental' mounds (Pierpoint 1980). At the Dorchester 'henge' (site II) the central burial is more elaborate (Atkinson et al. 1951). It is as if the agrios has been brought into the centre. This subtle transformation can be seen as the logical result of extending the domus outwards. As the domus became appropriated as a focus for a wider community than the domestic unit, it simultaneously changed in character. The central value of warring, the wild, and defence were emphasized in order to legitimate the expansion of domus–foris principles into new social domains.

Perhaps the most elegant example of this transformation is provided by the late Neolithic henges. Sites such as Dorchester (Atkinson et al. 1951) appear to demonstrate typological connections between causewayed camps, henges with interrupted ditches, and round barrows. There is little evidence of a gap in time between causewayed enclosures and the henges of the late third and early second millennia bc, and both are communal monuments for overlapping scales of aggregation, with related forms and functions. Indeed there are similarities with both the earlier causewayed enclosures and the earlier long barrows.

For example, henges are again involved in burial ritual. Pieces of human skull and long bone have been found at Durrington Walls, Mount Pleasant, Avebury, Woodhenge, and the Sanctuary (Braithwaite 1984; Wainwright 1975). It can be suggested that Stonehenge I recalls causewayed enclosures because of its causewayed ditch (Thorpe and Richards 1984). Certainly a primarily non-domestic function is implied for henges by the emphasis on alignments, by the links to upland stone circles, and the presence of multiple rings of posts at for example Woodhenge (figure 9.6). Indeed the formal similarity between the latter site and the long tradition of similar sites that I have described on the continent is striking. The underlying concern with bounding space while emphasizing access and entrance to that space is common in both the henges and causewayed enclosures in England. And once again, in some areas at least, henges are located away from settlement (Richards 1984; Bradley and Holgate 1984; Bradley et al.1984).

The specific similarities between henges and long barrows concern the emphasis on pig feasting that has been particularly associated with the forecourts of the long mounds. There is some evidence (Thomas 1987a) that henges are positively associated with meat-bearing parts of the carcass and with pig. Late Neolithic Grooved Ware pits in the Stonehenge area show a fall-off in the percentage of pig with distance from the Durrington Walls henge (ibid.). The link between henges and feasting is not found everywhere in lowland England (Thorpe and Richards 1984), but where such evidence does occur it suggests yet more specific parallels with the long barrows. It was noted above that in some long barrows cattle bones are associated with the inside and pig with the outside. At Durrington Walls, there are large variations in the proportions of pig and cattle, with pig dominating in the South Circle, and cattle in the North Circle (Richards and Thomas 1984, 205). At the Mount Pleasant henge cattle predominate in the interior, associated with pottery with more complex decoration, while pig are massively in the majority in the outer ditch (ibid., 214). In general terms, the symbolism of the

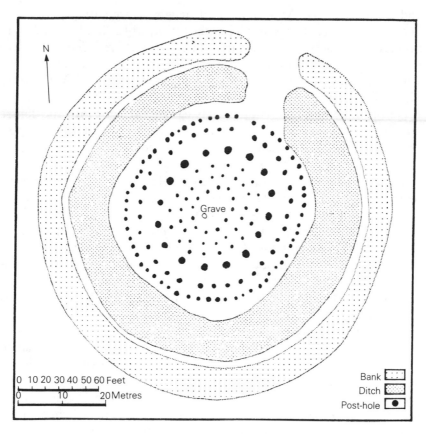

Figure 9.6 Woodhenge.
(Source: Wainwright and Longworth 1971)

henge circles is being overlain by other dimensions, including domestic animals and pottery in order to structure a wider 'whole'. But the specific nature of this structuring recalls earlier practices as seen not only in the cattle–pig opposition, but also in the cattle–pig/inside–outside relationship.

We still have too few spatial data to allow full understanding of the organization of space within the henges. However, in overall terms, the henges invite parallels with the *foris*, front ends of the earlier tombs, and with the increasing emphasis on the wild. As well as the importance of pig on many henges, a high proportion of wild species is found on henges and other Grooved Ware sites (Richards and Thomas 1984). At a number of henges a fascinating pattern has been found by Richards and Thomas (ibid., 214). Wild animals with no certain domestic counterpart, such as horse, red deer, roe deer, beaver, and fox are found in the South Circle at Durrington Walls, whereas bones of wild pig and wild ox are only found in the outer ditch. The same pattern occurs at Woodhenge and Mount Pleasant. It is as if unambiguous wild animals can be brought into the centre, but the entire fabric of the domus depends on maintaining an opposition between domestic and the wild. Wild pig and wild ox must therefore be kept to the margins.

Within such a constraint, the wild outside increasingly becomes the focus of activities in the later Neolithic monuments. The transverse arrowhead is the major arrowhead type found in henges (Green 1980) and I have already described the overall increase in arrowheads in later Neolithic contexts. Henges are often particularly associated with pig, which was associated with the foris–agrios in the earlier Neolithic, and with Grooved Ware which is itself linked to higher proportions of wild species (Richards and Thomas 1984). I have also discussed the burial of 'rich' males at the centre of some 'hengiform' monuments at Dorchester.

Thus although the henges continue and indeed emphasize salient features of the domus, they also incorporate more of the foris and agrios. I have linked the transformation between the domus and the agrios partly to defence. A remarkable aspect of the henges is that many of them invert the defensive function. The ditches of the causewayed enclosures are outside the banks. But the henge ditches often occur inside the banks. The defences now look inwards. This switch is one example of the way in which the outside is brought inside. The concerns with defence and the wild have been brought closer to the centre. The 'enemy' is within.

Another way to discuss this transformation would be to ignore the spatial and symbolic evidence and to emphasize the primary importance of changes in the subsistence economy in the later Neolithic. A major difficulty with this approach is that in the British Neolithic at least the economic and the cultural appear inextricably related. This problem may largely derive from the lack of excavation of clear domestic settlements in the later Neolithic in large parts of lowland England. Overall, there appear to be increases in percentages of pig in later Neolithic faunal assemblages (Bradley 1984, 64). In the Avebury region, sites with high proportions of pig in relation to sheep tend to have higher proportions of wild animal bones (Smith 1984). The spatial pattern supports links between sheep and open and closely managed settings, and between pig and woodland and scrub (ibid.). In the same region there is a general increase in the proportions of wild animals and pigs at the expense of sheep. But this apparent change through time may result from the fact that many of the faunal assemblages derive from 'ritual' sites.

Evidence of economic change is perhaps suggested by changes in settlement pattern in some areas in the later Neolithic. Extensive flint scatters often occur (Gardiner 1984) and in some areas, such as the Upper Thames, settlement expansion is visible (Thomas 1987a). Later Neolithic flint scatters tend to be larger and denser. They contain a wider variety of tool types and physically heavier items. They may reflect a rather less mobile settlement pattern. I would argue that these larger and tighter social groupings were formed through the use of domus–foris principles in the earlier and contemporary communal ritual monuments. The consolidated and expanded settlement pattern continued the idea of social agglomeration in close relation to the agrios. Similar domus–foris–agrios principles, extended across the landscape, may also have corresponded with economic intensification. Later Neolithic intensification might be suggested by the use of the ard plough, pollen evidence of land clearance, and examples of land enclosure (Bradley 1984, 64), but the dating and distribution of these phenomena are unclear.

Through time in the Neolithic there is an increase in labour investment in public monuments (figure 9.7). Presumably the numbers of people participating in these public works also increased. I have argued that the monuments show certain affiliations through time and that they obtain their meanings from the idea of monumental cultural control of nature historically derived from the domus. These meanings legitimate the increasing scale of social control and provide the discourse within which that control can be conceived and generated. As the domus reference is expanded beyond domestic or lineage production and as it becomes associated with fuller use of the resources of the environment and with economic intensification it has to be transformed to deal with the increasing importance of defence, warfare, and hunting. But at the same time that these latter attributes (the agrios) are emphasized in order to re-establish the authority of the domus, they can be manipulated so as to support new social strategies based on individual prestige and the warrior idiom.

The appearance of Beakers in the later Neolithic of lowland England illustrates again the transformation of cultural idioms. The pottery form termed Beaker in the first half of the second millennium

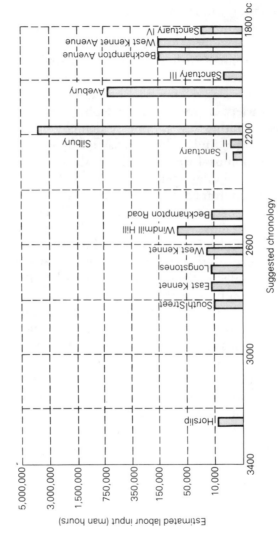

Figure 9.7 Estimated labour required to construct monuments through time in the Avebury region.
(Source: Smith 1984)

bc is rarely found clearly associated with other artifact types (Whittle 1981, 325). The associations that do occur provide a standard set including barbed and tanged arrowheads, perforated stone plaques (of unknown function but conventionally termed 'archers' wrist-guards'), 'basket ear-rings' and other gold ornaments, flint and bronze daggers, belt rings and buttons. Battle axes are associated with late Beaker graves (Braithwaite 1984). These various items are often associated with Beakers in inhumation graves, and it has frequently been suggested that male Beaker graves are somehow 'richer' than female graves (Whittle 1981, 328). An attempt by Pierpoint (1980) to quantify the 'fineness' of Beakers and the 'rich-ness' of their associations in Yorkshire certainly found that 'finer' Beakers and 'richer' associations occurred with adults more than with children, and with males more than females. Male and female Beaker graves tend to have different orientations (Pierpoint 1980; Thomas 1987a). It would certainly be possible to argue that the various attributes of the Beaker evidence, from individual burial to warring, hunting, and male display, encapsulate the emphasis on the agrios seen elsewhere in Europe. Beaker houses are small and show little evidence of domestic elaboration. The overall idiom is on the agrios.

Since the Beaker cultural phenomenon is so heavily dominated by one artifact type – the S-curved pot form with zoned decoration – it would be of interest to have information on the functions of this pot type. Decorated beakers do occur on settlement sites, often with a range of coarser and less well-decorated wares. It has often been assumed that the finer Beakers in grave contexts have a special prestige role, linked in some way to the drinking of mead or barley-beer. There has been little work on residues inside Beakers, but the contents have suggested a wide range of at least secondary uses: other beverages, sea shells, fish bones, a young person's skull, and a ladle (Whittle 1981, 327). Until more research on the food residues in Beakers and other contemporary pottery has been conducted, it remains difficult to discuss the social role of Beakers. For example, if it did prove to be the case that the finer Beakers found in graves had often been used in drinking rather than in eating, a contrast might be found with domestic pottery involved in food production. The complex series of stages used in preparing, mixing, or boiling solid foods in cooking-pots can be contrasted with many types of drink (e.g. milk) which are more immediately prepared or are prod-uced through processes of natural transformation (e.g. sour milk or fermented barley or honey). A culture–nature distinction might thus be created, with the finer Beakers associated with the more natural, 'wilder' side. The elaborate zoned decoration of the pots could then be seen as focusing attention on the natural and the wild, drawing attention to the ability to control the agrios through ordered decoration and the ordered etiquette that may have surrounded the social drinking of liquids.

Unfortunately the data are not available to allow these ideas about Beakers in relation to the social meanings of food and drink to be explored. Nevertheless the link between Beakers and the agrios is otherwise clear, as has been discussed above. It remains, therefore, to see how this idiom was expressed in relation to existing structures. I have already shown how the emerging emphasis on the agrios in the later Neolithic became inserted within the structures of the domus. And the same is true of Beakers, at least in many areas. In the Cotswold–Severn chambered tombs, Beakers are found both inside the tombs and in graves cut into them (Darvill 1982). More evidently, Beakers are found in relation to linear mounds, including the forecourt areas. Beakers are also found in association with major monuments. For example, in the Avebury region Beakers are associated with the stones of the West Kennet avenue, with the Avebury henge, and with The Sanctuary (Thomas 1987a). In the Upper Thames region Beakers occur in some henges in primary contexts (ibid.), while in the east of England, Beakers are found associated with other contemporary pottery types such as Peterborough or Grooved Ware (Cleal 1984).

Overall, therefore, Beakers emerge within the context of existing structures. They represent a development of a process in which the domus is gradually transformed from within by appropriating the ideas of the individual, the warrior, and the wild. And yet in at least one area of lowland England we do see a resistance to this elegant transformation, and a rephrasing of the dichotomy between the domus and the agrios. That area is southern Wessex where perhaps is found the most extreme expression of the monumentalism at the heart of the domus principle – Stonehenge. As a number of authors have noted (Bradley 1984; Braithwaite 1984; Richards 1984; Thorpe and Richards 1984; Whittle 1981), the first rich Beaker burials are located peripherally in southern Wessex, avoiding the major ritual monuments at Durrington Walls and Woodhenge. Beakers are not associated with henges until the later phases of these monuments. But ultimately, as elsewhere, Beakers are brought into the centre and are associated with the building of the first stone phase at Stonehenge itself. The stage has been set for the appearance of the rich Wessex graves of the early Bronze Age (Bradley 1984). The centralization of ritual activity seen in the construction and use of Stonehenge represents an incorporation of two historically opposed principles.

The opposition between the domus and the agrios in the late Neolithic in England is perhaps seen in the oft-noted distinction between the depositional contexts of Grooved Ware and Beakers. Although these two pottery types overlap in time and are both found on domestic sites, Grooved Ware is rarely found in burial while in some areas at least it occurs on henge sites. Beakers, on the other hand, frequently occur in graves, and as I have described, in southern Wessex they are rare on henges. Thus in Wessex at least, a distinction can be made between on the one hand Beakers which are found in similar types of deposits as used by a long tradition of Peterborough Wares, and on the other hand Grooved Ware. Thus Grooved Ware helps to define more closely the separation of the public ritual monument, closely associated with the domus, and burial monuments which were increasingly associated with the individual and the agrios.

Conclusion

As I wrote this chapter and as I approached what had to become an end to the book, the southern British evidence seemed to provide an appropriate conclusion to the processes described elsewhere in Europe. One fairly concise way of summing up those processes would be as follows. In the early Neolithic in Europe and the Near East the principles of the domus are tied to primarily domestic production. By this I mean that there is little evidence of levels of production beyond the domestic group. Domestic units are the main foci of productive tasks in south-east and central Europe, even if additional tasks involving joint labour (for example, in linear house construction) were increasingly undertaken.

Gradually through time however, there are indications of the organization of production at a larger community, perhaps including lineage, scale. Joint labour is invested in boundaries, defences, and enclosures in south-east and central Europe. The linear tombs of north and west Europe also seem to represent the labour of more than one domestic unit, in that the contemporary houses are small and more dispersed than the tombs. It is perhaps possible to talk here of a larger scale of production. Evidence for some degree of craft specialization is found widely in the fourth to third millennia bc in Europe (Chapman 1981; Bradley 1984). The direction of larger amounts of labour seems to have been beyond the domestic group. And yet the older symbolic principles of the domestic scale of production were used to create the new expanded community-scale production. It could be argued that the expansion of the domus, in particular its use in long burial mounds, resulted from a need to legitimate higher levels of productive organization.

Then in northern France and southern Britain the same process occurs again. The construction of the great monuments of Brittany and Wessex involved large amounts of labour. The monuments often suggest a degree of labour organization beyond the immediate local group. But this larger scale of production was again constructed through an extension of existing ideologies. The bank barrows, cursus, avenues, and henges simply extend the domus principle to a new level of social control.

Put still more simply, as increasingly large social entities are formed, increasingly large numbers of what Foucault (1977) has termed 'docile bodies' are created through transferring the idea and practice of domesticating the wild (or death, or decay, or the landscape) to the domestication of society. The domus thus continues through millennia as the discourse within which changing social relations of production are conceived and organized. As the scale of production increases, so the domus moves 'upwards'. Again, we might relate this change to the playing out of an abstract code in relation to changes in relations of production. Sherratt (1981) has shown that the later Neolithic in Europe is associated with an intensification of plough agriculture and a wider use of secondary animal products. These economic changes allow the use of a wider range of environments and the dispersal of small settlement units. Intensification and some degree of differentiation of production encourage specialization and independence outside existing structures of production. The now dispersed, more independent units of production break loose, developing opportunistic exchange links over widespread areas (Shennan 1986). They emphasize ideologies which historically have opposed the domus and which are more in line with a move away from ritual authority structures (Thomas 1987b).

Thus the agrios takes over a more central role, and as in southern Britain, domus and agrios are opposed and interplayed.

If I want to explain why the Secondary Products Revolution occurred, and why it had specific effects, I find it necessary to refer back to social strategies manipulating the domus–agrios scheme. I have argued in this book that the increased taming of the landscape in the later Neolithic is simply an extension of the older domestic-ation idea and practice, the aim being to extend social control competitively over ever larger social entities. The new secondary products' technologies and the associated expansion of settlement allowed the continuation of earlier domus strategies. But they also gave support to an older opposing idea and practice – the agrios. The gradual taming of the landscape in southern Britain is thus just part of a gradual long-term trend which includes what Sherratt has described as the Secondary Products Revolution.

Why is it then that the southern British evidence seems to provide an appropriate conclusion to my account? After all, the British sequence is closely similar to cultural sequences found elsewhere in Europe and the transformation from the domus to the agrios creates the springboard for the Bronze Age. I think the answer may partly lie in the degree of elaboration to which the domus has been subjected by the later Neolithic and early Bronze Age in Britain as well as in Brittany. The principles of linearity and monumentality can only be taken so far. Enormously long enclosures or enormously high mounds (such as at Silbury Hill) take the domus to an extreme. It is difficult to see what else could be done to recreate the idea of monumental intervention in nature and linear grading of space. Of course, this argument is not a satisfactory one. In other parts of the world, larger monuments were indeed constructed as part of a restructuring of the whole of society. It is often asked why Europe does not see, except on its margins in the Aegean, the rise of early 'complex societies' or 'pristine states'. It is at the point I have reached in my account that such developments might have been expected to begin to emerge in Europe. There is no simple answer to such a question, but I think one aspect of the answer also responds to my feeling that the British evidence provides a suitable conclusion to the European Neolithic sequence. However cleverly the domus facili-tates and incorporates the emerging centrality of the agrios, there always remains a clear social and conceptual opposition or distinc-tion. The opposition between domus and agrios was most clear in

SE Europe. But elsewhere in Europe a distinction seems to be retained between the collective, communal principles of the domus, associated with the control of esoteric knowledge, and the individual and the warrior associated with defence and hunting. However much these two aspects of later Neolithic society incorporate each other, they remain identifiably distinct and ultimately it is the warrior idiom that becomes dominant. I have argued for a long-term opposition between domus and agrios. It can be argued that the lack of full integration or unity between functions, between what Dumezil (1970, 1973, and 1983) terms the first priestly function and the second warrior function (see chapter 10 for the relationship between these functions and domus and agrios), never mind any separation from other functions such as domestic production and reproduction, prevented a full development of centralized power. And Brittany and Britain seem to show this best. Here the organization of labour for monumental construction reached its height, but still the old conceptual oppositions remain evident. I will return to these ideas in the final chapter, but it is at least clear from this brief account here that I am allowing a considerable role to conceptual structures in channelling or constraining the way in which social strategies can develop.

10

Beginning by Ending

I have already written one conclusion – at the end of the preceding chapter. But in fact the conclusion may already have been written at the beginning – in or before the first chapter. Despite my initial feeling of uncertainty about how or whether this book would develop, looking back it seems that the structures were perhaps already written in my mind well before the beginning. Now, at the end of the book, new dimensions and openings seem to continue onwards. The experience of the book activates the potential of the structures of thought and creates new thoughts in an endless sequence. The particularity of the book channels the structural sequence in certain directions. This last chapter is really the start of one of a series of other books – other uncertain forays in and through the structures that would bind us.

I, the writer, have been trying to ensnare you, the reader, in the structures of my thought. Yet I know that as you read, you will write your own structures across my words. I have tried to fix my thoughts in the objective and ordered flow of the book and in the concrete data of the past, in order to convince you, and myself, of their validity. So it is more that I, the reader, have tried to ensnare you, the writer, in past structures which are perhaps only present in us through the contemporary society which surrounds us. As I wrote I discovered structures in the prehistoric data, but was I only reading those data through structures which had already found me?

Did I write this book, or was it written through me? Many authors have the sense that someone is looking over their shoulders as they write, writing for them. We personalize everything – even the social structures through which we think.

And that is just the question. Are we today the products of long-term structures that play themselves out through us, or do we in some sense create the structures in the acts of reading and writing? Even the terms of the debate perhaps have a modern origin. Foucault (1973, 1977) has shown how modern conceptions of power and the individual have a specific historical context. The structures exist even in my asking the question about structures, as they do in questions concerning the relationship between structure and event, society and the individual.

For example, I ask whether structures in the present have led me to read and write the past in a certain way. Yet what *is* the present? The terms of all archaeological discussion about the relationship between past and present, about using the present to suggest hypotheses about the past, about observing dynamics in the present versus statics in the past, are preset by an assumed distinction. The comfortable certainty of a present which can be contrasted with a past allows the present to be used to test ideas about the past and it provides the basis of claims for scientific objectivity. Even if 'the present' is only a shorthand for the recent past in contrast to the distant past, the illusion is created of a present which we know and can control, administer, organize, and a past which is uncertain. And yet the present is only a construction. It can be argued that any act 'in the present' is always already past. It has to be past so that we can perceive it. Even our thoughts are past. Otherwise we could not know that we were having them. And that knowledge is itself immediately past, already available for reinterpretation in a ceaseless spiral.

Thought could therefore be described as the making of linkages between or the making of patterns within past events including past thoughts. The giving of meaning to the world is no more than a particular reading of it. Meaning involves making a relationship between things. When we say 'this means that', we are simply saying that we have just made a relationship, a real objective relationship between existing entities. Well, you might argue, what of the future? If there is no present, surely there is another component of thought — the future? In a sense the answer is yes, because intentionality involves looking forward. But even the idea of future is in the past. Our idea of future is already created in the past. It is constructed in the cultural debris within which we live. We create the future, we project forward, only in so far as we are making linkages between items in the past.

But our thought is always already past in another sense also. We do not simply make patterns in disorganized cultural debris. The past is already patterned and the linkages made in our thoughts are already made for us. For example, the idea of present and future have already been created for us and we fit new experiences, already past, into these existing structures of thoughts. Our readings have to some extent already been written.

This book came about through my fascination with the strength of the organizational structures through which we think and act. In the writing of the book itself I have tried to draw attention to this issue by, for example, using terms with Indo-European roots such as domus, foris, and agrios. By using these terms I have not wanted to write a prehistory of words or concepts – a long-term 'Begriffsgeschichte' (Brunner 1968, Koselleck 1985). I have not wanted to claim that modern words such as domestication, forum, and agriculture have roots in the Neolithic although I do think that such a claim would be reasonable. Rather, my use of the Indo-European terms results from a desire to show that the concepts through which we think the origins of agriculture are constructed in the past, perhaps even in the very distant past. I wanted to play on, to pun with words such as domus, domesticate, domestic, dominate, dome, dame and tame to show how our acceptance of certain ideas is partly dependent on the words and associated assumptions through which we think. Thus I assume it would have been more difficult to make the arguments in this book if the language I used did not link houses with economic and social processes. I doubt if I would have had the ideas expressed in this book without the linguistic stimulus. From one point of view my argument is thus language-dependent. Yet at the same time, I have been able to comment on the words and to choose which words to use. At least some degree of choice, of agency, seems to be involved. For example, I could have used the word 'oikos' instead of domus. This again conjures up links between houses and economic and wider social processes. The word economy derives from managing (*nomos*) a house (*oikos*). It refers to administration and is cognate with Latin *vicus* (village, hamlet), and with Sanskrit, Gothic, and Old English words for a house or dwelling. Benveniste (1973) argues that the Indo-European root refers to a social circle rather larger than the domus. Using the word *oikos* in this book it would have been possible to emphasize again the social dimension of the economic changes associated with the origins of agriculture. In addition, a more convincing or at least rather different link would have been provided between management of the house and the economy and management of larger village-sized social groupings. Once again the persuasiveness of an argument about the prehistoric past depends at least partly on structures of language which may have very early origins. But there is also some room for individual agency. I have had to choose which words to use and I have had to interpret the data in terms of those words. The outcome has always been to some degree uncertain.

The Tendency of Structures

I have tried in this book to look at European prehistory in terms of long-term structures, and in the summary below I will provide an even longer-term perspective. In writing the book I have become suspicious of the idea of inevitability. It seems possible to argue that the intentionality, the forward-looking component within the notion of 'acting' upon a world, itself derives from past structures. But it has remained necessary to retain some indeterminacy in structural change. The indeterminacy is suggested for two reasons.

First, I have not been able successfully to provide all the causes or conditions for major social and symbolic structural change. In examples such as the spread of agriculture into central Europe, the elaborate pottery decoration in Scandinavia, or the monumentalism of the British Neolithic I have had to accept that there is an uncertain, inexplicable interpretive component in human action. For example, the shift from the domus–agrios opposition in SE Europe to the more complex domus–foris–agrios scheme in central Europe makes perfect sense in terms of the spread of dispersed agricultural settlements into the relatively uninhabited loess areas of central Europe. But the change could not be predicted from the standpoints either of SE Europe or of what we know of the central European Mesolithic. The new emphasis on the foris in central Europe reinterprets existing social, economic, and conceptual schemes within the pragmatic processes of the spread of agriculture. I can attempt to understand or make sense of the domus–foris–agrios scheme without being able to explain or predict it. Similarly, the elaborate decoration of early MN TRB pottery in Scandinavia makes perfect sense in terms of the earlier Ertebølle emphasis on the symbolic elaboration of the non-domestic world and in terms of the increasing centrality of the foris, but it cannot be explained by those antecedent conditions.

The examples could easily be multiplied. But as a final instance, it is difficult to see anything in the social or ideological history of Breton and lowland British Neolithic groups that would lead one to predict the massive emphasis on enormous monuments. This cultural exaggeration and the extension of monuments to incorporate the wider landscape are certainly understandable in view of the desire to increase social group size and domination through the medium of the domus–foris concept. But the monuments can only be understood as a particular local and creative interpretation of widely found principles. All human action is meaningfully constructed, but there is an openness in decisions about which meanings to assign, which linkages to make.

Second, this openness derives from the fact that the use of social and conceptual structures in daily life has consequences, often unintended, and pragmatic effects which have to be interpreted in relation to existing structures. For example, the domestication of plants and animals has practical effects which have to be interpreted in terms of the social structure, leading to change in that structure. Or the pursuit of social dominance through the principles of the domus has the practical effect that economic intensification or settlement expansion become necessary, leading to the Secondary Products Revolution which has itself to be interpreted in terms of domus and agrios. Or the need to protect the interests of the expanding domus group has the pragmatic result that warring and fighting become more common and these consequences are incorporated into the agrios, leading to changes in the domus–agrios relationship.

In the last example, there is a likelihood that, because of the historical existence of the domus–agrios opposition, new events (increased warring and fighting) will be interpreted in certain ways and will have certain effects. Similarly, the Secondary Products Revolution involves economic changes that slot into and both reinforce and transform the domus–agrios opposition. Structures do not, therefore, determine the way events are acted out and interpreted, but because they are always already organized in certain ways, any manipulation of structures is constrained by their logic. Structures have a potential for certain directions of change. They have tendencies which may or may not be acted upon.

Any symbolic structure is organized into oppositions (high–low, front–back etc.). In some areas of life, such as that area today termed 'fashion', the pursuit of a single social strategy produces shifts within the symbolic structure (rising and lowering of dress lengths, for example). Thus a single social process might result in a shift from the domus to the agrios simply because as the prestige of one member of the structural pair is 'used up', so the alternative takes its place.

No necessary change in social strategy is implied. A new style, a new design, or even a new social structure, are adopted within a continuing strategy of social emulation simply because they were not used last time. Of course in most if not all areas of life, symbolic structural change also has to be appropriate within a given set of economic and social structures and it usually has practical effects which have to be taken into account. There were certainly many political considerations which made the shift from the domus to the agrios appropriate in the European Neolithic. While a particular set of structuring concepts remains as an appropriate discourse of power it has an in-built tendency resulting from the patterning of its parts.

Social and symbolic structures thus appear to 'play themselves out' even though they are ceaselessly being reinterpreted in relation to practical consequences and events in the lived world. Social and structural change only comes about through the structured reading of an earlier organized 'text' (Hodder, 1988). The construction of practical changes in lifestyle, such as village formation, can only be a reinterpretation of existing social and conceptual structures. Thus I have argued (ibid.) that the formation of villages in central and northern Europe was dependent on the construction of communal 'ritual' enclosures and on a particular reading of the idea of the domus. Similarly, the origins of agriculture had to be thought in socio-symbolic (domus) terms.

The notion that 'life imitates art' (for example, Bruner 1986, 69) is one version of this idea. More generally, in talking of revolutionary or political movements Koselleck (1985, 78) suggests that 'positions that were to be captured had first to be formulated linguistically before it was possible to even enter or permanently occupy them'. But since our verbal and non-verbal language is already structured, the capturing of revolutionary positions must itself be influenced by the organization of structures. Actions are trapped not only within the pragmatic world of logistics and consequences, but they are also caught within the tendency of structures. Structural tendency is not the same as structural determinacy. There is an opening left for action and contingency.

My writing of this book, as any book, any story, any history, any interpretation, is therefore a political act in that its words, its organization, 'envisage', encourage, create an opening for action in the world. By reinterpreting structures of thought in relation to the prehistoric data I have created new structures, new pasts in terms of which new events can be read and written. It has thus not been my concern merely to describe what happened in prehistory. Even if such a dry description without interpretation was possible, I would have been unsatisfied providing only data. I wanted rather to place the distant past within contemporary structures of thought in order to contribute and provoke. As Aristotle argues in the *Poetics* (II. 9), 'the poet's function is to describe, not the thing that has happened, but a kind of thing that might happen, that is, what is possible as being probable or necessary . . . . And if he should come to take a subject from actual history, he is none the less a poet for that; since some historic occurrences may very well be in the probably once possible order of things: and it is in that aspect of them that he is their poet.'

So I have tried to be the poet of the Neolithic of Europe, in that I have tried to show how possible events, such as the domestication of plants and animals and the formation of settled villages, became thinkable and plausible within existing cultural principles themselves constructed in relation to practice in the ceaseless interplay between structure and event. I have tried to show how what was possible was made probable, how changes were made acceptable in human terms, and how actions were constructed through existing but changing conceptual schemes. At the same time as contextualizing past events, I have been trying to make those past events appear probable and plausible to us in the 'present'. In doing so I have tried to erode the idea of a separate present and have focused on the degree to which our thoughts and actions are created through the past. By contextualizing ourselves in the past I have wanted to provide a new perspective that challenges some of the assumptions of the modern and post-modern world.

It is not difficult to argue that we live in a world which, in order to further mass consumerism and multinational corporations, draws attention ideologically to personal control, multiple choice, and the cult of the individual. My emphasis on structural indeterminacy is thus thoroughly post-modern and contemporary. But the European past that I have created, or that has been created through me, is not a decontextualized post-modern pastiche. I have tried, while pointing to examples of the regional interpretations of widespread structures, to show that those interpretations are themselves logically constructed over the long term. The long-term unfolding of structures in European prehistory is perhaps the main contribution that I have tried to make.

As Bruner (1986, 54) suggests, poets and historians make possible worlds probable, conceivable or desirable. 'Perhaps this is why tyrants so hate and fear poets and novelists and, yes, historians.

Even more than they fear and hate scientists, who, though they create possible worlds, leave no place in them for possible alternative personal perspectives on those worlds.'

The Duration of Conceptual Structures

At this point I wish to clarify some of the theoretical ideas I have been using in this book concerning the duration of symbolic structures. By considering in this way general anthropological theory at the expense of historical interpretations I am acting less like a poet and more like a scientist. While as a prehistorian the social impact of my writing is in making possible worlds probable through the process of contextualization, the writing of a scientist has social force through appeal to the non-contextual and universal. The aim is to provide general structures that can be used to interpret a wide variety of instances. The appeal to plausibility is precisely that the theoretical statements are widely applicable. The weakness of such a claim is that the general theoretical statements derive from particular historical contexts in the contemporary world. Nevertheless, attempts to clarify theoretical assumptions allow both contextual critique and the potential for wider implications to be followed through. The abstract ordering of the structures of thought within which we work contributes to the channelling of those structures in certain directions. In this way, general social theory plays an active political role.

My main concern here is to provide a theory which explains the long duration of structures. In most theories of society and social change a real world of objective structures is separated from a symbolic, representational, or subjective world. There is reference on the one hand to economy, conditions of existence, power (the 'real' control over others or over ourselves), domination, control of resources and wealth and, on the other hand, to authority, prestige, culture, symbols, and language. Dominance is then often given to the real, with the symbolic seen as secondary. Or dominance may be given to the symbolic but the latter is still separated from power such that in the end, in both views the symbolic is affected by, is contingent on, changes in relations of power.

It is perhaps language itself which forces us to categorize, separate and relate. I would argue that the distinction between power and symbol misconstrues the nature of power. For example, it might be assumed that the more I labour or the more people that labour for me, the more can I wield resources and power. But equivalent amounts of labour invested in or controlled by a coal-miner, a computer scientist, and an academic, for example, do not necessarily provide equivalent amounts of power because these different roles and persons are valued differently in contemporary society. In certain groups in East Africa today, however much labour women invest in crop production and however much they might control the agricultural product, male power based on highly valued cattle remains dominant. In archaeology it is remarkable that long use of the 'prestige goods model' (Frankenstein and Rowlands 1978; Bradley 1984) has ignored the way in which objects gain prestige. It is assumed that control of objects traded over long distances gives power. But restricted access to or control of objects only confers power if the objects are valued or given prestige. It is the idea of an object, nor the object itself, which confers power. As a final example, the use of force (towards non-elites, women, the young, etc.) only creates or supports positions of power if the beating or other display of force is socially sanctioned within a system of prestige. Thus systems of prestige and symbols of power are inextricably linked into organized networks (structures) of symbol/power relations.

So the very fabric of society, the relations of production, the dominance hierarchy, the systems of exchange can all be conceived as networks of symbols/powers. This is not to deny that objects are real in the sense that a pot has to be made out of something, made from clay available at a certain distance, etc. But it is to say that none of these 'real' structural constraints can play a part in society until they have been interpreted and valued within that society. A Neolithic tomb is both a valued representation of a social unit and it creates the social unit in the practice of its construction.

The long-term duration of symbolic structures is produced (a) by the fact that all social strategies involving dominance and subordination work within an existing symbolic network. Social change thus takes place within the tendency of structures. Equally, change of conceptual structures involves social and economic change which may be deemed expensive or risky. The conceptual structures, since they constitute power and prestige, serve the interests of actors within the social fabric. The potential for symbolic structural change is thus constrained by self-interest. Secondly, (b) the symbol/power network is only an interpretation of events. Its various strands are manipulated in making sense of unintended consequences and external influences. I have already argued for some indeterminacy in the relation between structure and events. The symbol/power structures are to some extent removed from the world of events. Indeed the most enduring structures may be those that are so general, simple or ambiguous, that they can be reinterpreted to justify or make sense of highly varied, even contradictory events and positions. The domus seems to be one scheme that was not only deeply embedded within primary areas of practical, economic, and social concern within Neolithic European society, but could also be continually translated into new contexts, applied in new ways, interpreted differently.

In order to demonstrate the duration of conceptual structures it may be helpful to return to my contextual reading of the prehistoric evidence and provide an overall summary which highlights the continuities involved. But this will be more than a summary because I wish to consider still greater expanses of time than have been covered in the main part of the book and to elaborate some of the themes that have been discussed so far in this final chapter.

More than a Summary

I remember once attending a lecture given by Grahame Clark in Cambridge. He put up a slide of a Lower Palaeolithic hand-axe and argued that the symmetry and order in this early object expressed a style and an aesthetic. Certainly hand-axes conform to a widely found code. They are perhaps the first clear evidence we have for the existence of an abstract stereotype used in the production of material form. Rules were used in producing earlier 'chopping tools' but the symmetry and extensive forming and flaking of hand-axes suggest a more complex 'style' (figure 10.1; Gowlett 1984). There was a repeated and abstract way of doing things that could be brought into play in particular cases.

Later it came to fascinate me that although we cannot be certain about the functions of the early hand-axes they are normally assumed to be heavy-duty tools. Perhaps they had multiple functions, but given their weight, size, and sharp edges one of their functions may have been to kill or butcher animals. Two examples from Hoxne in England have traces of meat polish (Champion et al. 1984, 34). Why was cultural elaboration invested in these heavy-duty tools more than on other artifact types?

A number of functional answers might be proposed, but I would like to consider an additional factor. The use of the first tools to kill animals has the function of objectifying the killing process. The existence of a durable tool that has been used in a kill, allows the process of killing animals to be abstracted beyond the particular instance of any one kill or any one dead animal. In other words, the existence of the tool creates or enhances the possibility of symbolic representation.

The stylistic and aesthetic emphasis on heavy-duty tools used in killing or butchering animals as well as in tasks concerning plant foods might then be seen to have several functions. First, the elaboration of and investment in these tools rather than others draw attention to the heavy-duty activities involved. The ordered flaking helps to create a certain prestige, a social desire. But equally, the cultural style obtains prestige from the use of the tool in procuring large sources of food, sometimes in situations that might threaten human life, such as in killing large or dangerous animals. Through the process of symbolic representation the act of using the tool can be linked to an abstract social code involving status and prestige.

Second, the development of a more elaborate representational system linked to the early chopping tools and hand-axes created a socially destructive potential. If a tool could be used to kill animals, it suggests the idea of killing other things such as other humans or even self. Consciousness and representation allow transfers of meaning. By a process of analogy, the objectification of the act of killing creates, increases, or reinforces the potential for human beings to destroy themselves and their society. Or at least the objectification allows such socially destructive acts to be thought, reasoned, and legitimated within an abstract symbolic code.

The heavy cutting tool and its sharp edge thus objectify both the desire for social prestige, and the violence within us that is potentially destructive of society. The stylistic or cultural elaboration of the hand-axes, partly derived from the desire for social prestige, creates a social order in the face of the potentially violent and destructive. It creates a common abstract code at the expense of the individual physical act; structure against and yet out of agency.

Thus right at the beginning of the European Palaeolithic a duality is created between the cultural (the flaked form) and the natural (the implications of the heavy cutting edge), between the ordered world of social representation and the physical violent world of the non-social. But also right at the beginning there is a contradiction, since

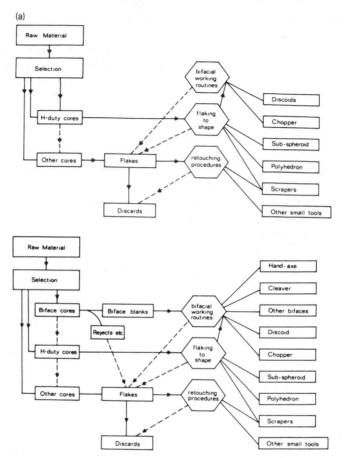

Figure 10.1 (a) The processes by which an Oldowan industry is made (upper) and the more complex processes involved in making an Acheulean industry (lower); facing page (b) the complex nature of biface hand-axe manufacture in the Acheulean.
(Source: Gowlett 1984)

the cultural is dependent on its opposite. The prestige of the cultural, its value, depends on the presence of an opposite – the danger of the wild. Thus at the centre of the cultural is an absence. The hand-axe both celebrates and excludes the wild.

Through time in the Palaeolithic, the same ideas are extended. For example, in the European Upper Palaeolithic there is a great increase in the range and diversity of projectile points, from Solutrean points to those hafted singly or in combinations on throwing spears. Bone

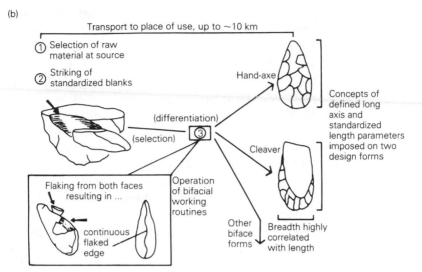

(b)

Transport to place of use, up to ~10 km

① Selection of raw material at source

② Striking of standardized blanks

(differentiation)

(selection) ③

Hand-axe

Concepts of defined long axis and standardized length parameters imposed on two design forms

Cleaver

Flaking from both faces resulting in ...

continuous flaked edge

Operation of bifacial working routines

Other biface forms

Breadth highly correlated with length

and antler points also were probably hafted. In these ways the prestige of the hunt was both created and abstracted into a general prestige within a broader cultural code. The prestige or value of parts of the cultural order were created through the act of domination in the wild. The 'desire' for this cultural order developed 'from below' in that it concerned basic fears and needs (the fear of the wild and the need for sustenance and protection), but it could also be used 'from above' to create respect for relations of power and dependence. I assume that the discourse between the cultural and the natural was used within social strategies to enhance the domination of certain age, gender, descent, and spatial groupings. The prestige of the cultural order could be used as the basis for social control. Equally, however, the ever-present wild on which that order depended could always be used as the basis for opposition, as could different conceptions of what it meant to be cultural. The prestige of the cultural against the dangers of the natural thus provided a discourse within which social struggles could be played out.

In this continual process of domination, resistance, and redefinition, the prestige of the cultural had ever to be reproduced. As the prestige of the cultural order was countered it had to be recreated. Thus from an early stage we can see the same discourse extended into other domains. For example, the natural process of individual human death was early enmeshed within a symbolic code. The earliest burials, of Neanderthal people, occur in south-west France and in Mount Carmel, Israel. Upper Palaeolithic burials in Europe have more decoration on the bodies, and mammoth tusk spears and tools in the graves. The common fear and the social danger of death are increasingly enveloped in a cultural meaning. The cultural protects, and in doing so it gains prestige – a prestige that contributes to the authority of the social and symbolic structures in which the burial has been enmeshed.

Much the same can be said for the early use of fire. The very existence of hearths in caves and settlement sites involves the localization and formalization of the use of fire within a cultural domain. This ordering and control of nature is used to protect and warm individuals and social groups, and perhaps to transform natural substance into cultural food in the process of cooking. Thus once again the prestige of the cultural and the socially ordered is created out of the control of the wild, and yet the danger of the wild, in being controlled, has been brought into the centre.

Indeed the whole subsistence economy of Upper Palaeolithic groups in Europe could have been organized through the same principles. In the extreme conditions of the last glaciation (about 70,000 to 10,000 years ago), Upper Palaeolithic groups (from about 35,000 to 10,000 years ago) had to maintain a high degree of mobility in many areas or had to follow other strategies in order to minimize risk (Champion et al. 1984, 60–1). The creation of the concept of risk and the need to organize the economy in relation to it provide further sources of support for the prestige of the cultural order. After all the 'economy' is a social and cultural mapping of order onto nature. And yet the very term 'risk' foregrounds the continued dangers within that imposed order.

Houses, too, particularly if they contain hearths and act as foci within economic systems, create cultural values through the incorporation and control of the wild. Sites such as Molodova I and Mezhirich in the Soviet Union (ibid., 73, Soffer 1985) contain mammoth skulls, bones, and tusks apparently incorporated into or associated with house or tent walls, or with the edges of work areas. The domestic context was further elaborated in other ways. For example engraved plaques are common in Upper Palaeolithic domestic contexts. In addition, the famous female figurines, often termed 'Venus' figurines, from the Upper Palaeolithic occur in debris from settlement sites (Gamble 1982). For example at Dolni Vestonice the most complete specimen was associated with a large hearth and a similar association occurs at the Abri Pataud.

The similarities of the locations in the 'Venus' figurines and the early Neolithic figurines, for example at Çatal Hüyük, are suggestive, particularly when it is noted that the Palaeolithic examples from certain areas are shown unclothed with the mid-body sexual and reproductive parts emphasized at the expense of the hands, feet, and head. But it is dangerous to assume any similarities of meaning on the basis of formal similarities across such great expanses of time. In the context of the Upper Palaeolithic data I have discussed so far, it is possible to ask 'why were women carved and moulded into a cultural form?' Since other instances of cultural elaboration concern the cultural ordering of the wild, 'were women, or the cultural category "female", perceived as wild or dangerous?'

Clearly no unambiguous answers can be given to these questions, even if they could have been given in the Upper Palaeolithic. But there are some properties of the figurines that are suggestive. As already noted, most areas in which cultural elaboration is found at an early date concern the confrontation of the wild with the cultural in order to create cultural prestige. The 'Venus' figurines are associated with some aspects of this process since they are found by hearths and since some have been formed by using fire to heat clay models. From an early date in the Upper Palaeolithic animal figurines occur, although this version of 'culturing' the wild does not reach a climax until the end of the Upper Palaeolithic. It thus seems possible that the culturing or ordering of the female form was part of a more general process of controlling the wild and the dangerous.

As Faris (1983) has noted, the 'Venus' figurines from parts of Europe do not represent women as labourers or as individuals with clearly defined facial characteristics. Rather, the female is sometimes represented as naked with the mid-body sexual and reproductive parts emphasized. It is tempting to conceive of the 'danger' of the female body as having been constructed in relation to menstruation taboos. As Testart (1986) has shown, many societies today make a metaphorical link between animal blood flowing free and human blood flowing free in menstruation. I have shown that in the Palaeolithic there is an increasing concern to surround the act of piercing an animal's skin with cultural elaboration, as projectile points are diversified and embellished. The act of killing is thus both powerful, constituting social prestige, and dangerous, a potential threat to the social order. The female body was associated with cultural elaboration. It too may have been seen as both powerful, in its reproductive role for example, and dangerous, in metaphorical and social terms (for example, in frustrating attempts at male domination).

It is difficult to identify gender roles in the Palaeolithic data and the evidence can only be claimed to be weakly suggestive. Nevertheless, this preliminary discussion, unsound as it is, usefully emphasizes the main point that I would like to make about the Palaeolithic evidence as a whole. Even if women, or some aspects of womanhood, were seen as wild or dangerous, there is nothing that is 'naturally' wild in them at all. Similarly, if we could link men to big-game hunting in the Upper Palaeolithic as we can in more recent prehistory, there is nothing 'naturally' wild or dangerous in manhood. Neither is 'death' or 'fire' necessarily wild. The 'wild' is not a 'natural' category at all. As I have argued it, the notion of 'wild' as a separate domain was created in order to oppose the 'cultural'. By categorizing and defining the wild as 'other', a prestige was derived from its control and embellishment, and through that construction of 'other', society could itself be built.

It is possible to argue that some components of the social and cultural construction of the 'wild' were built upon fears or dangers, for example concerning predators, which are identifiable in all animals. In the same way, the positive emotional and social values of sustenance and protection within a group have prehuman origins. Nevertheless, at an early stage in the Palaeolithic, the objectifications of a culture–nature distinction within stone tools allowed the creation of a symbolic order in which 'wild' could be *constructed* in relation to 'cultural'. From then on, basic emotions, fears, and desires were increasingly played upon in order to generate a social order.

There is a further aspect of this opposition which is dimly suggested by the Upper Palaeolithic data. In the Upper Palaeolithic, human and animal figurines occur and signs are engraved on limestone slabs. Soffer (1987) shows that the 'Venus' figurines date from 25,000 to 12,000 years ago, although there is some slight evidence for changes in style through time. The archaeological evidence for hunting, however, appears to increase with time. At the end of the Upper Palaeolithic, Magdalenian stone, bone, and other tools show an increased diversification with complex hunting equipment made out of small bladelets. The earliest barbed and tanged arrowheads occur at 18,000 years ago suggesting the use of the bow. There is an increased decoration of hunting equipment in the Magdalenian (Champion et al. 1984, 79). In particular, cave paintings, which promote a selection of big game animals, are concentrated in the middle to late Magdalenian (Jochim 1983), although precise dating is difficult.

Much of the wall painting is found deep within caves, away from occupation areas. In addition, as Faris (1983) has noted, there is little unambiguous depiction of settlement or domestic activities. In the cave painting the 'wild' is being categorized, separated, and controlled, while at the same time the prestige associated with the wild and its control is celebrated. The skill of the 'artists' adds to and derives from that prestige. Within the context of the emphasis on the prestige of the hunt, the 'art' further places that prestige within a wider social and cultural context.

I have suggested that the construction of the cultural in relation to the wild derives from a single process – the creation of social and cultural prestige through the separation and control of the wild. But at different times, in different ways this single process is given different expressions. The circumstances of the increased emphasis on the wild through time in the Upper Palaeolithic in Europe are uncertain. There is some evidence for a gradual increase in the number of animal species found on sites and a broadening of the resource base at the end of the Pleistocene, and this would be an understandable component in the symbolic elaboration of the process of hunting, differentiating between different animals and different resources as part of an increasingly complex cultural map. But perhaps the process worked in the opposite direction as well. The maximum extent of the ice was reached around 20,000 to 18,000 years ago, and animals would have provided the major potential resource in such conditions. The prestige of the hunt thus had a ready basis in the subsistence dependence on big game animals.

The Post-Glacial

About 12,000 years ago, the glacial megafauna disappeared as the ice retreated and as forests spread over Europe. Cattle, deer, and pig were found, with reindeer in the north. The new staples included plants with edible seeds, roots, nuts, and fruits from trees. The long-term trend to thicker forest reduced the variety and density of both plant and animal resources (Champion et al. 1984, 90–1).

Initially these changes are dealt with in Europe by continuing to elaborate on the importance and prestige of the hunt. There is settlement dispersal and poor evidence of houses which were presumably initially insubstantial. Rather than elaborating the domestic context, new ways are found of evoking cultural prestige in the act of the hunt. The reduction in the size of components of hunting tools began in the late glacial, but it is taken to a new extreme in the post-glacial. The piercing weapon is elaborated by setting the haft with small, minutely retouched flakes. With an almost scientific attention to the small and detailed, the cultural is increasingly imposed on the natural. As the bow and arrow are developed in late glacial and post-glacial times, the hunter is able to shoot from a greater distance and perhaps with greater accuracy at the quarry. There is an almost clinical distance and accuracy in the technology of the bow and arrow. In the post-glacial there is some evidence of controlled, selective hunting and the use of deliberate clearances in order to aid hunting.

In all these ways the cultural control of the wild increases as human–environment relationships become closer. The cultural prestige gained in the control of the wild is maintained, but as the cultural control is extended the importance of new types of behaviour increases. As the environment is artificially controlled and 'wild' herds are 'tended', all with the purpose of maintaining the prestige of the cultural in changing environmental conditions, an opening appears into which an alternative discourse can be inserted.

It is probable that the changing environmental conditions contributed to the transformation of the domus because the depleted stocks of large herd animals created a situation in which the prestige of the control of the wild had to be maintained by a more absolute and 'distanced' intervention in nature. This greater intervention logically involved the fuller imposition of a cultural order. The changing environmental conditions also had other effects. In many parts of Europe a dispersed settlement pattern in the early post-glacial was associated with the use of a wider range of resources. Through time this dependence on a variety of resources, partly produced by the disappearance of the large herd mammals and partly produced within social and cultural strategies (to be further defined below), may have allowed greater sedentism. Rather than moving to exploit large animal herds, a variety of resources could be harvested from one or fewer locations. Through time in the Mesolithic in many areas, the degree of sedentism and the sizes of main sites increase.

In order to understand this process of sedentism however, it is necessary to move beyond the effects of the environmental changes. So far I have suggested that the post-glacial economic, social, and cultural changes can be seen simply as responses to the retreats of the glaciers in the contexts of a set of social strategies based on the metaphor of the cultural control of the wild. Thus, while large herd mammals lasted in Europe the prestige of the wild could be used to maintain relations of dominance. But the solitary large mammals dispersed in the post-glacial woodlands could not in the long run be used as a basis for social prestige. A shift to prestige gained through the extension of the cultural order occurred. But this interpretation will not do. It does not account for the specific elaboration of the house, for the rise of the domus, for the importance of sedentism. A fuller discussion is needed.

I have already described processes throughout the Palaeolithic in which prestige was maintained through the ordering and embellishment of the wild. Hand-axes and elaborate hunting points, burial, and the control of fire all provide examples. Houses too were used as foci for the same metaphor of controlling the wild. The same process was extended into the post-glacial. Arrowheads were increasingly detailed and complex and through the Mesolithic houses became increasingly elaborate in the Near East. The same idea of controlling the wild was 'simply' extended to plants and animals, thus producing the 'origins of agriculture'. Plants and animals were separated from the wild, brought in and controlled within the cultural sphere, dominated in order to enhance social prestige by defining the cultural against the wild. But the extension was not simple and the results were not equivalent, because of the practical consequences of 'culturing' plants and animals. The 'culturing' of stone stools, the cultural encoding of wild animals within 'art', the 'culturing' of death in burial are not equivalent to the extension of the same process to the 'culturing' of plants and animals. The social and symbolic ordering of these latter aspects of the wild has consequences which are far-reaching. The ordering, controlling, and storage of plants, and the closer control of certain species of wild animal, lead to closer dependencies of certain plants and animals on humans and of humans on certain plants and animals. The separation of plants and animals from the wild population leads to genetic changes. In order to maintain or increase productive levels on the basis of such resources fields have to be cleared, fences built, food stored, etc. Humans thus become involved in longer-term commitments and dependencies. They have themselves become dominated by the circumstances in which they live, as the consequence of following a certain social and cultural strategy.

One consequence is that the prestige of the cultural order shifts its locus from intervention in the wild to the house. The emphasis on cultured plants and animals creates a separate domain, distant from active participation and hunting in the wild, and concerned more with storage, processing, planting, weeding, caring, and nurturing. Many such activities would have occurred in and around the house throughout the Palaeolithic and Mesolithic. But the potential is produced in the context of culturing certain species of plant and animal for the house to become the major locus for the idea of excluding the wild and ordering the cultural. Thus the split between the domus and the agrios is constructed from within the technology of agriculture and from an older scheme in which culture had been elaborated in relation to nature.

The various effects that I have described were manipulated within a social strategy. Throughout the Upper Palaeolithic and Mesolithic social groups were presumably competing in terms of feasting, exchange, and production, but power gained through these activities depended on the simultaneous manipulation of a set of values concerning the prestige of the cultural in relation to the natural. As resources changed at the end of the Pleistocene, shifts were required in productive relations in order to maintain relations of domination. One strategy that could now be followed was greater sedentism based on a wider variety of resources. This strategy allowed local groups to increase in size in order to produce more and so to participate more fully in processes of social competition. Following Bender (1978), this process of sedentism and intensification of production is another component in the mechanism by which wild resources are cultured and transformed.

A major concern of social groups would thus be to 'domesticate' people within settlements. This human control was achieved by using the conceptual, social, and economic structures. Death, for example, is brought inwards in order to foreground the dangerous and natural so that discipline and order within the settlement could be created. In the few cemeteries known in Mesolithic Europe, the graves are often near or within settlements – as at Vedbaek (Denmark), Tagus (Portugal), Hoedic and Teviec (Brittany), and Lepenski Vir (Yugoslavia). In the Near East too I have described how burials occur within Natufian houses. But the wild too was brought in and controlled. In chapters 1 and 2 I showed how wild cattle played an important role in domestic rituals at an early date at Mureybet. The wild was brought in to confront and thus create a social order. Ultimately the whole of the origins of agriculture is used both as a metaphor for domesticating society and as a mechanism for creating dependencies between people in the very practice of agriculture. As a more intensive delayed return system is embraced, so individuals become economically ensnared as they had been symbolically domesticated.

So the events at the end of the Pleistocene, including the adoption of agriculture and settled village life, are somewhat predictable given the cultural code that had been the basis for social prestige throughout the Palaeolithic. Although the consequences of following particular social strategies through a particular set of cultural principles may have been unforeseen and unintended, sedentism and the origins of agriculture are entirely unremarkable given the tendency of structures and the particular conditions within which these particular structures were played out. The origins of agriculture were initially thought within an older social and cultural code. The environmental events at the end of the Pleistocene were interpreted in terms of, or were read through an existing set of structures. The 'cultured' flaked hand-axe form had become the clinically detailed hafted tool. From there the step to the domus and the origins of agriculture was minimal, but the consequences were far-reaching.

It may seem that I have been courting an environmental determinism in this account. I certainly argue for climatic changes at the end of the Pleistocene being important components in the origins of agriculture. But I hope it is also clear that in my account agriculture would not have begun were it not for long-term processes that had been set in train by the first hand-axes. The gradual social and symbolic process of the dual elaborating and culturing of the wild had reached a certain point at the end of the glacial period. Only a few short moves were needed from complex hunting technologies to clearances in the forests as an aid for hunting and gathering to agriculture. The long-term symbolic and economic structures were manipulated within social competition for within- and between-group control and domination, production, exchange, feasting, and settlement formation. A particular conjunction between the structured process and climatic and environmental events at the end of the Pleistocene produced the origins of agriculture.

The early Neolithic

The 'origins' of agriculture thus reside in the conjunction between processes which have a long duration in the Palaeolithic and particular climatic and social events at the end of the last glaciation. I have suggested that economic domestication was involved metaphorically and pragmatically in creating docile bodies within larger productive units (termed by archaeologists 'settled' villages, or 'settlements'). The separating of the wild from the domestic, the creation of clearer distinctions in relation to the domus, was the primary process by which local groups competed and maintained their strategies of domination. The economic changes were just part of much wider processes. Many aspects of the wild were brought in and 'domesticated'. For example, in the eastern Mediterranean, human death, skulls, vultures, and wild animals were brought into the house. Indeed the linking of two or more aspects of the agrios in the house multiplies the force of the strategy. In the houses and on the walls of Çatal Hüyük, animal death is linked to human death, 'male' dangers to 'female' dangers. This juxtaposition enhances the prestige of the social and cultural order which confronts and controls the agrios. It identifies the domestication metaphor as the main mechanism for social control.

The house, the hearth and the pot were extensively employed in the culturing process and they became appropriate metaphors for the domestication of society. In areas such as SE Europe and the Near East in which it was the caring and nurturing aspects of domestic production that were emphasized, aspects of female biology (in reproduction and nursing) were appropriated symbolically. In other areas such as central and north-western Europe, the intervention in and exclusion of the wild were emphasized.

As the domestication metaphor and practice continued to be used through time in order to domesticate and dominate society, the culturally ordered domestic world was increasingly elaborated and separated from the agrios. For example, in several sites and areas human death was gradually removed from the house, and at Çatal Hüyük and Hacilar, the wall depictions of wild animals decreased. Wild animal bones were less frequently brought into middle Neolithic settlements. As social units expanded in size or gained in cohesion, the domestication metaphor increasingly became the discourse for between-unit relationships – the going in and the coming out, and the exchange of food. The boundaries around houses were emphasized and entrances and exits were elaborated. Pottery was increasingly decorated and caught within a complex cultural code.

The very separation of the domus from the agrios seems to have been used to exacerbate as much as to resolve tensions within the cultural scheme. Haudricourt (1962) has pointed to some of the types of conceptual conflict that arise with the domestication process. For example, domestic animals are separated from wild animals. They are brought into the orbit of the domestic world and are cared for, transformed from a wild into a cultural being. And yet they still have to be killed and eaten and treated as wild animals. The absent agrios at the centre of the domus is made visible.

Perhaps the most obvious way in which these internal tensions are used within social strategies in the European Neolithic concerns the relationships between individuals and groups. This social theme emerged as dominant in my account of the sequences in each region. In some areas and periods the relationship between the individual and the social is expressed in terms of elaborate individual households within uniform village plans. Certainly in the SE European Neolithic it is possible to argue for a largely domestic scale of production and a largely domestic scale of ritual. And yet the internal order is also used to create a wider scale of control and production. In other areas the individual–social tension is seen in the concern with the relationship between human flesh, the individuality of the flesh, and the social ordering of dry bones. There are many versions of this theme. For example, in the Near East the eyes and faces of dry, faceless skulls are remodelled in plaster. In SE Europe, there is a concern to mask the individuality of the face behind a literal mask. But by far the most common version is the reordering of human bones from which all individuality has been lost, into a social classification. While this practice is found widely, it is most common in the burial monuments of north and west Europe. The very construction of these mounds, involving communal labour, contrasts with the individual burials that are found within them in the early stages in many areas. Through time, however, the theme of the relationship between the individual and the social dominates the ordering of the bones within the tombs, resulting in highly evocative practices such as the reconstitution of skeletons out of the bones from separate individuals.

The initial concern in the Neolithic of Europe is thus to maintain the control of the cultural and the social over the natural and the individual. The prestige of the cultural continues to be maintained through dramas and rituals which evoke death, the wild, the individual and oppose these social dangers to a cultural order. A centre is created through an opposition. In SE Europe, for example, bucrania are brought into the house where they are controlled within a cultural order. In north and west Europe, human death provides an equivalent arena although here a wide range of cultural phenomena from the economic to the celestial are brought into conjunction. This establishment of a cultural order in the European Neolithic serves the purposes of social control.

The domus has, therefore, social and economic functions as well as an internal logic of its own. But I am not describing the history of a coherent whole, a set of normative rules, the domus. Rather, I am discussing opposed principles which are brought into eternal struggle in the social process. There is in the earlier Neolithic always a potential for individual fissioning, for transformations in gender relations and in the relationships between young and old. In all areas, this continual contest, centred around the relationship between the domus and the agrios, the social and the individual, leads to a gradual expansion of the domus. The prestige of the cultural over the natural is gradually extended into new domains. It has to be extended if social control is to maintain itself in the face of its internal tensions.

Perhaps the most elegant solution is found in north and west Europe where practical fissioning is incorporated neatly into conceptual structures. In a settlement pattern of largely dispersed and relatively short-term sites, the stable, long-term tombs become the foci for the repetition of rituals and the celebration of the domus. All the components of the dispersed individual lifestyles are brought together in the tomb. But in all areas, the domus is gradually moved 'upwards', away from the domestic unit. One way to explain this shift would be in terms of increasing scales of social control. Thus it could be argued that the domestic scale of production seen in the early importance of houses is later expressed by a 'lineage' mode of production in the enclosures and tombs, and finally in a regional scale of control as seen in the landscape monuments of Brittany and England. This process cannot be seen simply as an imposition of control from above, or as the subordination of individuals to the apparatus of central ritual authorities. Rather, the process works 'from the bottom up' in the sense that it is created out of common concerns. The domus is a system of representation, and it serves to confer value and prestige. The dominant social structures are thus embedded in a dominant value system in which truth and desire are conferred on, for example, dramas of cultural control, the linear ordering of the landscape, the movement through entrances into sacred places, and so on. Daily acts are thus given positive and negative values. They have a taken-for-granted truth, a self-evident prestige embedded within practical concerns for sustenance, dependencies, security, and exchange.

The pursuit of social dominance through the symbol/power network based on the domus and domus–foris resulted in settlement agglomeration, expanded group size and economic intensification as groups engaged in competitive production and exchange. But the historical process also produced ever larger monuments and larger-scale ritual organization in which the metaphor of the domus played a central role. This expansion in the scale or intensity of non-domestic labour organization not only reinforced the domus, but would also have had implications in terms of the overall organization of labour and dependencies. Social, economic, and symbolic or conceptual structures change dialectically. Each produces or entails the other but is reformed in the process. The various effects and implications of the expansion and extension of the domus suggest that any attempt to isolate a conceptual archaeology from a social or economic archaeology, to disentangle the cultural web, is fraught with difficulty.

The later Neolithic

What we know today as the gradual process of the Secondary Products Revolution can be seen as part of the same enterprise of expanding the domestication idea. It concerns the further domestication of the environment, a further culturing of the already cultured. Thus, additional resources obtained from domesticated animals allow settlement to expand further into interfluve areas. Cattle are yoked to pull carts, and the earth is scored with the plough. The domain and prestige of the cultural are in these ways extended. The increased use of ploughing and secondary animal products allowed dominant groups within the social system to maintain levels of production in those areas with poorer soils or higher levels of population. It also allowed the cultural to be taken to the natural. The domestication idea could be extended further into the agrios, creating new economic and social dependencies but also creating a new prestige for the domus – captured in plough marks under barrows or in double oxen burials.

I have already shown how the primary social concern in the early Neolithic was to establish the social in relation to the individual. The metaphorical strategy used was to deploy the cultural against the natural. One of the clearest expressions of the cultural in relation to the social group is seen in the early ritual and stock enclosures. Initially the boundaries around these enclosures dramatize coming and going, the inside versus the outside. The 'defences' at this stage are largely symbolic, separating the cultural from the natural and creating 'us' in relation to those outside, 'them'. However, the conceptual definition of 'us' is also a social definition of dues and dependencies. As the larger social group is increasingly defined so that parts of each household's labour are caught up in the construction of enclosures and in the maintenance of rituals within them, so the need emerges to defend the wider group's interest in a practical way. The symbolic defences become real defences. And yet what is defence except a return to 'the cutting edge of the hand-axe', to the celebration of violence, and the more recently defined agrios?

There are several ways in which the expansion of the domus leads to its ousting, suppression, or transformation. In other words structures, in their conjunction with events produced within those structures, are changed. A certain tendency of the structure is followed and varied effects are produced which act back on the structure. First, the importance of defence establishes the centrality of the prestige of the agrios, and opens up the potential for social groups to develop alternative strategies. Thus, warring, hunting, and the individual increasingly become important idioms for the construction and maintenance of social structures. Second, upwards and outwards expansion of the major expressions of the domus, away from the domestic unit of production, allows greater dispersal of individual household units. A potential is created for increased tension between the social and the individual. Third, the dispersal of settlements (involving a closer relationship with the agrios) is itself contrived in order to maintain the prestige of the culturally ordered and the monumental. The agrios continues to be 'brought in' in order to contrast with and to define the domus. The domus is associated with death (in linear tombs) and with wild animals (in settlements). The agrios has to be brought closer to the heart of the domus in order to maintain the social prestige of the domestication metaphor. But in the process the agrios is brought centre-stage.

In some areas the transformation from the centrality of the domus to the centrality of the agrios seems to be gradual and continuous. In many parts of north and west Europe, for example, it can be argued that there is a slow change in which the agrios is gradually inserted into the domus, and that even when the agrios dominates it still refers back to the domus. In SE Europe, on the other hand, the switch seems more abrupt, more revolutionary in nature. In either case the transformation is subtle and elegant. Indeed I have often found myself wondering at the artistry with which social actors read past texts in creating new versions. 'Indeterminacy' is a bland, 'objective' way of expressing the creative skill of social actors both in coming to a reading of past events and in writing new ones.

I do not want to leave the impression that the final return to the agrios resolves contradictions within the systems of power and prestige. In fact similar problems continue and new ones are produced. For example, the new system of prestige based on warring, hunting, drinking, and the 'male' (which is a social category, a stereotype, of which women may have been able to make full use), remains partly dependent on production within the domestic unit. More generally, the agrios remains dependent on its opposite – on an absent presence. As an example of tensions within the use of the agrios concept, it can be argued that in an agricultural society, domination depends at least partly on the existence of stable relations of production and exchange. Inequality is based on dependency and debt which are built up over time. The problem thus becomes in the late Neolithic in Europe, 'how can I maintain stable relations of production and exchange while at the same time emphasizing competitive warring?' In fact the very widespread similarities of the Corded Ware and Beaker assemblages, and the existence of what is called a 'package' of distinctive items, suggest that a solution was found – although it did in fact derive from an old solution, as old at least as hand-axes. The Corded Ware and Beaker data demonstrate the existence of rules, of a code surrounding hunting, drinking, and warring. But clearly we are not talking here of direct evidence of warring and hunting, but of the establishment of relations of dominance and exchange through the existence of a code, story, or myth which derived its prestige from an old idea – the celebration and fear of the wild.

In most areas in Europe it is difficult to identify any final synthesis between domus and agrios. Certainly the agrios is brought centre-stage through the domus. But, for example, individual burial with artifacts in round barrows is nearly everywhere opposed to either communal monuments or to agglomerated settlement. The early linear tombs contain individual burials, and the British oval barrows represent partial integration, but in the end the domus and the agrios are separated and made distinct. The control of esoteric knowledge about dry bones, celestial movements, and communal works is normally replaced by a thorough use of agrios concepts. Even in Britain where the domus is long retained as the basis for monumental construction, domus–agrios oppositions can be recognized.

Europeans and Indo-Europeans

I wish to use the recognition of long-term structures in order to contribute briefly to questions concerning the particular character of European or Indo-European society. The overall idea of domesticating the wild as a metaphor for social control is probably widespread, used outside the periods and area I have been discussing. Similarly, the symbolic use of the house within such a metaphor might well be common in social contexts with a primarily domestic scale of production.

But within these general ideas I have recurrently found in Europe and the Near East some version of the following structure.

| inside (back) | male | ?axe |
| outside (front) | female | ?pottery |

I have not wanted to argue that this was a determining structure. Rather, it has certain tendencies which allow room for reinterpretation in different contexts through time. The structure is widely available (like a grammatical construction in language) but it is only sometimes used. Therefore it only surfaces in the archaeological record in certain ways at certain places.

None of the evidence for this more specific structure is as clear-cut as I would like it to be. Perhaps the evidence is most secure in the SOM tombs (figure 8.2). But there have been traces of apparently the same structure in the Çatal Hüyük houses, just possibly at Lepenski Vir, in the Danubian linear houses and in the Scandinavian and British tombs. But in each area or context the structure is used rather differently. Thus in the examples just cited, the structure is given a spatial expression. As yet I have not been able to identify a spatial patterning of this type in the Breton tombs or in the SE

European Neolithic. There is, however, in the latter area an opposition within the house between a range of female-associated items
including pottery and, for example, bucrania or special axe deposits
(p. 85). The more detailed evidence awaited from SE Europe may
show that the same ideas were put into practice in rather different
ways. Other regional or temporal differences are more evident. For
example, at Çatal Hüyük the back, male area of the house is associated with death. Another version of this relationship between the
male back area and death is found in the tombs of NW Europe, but
in central Europe death does not appear to be associated with either
the back or front end of the house.

Even within one local expression of the same principles, the
structure does not appear to be hard-and-fast or all-embracing. Thus,
males and axes generally have associations not only with the inside
(back), but also with the outside and the wild, and gradually through
time these external meanings are given increased emphasis. By the
end of the Neolithic, the old back–front/male–female idea presumably remains as part of cultural codes, but it is not brought into
play in significant ways that we can identify. Similarly, the link
between female, front, and pottery found in the earlier Neolithic is
used to give meaning to certain aspects of social life (perhaps, for
example, providing food at feasts, nurturing, caring, domesticating,
receiving), but pottery and female can have both a domestic symbolic
focus and a ceremonial focus (as in the decorated Scandinavian
pottery and as in the depictions of women at the fronts of SOM
tombs). By the end of the Neolithic the link between the female and
decorated pottery appears to have been little used.

Much more evidence needs to be collected before the significance
of these initial findings can be assessed. Is it reasonable to argue that
there is some connection between the examples of a symbolic code
I have cited? Are they instances of a surfacing of a widespread
underlying structure, or are they chance convergencies? Were there
cross-cutting left–right distinctions? Does this specific structure, if
it exists, continue in time into the Bronze Age of Europe or even
later? Why does a very similar arrangement of Saami (Lapp) houses
into back–front/male–female occur into the eighteenth to twentieth
centuries AD (Yates 1989)? How common is this type of structure
outside the European arena? It is only when these questions have
been answered that it will be possible to evaluate the contributions
of this particular structure to the foundations of European society.

But one further intriguing piece of evidence comes from the Upper
Palaeolithic cave paintings. Far removed in time and inadequate in

terms of sample quality, this piece nevertheless allows the possibility of a larger jigsaw in which, as I have already argued, conceptual structures in Europe unfold over enormously long periods of time. Table 2 shows the percentages of males and females depicted in different parts of Palaeolithic caves (Bahn and Vertut 1988). Using strict sexing criteria to identify definite males, definite females, and uncertain 'neutrals', Pales and de St Péreuse (1976) had counted the frequencies of these categories in areas of the caves in daylight, obscurity, and total darkness.

The results show a tendency for female depictions to be located towards the fronts of the caves, in daylight, and for males to be more common towards the backs. Even the greater frequency of neutral depictions towards the back is reminiscent of the more ambiguous representation of males in the European Neolithic where female figurines and carvings are more common and where the male is often represented indirectly and ambiguously by, for example, axes.

The back–front/male–female structure is only one component in the Neolithic domus–foris–agrios structure that has been the main focus of this book, but if such continuities can be supported in larger data sets and if similar structures are not found outside Europe, European society will be shown to have developed through the unfolding of indigenous structures. Such a discussion is immediately relevant to another aspect of the long-term in Europe – the Indo-European problem. I will examine two issues concerning Indo-European language, social structure, and myth in relation to the domus–foris–agrios structure.

The first question concerns the Indo-European tripartite system 'read' by Benveniste (1973) in linguistic evidence and by Dumezil (1970, 1973, and 1983) in mythology, and supported or criticized

Table 2. Percentages of humans of different gender depicted in zones in Palaeolithic caves

	Female	Male	Neutral
Daylight	56.2	6.2	37.5
Obscurity	31.4	8.1	60.4
Total darkness	3.6	16.3	80.0

in a host of additional studies (see Littleton 1973 for a useful review). The tripartite system described by Dumezil is extremely complex. In simplest outline, Dumezil finds that in the ancient Indo-European-speaking communities of northern India there were three main social divisions plus a fourth subordinate group. The three main divisions consist of the Brahmans or priests, the warriors, and the cultivators. The ancient Sanskrit religious literature describes a pantheon of gods organized in this way. The first function concerns both legal and contractual administration as well as magical and religious practice. It thus involves two types of sovereignty. The second, warrior function, concerns youthful physical strength and the protection of society. The third, lowest function, concerns production and reproduction, plant and animal fertility, bodily well-being and comfort.

Dumezil argues that the same tripartite system can be identified among the Indo-Iranians in the fourteenth century BC, in Roman mythical history and in the Roman pantheon, among the Germanic-speaking peoples, especially the Scandinavians, and among the Celts. In general he argues that in these areas three-part divisions in mythology outlast three-part divisions in social organization.

Archaeologists for their part have long attempted to identify a spread of Indo-Europeans which could have produced the widespread similarities in Indo-European languages (see Littleton 1973, Renfrew 1987). Much of the discussion has concentrated on distributions of archaeological materials in relation to distributions of linguistic terms. Thus Gimbutas has linked the spread of the proto-Indo-Europeans to the expansion of the Kurgan pit-grave culture, for example in SE Europe around 2500 bc and with earlier waves of intrusion in the same area (Gimbutas 1970). Renfrew (1987) has argued that the Indo-Europeans spread through Europe with the spread of agriculture.

Many such archaeological studies employ a straightforward empirical methodology. Distributions of linguistic and archaeological traits are compared. Similarities in forms and distributions are assumed to represent some original real similarity in cultural or ethnic affiliation. Rather than this direct reading of the evidence, it is possible to argue for a more complex process in which Indo-European similarities were constructed as part of a social process. There may or may not have been some original Indo-European unity, but the cultural and linguistic similarities were produced in context-specific social interactions.

Thus 'the Indo-Europeans' may have been formed over the long term. To understand this process it is helpful to move beyond immediate empirical similarities to structural considerations. It is also productive to examine the archaeological evidence independent of the linguistic and mythological sources. The prehistoric account that I have provided in this book has described distinctions in the evidence which are reminiscent of Dumezil's tripartite system. But in the archaeological evidence the system does not appear suddenly from the outside. Rather, it is generated from within over the very long term.

The domus, in the original link to domestic production recalls Dumezil's third function. In its early Neolithic form, the domus concerns plant and animal production. It is also associated with bodily representation and particularly, as described by Dumezil, with the female form. Through time in the Neolithic, domestic production and reproduction are subordinated in the system of representation to equivalents of the second and first functions. It is not difficult to equate Dumezil's second warrior function to the long-term emphasis on the agrios that gradually comes to play a central social role in the late Neolithic. As for the first function, the magico-religious knowledge associated with, for example, the sorting of human bones and the organization of heavenly bodies could be identified as a dominant concern in the archaeological evidence from certain areas or periods. The linear tombs might incorporate the third function (as seen in the plough-marks), and the second function (as seen in the battle axes), but their main emphasis is on esoteric religious knowledge as in the first function. A similar first function attribution could be given to many of the enclosures, henges, etc. The tombs and enclosures also demonstrate the practical adminis-tration of social relations (first function) in the organization of large-scale construction.

It would thus be possible to argue that the Indo-European tripar-tite scheme emerged gradually and that it had reached its usually recognized form by the end of the third millennium bc. The structure emerged through the process I have described in this book. The widespread Indo-European similarities thus derive from a very early, and perhaps not specifically Indo-European, common origin in the Palaeolithic, allied with a process by which similar conceptual schemes were used to make social interpretations of similar conditions (such as the climatic changes at the end of the last glaciation). The consequences of these interpretations were again largely similar and were dealt with in similar changing ways. The common domus–agrios opposition was thus applied in varying ways through time. The first and third functions are different historical versions of the domus, resulting from different applications of the same principles. The second function is closely similar to the agrios.

My second Indo-European question concerns one way in which an Indo-European commonality may have been constructed in the later third millennium bc. It has long been assumed by archaeologists that the pit-graves which appear in SE Europe and the Corded Ware and Bell Beaker cultural traits which spread over most of Europe are the results of movements of people (itinerant smiths, pastoralists) or migrations (the Indo-Europeans). The attraction of such arguments is undoubted, since after a period of regional cultural diversity, a distinctive package of closely similar traits (such as beakers, battle axes, daggers, V-perforated buttons, inhumation burial under barrows) is widely found. Despite attempts made to describe the change to Corded Ware and Bell Beaker as an indigenous process (Clarke 1976a; Shennan 1986), in many areas of Europe, such as south Scandinavia, the changes are so abrupt that the migration hypothesis remains attractive (Kristiansen 1989).

Once again it seems to me that archaeologists are reading their data in too literal a manner. Material culture does not represent human behaviour, whether migration or indigenous growth, in a simple and straightforward manner. We need to see more clearly what material culture, like myth, represents. Certainly the Corded Ware evidence *appears* to *represent* a migration. The change is often sudden, the origin of several of the cultural traits can be found earlier to the east (Gimbutas 1970), and there is an increased emphasis on symbols of warring and aggression such as battle axes. But perhaps this appearance of migration was created indigenously as part of a social process.

I have argued that the Corded Ware phenomenon was generated within Europe as part of the rise to domination of the agrios discourse of power. Characteristic of that discourse are hunting, warring, male aggression, the individual, and the wild outside. It would not be inappropriate therefore if this new social discourse was joined to and further legitimated within a mythology and perhaps a practice of external origin. Perhaps material symbols referred to foreign powers and to their presumed warlike character in order to enhance the agrios idiom and in order to further the strategies of domination based on the agrios. In a comparison of Indo-European and Polynesian uses of the stranger-king concept, Sahlins (1985, 80) describes societies in which power is not represented as an intrinsic social condition. 'It is a usurpation, in the double sense of a forceful seizure of sovereignty and a sovereign denial of the prevailing moral order. Rather than a normal succession, *usurpation itself is the principle of legitimacy*' (Sahlins's emphasis). In a wide range of relatively small-scale societies 'the ruler as above society is also considered beyond it. As he is beyond it morally, so he is from the beyond, and his advent is a kind of terrible epiphany. It is a remarkably common fact that the great chiefs and kings of political society are not *of* the people they rule. By the local theories of origin they are strangers' (ibid., 78).

Although the ideology of the stranger-king or usurper-chief is not stressed by Dumezil, the notion of an incoming and terrible stranger-ruler who is ultimately absorbed and domesticated by the indigenous people is certainly part of his account of Indo-European mythology. In my view the widespread cultural similarities towards the end of the third millennium bc may have been produced by an early version of the stranger-king concept, itself generated within and part of the agrios idiom. In contrast to the earlier emphasis on village or tomb continuity, on indigenous domus links to the past, the new ideology emphasizes external novelty. In particular it emphasizes the wild, the aggressive, and the warrior. This is an ideology of dominant groups and it is notable that many of the most distinctive and widespread Corded Ware and Bell Beaker traits occur in 'high status' graves whereas domestic pottery, for example, often remains locally varied.

It is not only 'elite' items that change in the later third millennium bc. The stranger-ruler idea was only a component in the indigenous process through which the agrios became a dominant structuring principle. But the stranger-ruler hypothesis does account well for the observed changes and it directs attention away from insoluble problems such as whether migration 'really' occurred, or whether a few or many immigrants were involved. Rather, the hypothesis implies that the new usurper ideology was appropriate in a changing social context. As power ceased to exude from the pores of the common social body but came to be wielded by individuals, and as the concomitant ethic shifted from the domus to the agrios, so power came to be seen as foreign to society, derived from the outside, strange and unlovely. My emphasis on material culture as representation or myth thus provides a possible perspective on the construction of Indo-European unity. It is through such processes as the use of the stranger-ruler and agrios idioms that selective similarities in language, mythology, and social structure might be created over vast areas.

I recently came across a statement which reminded me of the encounter with the tall anthropologist which I described at the beginning of this book. In both cases someone I looked up to was inciting me to go beyond, to ask new questions. I was reading *Roland Barthes* by Roland Barthes, a writer and philosopher who had long fascinated me. The statement therefore had an authority it might not otherwise have had, even though it was only a passing comment in an account of his grandfather's garden in Bayonne. 'The worldly, the domestic, the wild: is this not the very tripartition of social desire?' (Barthes 1977, 9). The asking of this question raises the obvious point that I have not been able to answer in this book. Although I have argued for long-term continuities in Europe which may have contributed to the construction of Indo-European structures, I have not explored sequences in other parts of the world (such as China or the Americas) to find out whether my conclusions are local or whether they are universal, simply a fundamental part of human experience, including Barthes's reading of a childhood garden in Bayonne.

By referring back to the beginning of this book towards its end I provide a closure to the book, which is also an opening to others. This book can only be a first stage in defining the origins of European structures. I have defined a sequence in Europe. But whether it is a specifically European or Indo-European sequence must await comparative studies.

Things Are Not What They Seem

My final point is methodological. I have argued above that material culture often does not represent directly but only through poetry or myth. Thus migrations or indigenous development cannot be identified by archaeologists. But we can recognize instances in which the myth of migration or invasion is created partly through material culture. A similar point has surfaced at a number of points in this book.

Perhaps the issue has most frequently surfaced in the account of gender relations. This example also shows how activating structures of thought in relation to experience leads to restructuring of thought. When I began this book I had assumed that I would discuss gender relations in some depth, and in the first drafts of the early chapters I did indeed describe the changing role of women in the Neolithic in the Near East. But the flaws in this approach became increasingly clear partly because my own understanding of feminist issues in contemporary society gradually changed, partly because gender issues in archaeology had become more widely debated (e.g. Conkey and Spector 1984; Gero 1985), and partly because I could not justify my arguments in the prehistoric data. I noted, for example, that there were inconsistencies in my treatment of male and female representation. I had assumed that the return of the agrios in the later Neolithic expressed real male dominance, or that the occurrence of male symbols in the interiors of tombs indicated real male power, but I argued that the prevalence of female symbolism in the early Neolithic in SE Europe and the Near East probably mystified the subordinate role of women. I came to realize that it was possible to read representations of women as either representing 'real' power held by women, or as expressions of the lack of power held by women – their reduction to objects of desire. I came to see that I would have to extend the same principles to male representations. In the end I realized that I was not writing a book about gender relations, but a book about the way in which representations of gender relations were manipulated within more general structures.

It is rare that archaeologists can identify gender specific tasks and activity areas. Associations between women and pottery and men and axes in burials for example, or between spindle whorls, female figurines, and hearths in settlements do not necessarily mean that women made pottery or did the weaving or that only men cut down trees with axes. We cannot read such evidence directly in terms of gender relations. For the most part we dig up not how things were, but how people would have liked them to be.

Similarly, it is not possible to argue that changes in the percentages of wild animal bones on sites in, for example, the later Neolithic in Europe directly indicate economic change. It is equally likely that the bone-count changes result from wider structural transformations in which many aspects of the wild, the agrios, were brought into closer association with 'cultured' settlement areas. In the early Neolithic, for example in Scandinavia, the wild was separated in special activity camps. But gradually through time larger less specialized settlements were constructed. The strict boundary between the domus and agrios, as seen for example in the central European houses and enclosures, is ultimately broken down at the end of the Neolithic as elaborate houses, tombs, and enclosures disappear. Only when, for example, C12/C13 studies of human bones have shown that dietary change has taken place, can we begin to relate floral and faunal assemblage changes to economic change. But even then, a 'real' switch to, for example, eating more or less 'wild' fish, has to be understood within a broader cultural context in which bringing the agrios inwards, even into the body itself, is a social statement, a representation, a code.

As a final example of the poetic nature of material culture, I would throw doubt on the usual assumption that variations in social ranking can be monitored using archaeological evidence. Once again, human relations cannot be read directly in material culture. The occurrence of individual burials in large early tombs in Europe cannot be read as a simple expression of hierarchy. It is quite likely that these burials are concerned either to represent the group through the individual or to play on a structural tension between individual and society (the latter represented by the collective construction of the tomb). The appearance of defined enclosures, tombs, and smaller settlements in a regional site hierarchy in for example Scandinavia or central Germany does not necessarily imply a social hierarchy. Rather the different 'levels' in the hierarchy represent different expressions of wider social and symbolic structures. The individual burials under round barrows in the late Neolithic may well look 'richer', with more individual variation, but the change may be only apparent, caused by transformations in the domus–agrios structure. The earlier domus concerns with linear sequence, with body boundaries and the transformation of the flesh, with the durability of dry bones, and with the constraint of the individual within domus structures are replaced by an agrios emphasis on the individual. This social and conceptual change does not necessarily imply a greater or lesser degree of social ranking in the late Neolithic.

I have provided several examples, from migrations, gender relations, and the economy to social rank, in which material culture appears as an indirect and mythical representation of human relations. But the arguments should not be taken too far. The cultural representations cannot be contrasted with 'real' human relations. The myths, the representations are themselves part of reality; they are constructed within real social processes. It is therefore necessary for archaeologists to discuss these social processes, however difficult the discussions might seem. Thus I have in this book argued that at the beginning of the Neolithic real economic change occurred and I have argued that during the Neolithic larger social groups were formed in order to produce more significant scales of domination and social prestige. Such arguments are facilitated by the fact that material culture is not only abstract structure, it is also practice. Thus the construction of major monuments involves real increases in labour input and in the scale or intensity of social dependencies. The domestication of plants and animals involves, in practical terms, a delayed return for one's labour and the need for longer-term social structures. The protection of one's interest and resources involves practical defence and warring and the need for social and structural change to provide these everyday functions.

So in the end, as at the beginning, I find myself caught between conceptual, social, and economic structure and the practical consequences of their interplay. On the one hand, we dig up only representations which we read and write through a complex web of past structures that seem to enmesh us in all possible directions. On the other hand, we dig up the products of practical everyday behaviour, the outpourings of a pragmatic rather than a structural logic. I have tried to argue that while structures largely determine what we do, there remains a looseness between structure and practice – an opening that is filled by interpretation. Whether I have been successful in trying to bridge all sides of old arguments I do not know. The interpretive uncertainty, the looseness remains in the writing and reading of my text. At least, however, I have provided an interpretation which, structured and ordered within the practice of this book, can be reacted to.

References

Albrethsen, S. E. and Petersen, E. B. 1976. 'Excavation of a Mesolithic cemetery at Vedbaek, Denmark.' *Acta Archaeologica* 47, 1–28.

Andersen, N. 1988a, *Sarup*. Jysk Arkaeologisk Selskab, Moesgård.

Andersen, N. 1988b. 'The Neolithic causewayed enclosures at Sarup, on south-west Funen, Denmark.' In Burgess, C., Topping, P., Mordant, C. and Maddison, M. (eds), *Enclosures and Defences in the Neolithic of Western Europe*. British Archaeological Report S403.

Andersen, N. and Madsen, T. 1977. 'Neolithic bowls and lugged beakers with chevron bands.' *Kuml* 1977, 131–60.

Andersen, S. H. 1980. 'New finds of patterned Ertebølle artifacts from east Jutland.' *Kuml* 1980, 7–59.

Andersen, S. H. 1983. 'Patterned oar blades from Tybrind Vig.' *Kuml* 1982–3, 11–30.

Ashbee, P. 1970. *The Earthen Long Barrow in Britain*. London.

Ashbee, P., Smith, I. and Evans, J. 1979. 'Excavations of three long barrows near Avebury, Wiltshire.' *Proceedings of the Prehistoric Society* 45, 207–300.

Atkinson, R. J., Piggott, C. and Sanders, N. 1951. *Excavations at Dorchester, Oxon*. Oxford.

Bahn, P. G. and Vertut, J. 1988. *Images of the Ice Age*. London.

Bailloud, G. 1979. *Le Néolithique dans le Bassin Parisien*. Paris.

Bakels, C. C. 1978. 'Four Linearbandkeramik settlements and their environment.' *Analecta Praehistorica Leidensia* 11.

Bakker, J. A. 1982. 'TRB settlement patterns on the Dutch sandy soils.' *Analecta Praehistorica Leidensia* 15, 87–124.

Banner, J. and Foltiny, I. 1945. 'Neuere Ausgrabung im Kökenydomb bei Hodmezovasarhely.' *Folia Archaeologica* 5, 8–34.

Barstow, A. 1978. 'The uses of archaeology for women's history: James Mellaart's work on the Neolithic goddess at Çatal Hüyük.' *Feminist Studies* 4, 7–18.

Barthes, R. 1977. *Roland Barthes*. New York.

Bar Yosef, O. 1982. 'The Natufian in the southern Levant.' In Cuyler Young, T., Smith, P. and Mortensen, P. (eds), *The Hilly Flanks*. Chicago.

Becker, C. J. 1947. 'Mosefundne Lerkar fra yngre Stenalder.' *Aarbøger for Nordisk Oldkyndighed og Historie* 1947, 1–318.

Becker, C. J. 1950. 'Den grubekeramiske kultur i Danmark.' *Aarbøger for Nordisk Oldkyndighed og Historie* 1950, 153–274.

Becker, C. J. 1959. 'Middle Neolithic stone packing graves in Denmark.' *Aarbøger for Nordisk Oldkyndighed og Historie* 1959, 1–90.

Becker, C. J. 1973. 'Problems of the megalithic "mortuary houses" in Denmark.' In Daniel, G. and Kjaerum, P. (eds), *Megalithic Graves and Ritual*. Jutland Archaeological Society, Copenhagen.

Behrens, H. 1973. *Die Jungsteinzeit im Mittelelbe-Saale-Gebiet*. Berlin.

Behrens, H. 1981. 'The first "Woodhenge" in Middle Europe.' *Antiquity* 55, 172–8.

Behrens, H. and Schröter, E. 1980. *Siedlungen und Gräber der Trichterbecherkultur und Schnurkeramik bei Halle (Saale)*. Berlin.

Benac, A. 1973. *Obre*. Wissenschaftliche Mitteilungen des Bosnisch-Herzegowinischen Landesmuseums, Sarajevo.

Bender, B. 1978. 'Gatherer-hunter to farmer: a social perspective.' *World Archaeology* 10, 204–22.

Bennike, P. and Ebbesen, K. 1986. 'The bog find from Sigersdal.' *Journal of Danish Archaeology* 5, 85–115.

Benveniste, E. 1973. *Indo-European Language and Society*. London.

Biegel, G. E. 1986. *Das Erste Gold der Menschheit*. Freiburg.

Bogucki, P. 1982. *Early Neolithic Subsistence and Settlement in the Polish Lowlands*. British Archaeological Report S150.

Bogucki, P. 1984. 'Ceramic sieves of the Linear Pottery Culture and their economic implications.' *Oxford Journal of Archaeology* 3, 15–30.

Bogucki, P. 1987. 'The establishment of agrarian communities on the north European plain.' *Current Anthropology* 28, 1–24.

Bogucki, P. I. and Grygiel, R. 1981. 'The household cluster at Brześć Kujawski 3: small site methodology in the Polish lowlands.' *World Archaeology* 13, 59–72.

Bökönyi, S. 1962. 'Zur Naturgeschichte des Ures in Ungarn und das Problem der Domestikation des Hausrindes.' *Acta Archaeologia Hungarica* 14, 175–214.

Bradley, R. 1978. *The Prehistoric Settlement of Britain*. London.

Bradley, R. 1984. *The Social Foundations of Prehistoric Britain*. London.

Bradley, R. and Holgate, R. 1984. 'The neolithic sequence in the Upper Thames valley.' In Bradley, R. and Gardiner, J. (eds), *Neolithic Studies*. British Archaeological Report 133.

Bradley, R., Cleal, R., Gardiner, J. and Green, M. 1984. 'The Neolithic sequence in Cranborne Chase.' In Bradley, R. and Gardiner, J. (eds), *Neolithic Studies*. British Archaeological Report 133.

Braithwaite, M. 1982. 'Decoration as ritual symbol: a theoretical proposal and an ethnographic study in southern Sudan.' In Hodder, I. (ed.), *Symbolic and Structural Archaeology*. Cambridge.

Braithwaite, M. 1984. 'Ritual and prestige in the prehistory of Wessex c.2200–1400 BC: A new dimension to the archaeological evidence.' In Miller, D. and Tilley, C. (eds), *Ideology, Power and Prehistory*. Cambridge.

Bruner, J. 1986. *Actual Minds, Possible Worlds*. Cambridge, Mass.

Brunner, O. 1968. *Neue Wege der Verfassungs- und Sozialgeschichte*. Göttingen.

Buchvaldek, M. 1966. 'Die Schnurkeramik in Mitteleuropa.' *Památky Archeologické* 57, 126–71.

Burkill, M. 1983a. 'Social development in the early and middle Neolithic of north and east France.' Ph.D. thesis, University of Cambridge.

Burkill, M. 1983b. 'The Middle Neolithic of the Paris Basin.' In Scarre, C. (ed.), *Ancient France*. Edinburgh.

Burl, A. 1981. '"By the light of the cinerary moon": chambered tombs and the astronomy of death.' In Ruggles, C. L. N. and Whittle, A. W. R. (eds), *Astronomy and Society in Britain during the Period 4000–1500 BC*. British Archaeological Report 88.

Burl, A. 1985. *Megalithic Brittany*. London.

Case, H. 1969. 'Settlement patterns in the North Irish Neolithic.' *Ulster Journal of Archaeology* 32, 3–27.

Cauvin, J. 1972. *Religions Néolithiques de Syro-Palestine*. Centre de Recherches d'Ecologie et de Préhistoire, Saint-Andrée-de-Cruzières.

Cauvin, J. 1974. 'Les débuts de la céramique sur le Moyen-Euphrate: nouveaux documents.' *Paléorient* 2, 199–205.

Cauvin, J. 1978. *Les premiers villages de Syrie-Palestine du IXème au VIIème millénaire*. Lyon.

Cauvin, J. 1979. 'Les fouilles de Mureybet (1971–1974) et leur signification pour les origines de la sedentarisation au Proche-Orient.' In Freedman, D. N. (ed.), *Archaeological Reports from the Tabqa Dam Project – Euphrates Valley, Syria*. Annual of the American Schools of Oriental Research 44.

Cauvin, J. 1986. 'Le Moyen-Euphrate au VIIIe millénaire d'après Mureybet et Cheikh Hassan.' In Morgan, J. C. (ed), *Le Moyen Euphrate*. Strasbourg.

Cauvin, J. and Cauvin, M.-C. 1982. 'Origines de l'agriculture au Levant. Facteurs biologiques et socio-culturels.' In Cuyler Young, T., Smith, P. and Mortensen, P. (eds), *The Hilly Flanks*. Chicago.

Champion, T., Gamble, C. S., Shennan, S. J. and Whittle, A. 1984. *Prehistoric Europe*. London.

Chapman, J. 1981. *The Vinca Culture of Southeast Europe*. British Archaeological Report S117.

Chapman, J. 1982. 'The secondary products revolution.' *Bulletin of the Institute of Archaeology* 19, 107–22.

Chapman, J. 1983. 'Meaning and illusion in the study of burial in Balkan prehistory.' In Poulter, A. (ed.), *Ancient Bulgaria*. Nottingham.

Chesterman, J. T. 1977. 'Burial rites in a Cotswold long barrow.' *Man* 12, 22–32.

Childe, V. G. 1949. 'The origins of Neolithic culture in northern Europe.' *Antiquity* 32, 129–35.

Christie, P. M. 1963. 'The Stonehenge cursus.' *Wiltshire Archaeological Magazine* 58, 370–82.

Clark, J. G. D. 1975. *The Earlier Stone Age Settlement of Scandinavia*. Cambridge.

Clark, J. G. D. 1980. *Mesolithic Prelude*. Edinburgh.

Clarke, D. L. 1976a. 'The Beaker network – social and economic models.' In Lanting, J. N. and van der Waals J. D. (eds), *Glochenbechersymposion Oberried*. Bussum.

Clarke, D. L. 1976b. 'Mesolithic Europe: the economic basis.' In Sieveking, G. de G., Longworth, I. and Wilson, K. E. (eds), *Problems in Social and Economic Archaeology*. London.

Cleal, R. 1984. 'The later Neolithic in Eastern England.' In Bradley, R. and Gardiner, J. (eds), *Neolithic Studies*. British Archaeological Report 133.

Cohen, M. 1977. *The Food Crisis in Prehistory*. Yale University Press.

Conkey, M. and Spector, J. 1984. 'Archaeology and the study of gender.' In

Schiffer, M. (ed.), *Advances in Archaeological Method and Theory 7*. New York.

Coudart, A. 1987. 'L'Architecture dans l'approche anthropologique des sociétés néolithiques d'Europe centre occidentale.' In *Espaces des autres. Lecture anthropologique d'architecture*. Paris.

Coudart, A. and Pion, P. 1986. *Archéologie de la France rurale*. Paris.

Crawford, O. G. S. 1957. *The Eye Goddess*. Oxford.

Daniel, G. 1965. Editorial. *Antiquity* 39, 241–6.

Darvill, T. C. 1982. *The Megalithic Chambered Tombs of the Cotswold–Severn Region*. Vorda, Highworth.

Davidsen, K. 1978. *The Final TRB Culture in Denmark*. Copenhagen.

Dennell, R. 1978. *Early Farming in South Bulgaria from the VI to the III Millennia BC*. British Archaeological Report S45.

Dennell, R. 1983. *European Economic Prehistory: a new approach*. London.

Dennell, R. and Webley, D. 1975. 'Prehistoric settlement and land use in southern Bulgaria.' In Higgs, E. (ed.), *Palaeoeconomy*. Cambridge.

Dixon, P. 1981. 'Crickley Hill.' *Current Archaeology* 76, 145–7.

Döhle, H. J. and Stahlhofen, H. 1985. 'Die neolithischen Rindergräber auf dem "Löwenberg" bei Derenburg, Kr. Wernigerode.' *Jahresschrift für Mitteldeutsche Vorgeschichte* 68, 157–77.

Dohrn-Ihmig, M. 1974. 'Die Geringer Gruppe der späten Linienbandkeramik im Mittelrheintal.' *Archäologisches Korrespondenzblatt* 4, 301–6.

Dohrn-Ihmig, M. 1983a. 'Das bandkeramische Gräberfeld von Aldenhoven-Niedermerz, Kreis Düren.' *Rheinische Ausgrabungen* 24, 47–190.

Dohrn-Ihmig, M. 1983b. 'Ein Grossgartacher Siedlungsplatz bei Jülich-Welldorf, Kreis Düren und der Übergang zum mittelneolithischen Hausbau.' *Rheinische Ausgrabungen* 24, 233–82.

Donley, L. 1982. 'House power: Swahili space and symbolic markers.' In Hodder, I. (ed.), *Symbolic and Structural Archaeology*. Cambridge.

Douglas, M. 1966. *Purity and Danger*. London.

Duby, G. 1980. *The Three Orders*. Chicago.

Duhamal, P. and Presteau, M. 1987. 'Les populations néolithiques du bassin Parisien.' *Archéologia* 230, 54–65.

Dumezil, G. 1970. *The Destiny of a Warrior*. Chicago.

Dumezil, G. 1973. *The Destiny of a King*. Chicago.

Dumezil, G. 1983. *The Stakes of the Warrior*. Los Angeles.

Ebbesen, K. 1975. *Die jüngere Trichterbecherkultur auf den dänischen Inseln*. Copenhagen.

Ebbesen, K. 1979. *Stordyssen i Vedsted*. Copenhagen.

Edmonds, M. and Thomas, J. 1987. 'The archers: an everyday story of country folk.' In Brown, A. G. and Edmonds, M. R. (eds), *Lithic Analysis and Later British Prehistory*. British Archaeological Report 162.

Ellis, L. 1984. *The Cucuteni-Tripolye Culture*. British Archaeological Report S217.

Eriksen, P. 1984. 'The Neolithic settlement complex at Fannerup.' *Kuml* 1984, 63–76.

Eriksen, P. and Madsen, T. 1984. 'Hanstedgård. A settlement site from the Funnel Beaker culture.' *Journal of Danish Archaeology* 3, 63–82.

Evans, C. and Hodder, I. 1988. 'The Haddenham project – 1987.' *Fenland Research* 5, 7–14.

Evans, R. K. 1978. 'Early craft specialisation: an example from the Balkan Chalcolithic.' In Redman, C. L. (ed.), *Social Archaeology*. New York.

Faber, O. 1977. 'Endnu et kulthus.' *Antikvariske Studier* 1, 35–46.

Faris, J. 1983. 'From form to content in the structural study of aesthetic systems.' In Washburn, D. (ed.), *Structure and Cognition in Art*. Cambridge University Press.

Feustel, R. and Ullrich, H. 1965. Totenhütte der neolithischen Walternienburger Gruppe. *Alt-Thüringen* 7, 105–202.

Fischer, U. 1956. *Die Gräber der Steinzeit im Saalegebiet*. Berlin.

Fischer, U. 1958. 'Mitteldeutschland und die Schnurkeramik.' *Jahresschrift für Mitteldeutsche Vorgeschichte* 41, 254–98.

Fischer, A. 1982. 'Trade in Danubian shaft-hole axes and the introduction of Neolithic economy in Denmark.' *Journal of Danish Archaeology* 1, 7–12.

Foucault, M. 1973. *The Birth of the Clinic*. London.

Foucault, M. 1977. *Discipline and Punish*. New York.

Frankenstein, S. and Rowlands, M. 1978. 'The internal structure and regional context of early Iron Age society in south-western Germany.' *Bulletin of the Institute of Archaeology* 15, 73–112.

Gamble, C. 1982. 'Interaction and alliance in Palaeolithic society.' *Man* 17, 92–107.

Gardiner, J. 1984. 'Lithic distributions and Neolithic settlement patterns in central southern England.' In Bradley, R. and Gardiner, J. (eds), *Neolithic Studies*. British Archaeological Report 133.

Georgiev, G. 1965. 'The Azmak mound in southern Bulgaria.' *Antiquity* 39, 6–8.

Gero, J. 1985. 'Socio-politics and the woman-at-home ideology.' *American Antiquity* 50, 342–50.

Gibbs, L. 1987. 'Identifying gender representation in the archaeological record.' In Hodder, I. (ed.), *The Archaeology of Contextual Meanings*. Cambridge.

Gimbutas, M. 1970. 'Proto-Indo-European culture: the Kurgan culture during the fifth, fourth and third millennia BC.' In Cardona, G. (ed.), *Indo-European and Indo-Europeans*. University of Pennsylvania Press.

Gimbutas, M. 1974. *The Gods and Goddesses of Old Europe*. London.

Gimbutas, M. 1976. *Neolithic Macedonia as Reflected by Excavation at Anza, Southeast Yugoslavia*. Los Angeles.

Gimbutas, M. 1986. 'Mythical imagery of Sitagroi society.' In Renfrew et al. 1986.

Giot, P.-R., Helgouach, J. and Monnier, J.-C. 1979. *Préhistoire de la Bretagne*. Rennes.

Glob, P. V. 1949. 'Barkaer, Danmarks aeldste landsby.' *Fra Nationalmuseets Arbejdsmark* 1949, 5–16.

Glob, P. V. 1975. 'De dodes lange huse.' *Skalk* 1975, no. 6.

Gowlett, J. 1984. 'Mental abilities of early man: a look at some hard evidence.' In Foley, R. (ed.), *Hominid Evolution and Community Ecology*. London.

Green, H. S. 1980. *The Flint Arrowheads of the British Isles*. British Archaeological Report 75.

Gregory, C. A. 1980. 'Gifts to men and gifts to god: gift exchange and capital accumulation in contemporary Papua.' *Man* 15, 626–52.

Guyan, W. V. 1967. 'Die jungsteinzeitlichen Moordörfer im Weier bei Thayngen.' *Zeitschrift für Schweizerische Archäologie und Kunstgeschichte* 25, 1–39.

Haudricourt, A. 1962. 'Domestication des animaux, culture des plantes et traitement d'autrui.' *L'Homme* 2, 40–50.

Hibbs, J. 1983. 'The Neolithic of Brittany.' In Scarre, C. (ed.), *Ancient France*. Edinburgh.

Hodder, I. 1982a. *Symbols in Action*. Cambridge.

Hodder, I. 1982b. 'Sequences of structural change in the Dutch Neolithic.' In Hodder, I. (ed.), *Symbolic and Structural Archaeology*. Cambridge.

Hodder, I. 1982c. *The Present Past*. London.

Hodder, I. 1984. 'Burials, houses, women and men in the European Neolithic.' In Miller, D. and Tilley, C. (eds), *Ideology, Power and Prehistory*. Cambridge.

Hodder, I. 1986. *Reading the Past*. Cambridge.

Hodder, I. 1987. 'Contextual archaeology: an interpretation of Çatal Hüyük and a discussion of the origins of agriculture.' *Bulletin of the Institute of Archaeology* 24, 43–56.

Hodder, I. 1988. 'Material culture texts and social change: a theoretical discussion and some archaeological examples.' *Proceedings of the Prehistoric Society* 54, 67–75.

Hodder, I. and Shand, P. 1988. 'The Haddenham long barrow: an interim statement.' *Antiquity* 62, 349–53.

Hole, F. 1984. 'A reassessment of the Neolithic revolution.' *Paléorient* 10, 49–60.

Houšt'ová, A. 1958. 'Long barrows of the TRB culture in Moravia.' In *Epitymbion Roman Haken*. Societas Archaeologica Bohemoslovenica, Prague.

Howell, J. 1983. 'The late Neolithic of the Paris basin.' In Scarre, C. (ed.), *Ancient France*. Edinburgh.

Ilett, M. 1983. 'The early Neolithic of north-eastern France.' In Scarre, C. (ed.), *Ancient France*. Edinburgh.

Ilett, M., Constantin, C., Coudart, A. and Demoule, J.-P. 1982. 'The late Bandkeramik of the Aisne valley: environment and spatial organisation.' *Analecta Praehistorica Leidensia* 15, 45–61.

Ilett, M., Plateaux, M. and Coudart, A. 1986. 'Analyse spatiale des habitats du Rubané récent.' In Demoule, J.-P. and Guilane, J. (eds), *Le Néolithique de la France*. Paris.

Ivanov, I. S. 1978. 'Les fouilles archéologiques de la nécropole chalcolithique à Varna (1972–1975).' *Studia Praehistorica* 1–2, 13–26.

Jennbert, K. 1985. 'Neolithisation – a Scanian perspective.' *Journal of Danish Archaeology* 4, 196–7.

Jensen, J. 1982. *The Prehistory of Denmark*. London.

Jochim, M. 1983. 'Palaeolithic cave art in ecological perspective.' In Bailey, G. (ed.), *Hunter-gatherer Economy in Prehistory*. Cambridge.

Jürgens, A. 1979. 'Die Rössener Siedlung von Aldenhoven Kreis Düren.' *Rheinische Ausgrabungen* 19, 385–505.

Kaelas, L. 1981. 'Megaliths of the Funnel Beaker culture in Germany and Scandinavia.' In Renfrew, A. C. (ed.), *The Megalithic Monuments of Western Europe*. London.

Kahlke, H. D. 1958. 'Ein Gräberfeld mit Bandkeramik in Stadtgebiet von Sondershausen.' *Ausgrabungen und Funde* 3, 180–2.

Kaiser, T. and Voytek, B. 1982. 'Sedentism and economic change in the Balkan Neolithic.' *Journal of Anthropological Archaeology* 2, 323–53.

Kalicz, N. 1970. *Clay Gods*. Budapest.

Kancev, M. 1978. 'Fouilles du tell près du village Sadievo, département de Sliven.' *Studia Praehistorica* 1–2, 96–100.

Kaufman, D. and Ronen, A. 1987. 'La sépulture Kébarienne Géométrique de Névé-David, Haifa, Israel.' *L'Anthropologie* 91, 335–42.

Kempfner-Jørgensen, L. and Watt, M. 1985. 'Settlement sites with middle Neolithic houses at Grødby, Bornholm.' *Journal of Danish Archaeology* 4, 87–100.

Kinnes, I. 1979. *Round Barrows and Ring ditches in the British Neolithic*. British Museum.

Kinnes, I. 1980. 'The art of the exceptional: the statues menhir of Guernsey in context.' *Archaeologia Atlantica* 3, 9–33.

Kinnes, I. 1981. 'Dialogues with death.' In Chapman, R., Kinnes, I. and Randsborg, K. (eds), *The Archaeology of Death*. Cambridge.

Kinnes, I. 1982. 'Les Fouaillages and megalithic origins.' *Antiquity* 61, 24–30.

Kjaerum, P. 1955. 'A neolithic temple.' *Kuml* 1955, 7–35.

Kjaerum, P. 1967. 'Mortuary houses and funeral rites in Denmark.' *Antiquity* 41, 190–6.

Klindt-Jensen, O. 1957. *Denmark*. London.

Knörzer, K.-H. 1971. 'Urgeschichtliche Unkrauter im Rheinland. Ein Beitrag zur Entstehung der Segetalgesellschaften.' *Vegetatio* 23, 89–111.

Koselleck, R. 1985. *Futures Past*. MIT Press.

Kosse, K. 1979. *Settlement Ecology of the Early and Middle Neolithic Körös and Linear Pottery Cultures in Hungary*. British Archaeological Report S64.

Kristiansen, K. 1982. 'The formation of tribal systems in later European prehistory: northern Europe, 4000–5000 BC.' In Renfrew, C., Rowlands, M. J. and Segraves, B. A. (eds), *Theory and Explanation in Archaeology*. New York.

Kristiansen, K. 1984. 'Ideology and material culture: an archaeological perspective.' In Spriggs, M. (ed), *Marxist Perspectives in Archaeology*. Cambridge.

Kristiansen, K. 1989. 'Prehistoric migrations and the case of the Single Grave culture in Jutland.' Circulated paper for publication.

Kruk, J. 1980. *The Neolithic Settlement of Southern Poland*. British Archaeological Report S93.

Kuper, R. and Piepers, W. 1966. 'Eine Siedlung der Rössener Kultur in Inden (Kreis Jülich) und Lamersdorf (Kreis Düren).' *Bonner Jahrbücher* 166, 370–6.

Kuper, R., Löhr, H., Lüning, J., Stehli, P. and Zimmerman, A. 1977. *Der Bandkeramische Siedlungsplatz Langweiler 9, Gem. Aldenhoven, Kr. Düren (Rheinische Ausgrabungen 18)*.

Lakoff, G. 1987. *Women, Fire, and Dangerous Things*. Chicago.

Lane, P. 1987. 'Reordering residues of the past.' In Hodder, I. (ed.), *Archaeology as Long-term History*. Cambridge.

Larsson, L. 1982. 'A causewayed enclosure and a site with Valby pottery at Stävie, western Scania.' *Meddelanden från Lunds Universitets Historiska Museum* 4, 65–107.

Larsson, L. 1983. 'Karlsfält.' *Acta Archaeologia* 54, 3–72.

Larsson, L. 1984. 'The Skateholm Project.' *Meddelanden från Lunds Universitets Historiska Museum* 5, 5–38.

Larsson, M. 1986. 'Neolithization in Scania – A Funnel Beaker perspective.' *Journal of Danish Archaeology* 5, 244–7.

Legge, A. J. 1981. 'Aspects of cattle husbandry.' In Mercer, R. (ed.), *Farming*

Practice in British Prehistory. Edinburgh.

Le Rouzic, Z. 1933. 'Premières fouilles au camp du Lizo.' *Revue Archéologique* 1933, 189–219.

L'Helgouach, J. 1965. *Les sépultures mégalithiques en Armorique.* Rennes.

Lichardus, J. 1976. *Rössen – Gatersleben – Baalberge.* Bonn.

Lichardus, J. 1986. 'Le rituel funéraire de la culture de Michelsberg dans la région du Rhin supérieur et moyen.' In Demoule, J.-P. and Guilane, J. (eds), *Le Néolithique de la France.* Paris.

Lichardus, J. and Lichardus-Itten, M. 1985. *La protohistoire de l'Europe.* Paris.

Littleton, C. S. 1973. *The New Comparative Mythology.* Los Angeles.

Liversage, D. 1980. 'Neolithic monuments at Lindebjerg, northwest Zealand.' *Acta Archaeologica* 51, 85–152.

Liversage, D. 1982. 'An early Neolithic ritual structure on Sejerø.' *Journal of Danish Archaeology* 1, 13–18.

Lüning, J. 1982. 'Research in the Bandkeramik settlement of the Aldenhover Platte in the Rhineland.' *Analecta Praehistorica Leidensia* 15, 1–30.

MacCormack, C. and Strathern, M. 1980. *Nature, Culture and Gender.* Cambridge.

Madsen, T. 1975. 'Stone packing graves at Fjelsø.' *Kuml* 1975, 73–82.

Madsen, T. 1977. 'Toftum near Horgens.' *Kuml* 1977, 161–84.

Madsen, T. 1979. 'Earthen long barrows and timber structures: aspects of the early Neolithic practice in Denmark.' *Proceedings of the Prehistoric Society* 45, 301–20.

Madsen, T. 1982. 'Settlement systems of early agricultural societies in east Jutland, Denmark: a regional study of change.' *Journal of Anthropological Archaeology* 1, 197–236.

Madsen, T. 1986. 'Where did all the hunters go?' *Journal of Danish Archaeology* 5, 229–39.

Madsen, T. 1988. 'Causewayed enclosures in south Scandinavia.' In Burgess, C., Topping P., Mordant, C. and Maddison, M. (eds), *Enclosures and Defences in the Neolithic of Western Europe.* British Archaeological Report S403.

Madsen, T. and Jensen, H. J. 1982. 'Settlement and land use in early Neolithic Denmark.' *Analecta Praehistorica Leidensia* 15, 63–86.

Madsen, T. and Petersen, J. 1983. 'Early Neolithic structures at Mosegården, E. Jutland. Regional and chronological differences in the Danish Early Neolithic.' *Kuml* 1982–3, 61–120.

Manby, T. G. 1970. 'Long barrows of northern England; structural and dating evidence.' *Scottish Archaeological Forum* 2, 1–27.

Marinescu-Bîlcu, S. 1981. *Tîrpeşti.* British Archaeological Report S107.

Marinow, G. and Yordanov, Y. 1978. 'Preliminary data from studies of bone material from the Varna Chalcolithic necropolis during the 1972–1975 period.' *Studia Praehistorica* 1–2, 60–7.

Markotic, V. 1984. *The Vinca Culture.* Calgary.

Marseen, O. 1960. 'The Ferslev house. A cult building from the passage grave period.' *Kuml* 1960, 36–55.

Marshall, A. 1981. 'Environmental adaptation and structural design in axially-pitched longhouses from Neolithic Europe.' *World Archaeology* 13, 101–21.

Masset, C. 1971. 'Une sépulture collective mégalithique à la Chaussée-Tirancourt (Somme).' *Bulletin de la Société Préhistorique Française* 68, 178–82.

Maudit, J. 1977. La sépulture collective mégalithique de L'Usine Vivez à Argenteuil (Val-d'Oise).' *Gallia Préhistoire* 20, 177–227.

Meeker, M., Barlow, K. and Lipset, D. 1986. 'Culture, exchange and gender: lessons from the Murik.' *Cultural Anthropology* 1, 6–73.

Mellaart, J. 1965. *Earliest Civilisations of the Near East.* London.

Mellaart, J. 1967. *Çatal Hüyük. A Neolithic Town in Anatolia.* London.

Mellaart, J. 1970. *Excavations at Hacilar.* Edinburgh.

Mercer, R. 1980. *Hambledon Hill. A Neolithic Landscape.* Edinburgh.

Midgley, M. 1985. *The Origin and Function of the Earthen Long Barrows of Northern Europe.* British Archaeological Report S259.

Mikov, V. 1959. 'The prehistoric mound of Karanovo.' *Archaeology* 12, 88–97.

Milisauskas, S. 1976. 'Olszanica: an early farming village in Poland.' *Archaeology* 29, 31–41.

Milisauskas, S. 1986. *Early Neolithic Settlement and Society at Olszanica.* University of Michigan Press.

Milisauskas, S. and Kruk, J. 1984. 'Settlement organisation and the appearance of low level hierarchical societies during the Neolithic in the Bronocice microregion, southeastern Poland.' *Germania* 62, 1–30.

Modderman, P. J. R. 1970. 'Linearbandkeramik aus Elsloo und Stein.' *Analecta Praehistorica Leidensia* 3.

Modderman, P. J. R. 1975. 'Elsloo.' In Bruce-Mitford, R. (ed.), *Recent Archaeological Excavations in Europe.* London.

Moore, A. 1985. 'The development of Neolithic societies in the Near East.' In Wendorf, F. and Close, A. (eds), *Advances in World Archaeology* 4, 1–69.

Nandris, J. 1970. 'The development and relationships of the earlier Greek Neolithic.' *Man* 5, 191–213.

Neustupný, E. 1985. 'On the Holocene period in the Komořany Lake area.' *Památky Archeologické* 76, 9–70.

Neustupný, E. 1987. Comment. *Current Anthropology* 28, 14–16.

Nielsen, S. 1979. 'Den grubekeramiske kultur i Norden.' *Antikvariske Studier* 3, 23–48.

Nielsen, F. O. and Nielsen, P. O. 1985. 'Middle and late Neolithic houses at Limensgård, Bornholm.' *Journal of Danish Archaeology* 4, 101–14.

Nielsen, P. O. 1986. 'The beginning of the Neolithic – assimilation or complex change?' *Journal of Danish Archaeology* 5, 240–43.

Oates, D. and Oates, J. 1976. *The Rise of Civilisation.* Oxford.

Ørsnes, M. 1956. 'On the construction and use of a passage grave.' *Aarbøger for Nordisk Oldkyndighed og Historie* 1956, 221–34.

Ortner, S. 1972. 'Is female to male as nature is to culture?' *Feminist Studies* 1, 5–32.

Pales, L. and de St Péreuse, M. T. 1976. *Les gravures de La Marche: II, Les Humains.* Paris.

Paludan-Müller, C. 1978. 'High Atlantic food gathering in northwestern Zealand, ecological conditions and spatial representation.' In Kristiansen, K. and Paludan-Müller, C. (eds), *New Directions in Scandinavian Archaeology.* Copenhagen.

Pavlů, I. 1982. 'Die Neolithischen Kreisgrabenanlagen in Böhmen.' *Archeologické Rozhledy* 34, 176–89.

Pequart, M. and S. J. 1954. *Hoedic.* Anvers.

Pequart, M. and S. J., Boule, M. and Vallois, H. 1937. *Teviec.* Archives de l'Institut de Paléontologie Humaine, 18.

Pétrequin, P. and Piningre, J.-F. 1976. 'Les sépultures collectives mégalithiques de

Franche-Comté.' *Gallia Préhistoire* 19, 287–394.

Pierpoint, S. 1980. *Social Patterns in Yorkshire Prehistory 3500–750 BC.* British Archaeological Report 74.

Piggott, S. 1967. '"Unchambered" long barrows in Neolithic Britain.' *Palaeohistoria* 12, 381–93.

Piningre, J.-F. and Bréart, B. 1985. 'L'Allée couverte Seine–Oise–Marne de Vers-sur-Selle (Somme).' *Gallia Préhistoire* 28, 125–70.

Pleinerová, I. 1980. 'Cultic features of the late Neolithic period excavated at Březno, NW Bohemia.' *Památky Archeologické* 71, 10–60.

Pleinerová, I. 1981. 'The problem of ploughmarks in the Early Neolithic enclosure discovered at Březno, NW Bohemia.' *Archeologické Rozhledy* 33, 133–41.

Pleslová-Štiková, E., Marek, F. and Horsky, Z. 1980. 'A square enclosure of the Funnel Beaker Culture (3500 BC) at Makotřasy (central Bohemia): a palaeoastronomic structure.' *Archeologické Rozhledy* 32, 3–35.

Powell, T. G. E., Corcoran, J. X. W. P., Lynch, F. and Scott, J. G. 1969. *Megalithic Enquiries in the West of Britain.* Liverpool.

Preuss, J. 1980. *Die Altmärkische Gruppe der Tiefstichkeramik.* Berlin.

Pryor, F. 1987. 'Etton 1986: Neolithic metamorphoses.' *Antiquity* 61, 78–80.

Raczky, P. 1987. *The Late Neolithic of the Tisza Region.* Szolnoc County Museums, Budapest.

Randsborg, K. 1975. 'Social dimensions of early Neolithic Denmark.' *Proceedings of the Prehistoric Society* 41, 105–18.

Randsborg, K. 1986. 'Women in prehistory: the Danish example.' *Acta Archaeologica* 55, 143–54.

Rasmussen, L. W. 1984. 'Kainsbakke A47: a settlement structure from the Pitted Ware culture.' *Journal of Danish Archaeology* 3, 83–98.

Ray, K. 1987. 'Material metaphor, social interaction and historical reconstructions: exploring patterns of association and symbolism in the Igbo-Ukwu corpus.' In Hodder, I. (ed.), *The Archaeology of Contextual Meanings.* Cambridge.

Reed, R. C. 1974. 'Earthen long barrows: a new perspective.' *Archaeological Journal* 131, 33–57.

Renfrew, C. 1973. *Before Civilisation.* London.

Renfrew, C. 1987. *Archaeology and Language.* London.

Renfrew, C., Gimbutas, M. and Elster, E. S. (eds) 1986. *Excavations at Sitagroi.* Los Angeles.

Richards, C. and Thomas, J. 1984. 'Ritual activity and structured deposition in later Neolithic Wessex.' In Bradley, R. and Gardiner, J. (eds), *Neolithic Studies.* British Archaeological Report 133.

Richards, J. 1984. 'The development of the Neolithic landscape in the environs of Stonehenge.' In Bradley, R. and Gardiner, J. (eds), *Neolithic Studies.* British Archaeological Report 133.

Rollefson, G. O. 1983. 'Ritual and ceremony at Neolithic Ain Ghazal (Jordan).' *Paléorient* 9 (2), 29–38.

Rollefson, G. O. 1986. 'Neolithic Ain Ghazal (Jordan): ritual and ceremony, II.' *Paléorient* 12 (1), 45–52.

Rowley-Conwy, P. 1980. 'Continuity and change in the prehistoric economies of Denmark 3700bc to 2300bc.' Ph.D. thesis, University of Cambridge.

Rowley-Conwy, P. 1984. 'Middle Neolithic economies in Denmark and southern England.' *Kuml* 1984, 92–112.

Rowley-Conwy, P. 1985. 'The Single Grave (Corded Ware) economy at Kalvø.' *Journal of Danish Archaeology* 4, 79–86.

Rowley-Conwy, P. 1987. 'The interpretation of ard marks.' *Antiquity* 61, 263–6.

Sahlins, M. 1985. *Islands of History*. New York.

Saville, A. 1984. 'Preliminary report on the excavation of a Cotswold-Severn tomb at Hazleton, Gloucestershire.' *Antiquaries Journal* 64, 10–24.

Savory, H. N. 1977. 'The role of Iberian communal tombs in Mediterranean and Atlantic prehistory.' In Markotic, V. (ed), *Ancient Europe and the Mediterranean*. Warminster.

Scarre, C. 1983. 'A survey of the French Neolithic.' In Scarre, C. (ed.) *Ancient France*. Edinburgh.

Sevic, R. and Kostic, N. 1974. 'Vojvodina in prehistory.' In Brukner, B., Jovanovic, B., and Tasic, N. (eds), *Praistorija Vojvodine*. Novi Sad.

Shanks, M. and Tilley, C. 1982. 'Ideology, symbolic power and ritual communication: a reinterpretation of Neolithic mortuary practices.' In Hodder, I. (ed.), *Symbolic and Structural Archaeology*. Cambridge.

Sharples, N. 1985. 'Individual and community: the changing role of megaliths in the Orcadian Neolithic.' *Proceedings of the Prehistoric Society* 51, 59–74.

Shennan, S. 1986. 'Central Europe in the third millennium bc: an evolutionary trajectory for the beginning of the European Bronze Age.' *Journal of Anthropological Archaeology* 5, 115–46.

Sherratt, A. 1981. 'Plough and pastoralism: aspects of the Secondary Products Revolution.' In Hodder, I., Isaac, G. and Hammond, N. (eds), *Pattern of the Past*. Cambridge.

Sherratt, A. 1982a. 'The development of Neolithic and Copper Age settlement in the Great Hungarian Plain. Part I: the regional setting.' *Oxford Journal of Archaeology* 1, 287–316.

Sherratt, A. 1982b. 'Mobile resources: settlement and exchange in early agricultural Europe.' In Renfrew, C. and Shennan, S. (eds), *Ranking, Resource and Exchange.*' Cambridge.

Sherratt, A. 1983a. 'The development of Neolithic and Copper Age settlement in the Great Hungarian Plain. Part II: site survey and settlement dynamics.' *Oxford Journal of Archaeology* 2, 13–41.

Sherratt, A. 1983b. 'The secondary exploitation of animals in the Old World.' *World Archaeology* 15, 90–104.

Sherratt, A. 1983c. 'The eneolithic period in Bulgaria in its European context.' In Poulter, A. (ed.), *Ancient Bulgaria*. Nottingham.

Sherratt, A. 1984. 'Social evolution: Europe in the later Neolithic and Copper Ages.' In Bintliff, J. (ed.), *European Social Evolution*. Sheffield.

Sherratt, A. 1986a. 'Wool, wheels and ploughmarks: local developments or outside introductions in Neolithic Europe.' *Bulletin of the Institute of Archaeology* 23, 1–16.

Sherratt, A. 1986b. 'The pottery of the early Bronze Age at Sitagroi.' In Renfrew et al. 1986.

Sherratt, A. 1987. 'Cups that cheered.' In Waldren, W. H. and Kennard, R. C. (eds), *Bell Beakers of the Western Mediterranean*. British Archaeological Report S331.

Simonsen, J. 1986. 'Settlements from the Single Grave culture in NW Jutland.' *Journal of Danish Archaeology* 5, 135–51.

Skaarup, J. 1982. 'The excavation of a passage grave site at Himmelev, central Zealand.' *Journal of Danish Archaeology* 1, 19–30.

Smith, R. W. 1984. 'The ecology of Neolithic farming systems as exemplified by the Avebury region of Wiltshire.' *Proceedings of the Prehistoric Society* 50, 99–120.

Soffer, O. 1985. *The Upper Palaeolithic of the Central Russian Plain.* New York.

Soffer, O. 1987. 'Upper Palaeolithic connubia, refugia, and the archaeological record from Eastern Europe.' In Soffer, O. (ed), *The Pleistocene Old World. Regional Perspectives.* New York.

Soudský, B. 1962. 'The Neolithic site of Bylany.' *Antiquity* 36, 190–200.

Soudský, B. 1969. Étude de la maison néolithique.' *Slovenská Archeológia* 17, 5–96.

Sprockhoff, E. 1938. *Die Nordische Megalithkultur.* Berlin and Leipzig.

Srejović, D. 1972. *Europe's First Monumental Sculpture: New Discoveries at Lepinski Vir.* London.

Starling, N. J. 1983. 'Neolithic settlement patterns in central Germany.' *Oxford Journal of Archaeology* 2, 1–11.

Starling, N. J. 1985a. 'Colonisation and succession: the earlier Neolithic of central Europe.' *Proceedings of the Prehistoric Society* 51, 41–57.

Starling, N. J. 1985b. 'Social change in the later Neolithic of central Europe.' *Antiquity* 59, 30–8.

Startin, W. 1978. 'Linear pottery culture houses: reconstruction and manpower.' *Proceedings of the Prehistoric Society* 44, 143–60.

Startin, B. and Bradley, R. 1981. 'Some notes on work organisation and society in prehistoric Wessex.' In Ruggles, C. and Whittle, A. (eds), *Astronomy and Society in Britain during the Period 4000–1500 BC.* British Archaeological Report 88.

Strömberg, M. 1971. *Die Megalithgräber von Hagestad.* Lund.

Taborin, Y. 1974. 'La parure en coquillage.' *Gallia Préhistoire* 17, 101–79.

Testart, A. 1986. *Essai sur les Fondements de la Division Sexuelle du Travail chez les Chasseurs-Cueilleurs. Cahiers de l'homme* 25.

Thevenot, J.-P. 1985. 'Informations archéologiques: circonscription de Bourgogne.' *Gallia Préhistoire* 28, 171–210.

Thom, A. and A. S. 1978. *Megalithic Remains in Britain and Brittany.* Oxford.

Thomas, J. 1987a. 'Relations of power. The Neolithic of central southwest England.' Ph.D. thesis, University of Sheffield.

Thomas, J. 1987b. 'Relations of production and social change in the Neolithic of north-west Europe.' *Man* 22, 405–30.

Thomas, J. 1988. 'The social significance of Cotswold-Severn burial practices.' *Man* 23, 540–59.

Thomas, J. and Whittle, A. 1986. 'Anatomy of a tomb – West Kennet revisited.' *Oxford Journal of Archaeology* 5, 129–56.

Thorpe, I. 1984. 'Ritual, power and ideology: a reconstruction of earlier Neolithic rituals in Wessex.' In Bradley, R. and Gardiner, J. (eds), *Neolithic Studies.* British Archaeological Report 133.

Thorpe, I. and Richards, C. 1984. 'The decline of ritual authority and the introduction of Beakers into Britain.' In Bradley, R. and Gardiner, J. (eds), *Neolithic Studies.* British Archaeological Report 133.

Tilley, C. 1982. 'An assessment of the Scanian Battle-Axe tradition: towards a social perspective.' *Scripta Minora* 1981–2, 4–72.

Tilley, C. 1984. 'Ideology and the legitimation of power in the Middle Neolithic of Southern Sweden.' In Miller, D. and Tilley, C. (eds), *Ideology, Power and Prehistory*. Cambridge.

Todorova, H. 1978. *The Eneolithic in Bulgaria*. British Archaeological Report S49.

Tringham, R. 1971. *Hunters, Fishers and Farmers of Eastern Europe, 6000–3000 BC*. London.

Tringham, R., Krstic, D., Kaiser, T. and Voytek, B. 1980. 'The early agricultural site of Selevac, Yugoslavia.' *Archaeology* 33, 24–32.

Tringham, R., Bruckner, B. and Voytek, B. 1985. 'The Opovo project: a study of socioeconomic change in the Balkan Neolithic.' *Journal of Field Archaeology* 12, 425—44.

Twohig, S. 1981. *The Megalithic Art of Western Europe*. New York.

Ucko, P. 1969. *Anthropomorphic Figurines of Predynastic Egypt and Neolithic Crete*. Royal Anthropological Institute Occasional Paper.

Verron, G. 1986. 'Les civilisations neolithiques de la Normandie.' In Demoule, J.-P. and Guilaine, J. (eds), *Le Neolithique de la France*. Paris.

Vyner, B. E. 1984. 'The excavation of a Neolithic cairn at Street House, Loftus, Cleveland.' *Proceedings of the Prehistoric Society* 50, 151–95.

Wainwright, G. 1975. 'Religion and settlement in Wessex, 3000–1700 BC,' In Fowler, P. (ed.), *Recent Work in Rural Archaeology*. Bradford-on-Avon.

Wainwright, G. and Longworth, I. 1971. *Durrington Walls: Excavations 1966–1968*. Reports of the Research Committee of the Society of Antiquaries of London 29.

Wamser, L. 1980. 'Eine gefasshaltende Idolfigur der frühen Linearbandkeramik aus Mainfranken.' *Jahresbericht der Bayerischen Bodendenkmalpflege* 321, 26–38.

Waterbolk, H. T. and Van Zeist, W. 1978. *Niederwil, eine Siedlung der Pfyner Kultur*. Bern.

Wheeler, R. E. M. 1943. *Maiden Castle, Dorset*. Reports of the Research Committee of the Society of Antiquaries of London 12.

Whittle, A. 1977a. *The Earlier Neolithic of Southern England and its Continental Background*. British Archaeological Report S35.

Whittle, A. 1977b. Earlier Neolithic enclosures in north-west Europe.' *Proceedings of the Prehistoric Society* 43, 329–48.

Whittle, A. 1981. 'Later Neolithic society in Britain: a realignment.' In Ruggles, C. and Whittle, A. (eds) *Astronomy and Society in Britain during the Period 4000–1500 BC*. British Archaeological Report 88.

Whittle, A. 1985. *Neolithic Europe: a Survey*. Cambridge.

Whittle, A. 1988a. 'Contexts, activities, events – aspects of Neolithic and Copper Age enclosures in central and western Europe.' In Burgess, C., Topping, P., Mordant, C. and Maddison, M. (eds), *Enclosures and Defences in the Neolithic of Western Europe*. British Archaeological Report S403.

Whittle, A. 1988b. *Problems in Neolithic Archaeology*. Cambridge.

Willerding, U. 1980 'Zum Ackerbau der Bandkeramiker.' *Materialhefte Ur- und Frühgeschichte Niedersachsens* 16, 421–56.

Winn, S. M. M. 1981. *Pre-writing in Southeasten Europe: the Sign System of the Vinca Culture ca 4000BC*. Calgary.

Woodburn, J. 1980. 'Hunters and gatherers today and reconstruction of the past.' In Gellner, E. (ed.), *Soviet and Western Anthropology*. London.

Wright, G. A. 1978. 'Social differentiation in the early Natufian.' In Redman C. L. (eds), *Social Archaeology*. New York.

Yates, T. 1989. 'Habitus and social space: some suggestions about meaning in the Saami (Lapp) tent ca. 1700–1900.' In Hodder, I. (ed), *The Meanings of Things*. London.

Zápotocký, M. 1966. 'Streitäxte und Streitaxtkulturen.' *Památky Archeologické* 57, 172–209.

Index

(Index compiled by A. L. Gibbs)